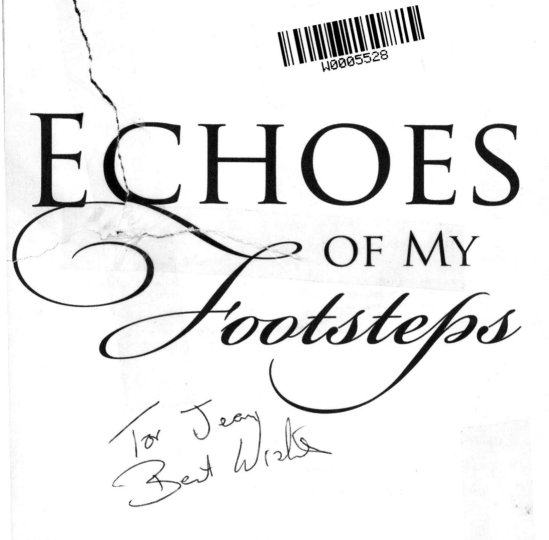

ECHOES
OF MY
Footsteps

*For Jean
Best Wishes*

ROY PHELPS

outskirts
press

DEDICATION

My book is dedicated to the memory of my brother, Colin Phelps, who passed away in November 2021 due to the Covid-19 virus. From 1966-1970 he served with honor in the United States Navy and the United States Marine Corps as a Medical Corpsman in the Vietnam War saving many American lives. The men in his platoon called him Doc Limey. He was a true American who did his duty for America and served his country with bravery and pride. He was a real hero.

ACKNOWLEDGEMENTS

My thanks to my family for their support and assistance in creating this journey of my life. To my wife Patty for proofreading and editing the manuscript and my daughter Carolyn for her valuable insight and suggestions. Thank you.

Table of Contents

Prologue...i
1937...1
1939 11
The Gas Works 15
1939-1940, Preparation for War 16
The Battle of Britain...25
1940, I am Evacuated Out of London 29
St. Peters Church 40
1942..51
1943..54
1944..59
D Day, Invasion of Europe 88
1945, The War is Over..89
June 1946, I am Back Home...96
1946, My Dad Has Come Home 98
1947, An American Care Packages Arrives....................108
1947, I Started School 110
1947, My Dad Becomes Very Ill 118
1947, My Dad Dies of Lung Cancer 123
1948, I was 11 Years Old...133
1949, My First Real Job 145
1949, The Great Fogs of London 150
1950..152
1950, My New School..163
1951, I Am Age 14 173
1952..183

May 1953, I was Age 16 188
1953, Graduated from School 191
1953-1954, I am Now 17 206
1954...210
March 1955, RAF Induction 220
June 1955, RAF Compton Bassett 245
August 1955, RAF Bletchley Park, Bedford...................................254
1957...258
1957, I Was Now a Civilian..260
1958, April 267
1958, I Arrived in America...286
1959-1960 316
1960, My Visit Back to London...321
1960, My Trip Across Country 326
1961, Back in NYC...367
April 1961, A Second Beginning...370
1963, Lithographic Institute, Tennessee.......................................381
1963-1964 398
1965, I Started My New Sales Career..400
1965...402

Prologue

THEY SAY THAT there are good times and bad times in a human life and I began my life at the beginning of some very hard times for most of the world. It was a period of time that would be recorded as the worst in modern human history that decidedly brought great changes to the world. Who would know how many people would be killed, die of starvation and live in brutality, that the whole social fabric of Europe would be changed forever? Countless lost their homes as well as their places of business.

I write this book hoping that the history of the Second World War will not become just another piece of history. Would anybody in future generations really care how many people worldwide it uprooted, killed or maimed for life both physically and mentally? Present statistics say that each day about one thousand American World War II veterans die of old age or other ailments related to their war wounds.

This conflict would change the world forever and it also changed my life. Much has been written in the past about this period. I hope that by relating my own personal experiences as a child during that time that I was a forced evacuee from the city of London during the air raids on London and other British cities by the German Luftwaffe in 1940. Enduring five long years of being apart from my parents and family and being raised by a surrogate mother and father did change my future life. It has been suggested that the first five years of a child's life will establish their mental and spiritual attitude for the rest of their lives. I can personally attest that this is true. I probably would not be the same person I am now had I not been pulled away from my mother and father during those important formative years for a young child from the age of three years until after the war ended at age eight years.

The horrific bombing on innocent civilians would not only be of historical interest, but my personal testimony as to what it really was like growing up in London during these times. From 1939 until final victory was won for the allies in 1945, there was an unconditional surrender by the Germans and Japanese dictators.

The British people began to slowly recover after 1946 from the effects of those six years of man's inhumanity to man. Those six years contained so much hardship for the people of Britain and its wounds would only slowly begin to recover during the early 1950's with the removal of food coupon books and the personal identity cards, which were issued to everyone to show when permission was given what they can eat and where they can travel.

After war's end when I was returned to my family, I did have serious problems in living a life I did not know or understand. I had lived in the country during my growing years and came to love the countryside and village living. Having to return to the city of London as a child I did not like the crowded city neighborhood after living the wide open spaces of the English countryside for over five years.

I returned home at the age of eight. My mother was at the time taking care of my newborn brother, but soon I had the job of taking care of my baby brother myself. My mother had to go to work in a factory from eight in the morning until six at night. I spent following years with my mother and younger brother Colin getting to know how to live in a city that after existing for two thousand years had almost died, but like the Phoenix of ancient history London raised itself up again more vibrant that before.

With bricks and other debris blocking the roads at wars end it is difficult for an eight year old to really understand why this happened except to say that I had a great time after I was allowed to go off on my own in later life's adventures in a country called America. I will describe in this story my early life which was lived under very difficult circumstances. I completed my schooling from the normal age allowed by law at a school that was not a good school. It was in an old building built for education in the early 1900's with a lack of good educated school teachers and a socialistic society. Most qualifying teachers at that time were in the military so there was a shortage of teachers.

After I finished school at the age of fifteen, I had to go to work. I started working for a small printer for two years and by the age of 18 I joined the British Royal Air Force which changed my whole way of life with its stark military discipline that I learned to keep for the future. I really enjoyed my time during that period of my life. It toughened me up for what lay before me.

I really became an American, at least in spirit, while I was still in the British Royal Air Force. For a period of time during my service I was temporally attached to a combined RAF/American Air Force base in the north of England. It was during this period of time of my service that I had my first contact with Americans that caught my imagination at the RAF/USAF Chick Sands Air Base. That imagination eventually grew and directed me to America one year later after my honorable discharge from the RAF in 1957.

I went back to work after I was discharged from the RAF and tried to go back to civilian life, but I had changed while in the military. I was more independent and confident in myself to go to other parts of the world. My American Air Force friends at USAF Chick Sands suggested many times while I was at their base that I would fit in well in America and urged me to visit. Visit New York they said and give it a try. Go see if there was a fit for me in a new country like America and its different and wonderful opportunities. After going through all of the formalities of obtaining a permanent resident visa to stay and work in the US, I was on my way to a great lifetime change. It took many months to get my visa to be able to work and stay in America and after my final interview in the American Embassy in London I received my visa. Soon I was on my way to the New World, on towards a new life in America.

After my departure from the docks of Southampton, England during my voyage across the ocean on the liner Queen Elizabeth on April 23, 1958 I began to feel a personal change in myself. As we sailed past those great white cliffs of Dover, as many other passengers had done in the past for hundreds of years, I felt I was no longer an Englishman but a re-born spirit as an American.

I eventually did very well in America and became a US citizen and became a business man in the city of New York. My job involved traveling across America, flying coast to coast on business, and traveling all over America. I did not know it at the time but I had a future lifetime of opportunity, it was offered and I grabbed it and loved every moment of it. I was inspired and encouraged to write this book by the many Americans across the country that I had met during my business contacts and travels during the next forty-five years.

My American customers kept asking me what was it really like as a child during the London blitz? What was it like being bombed night and day and possibly losing your home and watching the damage done to other homes and buildings night after night? They kept suggesting to me whenever we discussed the war that I should write a book about my experiences, which surprised me that they thought it was an interesting enough subject to write about. They even declared that if I wrote a book, they would certainly like to buy a copy. So here is my story about myself in two different countries, England and America. I hope that you find my story interesting and enjoy reading some of the incidences in these personal travels of a young man who was not satisfied with what he had, but always hungered for something better.

1937

I WAS BORN on January 6, 1937 at 34 Hove Avenue in Walthamstow in the county of Essex, England during the early hours of the morning to my parents Ivy Irene Phelps, known as Ivy, and my father Edwin Paul Phelps, known as Eddie. I was named Roy Edwin George Phelps. The name of Edwin was my father's middle name. I was also named George after the then King George the Sixth, King of England. Edwin is an old English name written as Edwyn Phelps.

They told me I was born on a typical, English January day for the south of England. Usually there was no rain from the west winds, but wind and rain from across the North Sea from the continent of Europe could make life cold and miserable for just about everyone. They say I was born precisely on time as predicted by the midwife who delivered me. That might mean something indicative of me, since during my whole life I have had a passion for being always on time. To this day I hold my commitments and promises very seriously both in business and my private life.

It was an old English custom in those days that when a baby is about to be born, prior arrangements would have been made to hire a midwife who was experienced in birthing babies, which allowed mothers to have their baby delivered at home. A midwife was also known as a birthing mother so I did not arrive in a high-class hospital with a nurse tending to my mother, but arrived in an apartment bedroom that was the best my parents could afford. Hot water had to be boiled in the house. It was said that this was strictly female business. Men were not encouraged to be involved and stayed away spending time in the local pub with their friends toasting the new arrival coming into this world. A midwife in England at that time basically substituted for a baby doctor and was highly trained to birth a baby. A doctor sometimes was there at the birth, but preparations were made by the local midwife who lived in the neighborhood that offered the kind of service to mothers in waiting as it was delicately called in those days. It was always somebody that was well respected in the neighborhood and competent in this kind of operation in birthing babies. I was also told later in life that I was born with severe bronchitis and very nearly died at an early age.

Up until the time when I left England to go to America, I continued to have severe coughing fits, congestion and very bad bronchitis and bad colds. It was believed that this was due to the damp and wet weather that continuously plagued England. When I lived in America the climate is much warmer and drier so when I did finally leave England and live in America the colds and cough totally disappeared and I was free of that curse forever. The wet English climate was the cause and I dreaded the time when I caught a bad cold because I immediately went into bronchitis with severe coughing and coughing up mucus from my lungs. When I coughed, I seemed to whoop as I tried to catch my breath and my chest hurt so badly so at times they thought I had whooping cough. I also had what they called fits as a child. Nobody really spoke about it during my older childhood, but my mother said I would lie on the floor and curl up in a fetal position and lose consciousness. The local doctors did not know what caused this saying that I would probably grow out of it.

My father, Eddie Phelps, was a retail food salesman in a grocery store. The store was called Bache's and the owners of that store were family friends of my father for a long time prior to my birth. Prior to World War II he worked there daily for many hours for the store selling produce. This grocery store was owned by Jack Lyons and his wife Beryl and the shop was located in a street market called Walthamstow High Street which was a long narrow street about a mile long. Jack Lyons was a very severe looking man, rough of nature and had an aggressive red facial look. He had a hawkish looking face, which showed that he did not have too much patience with anybody that crossed him, as I was to find out later when I was given a job to help out in the store on Saturdays as a teenager.

Walthamstow High Street is a narrow cobblestone road wide enough to barely be able to allow a small truck to pass between the shops on either side, which had street vending carts lined up on each side of the road outside of their particular shop, cart wheels in the gutter. Each shop had a large cart outside as an extension of the store itself with the same produce loaded up with all of the products available in the main store. These carts or barrows were there as a convenience to shoppers to save time by not going into the store. The barrow cart had a tight tarpaulin covering the cart as a roof to prevent rain falling onto the displayed produce and the salesman.

The High Street itself looked not much larger than a wide alley and the street was always crowded with shoppers especially on a Saturday which was considered a market day. It was so crowded that it was almost impossible to pass other shoppers in the middle of the road without bumping into someone. It was an open market with all kinds of stores and products, all kinds of trade from ice cream parlors, grocery stores, and fish and chip shops that lined both sides of the road. On each side of the street were other stores that sold just about everything from food to furniture, bacon, eggs, canned goods and biscuits. The stores lining each side of the street were all brightly lit inside with long counters reaching far into the back of the store.

My mother worked behind one of the counters inside the store for many years especially during the war years and I did some Saturday work there in later years when I was a teenager. Looking for some extra money on a Saturday, I would stand alongside the cart and try and sell biscuits and eggs. The people that were out shopping sometimes did not want to go inside the store. They only wanted to window shop and bought only what they wanted that day. There was very light car traffic on the street and once in a while a car would make its way slowly through the crowded street.

The Lyons family were good friends of the Phelps. I mention the store in this early part of this story since it would later play a larger part in my later years. My mother worked in this store during the dark days of the war during the bombing. There were ration books given to the store keeper when a buyer bought food because the government was rationing all people for food and other essential items. The ration book as it was soon to be named was a small printed book card which you had to tear off tabs on the ration card showing that you had been given your ration of eggs, meats and other items that were in very short supply. To apply to get a ration book you had to go to the town hall applying in person for your ration card with your identity card issued by the government.

My dad Eddie and his sisters were born and raised just a few streets away from the grocery store on South Grove Avenue, still in the town of Walthamstow. They lived in three separate family flats (apartments) on South Grove Avenue where my paternal grandmother and grandfather lived surrounded by their children and older members of family. Each member of the family lived practically next door to each other and was very socially close to each other. This was very typical of families in those days since few people moved away from their family or from the local area where they were born and raised. At one end of South Grove Avenue was a large brewery making beer. There was always the strong aroma of beer while it was brewing day and night. My dad worked hard and sometimes had two jobs, one working at the grocery store during the day and then he worked at the brewery at nights or in his spare time. He always worked somewhere. He always had a job doing something somewhere for extra money to pay for any extra bills that came up.

The neighborhood consisted of row houses or flats as we called them and all were attached to each other with side roads crossing to make blocks of flats. That was normal in most cities of Britain where few working class British people owned their own homes. These flats were initially built to house the working class or blue collar workers who usually rented their flats and were owned by a Consortium Company. The renters worked in the local factories, local stores and shops or commuted into the city of London by bus or by train. There was no hot water available in any of these flats and living quarters and consisted of an upstairs and downstairs flat. Out in the back yard there was a small garden that sometimes had a chicken coup with chickens located alongside of the garden fence on either side, in low screened boxes, and us kids used to gather fresh eggs each morning, which were in special nesting boxes. In the morning when visiting grandma, us kids would rush out to the back garden and bring in fresh eggs for the breakfast table. Although as a three year old I did not do much of that.

Other men had racing pigeons in boxes located in their backyard and each night they would let them out. It was fascinating to see them released when they flew like a flock of geese. They would fly around and around until they returned home to their pigeon boxes. I could never understand how they managed to find their way back. I suppose that is why they are called homing pigeons.

Walthamstow High Street was and still is an open market street that extended over a mile to the other end of High Street, where it ended at the Walthamstow public baths. The public baths are where most people took their weekly bath. This bath house consisted of a long corridor with large numbered bath stalls on each side of the corridor. Behind each door was a bath tub with two taps or faucets, one tap for hot water, the other cold. As soon as one stall had been made vacant and cleaned by a large mop the attendant would call out to the next person in line. In later years after I returned from evacuation, I brought my own towel and change of clothing in a bag then stepped into the stall closing the door behind me, watching the hot and cold water streaming out of the taps in the far end of the tubs. When the water was just right for hot and cold you shouted out to the attendant that the numbered stall that you were using should be turned off. I then attended to myself in taking a bath. As the water cooled, I would call out again loudly to the attendant that I wanted more hot water in the numbered stall that I was using so again he would send in more hot water. There was also a swimming pool there for those that wished to take a swim. In fact, it really was just like a YMCA. We did not usually take a bath at home since the rooms were too cold. Most homes did not have a bathroom, just an outside flush toilet at the back of the house. I do not remember much of this period during the early years of my life. I mention it only as a background to my later postwar connections where my father's family lived.

There are some photos of me as a plump baby being photographed in portrait style at the local photographers. Since very few people owned a camera other than a box Kodak Brownie camera, it was a tradition for a baby and other important photos to be photographed by a professional photographer in his studio each year. I was photographed sitting upright on a cushion looking like I was ready to topple over any moment. This I do not remember, but I do remember being tucked into a pram (short for perambulator) and listening to the rain beating down on the roof of the pram. Even to this day I still enjoy listening to the rain beating on the windows or roof, giving me some sense of comfort and security that I felt while being pushed around by my mother in the rain.

My father was a great provider during his short life and he was not afraid of hard work, working two jobs at the same time to make extra money for his family. He was very family conscious and was a great father. He passed away in 1947 at the age of 39 years due to lung cancer, caused by his job in the Army during the war years where he worked in chemical warfare and ammunitions for the British Army in the Royal Engineers. Although I do not remember him during the first three years of my life, I do remember my father taking me to the Clapton dog race-track and I have memories of seeing the entrance to the Greyhound Dog Track buildings all painted in white. Flags were flying above the entrance. He would lift me up and put me on his shoulders calling me a Flying Angel and hold my arms up in the air as if they were my wings.

My mother Ivy, whose maiden name was Went, was born in a near-by town of Clapton where my maternal grandmother Rose Went and grandfather William Went lived. I was told he served in the Army during the First World War and was gassed in the trenches but I never saw any effects of this gassing. These two towns of Clapton and Walthamstow were quite close together by only about four miles. To visit each other meant catching two trolley buses. Trolley buses were like regular buses, but were electric driven and had two poles attached from the roof of the bus to the overhead electric wires which powered the bus. There were other buses but they were diesel driven. Sometimes when the trolley bus turned corners too sharply the poles came off of the overhead wires causing the bus to lose power. Then it was the conductor's job to pull a long bamboo pole from a long tube located under the bus and reach the overhead wires with the bamboo pole to restore the buses connection to the overhead electric wires. Later, as I grew older, I could never understand why the conductor did not get electrocuted when he attempted to do this.

Prior to her marriage to my father, my mother lived with her parents and brothers and sisters in Clapton. The family was large with seven children who ultimately became my uncles and aunts. My maternal grandparents lived on Pedro Street in the London Borough of Clapton. Although technically Clapton was within the county of Essex, it had been annexed by the giant borough of London, a borough being part of greater London that expanded from the center outward of the city into the surrounding suburbs and countryside.

I was born in a flat on Hove Avenue in the town of Walthamstow in January 1937, but I only lived there for about a year after I was born because my parents were lucky enough to rent a Warner's flat in a nice area in the next town over called Leyton which was about four miles away from Walthamstow. Not too far from my paternal grandparents and about equal distance from Clapton was where my maternal grandparents lived. Family ties were very strong so it was important to everyone that we all lived reasonably close to each other and rarely travelled outside of our area.

Most families wanted an easy enough distance to ride on a bus or to walk the distance when visiting each other. The term that we used to say on a Sunday afternoon was let's go "knock up" Aunt Jenny, meaning to knock on her front door to see if she was home. We had no telephones in those days to call ahead and confirm that they were home. Many years later when I went to America, I got myself into a lot of trouble using that phrase since it had an entirely different meaning.

At that time my dad was still working as a food salesman at Baches, the grocery store on Walthamstow High Street. It was not a good time to bring up a child because the world was preparing for a war with Germany and as of September 1939 two years after I was born my dad was drafted into the Army at the age of 31. He was inducted into the Royal Engineers Regiment. His job was to be responsible for building Bailey river bridges and de-activating bombs. His rank was Sapper Engineer Phelps. He also installed on many beaches tank traps prior to the pending invasion of Britain.

My mother told me in later years that her father William Went, who was my maternal grandfather, was very rough after he and his friends had had a few drinks at the local pub. Uncle Will, the oldest son was named after his father William Went. William, who died late 1936, taught my Uncle Harry to ride a motor bike and taught him all about electricity so that he could be an electrician. In later years after the war ended Uncle Harry had to leave his electricians job because he had to work through attics and he developed a heart condition. Aunt Ida's brother Bill got him a job as a city bank courier. Bill whose job was with the stock exchange and his boss was Lord Ritchie of Dundee. Somewhere there was a connection to an American company called Cargill, but I never did understand what kind of company Cargill was and what they did.

When my maternal grandfather left work at the end of the work day it was said that he would stop in at many pubs until the last pub closed at 10:30 pm. It has also been said around the family that he walked home from Islington and never missed a pub on the way back home before closing time. After the pubs were closed my grandfather would come home to his family. My grandmother waited with her children and they would sit at the top of the stairs waiting for him to come home drunk from the pub. They would hear him coming along the street, singing baldly songs with his friends. The children were very nervous as they waited for him as he unlocked the front door. I was told that he would first sit in a chair facing my grandmother Rose in the kitchen glaring at her as he slowly took off his large hob nailed boots. As soon as he took off the first boot he would throw the boot at my grandmother which hit her and then he threw the other boot at her. I only heard about these incidents years afterwards and it was hard for to believe that this was the same person since my grandfather was always good to me and his other grandchildren. However, since I was away during my formative years, I really had no contact with my family until the war ended in 1945 when I returned back to London.

We lived in a flat on Clementina Road in Leyton so my mum and dad were lucky to get such a nice flat. All applicants had to get on a list for housing and usually few were ever available unless you had some influence with someone to push you up to the front of the waiting list.

The kitchen was a cozy room set aside and used as a family room with an iron stove and an oven which was used for both heating and cooking. The front room was only used for when company called or if there was a family party. In the front room was located the best furniture, always a display of a glass cabinet full of best china usually heirlooms, plates, cups and other nick-knacks. The china was only used on special occasions.

In England in those days a piano was part of the front room furniture. At least one of the family members was taught to play the piano at a young age to be able to grow up and make music for the family when there was a family gathering. In this room was a large rollaway carpet located in the center of the room. The carpet was always rolled up when a party was planned and there was room enough for the whole family, uncles and aunts to sing around the piano and dance the knees up dance, Knees up Mother Brown. Some of my English readers may remember that.

My mother Ivy Went was born January 17, 1910. She was a twin, but not identical, since the other twin was her brother Tom, who became my Uncle Tom. His trade was a typesetter on one of the national newspapers on Fleet Street in London. During the year of 1937-1938 the first of five grandchildren arrived to my grandmother Rose and William Went. Each one of her children produced the first round of children which I happened to be one of. I had five uncles and aunts each producing one child. After the war when my uncles returned home from the Army the second round of children were produced. I had four cousins, Maureen, Malcolm, Ronnie and Anne all about the same age as myself. After the war that number doubled as the second generations round of cousins were born, Colin my brother, Roger and others.

I am not sure how my parents met but my mother said that one evening she was out with her girlfriends walking down the street. Walking towards them was a group of boys and one of these boys was Eddie, my father to be. He was whistling the theme song of Laurel and Hardy from the movie they saw. That is how they met and soon after they went to dances and movies until they finally got married at All Souls Church, Clapton in 1934. Most of the children of my grandmother married about that same time. They all produced their first child during a period of 1937-1938 prior to the Second World War which began in September of 1939.

I did not know my Uncle Will who died in the 1930's and I am not sure if he was married and had children. Tom, who was my mother's brother, married another Ivy who produced two children named Ron and Pat. Maud married Charlie who produced Maureen and Roger. My mother Ivy produced me and later Colin. The youngest sibling was Harry who married Ida, but they did not have any children. After the war was over each of my uncles and aunts produced another child which would in later years be called one of the first post war baby boomers.

On my father's side of the family was the Phelps. They lived about five miles from my mother's family in the town of Walthamstow. The family lived on South Grove Avenue. This Avenue had houses that we called a ribbon row house. These were homes that were connected to each other like a piece of ribbon and were not detached from each other. The Phelps family consisted of John Ambrose Phelps, my grandfather, who was a sewing machine mechanic for Singer Sewing Machine Company. My grandmother's maiden name was Ellen Arrah. My paternal grandparents produced one son Eddie and three daughters Matilda, Margaret and Hilda.

1939

I DON'T REMEMBER much about 1939 since I was only two years old, but what I do know is that it was a very bad year for everybody in England. This was the year when war had been declared against Germany and when my dad was drafted into the Army. He was drafted during early 1939 and off he went to war leaving a wife and baby behind. I do not remember him much prior to him going into the Army except I remember he would put me up on his shoulders whenever we went for out for a walk and hold my small hands. He always managed to have quality time for me. He liked lifting me up and putting me on his shoulders and laughing as he played with his only son at that time. That I do remember well since it has stayed with me all of my life. I will always remember him as a loving and caring father whose first concern was to his family before his own needs.

He defused bombs and later was involved in the development of chemical warfare, which eventually caused his death of lung cancer in 1947. This occurred just after he returned after the war and right after he returned home after the war ended. This we believe were the chemicals that he came in contact with during his service in the Army and caused his cancer.

During this period of 1939 was called the phony war since each side continued talking and politically threatening each other across the English Channel between their leaders, but nothing was really happening except using this time to prepare for war by calling up men for training and making war machines. Threats of war were continuing to be made, but each country knew it was surely coming soon enough and each country was using this time to build up their weapon resources.

They drew on young men ready for the draft into the various military services, training them until the time really came when we were finally at war.

My mother's side of the family consisted of her four brothers. William the eldest, known as Will named after my granddad, died in the mid 1930's. Harry the youngest was born 1917 and was the most educated son joining the Army in a higher grade position. Tom who was a twin to my mother was born 1910 and he did not go into the military. My mother's sisters were Rose the eldest, Maud, the one in between. Aunt Maud's husband Charlie was also in the Army and they were all inducted at about the same time together. I believe he was inducted into the Pioneer Defense Corps.

On my father's side was the Phelps family and my dad went into the Army for the Royal Engineers. My Uncle Cyril who at the age of nineteen volunteered and joined the Royal Air Force as aircrew tail turret gunner on a Lancaster bomber was shot down and killed over Germany in 1942. This incidentally helped me in later years to be accepted into the Royal Air Force which allowed the next generation to go into the Royal Air Force and continue their family tradition. But that will come later in my story.

At the end of Clementina Road where we lived was a huge gas works which belched out smoke. It cooked the raw coal, extracting gas out of the coal, then the gas was then pumped into gas lines direct to family kitchens and then we used the gas stove for cooking food. At night it looked like the fires of hell with the clanking of the huge overhead railway gondolas filled to the brim of coal to be dumped into the roaring furnaces to be cooked. The smell was bad and the noise was worse since all night the clanking of machinery went on day and night. I will get more into that as we go through the later years of my life.

There were about a thousand Warner flats laid out in a type of building grid all built in the same design and were owned by a company called Warner's. The huge development was a Warner subdivision and they were the ones who we paid the rent. These flats were ribbon style apartments connected to each other with one flat upstairs and one downstairs, all of the same design. They were laid out in large two-story blocks and were actually very nice for that period of time. It was a very nice neighborhood to live and play. Each flat had a private front door where each led to either upstairs apartment or direct downstairs into the lower apartment.

We had our own front door leading directly upstairs to our living area. The apartment had two bedrooms, a front room facing the street (used only for special occasions) and a scullery (kitchen) which had a built in large, round brick-fired copper boiler to boil and clean our clothes. There was a small fireplace grate built into the bottom of this copper to burn coke fuel for heating the copper water bowl at the top. Water would boil into the large top bowl that was about three feet deep where you put the dirty clothes in to boil. When the water was good and hot the housewife would then put in the lye soap, which caused their hands to become red. When the clothes were boiled, the housewife would then use a washboard to scrub the clothes with lye soap, one article of clothing at a time directly out of the boiler. When the clothes were boiled and washed, they were then put through a large wringer. This consisted of two tightly joined wooden rollers on top of each other with no gap in between and iron gears at the sides to squeeze out the excess water in the clothes. The clothes were then hung out to dry in the back garden on long clothes lines. Each article of clothing was held firm on the clothes line by a clothes pin. Everything was hung out to dry in the back yard clothes line for everybody to see even lady's underwear, which was truly a sight to be seen.

In our scullery was an old gas range where the food was prepared. It was not the kind of a kitchen an American would recognize or would want to have their food cooked and prepared on. In this room was also a small room set aside for a toilet, which was a chain-pulled flush toilet filled with a water tank at the top with a chain hanging down to flush. The gas range was on the right side of the room fired by gas extracted by the local gas works from coal into desiccated coke. In the corner was a large tall closet used as a coal bunker where all the coal was kept to light the fires in each room. It had an open fireplace to put coal or coke into the grate and lit for room warmth.

The coal delivery man, whose face was covered black with coal dust, delivered our coal with his horse and cart. He would first have to come up the front stairs from the street carrying a heavy sack of coal on his back and deliver the coal into the upstairs bunker. When he delivered the coal into the bunker there was a roar that sounded like thunder. We usually contracted for about four sacks of coal each with about 100-weight in pounds every week.

On the right side of the scullery were stairs leading down to the back door into a small back garden. The scullery was dark and gloomy with the smell of coal from the coal bunker at the back which seemed to find its way throughout the house. I discovered later that the smell of coal was the gases escaping from the coal bunker into the kitchen into the air that we eventually breathed into our lungs.

My mother cooked for us in that room and carried the food into the living room that was at the back of the apartment overlooking the garden. We had an open fireplace and mantel shelf but we never used it. On the mantle shelf above the fireplace was a nice clock that chimed on the hour. This was our living room where we ate and spent much our leisure time listening to the radio. In the front room we had a small piano and a glass cabinet filled with delicate china plates and cups of the same design that were never used unless company came calling and our visitors would then be invited into this front room for any visiting or a family party. My mother and her twin brother Tom both played the piano. In later years we had a great many family parties which I will address later in other upcoming chapters. Some of our favorite lunches and sometimes dinners were eating bread and beef dripping sandwiches.

The Gas Works

MOST FAMILIES DURING those days had an open-hearth fire which was fueled by coke. To describe what coke was in those days was when a large piece of coal was cooked by tremendous heat it sucked out all of the gas that was in the piece of coal. Then the gas was piped into the homes for the family cooking. When this occurred all that was left of the piece of coal was a desiccated piece of coal, changed now and called coke. Down the street from our flat was a huge gas works which was a manufacturing facility of turning coal into coke and gas for cooking fuel. This is not natural gas as we know it, but manufactured gas. The gondolas would be running all night with the fires looking like hell and smoke would be pouring out of the furnaces into the air.

There were huge furnaces fired up as the coal was tipped into the furnace from the moving gondolas as the heat then was sucked out of the gas which was then piped into the homes of Londoners as cooking gas. It was nothing like the natural gas that we use today, but raw coal had to be cooked first by emptying out into the atmosphere Sulphur and other bad gasses. What was left of the original coal was a piece of coal that was full of tiny holes and very dry. This end product of coal and gas was used as fuel in the fireplaces of the people because it kept a smoldering fireplace in the house all through the night if it was banked up enough. Most of the residences used this instead of raw coal and the gas was used for cooking.

1939-1940, Preparation for War

WHEN WAR WAS finally declared in September of 1939, militarily events began to move quickly to become an active war. Preparations had to be made very quickly for a pending terrible conflict that would later be called World War II. Everybody including civilians was issued a personal gas mask. I was issued a red children's gas mask. The face mask was designed as a Mickey Mouse rubber mask with two big round glass eye sockets and a floppy flat red nose. I was instructed to carry it at all times with a thick string over my shoulder in a small square cardboard box. It was ordered by the government that all civilians should carry the gas mask at all times in case of a gas attack, which was fear and apprehension left over from the First World War when mustard gas was used in the military trenches in France. Most people feared that it would be used on civilians if an air war was conducted in a future aerial bombing.

All public buses had a straw-based taped window covering which stretched across each bus window to prevent the window from blowing out during a blast of a bomb shredding glass over the passengers. The blackout was strictly enforced every night. Every door and window had a curtain pulled across to prevent any light from escaping and to prevent any enemy bomber aircraft seeing any a small light from the air.

Older men, who were too old to be inducted into the armed forces, were designated as air raid wardens. They wore an Army type uniform with a tin helmet and were armed with a flashlight. The air raid warden had a designated area or a beat to walk in the neighborhood and if he saw any chink of light coming from a window he would shout out in a very loud voice to put out that bloody light!

All the cities of England were blacked out as were all shops, music halls and movie theaters. All theaters then began immediately to shut off all of the outside lights except one, the Windmill Theater in London which was a so-called naughty vaudeville theater in the West End of London. Their slogan during the war was we never closed playing all through the war years although they did turn off their front Marquee lights from the street. No light was allowed at all to leave the building.

Street lights were turned off and torches (flashlights) were absolutely necessary to find your way along the streets. In most streets there were some special street air raid shelters built above ground just in case people were caught out on a street away from home. It was easy to be caught out on the streets during an air raid when falling shrapnel from exploded gun shells came raining down from the air after they were fired.

As kids after a raid we would go out and pick up these broken shell cases that had been sent down to kill us. We would pick them up and use them as souvenirs. Being built above ground some of these shelters did not help much with a direct hit by a bomb, but it did give protection from airborne shrapnel and exploded bombs. That was one of the greatest fears for civilians, shrapnel from exploding bombs killing and injuring people.

England was preparing for war but I was still very young and did not really know that we were on the verge of a worldwide disaster that would socially turn the world upside down. It has been reported in recent years millions of people died in this coming conflict that was bearing down on Europe. That is today a conservative estimate, probably more in fact if a final tally was ever made. Nobody really knows how many had been killed at the end of the war until some years later. I believe that the final count will be more.

Everyone was issued a national identity card which must be with you at all times and was also given a ration book. This allowed the local grocer to tear off coupons only to the amounts allowed since food was in short supply and in the coming years would get even worse. The ration book was for all commodities such as petrol (gasoline), butter, eggs, meat and other items that were in short supply.

This lasted for the duration of the war and even for a few years after the war had ended. Travel was restricted for civilians since the Army needed the railway cars to move troops around the country. It was difficult for civilians to get a travel warrant from the government unless it was for a special reason.

The police did many defense practices to prepare for the coming air raids they knew were sure to come, as well as preparing for many casualties. Other war preparations were built. One was that an air raid shelter had to be built in everybody's back yard. This official shelter was called an Anderson air raid shelter. To build this shelter was the responsibility of the owner or renter of the apartment. The materials were given free to each renter by the government and the owner had to apply for the materials at the town hall offices to be delivered. There were very few able bodied young men to do this labor since they all had been inducted into the armed forces training for war by 1939 and early 1940.

These are the directions that the Anderson shelters were to be built. First, dig a large hole in the back yard about fifteen feet long and ten feet wide. The depth into the ground would be about six foot deep. The joke going around was that it was six feet down, about the depth of a grave. Then pile all the earth from digging this hole and keep it separate. The corrugated iron had a curve at the top would each serve as a roof as each curve met from opposite directions. The sides also were made of corrugated iron so that when it was installed it would make it an iron shelter buried six feet down into the open hole. When this was completed all of the excess earth and dirt taken from digging the hole was piled on top of the iron shell roof to protect from a bomb blast. Below ground level was relatively safe from bomb blast except for a direct hit. Inside the shelter they installed slatted wooden flooring to help with the water drainage. There were bunks on either side making it feel damp and had an odd moldy smell. To this day I can still smell that damp earth smell whenever I go into a cave or some old building. The insides of the iron shelter would sweat with droplets of water dripping down the sides. The inside lighting would come from oil lanterns which we called hurricane lamps. When these lamps were lit, fumes would rise into the enclosed space and it was dangerous with possible carbon dioxide in the shelter. When the shelter was finished it was a fairly good bomb shelter against bomb blasts, but was of no help if the bomb exploded nearby or took a direct hit.

When the shelter was completed, and since English people are avid gardeners, they planted flowers and plants on top of the shelter with the excess left over earth. Then they covered the top of the air raid shelter making the roof into a garden of flowers and vegetables that could be used as the food when shortages began to start. The space for the occupation of people allowed in the shelter was limited to about six to eight people.

During the month of September 1940, the bombing began with a vengeance, with night time bombing of London every night. The air raid sirens began to wail hour after hour as the bombing blitz began. The whistle of the bombs falling was frightening, but waiting for the bombs to make a hit maybe somewhere close by was even worse.

This was the first time that Germany began the bombing of civilians in London, but there was much to more to come. After the war ended it was discovered in captured documents that it was a navigational error on the part of one German bomber pilot squadron leader who by poor navigation led the attack on London by mistake. It also was said that Hitler was not too pleased with this pilot who was severely punished since history also said that he was not in favor of bombing British civilians. He only wanted complete control over the other continental European countries.

The first air raid warning siren that we heard was a warbling sound, an up and down, high-pitch low-pitch sound. When this was heard night or day, my mother picked me up out of my bed and went immediately down into the air raid shelter and we lived there every night. I remember seeing the search lights in the night sky looking for German bombers and the roar of low flying aircraft, the explosions rocked the ground and filled the air with sound and smoke and in the air raid shelter was the smell of sweat from absolute fear.

Interestingly enough one of the major targets for the German bombers was the gas works that were at the bottom of our road. Nearby was a huge railroad martialing yard that ferried both troops and material by rail to aid the war effort. It was a juicy target for the bombers, but they missed it on each bombing run which shows how bad their training was at that time, but it soon improved. People were being killed and losing their homes by firebombs called incendiary bombs that were also being dropped by the bombers. These incendiary bombs were meant to create fire storms.

In 1940 in most cases, it was the killing or maiming of the people who did not go down into the air raid shelters. Everything was on fire because of the incendiary bombs that used liquid fire instead of an explosion. When the bombing was completed and the bombers were gone then the siren for all clear sounded which this time gave a single long one note soothing wail that would last for about ten minutes. People who came out of their shelters at this sound when the raid was over sometimes found that their house had been bombed and destroyed, they had no home to return, just piles of smoking rubble in the streets. There were fireman trying to put out fires and ambulances racing along the streets their sirens blaring. Air raid wardens were looking through the rubble for anyone that could have survived and remove the dead bodies from the piles of burning rubble from within the bombed building. Imagine if you can that it was like each night of the bombing was like New York's 9/11 all over London every night, three thousand dead every night.

The adults in the shelter were very scared although I do not personally remember being scared, but only being interested in what was going on. Although I was quite young at three years old, I was old enough to understand what was going on. I do not remember having any actual fear of the noise of the bombing and the big guns firing, but I remember understanding that it was a serious situation. I was very confused as to why this was going on in my life, but then I did not really understand anything better at that age. It was for me like hearing a modern day heavy thunderstorm with the lightning and sound of thunder, but this was no thunderstorm for sure.

I remember each time I was in the air raid shelter during the London blitz of September 1940. I could smell the odor of wet soil from the newly dug holes in the ground, the smell of bomb cordite above the ground and feel the earth move beneath me as I lay in the bunk. I remember also when someone parted the door curtain seeing the massive searchlights that were crisscrossing the night sky searching for enemy planes that had dropped bombs on civilians destroying whole neighborhoods in one single raid. The German aircraft also used a delayed explosive called land mines so that the device exploded after the raid, while the fireman was trying to put out the fires and rescue anyone that had survived. This killed more people who were just trying to help.

I also remember hundreds of huge grey barrage balloons that looked like a giant grey elephant which was filled with hydrogen gas. The balloons were as large as a house and usually tied to trucks with large roll-up wire wheels that wound the steel wires to let the balloon go as high as possible. The purpose of these balloons was two-fold. One was to get the aircraft tangled in the wires that tied the balloon to the truck to prevent the Stuka dive bombers to dive and get tangled in the wires before their target and second, to be caught near a balloon when its hydrogen gas inside the balloon exploded on their run to the target. The great docks of London were an important target to the German bombers since that was where the merchant ships docked after crossing the Atlantic bringing in food from America. Everyone had a good laugh seeing the wardens running after the trailing ropes of these huge elephant barrage balloons when they got loose dragging their tie ropes across the house roofs.

During the war many people would go down the tube station (underground train) which was 300 feet deep down into the earth. They named it the iron lung. Sometimes when my Uncle Bill came home on leave from the Army he arrived at his subway station to get off, where there were many people sheltering from the bombs with their bedding getting ready to sleep there overnight. Bill enlisted in the Army under age and many did that to get out of severe poverty left over from the great depression by joining the military.

My mother now had to find work to keep us in rent and food and since dad's Army pay would not cover living expenses so she went back to Bache's to work at the counter inside the shop. I had to be cared for which is like a present day term for daycare. There was a woman friend of my mother's down the street who was minding about five or six other children, so I was included in that bunch of children. I remember climbing over the top of the air raid shelter that had been built in her back garden, but I also remember I did not like this woman too well.

These kids that were being minded were really rough kids and whenever this woman was not around some of the kids were wild and they tried to attack me by kicking and punching me around. It was not a happy scene, but I was too young to complain to my mother what was going on during this day care.

My mother worked very hard for a small amount of pay. To get to Walthamstow High Street and Bache's she had to catch a trolley bus to the top of Markhouse Road and pick up another bus that went to Walthamstow, to Batch's store. They sold just about any produce, chicken's eggs, duck eggs, cookies, general groceries and other items. She worked the cart which was meant to appear to be a special sales cart with prices that were supposed to be lower than inside the shop. It tried to catch the attention of the passersby that had no intention to take the time in going into the store. The person that worked the stall as we called it was constantly on the move. She would be like a super fired up car salesman, who would put eggs in a bag and chase after the housewives passing by on the sidewalk, fast talking to offer eggs and cookies and trying to persuade them to buy a dozen eggs. She would call out, hey lady, look at these wonderful large eggs and biscuits. This is what my dad did prior the outbreak of war in 1939 before going into the Army.

My mother worked at Bache's shop during the blitz bombing and throughout the war until my dad was discharged from the Army in 1946. She would take the bus even if there was an air raid in progress. I asked her once after the war, why she did this during an air raid and she said it didn't matter since if she was going to get killed by a bomb, she couldn't help it and had to just carry on. I mention this at this time since it had an important part in my story in my teenage years.

The house windows were blacked out by pulling black curtains across the window to prevent any light showing outside. Supposedly if enemy pilots in bombers would see light from uncovered windows if would give them a target. I do not see how an airplane moving at 200+ mph would see a chink of light to help them find the bomb area, but I think this was done to calm down the people. Actually, we all found out after the war from those German pilots that targeted London that they just followed the river Thames during a moonlight night when the moon was shining on the river directing them to their target to the center city of London and just bombed it.

My mother, whose maiden name was Went, came from a suburb of London called Clapton where my maternal grandmother Rose Went and paternal grandfather William Went lived. It has always been accepted that the family name Went was originally German, Wentz. Only recently it has that been proven incorrect and that the name of Went had been changed by my great, great, grandfather in the late 1800's from the original name of Frakes to Went, but that is ahead of my story. My grandmother owned a three or four level house built ribbon style and lived there until she died in the 1970's. It was the same kind of building for miles around. My grandmother's house was in excellent repair, three or four stories high. At an earlier time, my grandmother had what they called gas mantels which were small white lacey lamp bulbs which burned the gas and gave light to the rooms. That was before there were electric light bulbs. Most of the families in those days all lived close together so it was easy to visit each other. The back yard or garden as we called it was about fifty feet deep backing on to the next row of houses on the next street and about thirty feet wide.

My Uncle Harry and Aunt Ida lived in a neighborhood street and my Uncle Tom, who was a twin to my mother Ivy, lived upstairs in my grandmother's house until both Tom and Harry were called up to join the Army and were drafted into the various branches of the armed service for the duration of the war. At the back of my grandmother's house there was a concrete pathway leading out from the back door. To the left was a chicken shed on one side and flowers and vegetables on the other. There were about twenty chickens in the shed producing fresh eggs each day. Also, a crowing rooster was in the chicken coop and would crow early in the morning.

The house had no hot running water. The toilet was part of the house attached at the back but to get to the toilet you had to go outside first. It was a flushable toilet with a chain that you pulled from a water tank located at the top of the wall. This facility was always called the loo and still is. It was connected to a public sewer under the street. Although it was considered normal in those days in London to have a flushable toilet the system, at my Grandmother's house it was quite unique and could be called quite posh since most homes had only an outhouse.

To take a bath home style you brought in a galvanized tub bath which was usually hung from a nail on the garden fence. For getting hot water you had to boil a whole lot of water and pour it into the tub in the scullery and bathed there. In case the term the scullery is unknown to my reader, it is a room kept away from the kitchen where most of the cooking was done but also was where the laundry was done. Keep in mind also that there was no central heating in any of these homes. To take a bath in the cold scullery took a lot of preparation. Because there was no heat in the home except small open fireplaces, both hot water and cold were needed quickly. To take a bath in those days was to quickly undress, get in the tub, scrub and quickly dunk in cold water to wash away the soap and dry off quick before the cold air reached your body. You had to be quick on your feet for sure!

There had not been much civilian bombing during the First World War, but since 1918 aircraft had grown much more sophisticated so the government was expecting heavy bombing when this new war began. The government was giving all kinds of directives to the people to prepare for war such as evacuation of children from the city and building shelters in the gardens. Everybody was preparing for the eventual conflict which was being considered as a continuation of the World War I from 1914-1918.

The Battle of Britain

BY THE TIME I was three years old I started regular school. All the schools in the London area were named after the street it was located. My first school was on the next street over from where I lived, the street was called Perth Road, so the school was called Perth Road School.

My first grade teacher was a very portly lady called Mrs. Gould. She was a little on the heavy side and very severe looking and strict. She took no nonsense from any of her pupils and had no qualms in rapping the boys over the knuckles with a wooden ruler. The girl's punishment for any misbehavior was a slap on the legs with the ruler.

I remember that she always came to school each day dressed in drab colors, with a long dress with plenty of white lace around the top and black button-up shoes. She taught us how to read and write when we were only three years old. I do remember vaguely the classes she taught were basic math, English and geography. I stayed at the school for about a year until after the London Blitz which began September 1940 when I was evacuated out into the country about 25 miles away in the county of Essex.

One night during late September 1940 I remember an air raid siren going off in the middle of the night. The warning siren had a starting low pitch intense wail, moving slowly up the scale until it was screaming in a high-pitched constant wail. I remember my mother picking me up and laying me over her shoulder and going down the stairs to the back door to the garden and out to the air raid shelter in the back yard. I recall the sky being bright red from the thousands of fires caused by falling bombs. There were also lots of flashes lighting up the sky and anti-aircraft guns trying to knock out the invading bombers. Not only were they dropping explosive bombs, but dropping bombs that were called incendiary bombs. These bombs were really fire bombs that were made to cause civilian deaths at the same time as destruction of their homes and factories by fire. They also used these weapons to destroy people in their homes by burning the houses and the people inside them.

The sky was filled with beams of searchlights slowly sweeping the sky looking for any aircraft. As these searchlights swept the sky, they would suddenly find one of the bombers caught in the cross hairs of three or more searchlights. The German aircraft appeared in the night sky as a silver light and suddenly the sky would be filled with arching red lines of tracer bullets, like rockets in a firework display, as the defensive artillery guns zeroed in on the aircraft sending it crashing down into the burning city. Sometimes the aircraft blew up in midair causing a flash of light. The tracer bullets reached up from the ground directing the larger guns to shoot down the aircraft. There was a puff of flame and down came the German aircraft.

I could hear the heavy drone of many aircraft passing overhead. Everywhere in the sky explosions of bombs in the far distance appeared to me to be getting closer. The sirens high pitched warning sound was troubling. To this day whenever I hear a fire whistle warning start up, the memory comes back and a shudder goes down my spine. Down the stairs to the shelter we went, my mother putting me on the lower bunk thinking it was safer.

I remember hearing the bombs coming closer, but after a while the German aircraft turned around and went back to Germany. After about an hour the all-clear siren sounded off. This sound was quite different from the warning siren since its pitch was more calming. Just one high level pitch wailing on one note, to let people know that it was all clear for the moment and could they could leave their shelters for now and return back their homes. I was told that this went on for about four weeks. Every night they came back and every night we went down to the shelters in the garden. During the day we could see the contrails of aircraft of British fighter spitfires of the Royal Air Force engaging in dog fights in the sky shooting down the bombers. This was called the beginning of the Battle of Britain. The Royal Air Force was using every aircraft at their disposal to shoot down the bombers since they knew that the Germans were trying to control the skies prior to an invasion of England. Germany had the invasion plans in place and ready to cross the channel to invade England.

By this time the bombing each night was becoming intolerant. The spitfires of the RAF were shooting down as many bombers as they could, but the amount of fighter aircraft was getting smaller as so many had been shot down in defense of London. There was always the sound of machine guns chattering away up in the sky as the RAF fighters were firing at the German aircraft heading back to their bases and leaving their vapor trails high in the sky.

Other English counties further up north far away in the industrial Midlands were bombing targets such as Birmingham and Sheffield where the manufacturing factories were being targeted by the German Air Force with daily and nightly bombing to destroy the industrial might of the British homeland. England was expecting a German land invasion from France by the Germans armies at any time. The German targeted the factories, gasworks and manufacturing facilities of London firebombing with air raids every day and night.

Thousands of civilians and children were killed each night during the bombing so it was ordered by the government that the children must to be removed from the city of London and by government decree all children must be evacuated out of the city and out of harm's way.

I have been told since then that the fires set in London were so hot that the fires created firestorms that quickly consumed all the oxygen in the air towards the center of the fire. Sucking into the fire like a vacuum not only cars and buses but people such as fire fighters and other people that were trying to put out the fires. There were so many civilians being killed nightly by these raids, including many that were leaving the city to the countryside where it was safer from the nightly bombing.

So severe were these attacks that the British government made a law that all children must be evacuated out of the city into safer parts of the country. They sent as many children as possible out of the city in a great evacuation. There was an official government letter sent out to all parents ordering, that at a certain date and time to be soon determined, each child must be brought by their mothers to one of the many terminal railway stations in London for evacuation out of the city of London out of harm's way. The parent was told in the letter that each child should only bring one overnight change of clothing and must bring their gas masks carried over their shoulders. They also allowed a small suitcase for personal belongings. My gas mask given to me was a red colored Mickey Mouse gas mask designed with large eye holes and a floppy nose. We all had fun trying it on. When all the children were assembled at each railway terminal their names would be checked against a government serial number as to their ordered destination and they would then board their designated train used only for evacuating children assigned by a previously selected destination. This was not too well organized since many parents did not know where their children were going or where their final destination was to be.

The mothers were told that their child would mail back a postcard notifying generally where the place where they had been evacuated. Many parents did not send their children away since they had heard of horror stories of lost children. They made their own private arrangements to evacuate their children, sometimes to a family member that had property outside of London or to friends. After the war ended there were many lost children and many parents did not know where their children had been sent and some parents never saw their children again.

The railway terminals in London were Euston Station, Paddington Station, St. Pancras Station, Fenchurch Street and Waterloo Station where the children's trains left for their many destinations to all over the country. Only children were put on these trains and they did not stop at any station in between London and its final destination. The children had to be moved out of the city of London where the casualties were so high and death was everywhere. Some were sent to the counties of Devon and Cornwall in the southwest of England and to the open countryside out of danger where the Germans did not drop their bombs on civilians. My mother did not want me to be evacuated by the government to just anywhere in the country especially after hearing the horror stories of permanently lost children.

To travel to Thundersley from my home in Leyton was to catch a steam train from the Leyton train station and travel to a town called Barking about ten miles away. At that station we were supposed to change trains to connect to another train to go to Benfleet station where we would take a bus to Bread and Cheese Hill where Mrs. Heath lived. We arrived at the first stop at Barking Station but somehow my mother thought we had to stay on the same train to Benfleet. The train pulled out of the station but only into the train yards and made preparations to turn around and go back to London. The conductor walked down the train, saw us still sitting there. He said we were on the wrong train and he walked us back down along the tracks to the station where we caught the next train to Benfleet station.

We then had to walk from Benfleet Station through the village of Benfleet to board a bus which I remember was painted a bright yellow. The upstairs part of the bus was open and did not have a roof and the seating was completely open. After about a half hour ride, we arrived at the bottom of a steep hill called Bread and Cheese Hill. There was a bus stop at the bottom of the hill at Kent's Hill Road where we got off the bus. We walked up the hill to a small country lane which was named Rhoda Road. This was an old unpaved country lane and since there wasn't any road paving, there was just muddy ruts where cars had once tried to drive up the short lane. After a short distance we came to the bungalow, which I would soon call my home for the next five years and I sometimes still call it my home to this day. It was such a different experience since there were very few houses and everywhere there were fields and hedgerows of thick bushes. The air was clear and there were no bomb craters that I could see. This is where my life was completely changed by this lady who became such a good woman to me in the next five years.

Mrs. Heath was not at home when we arrived at the bungalow, but her husband Jack Heath was there and he told us that she was up at the church sports field where she was umpiring a football game with the Boy Scouts. After retracing our steps and crossing the main road to the opposite side of Rhoda Road we went right to St. Peters Church which was located upon a small hill. I clearly remember at age three and half years old climbing the high steps up through the many old graves to the church yard to the top of the hill where the St. Peters Church had stood for the past 1,200 years. In the field next to the church rectory at the top of the hill we saw boys playing football (soccer) and seeing a rather stout lady in the middle of the game blowing her referee whistle as the boys were kicking the football around and she was acting as a referee to the game. When she noticed my mother, she blew her whistle to end the game and came over to us. I was then introduced to my future surrogate mother. I only recall those few moments at that time. What I did not know was just how much this small, very old church would play in such a large part of my life for the next five years. This will be the last time I would call her Mrs. Heath and from now on she would be called auntie. The game was now finished and we walked together back to the bungalow.

I do not remember much after that except we arrived at the bungalow. We talked a little and sort of got to know each other for the first time, not real strangers but not yet acquainted. I was only a 3 and a half year old toddler. We had some tea and some cookies after which, my mother said it was time for her to go home. I suddenly realized that she was now going to leave me here alone with a stranger in a stranger's home. I do not remember much after that other than saying goodbye to my mother with a few kisses and a few hugs. I might have been in some sort of shock, but I was holding back any emotions about my mum leaving. I suspected I did cry but I do not remember much if I did but by her leaving, I did feel a great sadness. We all walked together down the lane to the main road where my mother would catch a bus to go back to Benfleet train station and home. I watched my mother walking down the hill towards the bus stop. The bus would take her back to Benfleet train station and there she would catch a train back to Leyton and then home to my old home but it was no longer my home.

It was very difficult to get a travel pass in those early days of the war. The Army needed railroad transportation and they were the priority passengers on all civilian transport so she had a civilian reservation for a special civilian and had to be on that train. I had been left behind and this bungalow was now my home. I can still see that sad scene vividly in my mind as my mother walked down the hill watching her getting further away from me, the bus arrived and she was gone. I was only able to see her a few times during the next the five years of war. I saw my father only twice in five years before the end of the war.

I had arrived at the bungalow, my future home and although I was sad, I did not cry. I probably just accepted the change. She had a dog called Tess which made me feel a lot better as little boys do with a small dog. All the years I lived in Thundersley, Tess and I were pals and always enjoyed our company, joining us on our evening walks up the lane. I would throw a stick and away she would run and pick up the stick and bring it back to me. I would hear birds singing all day since in my old home we had no birds to sing other than pigeons. I really loved the singing of the birds in the woods next to the bungalow listening to the woodpecker pecking away at a tree and the cuckoo bird.

The bungalow where I was to live was very small, but it had a very large garden that extended up a hill at the back with an apple orchard on the left side and heavily grown woods on the right side. The bunga-low consisted of one bedroom, one living room where the front door was located and another living area where we actually lived. There was a large cast iron coal stove in the living area that was used for cooking which was attached to a large iron oven. There was no other heating available in the house. Cold water for cooking and bathing was from a hand pump well outside of the house in the back garden.

The furniture consisted of a rocking chair by the stove for Uncle Jack, another chair for auntie and on the other side of the fireplace I had a small chair in front of the fire. We toasted bread in front of the open stove fire on a table fork where there was a frontal grill. My auntie hand cut slices of bread from a loaf, toasting the bread brown at the fire grill or sometimes we would put butter on the bread and put it in the iron oven of the stove with melted cheese on top. That is why I enjoy grilled cheese for a meal to this day. There was a small table over by the window facing a small field looking towards the main road. This was our dinner table which we used for all our meals. Looking out of the window I could see three evenly spaced high poplar trees that seem to have been there forever and probably had been growing there for a long time. They were there when I arrived and were there when I left five years later. Unfortunately, they are not there anymore.

Next to the bungalow on the left side was a raspberry cane bush garden area where there were many raspberry bushes that each summer produced tasty red raspberries. There was no kitchen for the bungalow, just a lean-to shed with large glass windows. It almost looked like a small greenhouse. Outside the bungalow, out back, there was an old primer hand pump attached to large covered natural water well. The pump had to be primed first by pouring water down the top of the pump then you would pump hard until you felt the water pressure build in the pump. At that point the water came out of the pump from the well from underneath the ground and it was very cold water. This had to be pumped by hand into a bucket then brought into the scullery for all our water requirements.

The scullery was quite an important part of the house because auntie did some cooking on an old electric range out there such as boiling water for tea and for our main meals but we also used the scullery for bath time. To take a bath we used an old galvanized bathtub that had multiple uses for washing clothes and bathing. There was no central heating in the bungalow so when it was bath time it was usually very cold, so off came your clothes very quickly and you would get into the warm water in the tin tub. Being only three years and a half, I was bathed by my auntie.

At the two corners of the house was a square water catcher tank and a barrel shaped container which we called water butts. This caught all the rain water run-off from the roof for any future time when water was scarce. Because of the wet climate the water butts were usually full with crawling and tiny swimming worms in the water like centipedes and other insect life. She did not use this water for cooking or drinking water, just for general house cleaning.

Since there was no running water in the house, we used an outhouse for a toilet which I remember had a very bad odor. The outhouse was a small bricked building that had once been built as an air raid shelter. It was now an outhouse with a wooden bench with a circle cut out in the center for a seat and a bucket underneath. There was a piece of sacking for a curtain at the door for privacy. To go outside in the middle of the night alone in the dark to use the toilet for a small boy was daunting. It seemed there were ghosts and wild animals everywhere waiting to pounce on me. I was always happy to get back into a nice warm bed and feel safe again. I kept those demons away as best I could. A flashlight or torch as we called it then was absolutely necessary and a fast run back to the bungalow after my business was done.

In winter it was a race to get back into the warmth of the house and a warm bed. I could hear owls hooting as I ran back to the house and in summer frogs croaking all night. My bed was a small rollup camp bed that was rolled to the back of the room. It was a regular couch during the day but when bedtime came along it was rolled up into four sides like I was in a cocoon. The reason for this was that auntie believed I would be protected from all sides by a mattress if there was any bombing nearby and shrapnel could hit me as it passed through the house.

There was a small fireplace in the room where I slept but it was never used. A mantle shelf over the fireplace had strange looking items sitting on it and a large old-fashioned dresser and mirror was on the opposite side of the room. At Christmas time it was decorated with pearl like ornaments that hung down from the top in a decorative way. Before I arrived it probably was a sitting room when guests or friends would visit.

To keep warm in bed during the winter auntie would take an ordinary building brick and put it in the oven to heat it up. When it got hot enough, she would wrap a towel around the hot brick and put it in the center of the bed. This warmed up the bed in the middle but that left the other end of the bed very cold. The thing to do was as soon as you pulled on your pajamas to escape the cold you then pushed down the wrapped brick so that you could put your feet on the brick and keep your feet warm which slowly warmed up the bed. There was a time when my teeth chattered with cold waiting for the bed to warm up. It was so cold!

As soon as I had settled into my new home auntie began making arrangements for me to attend school at the Rush Bottom Lane Elementary School. This was located off the main highway just about half mile away from Tarpot's Corner. Auntie took my hand and we walked down Bread and Cheese Hill past Kent's Hill road to Tarpot's Corner to school. I believe the village was called Tarpot's because of the pub on the corner was called The Tarpot. The village took its name from the pub. Even after we had arrived at Tarpot's corner there still was a long walk through the fields to the school where I attended for over five years. The school was very small with three classrooms. Auntie took me and she spoke to the head mistress. We met her in her office and had a talk with her and she said that the law was quite strict, war or no war, children had to go to school at age three or older.

I started school two weeks later with auntie walking me all the way to school on my first day. The school building was made of black creosoted wooden planks and had only three class rooms, two for lessons and one for general assembly. Every morning we sang the national anthem God Save the King and said prayers. Outside on the other side of the sports field was a long brick building. This was the air raid shelter for all of the school children which totaled only about forty. There was a large elm tree in the front of the school where in the summer we had lessons outside sitting under the tree in its shade. There were not many children from London, in fact I think I was the only one. They were mostly local children and my London accent stood out like a sore thumb with the other children. They called me a city boy and a Londoner. I was very embarrassed and wondered if I would ever fit in.

School hours were from 9:00 am until 4:00 pm and the school curriculum was very intense. My first day there was uneventful and I had no real problem with any of the other students. We had hot school lunches and we did not carry any books. All of the books were left at school. I was there on my first day when the air raid warning began to wail and out we went to the air raid shelter and I was beginning to think that it was not that much different if I had stayed in London. Anything about our lessons was left on our desks which we put inside when we left for home.

I did fairly well at school since I could read and write in long hand at the age of three. There were only three teachers at the school, all women. We had the same teacher for every subject. They were all women since all of the men were away in the armed forces fighting the Germans. We had hot lunches in the assembly hall which is where I believe I first became a vegetarian. I was sitting at the table one day looking at my plate of mincemeat next to a girl who began eating her meal. Mincemeat is where a chunk of meat and gristle gets ground up into a long mush of meat. Nobody knew just what was being ground up back in the kitchen. I watched this girl eat her mincemeat when she suddenly threw up all over the table. The smell was so very bad I could not touch any more mincemeat that day. I tried so hard the following days to eat some mincemeat, but felt like throwing up each time I tried to take a bite. I remember now why I do not eat meat, remembering that little girl being sick. I was taught by my Auntie Ellie not to harm animals and care for them and I still adhere to that reasoning. She was an environmentalist in those early days, she just loved all animals. She kept reminding me that every animal should be free from pain and suffering.

I lived in the small village of Thundersley in the county of Essex. Usually each village had its own church that was as old as the village itself as was our church of St. Peters. The church of St. Peters was built originally in the 7th century, and burnt down by the Vikings. In the 8th century it was rebuilt as a Saxon church with a Saxon pointed steeple. It rang its three bells in a high, medium and low rhythm on Sunday morning and was located on top of a three hundred or so foot hill. All churches at that time were built on a hill as a lookout for the Vikings and warned other churches. If an enemy would be seen approaching, the next village would light a bonfire on their church hill to warn others that Vikings were on their way.

On the chancellery door to the church is a two-foot-thick door to enter the church. On this door are large nail holes. These nails must have been quite large especially for what they were used for. When the Vikings were on the march and warning had been given by the next village that they were coming, the villagers would all hurry into the church and since the church was made of stone it was reasonably safe for the villagers. If some of the villagers left it too late to get into sanctuary of the church they were caught by the Vikings, skinned alive and had their skins nailed to the door of the church. It cannot be imagined in these modern times how the villagers inside the church in safety would hear the human skins being nailed into the church door. The village would then be put to the torch and domestic animals driven away for food. To this day if you look closely you can see in that huge oak door the large nail holes that would hold up the skins of the villagers who got caught.

The social life in Thundersley was very strong in those days since most events worked around the church and its activities. There were women's sewing circles, the cubs and scouts. We put on plays and musical evenings for the congregation. They also arranged garden parties in the summer and magic lantern shows in the winter. I remember the church being so cold since it was built of stone and there was no heating of any kind.

I was a kind of mascot for the cubs. We would go each Sunday to church parade and marched into church. I was too young to join the cubs, but somehow she fixed it. I marched in front of the group. Behind me came an older cub scout who carried the totem pole with a model wolves head at the top of the pole and all the ribbons and medallions hanging down from the head. Beside him came another cub who carried the British flag, the Union Jack and I longed for the day when I could be the one to carry the flag of my country.

As the year of 1943 came to an end the bombing became less and some nights there were no air raids. When the air raid siren did sound, we ran across the lane, into the garden and climbed down the steps into Mrs. Willis's air raid shelter. German aircraft were being shot down in increasing numbers since now the RAF and the USAF had control of the skies. This was because of a new detection device called radar.

Although at night there were the occasional raid so it was not unusual that on my way to school in the morning, I would hear high in the sky a stuttering sound of an aircraft engine and see in the distance a Messerschmitt 109 that had been hit, trailing black smoke and seen crashing in some farmers' field. There was debris all over the roads after an air raid. Hot shrapnel which was shell casings from defending guns from the attacking bombers or from the defending RAF fighter pilots trying to shoot them down. Radar was being developed although it was in its infancy.

This was now more accurate to find opposing aircraft so some sort of defense mechanism had to be invented to disrupt the radar scopes of the aircraft. The Germans had discovered that by dropping strings of long silver foils by aircraft they would upset the electronics of defense radar.

My auntie was very active in the cubs and Boy Scouts. She was also very active in local civil events. This was due to the fact there were a lack of men at that time because all of the men were in the military service. She was probably one of the most prominent women in all of Thundersley society. She was the leader of two cub packs and two scouts' groups, both were sponsored by St. Peters Church. I grew up from the age of four years old very close to the scouting movement. Auntie ran her life under the premise of the scouting code of honor and tradition. I would have to attend the meetings with her and learn the cub and scout code of honor. She would always know when I was not telling the truth and she knew my weaknesses, if I told a lie or when I made a false answer to her question, she asked me to raise my hand to my forehead, three fingers raised and say scout's honor. If I was guilty, I could not lie so I would tearfully admit that I was not telling her the truth. I was then punished anyway. The scouting code was very strong in me and still is to this very day. She was the cub mistress and scout master of St. Peters Church and very much involved in the politics of the church with the Reverend Mailey, the vicar of St. Peters Church.

St. Peters Church

THIS CHURCH WAS 1,200 years old and named after Saint Peter the Rock in biblical terms. Village life revolved around this church and the religious denomination was Church of England, the Anglican Church or in America it was called the Episcopal Church. For the past four centuries the crown had changed faiths. After King Henry the 8th was divorced and remarried, he called the national religious faith in England the Church of England. Some of my readers may have noticed that on the Episcopal Church emblem in America is a small red cross on the shield. This is the red cross of Saint George, the slayer of the dragons and national symbol of England.

The church services that I attended were compulsory to me since Auntie Ellie was also a Sunday school teacher for the church. I was really too young to join the cub scouts since I was just four years old now. A boy had to be seven years old to join the cubs so my auntie made me their mascot. She was the cub leader and I suppose she made the rules so I became a cub scout at the age of four years old. I wore a green jersey with a blue scarf. At the point corner of the scarf was the cross keys emblem of Saint Peter, the keeper of the keys to heaven.

The bells of St. Peters rang Sundays at 7:45 am calling all of the church goers to Sunday morning service. All cubs and Boy Scouts had to attend unless they were sick. After the morning church service, we all retired to the church hall and worked on our badges and other things we had scheduled to do. We would assemble there early every Sunday morning where we would march the half mile to the church for eight o'clock holy communion and prepare to march like young soldiers to the church with our flags flying and me carrying the wolfs head totem pole.

Ahead of the marchers was Auntie Ellie dressed in a khaki dress reaching down almost to her ankles with a military type safari type blouse and man's necktie around her neck. She wore scouting ribbons on her chest with many badges crediting her with certain decorations of service and achievements. Auntie Ellie marched first at the head of the parade leading the marchers and I was carrying the totem pole with the wolves head at the top and all the draped ribbons falling down like an Indian totem pole. I felt very proud! Behind me came an older boy pounding a drum which he carried across his chest. The drum was to keep the marchers in time with their feet. There were always people on the sidewalks watching us march to the church with a few cheers and hand waves to urge us on. There were about fifty members of her cub group of ages seven up to twelve and we usually had at least thirty to forty boys marching each Sunday. That was considered a good turnout.

Everybody had to turn up for Sunday parade since it was well known that my auntie was a stickler for not only being on time, but all must show up for the church parade. I can still see her now in my mind marching along in front of me turning her head to see that I was following her and that the rest of the parade was following me. We would be carrying full colors which were the Union Jack, the British flag, the troop flag and the flag for the county of Essex. We were very military since she drilled us like any determined drill sergeant and during the week we would practice again at our Wednesday evenings meetings. She was a Sunday school teacher so during the afternoon on Sundays I had to attend Sunday school. We were back at the church again at six pm for the Evensong church service in St. Peters Church.

Thundersley is a very old village and had a very long history. All functions seem to circle around the activities of the church. There were many events that were very important for war time civil morale. We attended fetes which were small outdoor country fairs. We had some merry go rounds which were like a small carousel. There were side shows and one was a coconut shy. This was when a coconut was put up on a pedestal positioned in a large wooden cup and then someone tries to knock it down with cricket ball.

The vicar of St. Peters at that time was the Reverend Mailey. I seem to remember him as a stout, silver grey haired man with a ruddy face, somewhat typical of the look of a US senator that was depicted in many American movies. I remember him as a very nice but pious man who was very soft spoken and looking very old to me. I think he was about sixty plus years at that time, which to me was very old. Saint Peters Church was also very old in itself since it was built in the 7th century in Saxon England. England at that time was ruled by the Saxons who actually came from Saxony in Germany. It was burnt down by the Vikings around the 8th century and rebuilt in that year as St. Peters.

The church logo was a pair of crossed keys named in the biblical testament of St. Peter. He held the keys to the gates of heaven. On our green Cub Scout uniform, we had neck scarves which hung down to a point at the back of the shoulder where there was a pair of embroidered cross keys depicting that we were from the parish of St. Peter of Thundersley. The front of the scarf was clasped together by a wide small leather band called a woggle.

I am mentioning this because the two greatest parts of my life in Thundersley during the war years revolved between scouting and St. Peters Church. I do not remember much about the school days during those five years except the continuous interruptions of our classes when the air raid siren sounded off and then having to run quickly across the lawn of the school to the air raid shelter that was set up for the children. They had benches running the length inside of the shelter but no desks so the teacher had to resume her class under the worst conditions trying to teach over the drone of aircraft overhead on their way to bomb London 30 miles away. Because of these interruptions we did not learn much during this very important part of my education although my auntie had already taught me how to read and write in long hand.

It was a long walk to school which took almost an hour round trip every morning. When we got nearer to the school, I would see walking down the road towards the school all the children walking to school. Girls in starched dresses and the boys all wore grey flannel short pants and shirts with school colored design ties. Most of the girls wore very plain blue gingham dresses some with flowers printed on the dress. One girl I remember wore a blue gingham blouse. I do not recall her name but she had a lisp and the other girls made a lot of fun of her, it was not very nice of them but I suppose children are children. I also remember there was an open drainage ditch along the countryside road and I would stare at the water as I walked along to see if I could see any fish.

Near the school gate was a huge old elm tree. During the rare sunny days of England, we had lessons held under the elm tree in its shade. I visited the school fifty years later and the tree was still there. It was a very pastoral scene since there were very few houses. The whole countryside was mostly made up of all dairy farms with squared off fields and divided by large hedgerows of blackthorn and blackberry bushes where we used to go blackberry picking in the fall, almost impossible to pass through the hedges because of the dense thorns.

I was at that time what one might be called today a loner. This has followed me most of my life. I never had problems not being part of a group of friends, I did not mind being on my own. I had made myself completely independent and I was quite content to be on my own. This could be considered a positive and an independent attitude, but it also cost me the inability to look for friends. This would affect me later during my life. I was happy with people, but also happy with or without friends. Once I left school and returned back to the bungalow there were no small kids of my age around that area to play with so I made my own enjoyment.

There were lots of cattle and sheep in the fields and I remember that it was kind of relaxing. Every day I would be dressed by my auntie and I left on my own from the bungalow to walk down the lane to the main road, down Bread and Cheese Hill to the bus stop and I got to school by 9:00 am. Most of the houses were small bungalow types with only maybe one or two bedrooms. The countryside was very green and serene. I remember that there were not many people out and about. Most of the people I saw were women since all the men had been drafted into the Army and were away in the early days of the war. I always remember walking the three miles to school watching the air battles going on above my head listening to the chattering of machine guns and the watching the aircraft trying to shoot each other down and sometimes one or more would be trailing black smoke when it was hit and heading for the ground somewhere.

My auntie would work with the scouts and cubs almost every day of the week and she was such a busy person. She really was a good woman but very strict. I had not learned too much about bad words since I had little contact with other children. Bad language was forbidden at school and my auntie made sure that I never said anything improper at home. We lived in a very wet country where it always seems to rain. The grass was lush and green and plants and trees grew very quickly. It rarely snowed in the county of Essex because we were so near the mouth of the river Thames, so being near the coast the weather was mild and affected the climate. I would say that the climate was about the same as in North Carolina. One day it started to snow, the snow coming down quite heavy and beginning to settle on the pathways. I was so excited to see snow coming down out of the sky and just lost control of myself and blurted out those terrible words that would cost me my dinner. I cried out, auntie, auntie it's snowing like hell! Well, my auntie looked at me like I had never seen her look before and she grabbed me by the collar of my coat, wacked my backside hard with a slipper, grabbed my left ear and pulled me out into the scullery. She put a large bar of Lifebuoy soap in my mouth and stood me in the corner of the room for about two hours. She then washed out my mouth with soap and water. Sometimes I can still taste that soap in my mouth and was actually blowing bubbles out of my mouth for hours afterwards. I was a bad boy. She then took me into the middle room where my small bed was located and said that for dinner, I would have nothing to eat but bread and water. She actually brought a tray of bread slices and a glass of water. Today, here in America, that probably would be cause for the police to be called and she would have been accused of child abuse!

As I mentioned before we had a real nice dog named Tess. She was a tawny, white haired English Terrier, except she had slightly brown ears and she and I became friends for life. We were always together and one of the happiest parts of my childhood was for us to go out on our evening walks together with my auntie who carried a hickory walking stick with a hand carved bull dogs head on the end.

Her husband, Uncle Jack, did not come on any of the walks since he was a mentally ill invalid staying home most of the time, sitting in his rocking chair by the fireside singing songs and gazing into the fire in the iron stove. He was in another world. He occasionally said something to me but most of the time he was inside himself. He never had much contact with me except when we were sitting by the fire with a large blanket wrapped around him.

My auntie was a great story teller and would make up stories when I went to bed. Just an ordinary story would become a wondrous tale for a young boy. She had this story that she knew that I passed down to my daughter many years later. The story was called Tommy and the Bubble. The story was a continuous story, different each evening, about a boy called Tommy who would be just ready for sleep when he would hear a tapping on the window pane. Tommy would slowly pull the curtain aside where he would see a giant soap bubble outside his window. Sitting inside was a little old man. The man would say come on out, we have to help someone tonight. I would climb out of the window into the bubble and fly off across the lawn and higher than the trees. We were so high that we could see the bungalow way below us. I could see the houses below and off we would go on another great adventure. We would then fly to a place where we knew that someone was in trouble and we would then go and help them. I remember that the story seemed so real as we flew over the house tops. When I had been tucked up in bed I would listen to the wind in the woods at the side of the bungalow. They would make that mysterious sound of wind whooshing along making their dead leaves rustle. During the winter, I would still hear the wind but it would be different now since the leaves had gone and I could only hear the branches moving against each other causing a mysterious groaning sound as if the trees were wishing for summer to return and looking forward to spring again.

One of the sounds of summer I missed was the song birds. I loved to hear the birds singing their special songs and it seemed that they learned one song each year that they have lived. In the summer mornings just before dawn we would hear only silence, but as dawn approached a single bird would start chirping, then another, and before long a whole chorus of birds would awaken and the dawn chorus would begin almost like a symphony but only a symphony that nature could provide.

I think that England has cornered the market for the incredible variety of song birds. There are other bright colored birds but not like the song birds of England. We have here in America bright red cardinals, blue winged blue jays and humming birds hovering over a flower drinking its nectar. There is also a yellow bird like a canary that flies around our garden. Other states have different species and different colors. Large predator hawks drift on the thermal winds and the wind drafts slowly spiral down so beautiful and so slow and easy going until they see below with their excellent vision their next meal and then they drop from the sky and attack. From that great height with their eagle eyes, they see their evening meal and strike. I sometimes watch British TV here in America. One time on an English TV show that was being filmed outside in a garden in spring, I would hear the rapture of all the different song birds singing their songs that I remembered. It seems here in America the bird's just chirp, caw and screech and have some song birds, but not like they do in England.

In England the birds truly sing their songs to the best of their ability. In the background one keeps hearing the cuckoo bird, cuckooing around the trees and woods. The cuckoo is a bird that is the lazybones of the bird world. Whenever she sees another bird's nest with eggs in it, she quickly drops an egg from hers into the clutch of eggs in the nest and then allows the other bird's parents to raise her young as well as their own. In the woodlands in between the tympani of other bird songs one can hear the cuckoo calling from the woods, cuckoo-cuckoo. To the best of my knowledge, we do not have the cuckoo bird in America.

While we were walking my auntie would tell me stories of how things used to be in the old days. She told me some of the books she had read and little bits of information that would make all the characters of the book come alive. She would read to me all of the Dickens books. One book I especially like is Great Expectations. One of them was written about the area where we lived near the Benfleet marshes and it was called Great Expectations. The story was about an old lady that lived in a large old house on a hill. We also had an old house up on the hill where two elderly sisters, the Howard sisters, lived and they were both somewhat recluses. These sisters never seemed to come out of the house to see the outside world. The difference was that in the book there was one old lady and one young girl. Behind our woods there were two older sisters that lived in the Howard House way back in the woods behind where our bungalow was located. When we walked up the lane, we would pass the wooded bottom property that was overgrown on the forest floor. Overgrown and way up on the hill stood the mansion where the Howard sisters lived. It was very spooky I recall especially in the autumn when the winds blew sighing through the dark woods. My auntie would tell me that the big house was haunted and nobody ever went into the upper grounds of the property. I met them once and they seemed nice enough ladies in the daylight but you never know what lurks in the darkness of night of an old dilapidated house with a spooky history.

As we walked on one of our evening walks we would talk about the history of England, of the Vikings sailing up the river Thames in their dragon boats from Scandinavia, burning and pillaging the Saxon villages from town to town. She also talked about geology. I do believe she knew about plate tectonics even before anyone else did because she asked me to look at a world map showing me all the continents looking like a puzzle of each continent butting up against the other like a jigsaw puzzle ending with one super continent. She taught me how to read and write long hand at the age of three. I still have samples of my letters I had written to my mother thanking her for my new shoes and yes, say love to daddy who was still in the Army somewhere, but we did not know where.

On one of those beautiful rare sunny evenings when we had decided to go for a walk, Tess would be so excited to know that she would be going for an evening walk. My auntie would say to Tess let's go for walkies. Tess would be so excited she would go over to the hook where the dog's leash would hang and pull it down. She was never on a leash since we lived in the country and in those days, there were no local laws to keep a dog on a leash, but she would hold it in her mouth as were ready to leave for our walk.

We would walk up the lane first which was very picturesque. It truly was a wooded, earthen lane since it could be called a road but it really was just a country lane. At some time, cars had driven up the road but vary rarely would I see a vehicle driving up. It was a road in name only with muddy ruts in the middle of the road and a small well-worn pathway located on the left side for people to walk. This lane would forever be in my mind because it was so beautiful with its trees and forest on both sides of the lane. There was elm, oak and walnut trees.

During the spring the forest floor would be carpeted with wild bluebells, my favorite flower. The forest floor was covered with them and they looked so beautiful with their blue bells hanging from the stem of the flower. There were also primroses scattered around the forest floor with their yellow flowers. I also remember on the front garden some plant auntie called London Pride which flowered, but was really like a large leaf plant.

As we walked up the lane, we had two direct neighbors who were quite different from each other. These were the only people in the immediate neighborhood. The first and closest was Mr. and Mrs. Willis who lived in a real brick house across the road from our bungalow and where we would run to whenever an air raid approached. To me Mr. and Mrs. Willis were very old and lived in an old house on a large piece of property opposite our bungalow. They were probably about sixty years old or so. During the five years I lived there I never did know their actual names. They had approximately four or five acres of woods surrounding the house with a large garage at the back. Inside was a family car. I had never even sat in a car before and they would let me sit there like a king. They never used it because of the rationing of gas during war time. The garden was designed as an old English manor garden. To the one side of the house was a pathway that led down to a large area that had a large grass circle which dropped down to a sunken lawn with flowers growing around the circle. Rose bushes were everywhere. The entrance to the sunken garden was led by three small steps down with an overhead trellis covered in rambling roses. To this day I have a deep appreciation of any kind of rose, rambling or full rose.

They had an air raid shelter at the back of their house and after the first sound of the air raid warning my auntie would wake me up and carry me over to Mr. and Mrs. Willis as the siren sounded. We would open the door to the shelter and climb down the steps into the shelter then close the door. She would then put me in one of the bunks while waiting to hear the coastal guns begin to start to fire up as the German bombers appeared after crossing the English coast. After that then came the droning of the German aircraft bombers on their way to bomb London. Their engines sounded distinctly like a heavy motorcycle engine and were quite different from the sound of the Allied bombers engines that had a much smoother sound.

One of the fondest memories of growing up with my auntie was twice a year she would say Roy let's see how you measure up. My auntie would stand me up against the living room wall behind the door where the wall was covered in wall paper. Each time we wanted to find out how much I had grown she put a ruler at the top of my head to mark the spot on the wallpaper. She would then write on that spot the date and my height. Looking back now I wish I had that piece of wallpaper with all the notations on it but it was torn down during the later years of 1990's to be replaced by a larger house which was built on the property site.

A few years after the war was over, I did return to visit my auntie when I was about 10 years old. I would take the train on my own. My mother was not pleased that I did that because I think that she thought she was losing me to my wartime surrogate mother, but still she was my surrogate mother for all those years in Thundersley. Whenever I did visit Auntie Ellie after the war was over, I felt more at home in Thundersley than I did in London. It was very confusing for all of us, since I enjoyed coming home to be with my mother but I had been away for such a long time. Each time I did go back to visit Auntie Ellie after 1950 we would look at the wall where she had marked my growth history of over the past seven years and we would both laugh to see how small I was when I first arrived at her bungalow. At three years old I was quite a small child.

I was still very young and I was either playing up at the top of the garden or exploring in the woods. Even when the times were not so good, we found so much joy walking that small country lane called Rhoda Road. Auntie Ellie and I would play a board game in the winter called Benedicto. It was a game that was put out prior to the war by the Benedict Pea Company that sold garden peas. The board game was of course an advertisement for their pea products. One of my small duties for my auntie was to bring a wheel barrow from her house to the stable and fill it with horse manure for her vegetable garden located at the back of the bungalow. She grew potatoes, lettuce, radishes, horse radish and onions.

Walking up the lane towards the top of the hill we would pass Captain Barton's stables located on the right side of the lane. He had four horses in his stables. One horse was named Raja and I remember that on many of our evening walks up the lane we would stop in at the stables and speak with Captain Barton. Captain Barton was a typical retired military gentleman who dressed in tweeds and high boots and he talking with a sharp staccato voice that was used to issuing orders to his troops. I did not know if he really was a captain but he was a man that had a very ruddy face, wore English tweeds and a mustache and was a very imposing man. Something like a typical English squire. He owned four horses. I do not remember if Captain Barton used the horses for horseshows. There were no horse shows that I knew of since all activities were kept to a minimum because of the strict wartime laws. I only remember the horses were kept in their stable and it was part of our walk routine to stop in and see them whenever we passed their stables. My auntie always carried some cubed sugar and apples from the orchard that grew adjacent to our back garden. She allowed me to feed the horses using my open hand and gave each horse his apple or some cubed sugar to each of the four horses that Captain Barton owned.

I recall that during the summer months we would take our evening walks up the lane. She did not really need a walking stick to walk, but in the tweedy set of an English rural countryside it was quite common for an English lady to walk with a walking stick during an evening walk and we were all really part of the local tweedy set. This stick was really special since it had a bull dogs head carved into the top of the handle of the stick. The carved dog had brown glass eyes inserted in its head. I often wonder where that stick is now.

1942

I WAS ABOUT five years old now and beginning to understand many things as to where I was and who I was. I always enjoyed those evening walks when it was warm and sometimes sunny. I still recall the lovely smell of the blue bell flowers growing wild in in the woods and Miss. Howard's forest floor that was almost like an addiction. Tess would be running around us barking and having a grand time. Bluebells really are a wild flower growing in the woods but to me they are beautiful and I still look for them whenever I return to England in the spring and breathe deeply their flowering smell. The lane led up to a small hill with woods on the left which was the Howard sister's property, and Captain Barton's stables were on the right.

There were very few houses or people that were living in that area. There were plenty of trees for me to climb but there were no houses on that lane except ours and the Willis's until we reached the top of this slight hill. There you could see for about fifteen miles to the horizon. In those days there was nothing but fields and hedgerows of blackthorn, rose hips and raspberries.

All of these lovely sounds followed us up the lane on our evening walks. These walks I had with my auntie made our walks like an interesting classroom. She would talk to me and tell me stories about the local history about how the Vikings from Scandinavia would sail up the river Thames. Burning and pillaging the local villages, killing the village Saxons, stealing the food and livestock that was used by the villagers. This was about the year 800-1000 AD. She also talked to me about King Arthur and the knights of the round table, about chivalry, teaching me lessons about always doing the right thing no matter how difficult it was to do but just to do it right and doing it well. Follow Camelot she said, it is still alive and well. She really knew her history and later in this story as I grew older, she would get more serious in talking about the science, history and geography. I discovered that she had a very good education for a woman at that time. She had gone to college in the 1920's and later her parents had sent her to a girl's finishing school in France. I was now about five years old and well-adjusted to living a rural life in the country.

I had not seen my mother since I had been brought to Thundersley. My father was still in the Army and I had not seen him for a long time. We wrote letters to each other but I did not see them. I was left alone to do what I wanted although I will say that I knew I was still under supervision. I was becoming aware of myself just by listening to my auntie, but my only one regret was that I still had nobody to play with. None of the neighbors had children and the school was so far away from home and that most of the children lived nearby the school. I did not really mind too much because I found that I was fine playing on my own and did not really need any friends. I climbed trees and played Robin Hood. I made a bow and arrows and learned to shoot a bow on to a target quite well. I had friends in the scouts, but they were older boys.

There was a large tool shed set aside alongside of the bungalow and I was forbidden to open the door because of the sharp tools that were inside. I did open it once and I got paddled on my backside for doing so. There was an orchard that ran alongside of the property that had apples and green gages, which is an English fruit. I would go scrumping, picking fruit, over the fence into the orchard and climb the trees and pull off some of the fruit.

At the top of the garden was a bench where I would sit. The small hill leading down to the house was quite steep and looked down on the bungalow below, which appeared to me to look very small. I would sit for hours on that seat. Day dreaming of how things used to be with knights riding up the castle ramp to the portcullis with their large war horses and broad swords, their flags flying as they followed in line through the castle gate. I imagined Vikings running amok through the villages up to our beloved St. Peters Church. All of this would be stolen from my mind when I would suddenly hear a steady drone of aircraft in the distance, the coastal defensive guns firing off and my auntie calling out loud for me to me to come down immediately to the house and we would then go over to Mrs. Willis air raid shelter and shut the door.

1943

WHEN I WENT to school each day, I had to walk about three miles down Bread and Cheese Hill and cross the road at Tarpot's Pub. As I walked to school, I could see in the clear sky above me the vapor trails of the aircraft that were on their way to bomb London. I could also see the looped vapor trails of the spitfires of the RAF fighter planes shooting down these bombers. From the ground I could hear the chatter of the machine guns from both the bombers and the fighters. I could see the smoke coming from some of the bombers as they were being shot down as I watched to see the flash of fire from the aircraft and see it spiral down to the ground in a violent explosion. In comparison to today's modern fighter aircraft, they were flying very slowly so it was like watching the air battles in a slow-motion film as the British spitfires spun up, loop up and down to shoot down and kill these bombers heading for London. Some aircraft on both sides were hit and down went the destroyed aircraft in fire and smoke hitting the ground with a boom and flash of fire.

Sometimes we saw parachutes dropping from a destroyed bomber or spitfire and we all tried to find out where the plane had crashed and where the pilots had parachuted. We would have a policeman visit the school and he would lecture all of the students, saying if we saw men wearing a strange uniform, we must tell our mums and she would then call the Home Guard. They would then look for the downed pilots even though the Home Guard may have not been armed and the pilot usually carried a side arm. In most cases the crashed pilot if not killed would emerge from his crashed aircraft injured and surrender as soon as possible. They would prefer to be a prisoner of war in England than dead.

One of the favorite hobbies of English boys was to have a butterfly collection. It may sound cruel to children these days but seventy-five years ago things were quite different. Boys would attach a fine meshed material to a round metal collar to make a net, then attach that collar to a long bamboo cane and out you would go into the fields trying to catch the various types of butterflies fluttering around that were so abundant. We would run across the fields chasing down the butterflies using our net to catch them. When we caught a butterfly, we would quickly drop it in the jar that had a perforated hole, screw the lid to allow air to get into the jar and keep the butterflies alive until we arrived home. We would then pin the butterfly to a flat board as part of a collection along with the others we had collected. This was not the most humane thing to do to a living butterfly but we did not know any better in those days. Besides it was fun chasing across the knee-high grass fields of Thundersley watching the grass hoppers jumping up in front of you as you ran to catch this fluttering butterfly with the warm sun on your face. It was a happy time for a young boy growing up in Thundersley.

It was fun, but not for long because the Germans had other bad ideas for this English pastime which was used to break the will of the English people and terrorize their children. They made a special kind of bomb that would kill children when they were catching butterflies. While the young English boys were happily pursuing their butterfly collection, they built a new bomb. It was called a butterfly bomb, directed only at killing or injuring young boys who were just collecting butterflies for their butterfly collection. Many kids were maimed and died because of this. They made millions of these special child killer bombs by making a long heavy ended stick with a painted butterfly at the top. At the heavy end, a spear pointed arrowhead would land sticking in the ground with the butterfly top just showing above the grass. They were designed to drop thousands from each bomber from a great height landing with the stick upright in the ground with up to three quarters of its length sticking up in the ground. At the top of the stick where the feathered flight would be on an arrow there was a painted model of a colored butterfly attached to a sensitive bomb trigger. The small anti-personnel explosive device was loaded on the arrowhead of this shaft powerful enough to kill a boy who was chasing butterflies. When an unsuspecting young boy was out in the fields catching butterflies for his collection, he would swipe at this butterfly that was sticking up on the top of a stick that was stuck in the ground. Upon seeing his perfect butterfly, the boy would try and catch it with his net that hit the trigger of the bomb. The bomb would explode and kill or injure the boy or anybody close to him. Thousands of young boys in England were killed and it got so bad that the government banned the sport of butterfly collecting for the duration of the war. At school there were posters on the bulletin boards with pictures of these butterfly bombs as a warning to beware of touching them and tell the adults in the family where they had seen them. Even though we were out in the country it was no longer safe.

The German bombers would make daylight raids from occupied Belgium, Holland and France. The distance from those countries by air was very short, just an hour or so flying time. Both day and night they would be on their way to bomb London and we in Thundersley were in the middle of their bombing runs from Europe in the east, over our heads onwards to the west and London to kill more civilians.

I was about five years old now and I remember one special air raid. Whenever an air raid siren sounded it was time to head for the air raid shelter. The Germans were beginning to lose the war and the German Luftwaffe bomber pilots were ordered not to return with their full bomb loads. Thanks to the RAF the German bombers found it difficult to reach London due to our air defenses. Since they were not allowed to return to airfields with their bomb bay still full, they just dropped their bombs anywhere in England as they left to return to their bases. Thundersley was on their return route back to their bases in Europe.

We had an arrangement with Mrs. Willis who lived in the big house across the lane from our bungalow that when the air raid siren wailed, we could run across the lane and into her garden where she had a large underground shelter that had been built prior to the outbreak of the war. That night was a particularly dark night with no moon. I awoke to the sound of the air raid siren that had a high pitch and low pitch indicating it was an air raid warning. I was quickly told by my auntie to get over to the shelter and using flashlights in the darkness we ran out of the front door. We ran across the front lawn and over the muddy lane into the garden of Mrs. Willis where the shelter was located. I looked up at the night sky and I will never forget the sight of those great search lights that were sweeping the black sky with their beams of light. The sky was full of these searchlights. I could hear the coastal guns firing in the distance as the German bombers approached the coastline of England where the coastal batteries of powerful defensive guns were firing and sounding the alarm. The main squadron of bombers had not yet arrived however since the forward patrol of their pathfinder aircraft would precede them seeking out the targets. Searchlights were sweeping the sky and I could see the red tracer bullets being fired by our defense gunners to work the tracers and find an enemy bomber to shoot down.

I saw all the searchlights come together to a small point of silvery light where they had caught an enemy bomber in the convergence of the pencil shaped searchlights. I saw the reflection of the plane in the crosshairs of the searchlights. I could see the red tracer bullets rising up to the apex of the silver light from the searchlights. The tracer shells were now arching up towards that small silver spot where the aircraft was about to be hit. Suddenly they got a confirmed hit and the plane suddenly exploded in midair, slowly falling to the ground. It had crashed in a field of some farmer. I was not sure if the airman survived. The booming of guns in the night sky and being lit up by the anti-aircraft shells that were exploding, lighting up the sky with light and the sound of battle was an event I would never forget. We did not hear any noise other than the sound of German bombers passing overhead and the attacking aircraft of the RAF to bring down the bombers before they reached London, which was only a short 23 miles distance away. The coastal defensive guns were trying to prevent the bombers from reaching London. To reach London all that the German bomber pilots had to do was to follow the river Thames shining brightly on a moon-lit night. It was like directing the bombers as runway lights at an airport, straight into the heart of London. The bad situation for us in Thundersley was that we were living near the mouth of the river Thames and the aircraft flew right over us on their way to London so the air battle was only about 17,000 feet above us in Thundersley.

When we reached the safety of the air raid shelter Mrs. Willis and the older Mrs. Willis from the other side of the woods was there. We entered down into the air raid shelter and again I smelled that dank earthy smell. On the other side sitting on the other bunk were two elderly women holding hands and crying as the sound of the aircraft overhead reverberated through the ground. There were the two Mrs. Willis'. One lived across deeper in the woods. She had to be about 70 years old and to get to the shelter from her home she had to walk through the dark woods with only a small flashlight to guide her. She was shaking and crying in the shelter, holding hands with the other Mrs. Willis who was also scared to death of the battle raging over head. Mrs. Heath was a strong a woman in spirit and she was holding the two women trying to comfort them.

I did not personally recall any actual fear myself, other than I did understand what was going on. I was really looking forward to looking for some hot shell shrapnel when the air raid was over to collect them as souvenirs. Shrapnel was the broken exploded pieces of bomb shells and shells that had come out of the defending guns on the ground or from the enemy aircraft. They were very hot and I had to be careful when picking them up when my auntie was not looking.

There were also silver streamers of material to find on the ground that were about four inches wide and six feet long. These strips were made of reflective aluminum foil and were dropped by the bombers to disable their enemy radar signals. After the bombers had passed over on their way to London, we had to wait for about one hour for the German bombers to return from London after their bombing run was over. The pilots were not allowed to return to base with a full bomb load to their European bases so if they were not able to drop their full load on London or were unable to reach their target, they would drop their bombs on any English towns and villages on their way back to Europe just to get rid of the bomb loads. We waited for their return and soon we would hear the slightly low stuttering sound of German aircraft approaching and then the high-pitched whine of the bombs falling through the air and detonating all around us. Everybody's nerves were on edge and the women were holding hands and crying again in terror until the German bombers had passed over and the all-clear siren would sound of and I would be taken back to the house to my bed and realized that we had survived another bombing.

1944

AMERICA HAD MANY Air Force air bases in England located all over the country. One of the saddest parts of the war that I witnessed was during the 1942-1945 years. That was when we witnessed thousands of US Air Force bombers flying in full formation on their way to bomb Germany. It would be hard to imagine these thousands of aircraft that we could see in the sky all at once, all in perfect formation with their contrails fanning out behind leaving giant streaks of white contrails in the sky. They would start to arrive overhead usually about 9:00 am. A quiet country morning was shattered by the growling sound of engines far off to the west. The growling turned into a rumble and slowly these giant B17 bombers of the US 8th Air Force appeared over the horizon and flew overhead with a great roar of their engines. We would try and count them as they flew over, but I kept losing my count and had to start over again. The sky was filled with these aircraft heading east to bomb Germany and other parts of occupied Europe. We cheered them on and wished them luck.

Squadron after squadron would pass overhead, all in perfect formation, taking at least an hour to pass over and disappear into the eastern skies on their way to bomb Hitler's Germany in retaliation for their bombing of London. As kids we went crazy in the school yard yelling and whooping at this marvelous sight. Suddenly, all was quiet again and all we could hear was the buzzing of insects in the grass watching the grasshoppers jump in the grassy fields. We knew that it would take about two hours for them to get to Germany, drop their bombs and do their return flight, and sure enough about two hours later we began to hear the murmur of aircraft engines in the distance. This slowly became a roar as they again passed over us in the English countryside. We did not whoop and shout this time because within their formations there were many large gaps where there were no aircraft. Those aircraft were missing, out of formation and had been shot down over Germany and would not return to their bases, nor would their pilots ever return back to America. It was sad because there were so many gaps in each of these formations.

The sound changed to a roar as they flew over our heads at about 10,000 feet but this time the roar was not the same. Some of the aircraft engines were faltering and the engine sounds was not a steady drone as when they left. Some were trailing smoke and some fell out of the sky and crashed. Sometimes we would see the planes catch fire and we began to look for parachutes and cheered when we could see that there were at times ten or more parachutes floating down from the sky. Sometimes we would see no parachutes and we could hear a crash from some distance off and knew that those USAF airmen would never see America again. We wonder just how these men of the allied countries did their jobs so well without the complaining and whining of having to get up again the next day and do it all over again. The Royal Air Force flew the night missions so we only heard their engines roaring overhead at night.

There were reports that there was some difficult situation that was developing between the two Allied Air Forces because the Americans bombing missions was scheduled during the daylight hours which was far more dangerous. The RAF bombed by night under cover of darkness. Since that time, I have heard that historically the American Air Force were complaining that they had the most dangerous time to fly over the target during the day which was probably true. The bomber commanders on the ground of both countries had to be true diplomats to calm everybody down and become one battle air group both day and night to win this war.

The Germans bombed both day and night and it seemed to me that when I had just got off to sleep, I was awakened by my auntie and off we went back into the air raid shelter. I was now about six and did not need to be carried across the lane to Mrs. Willis's shelter. In the few short minutes, it took to cross the lane I would look up at night and see the blazing light in the night sky. At night the ground search lights were like huge beams of light sweeping across the sky from left to right and on the other side of town there were other searchlight crews doing the same thing but in the opposite direction. All trying to pin point that tiny dot of silver light that was a German bomber and then up would shoot the red tracer bullets arcing their way up to where the two or three searchlights had caught a bomber in the cross hairs of the searchlights and the flak guns fired off with such a loud noise to bring the enemy aircraft down. It was like a modern firework display, but so much deadlier. As the shells burst, they shattered into tiny pieces and people were killed just by being struck by one of those pieces if they were out on open ground. There was the sound of bombs bursting and the rattling of guns coming from the RAF fighter spitfires. It looked like the sky was on fire with the flames and the bombs bursting far away in the distance.

Since we were on the first part of England that German bombers flew over, we first heard the loud explosions of our coastal guns firing off telling us that they were getting closer and crossing the English coast. Strangely the German aircraft engines had a different sound than the allied aircraft. Their engines had a stuttering sound as they flew overhead while the allied aircraft had a continuous drone so we began to recognize what aircraft was flying overhead.

In the air raid shelter the two Mrs. Willis' were doing their knitting and talking about the plans for the church events with my auntie not knowing if we would survive the raid to participate in any event. The women were always crying and holding hands as the explosions continued for over an hour before the aircraft were either shot down or returned to Germany. An air aid shelter was not much protection since either a direct hit by a bomb or a near hit the depth of the shelter would not protect those inside. It did protect the blast if a nearby bomb hit so it was better than being unprotected in the house.

I had an Aunt Rose, sister to my mother, who lived in the southern part of England in a beachside town called Deal in the county of Kent. A letter came for me and to my delight it was my mother who wrote that she had received travel papers and that she would soon be coming to see me in a few weeks. We were going to visit my Aunt Rose in Deal in the county of Kent. My mother had managed to acquire some travel papers for us to go visit her since the bombing was becoming less and the threat of invasion from the Germans had been reduced. All of my mother's side of the family was going to be there except those that were serving in the military.

A few days later my mother arrived at the bungalow and packed up some clothes for a short time and we went on the train back to London's, Fenchurch Street Station terminal. We took the underground (subway) across to the other side of the city to another railway terminal, Waterloo Station, and we caught another long-distance train to the seaside town of Deal which is in the county of Kent near Dover.

I remember seeing the train packed with men with all different foreign uniforms for the Navy, Army and Air Force. Since the train was basically a troop train, there were few seats available for civilians. It was what we called a corridor train with the corridor running down one side of the cars with individual compartments alongside of the corridor. We arrived at Deal station and headed for my Aunt Rose's ribbon type flat. My three cousins, Maureen, Malcolm and Roger were also there so it was a little cramped but we all seem to manage. My Aunt Rose was a stout woman that did not have the usual London accent. We went on walks across to the beach frontage boardwalk, which was only about a half mile away from the English Channel facing occupied France. Because of mines planted on the beaches we could not go on the beach until after the war was over.

There was a huge medieval castle nearby and we went there to play knights on the ruins of the castle. Also, there were military barracks of the Royal Marines located nearby. The sea and sky always looked gray and there was no sand on the beach, just small pebbles which sounded like a roar as each wave carried more small stones onto the beach.

Along the beach were all the defenses of war. Earlier on at the beginning of the war England had been threatened to be invaded by Hitler which fortunately for us was put off indefinitely by the Germans. The distance between England and France is only 21 miles so on a clear day you could see Calais, France. All along the beaches of Southern England were protective huge concrete tank traps built side by side to prevent any invading tanks getting through to the land. The beaches were all mined and there were large painted signs of a human skull that warned that this was a dangerously mined zone and nobody was allowed to go on to the beach.

On the other side of the English Channel were the same defenses for the Germans but they had some huge 88 millimeter guns installed on the cliffs of France. The range of these huge guns was over thirty miles, so on occasion they would fire huge shells across the Channel to hit some of the civilian homes along the English south coast.

They shelled every evening just to keep everyone on edge. When that happened during our visit us cousins were pushed under the stairs for safety. Suddenly on the first night we heard a whooshing sound and a loud explosion. Immediately, the adults grabbed all of us cousins and pushed us deeper into the compartment under the stairs.

The whooshing sound of the great artillery shells arching across the town and exploding with a loud bang put our nerves on edge, but after a while we got used to it and as suddenly as it started it would stop. We all had a great time at Aunt Rose's home and after a week it was time to return to London so we all climbed aboard the train to head back to London. As we entered the southern part of suburban London, we began to see more damaged houses and factories that had been destroyed.

When we arrived at London's Waterloo terminal station, we could see so much damage. The Germans now had a new weapon called a V1 which we called a doodlebug. This destroyed complete blocks of flats in one bombing killing hundreds of people living in that block. As we pulled out of London's connecting railroad station, Fenchurch Street, on our way back to Thundersley we could see by looking out of the carriage window the terrible damage done to the city of London by the bombs. It has been estimated that one million civilian homes had been destroyed with most of them housing at least three civilians in each house. Doing the math, three million Londoners were either killed or injured. We then changed trains for me to go on the train to Benfleet, back to my Auntie Ellie and my normal routine that I had for over four years.

Each evening at 6:00 pm we would bring our chairs around the radio set to listen to the news from the BBC. My Uncle Jack was incensed by the news and he would put his face close to the loud speaker of the radio set and cup his hands around his ear to intently listen to the news.

The only radio station available was owned by the British Broadcasting Company known as the BBC. It was a total monopoly and some say it was owned by the government. The BBC only had two stations. There were no commercials on either channel.

One was the BBC itself that broadcasted serious music, news programs, interviews etc. and then there was another channel called the BBC light program. Light, meaning not so severe as the regular BBC, although looking back it was not that much different from the first program. The light program played mostly light music that was semi classical and had programs that were like Vaudeville sketches with famous comedy teams such as Arthur Askey and others. They also played American dance band music. My auntie rarely allowed me listening in on the BBC light program.

The news introduction was made because in war time by law it always must identify the person who was reading the news first and then after his introduction came a list of coded messages for the Resistance in France or other parts of occupied Europe. Always at the beginning of the newscast there would be the sound of a drum, drumming out the Morse code letter V for victory. It was based on the first four notes of Beethoven's fifth symphony. It went something like this. First the drum of three dots and one dash, three times V for victory: dum-dum-dum-dum. The announcer would then say this is the BBC news from London and this is Stuart Hibbert reading it, but first some messages: the fox is in the chicken house, repeat, the fox is in the chicken house and the cat has not come home. These messages continued for a few minutes until all of the coded messages had been sent out. Then came the bulk of the latest news.

England is only 21 miles from Dover to Calais in German occupied France so these messages were sent out to give orders for groups of resistant fighters in this kind of code. The recipients of these codes knew what each coded message was meant for them. If their coded message came through then they would go out on an operation of sabotage against the Germans or any other orders that was activated by a message on the BBC evening news. One evening at six we were listing to the newscast and heard the news that Hitler had been killed in an assassination attempt. Everyone thought that the war soon would be over because of this but then the news said it was a mistake and he was only injured by a planted bomb.

One of the happiest times of my residence in Thundersley was the excitement of sledding down the Green Hill. It does not snow very often in southern England, but when it does there is great excitement because there usually is just enough snow to go tobogganing down Green Hill. This was a small hill that sloped down to the major road that joined the highway at Bread and Cheese Hill. We would take our sleds up to the top of the hill which was ice bound and prepare to ride down the snow-covered hill. At the top where we started was usually worked by the big boys into icy conditions which would give us a start. Half way down the hill was an old bomb crater with dirt built up high along the sides of the crater. The plan was to direct the sled towards the crater hit the bump and go airborne over the crater. Doing this made us feel like we were flying and of course was quite dangerous, but when you are young you think that you become immune to danger. There were about fifteen boys and a girl taking this slide into oblivion, but the hardest part of this sport was the return journey up the hill since it was snowy and slippery at the top and Green Hill is quite steep. I believe that hill is still there and when it snows, they still sled down.

My auntie had a sister that lived in Hadleigh the next village over to us on Shipwrights Drive. Her name was Beatrice, but was called Aunt Bea. After the visit to Aunt Bea, auntie and I would go a little further on down the street heading for the picnic grounds on the grass at Hadleigh Castle which was located overlooking the Thames estuary. As we were sitting on the grassy mounds of the castle my auntie would begin to tell me stories of Hadleigh Castle.

The castle was built on a hill around year 1100 AD and was active for about five hundred years and prior to its overthrow it was a main defensive part of England. It protected the entrance of the Thames estuary the entrance to the river to the city of London. The castle was at one time a very important defensive castle that overlooked the entrance of the river Thames which wound its way towards central London. First it was the Vikings that were attacking. After that came the Spaniards who were at war with Elizabethan England and were threatening to send a Spanish Armada of ships to invade England in year 1588. At that time there was four standing towers and a central keep but as the years went by the castle started to break up, so while I was there that time only one tower was left and some other rubble. Sitting there with my auntie I imagined these knights on their large war horses and battle flags flying, knights in full armor riding up to the gates of the castle. Only one tower is left now among other remains, but I still would go up into the tower and peak through the only barred window.

During the month of October of each year was the time we would go gathering chestnuts in the woods at the top of Bread and Cheese Hill. October was the beginning of winter and the chilly winds would come blowing in off of the sea coast from Europe and it was quite cold. Early in the morning after a night of gale force winds my auntie would wake me up to put some warm clothes on and we would walk up Bread and Cheese Hill, then into the woods. Thundersley was built around a hill alongside the old Southend Road winding its way up the hill. To the left of the highway were big trees of elm and oak that would stretch all the way up to the top of the mount. During October these chestnut trees would drop their chestnuts after a high wind. My auntie and I would walk through the woods, she wielding her big bulldog head walking stick and me running around with my dog Tess. We would go around picking up chestnuts filling the bag that we brought with us. The forests floor was covered in deep autumn leaves that had fallen off the trees sometimes a foot deep and I would roll myself in the leaves enjoying the wonderful odor of withered leaves.

Even today I enjoy the smell of autumn leaves. We would take these chestnuts home providing us with great snacking during the winter months. We would shell the chestnuts and put them in the hot oven of the iron cooking stove. The odor was wonderful as they slowly cooked and when ready we would quickly let them cool and break open the shell and eat them. With the chestnuts my auntie would also slice off some bread, butter the bread and put them in the oven and few minutes later out would come delicious slices of hot buttered bread.

Another type of horse chestnut was similar to chestnuts that you eat, but these nuts are hard and we had a different use for these nuts. We called them conkers. One of the games that gave a great competitive spirit for young boys was the game of conkers. A conker was the inside nut of a horse chestnut tree that had been shed and fallen to the ground like a chestnut. We would harden the nut in many secret ways, one was to put some vinegar in a cup and put the conker in the cup. I let it stay in the cup for a few days. Put it in an oven and let it harden until it was as hard as concrete. Then, drill a hole through the center of the nut. We would then run a string through the hole tightening a knot at the end of the string to prevent the conker from falling out. We then had the hard nut at the end of a string. We would challenge an opponent. One boy's conker would hang by the string, hanging undefended. At the bottom and in turns the other boy would try hit the conker with his conker to try and split it which would then give the winner a point. I would aim my conker and strike hard my opponent's conker hoping that it would be softer than mine and break into pieces. The accounting of each breakage operated on the honor system, so if I broke five other boy's conkers, my conker would be called a fiver. We made all sorts of mixtures to make the conker hard. If a boy was proven guilty of cheating on how much conkers he had destroyed he would be sent to Coventry which meant nobody was to speak to him for so many days. This was just a term of speech. To have this punishment was very devastating to a young English boy where honor and duty was as important as life itself so not too many chanced to be caught cheating.

Once a week we would walk up Bread and Cheese Hill to the butcher shop on Kenneth Road to buy some meat. Nobody had refrigeration in those days so the meat that had been chopped into lengths while it was hanging from hooks from the ceiling. Looking back to those years, I often wonder if anybody got sick. There were flies everywhere, especially a type of fly called a blue bottle. It was a large fly colored blue and green attracted to dead meat. Hanging from the ceiling were strips of fly paper which trapped hundreds of flies landing on the sticky surface of the fly strip. I thought at the time and still do that it was a cruel way to kill flies. To kill bad flies and other insects we also had a brand of spray called Flit. A container was filled up with Flit and pumped out like a spray that came out of a round container. This container held the liquid spray and the by pushing down on the plunger like a bicycle pump it sprayed out the fly killer. Looking back now, I wonder if this spray may have caused cancer killing more people than flies. The butcher wore a traditional striped blue and white apron and wore a straw hat like a boater style. I remember seeing him grabbing a huge piece of meat in one hand and a meat cleaver with the other. He would bring the meat to the butcher block and seconds later he would be weighing the piece of meat on the scales ready to be wrapped in a sheet of newspaper. I think it may have been at this point when I saw rabbits hanging dangling on a hook from the ceiling that I decided not to eat meat. Rabbits at that time were quite a delicacy and many farmers went out with their guns to shoot rabbits in their fields and eat or sell them.

I enjoyed going to the butcher shop with my auntie because while we walked, she would always talk to me about history and astronomy. I was still going to school during the week but we did not learn very much because of the constant moving in and out to the air raid shelter for some hours and then returning to the classroom and trying and pick up where we left off.

Going out for a walk with Auntie Ellie gave me more education than any school teacher could have given me because she made it come alive in the way that she described a living history and geography. Sometimes we would often go up to St. Peters Church just for a walk in the evening. My dog Tess loved to go out on walks, once outside she would always be at my side running all around happy to be out with us on walkies. To walk to the church from our cottage we would first open the front garden gate of Standish Villa, which was the name of our bungalow and walk down the lane towards the main road. After crossing the main road, we would continue walking up the lane towards the church, walking past woods and fields down into a dip in the lane to a small stream with a wooden bridge crossing the stream. Crossing over the wooden bridge I would love to look down into the stream to see if I could see any fish. I never did see any fish in that stream, but never gave up looking.

Along this rutted country lane appeared some cottages on the left which had beautiful gardens and in the garden of one of the cottages there was a talking parrot. I imagined that a witch lived in that old thatched cottage with the parrot outside in its cage. On our right was the house of Mr. and Mrs. Saunders who lived in one of the newer houses in the area. Then we could see the open fields pointing the way towards the church. Sometimes we would walk across this field alongside of the church and see the grasshoppers jumping ahead of us as we walked through the grass. I could smell the sweet smell of recently mowed grass and to this day when I smell newly mown grass I have a nostalgic moment reliving my childhood in this the lovely countryside of Thundersley in the county of Essex.

One time at this same field we held a scout's camp, pitching out tents high up on the hill overlooking the Essex countryside. As far as the eye could see were all fields. Since the church was on a hill, we would have to pass through the old church gate. A gate is the entrance to the churchyard itself and is a wooden gate with a small roof that was the entrance to the church perimeter. Passing through the gate and climbing up many wooden banked up steps supported by wooden logs we were able to reach the top of the hill, huffing and puffing with great effort. At the top of the hill lay before us the very old church of St. Peters.

At the top of these steps alongside of the church stood a very old oak tree which had a hollowed-out trunk. History relates that during the 1600's King Charles the First, hid in the trunk of this same tree to evade capture by Oliver Cromwell's Roundheads during England's great civil war. It was during the English civil war when Cromwell's Army managed to topple the Stuart monarchy and for the first time in English history the country fell into an actual dictatorship for about twenty or more years until the monarchy was restored by the House of Stuart.

Passing by the tree there are some very old graves surrounding the church. These graves were first interred when the church was built in the early 7th century. The graves that surrounded the church today are still marked by the name of its occupant, indicating the year of birth and death. My auntie and I would walk around these grave markers and we would see graves of people that had been born in 900 AD and died 945 AD. Others were dated in the 12th and 13th centuries. The dates were still legible on the head stones, although faded with age and covered with moss. As we walked around the churchyard my auntie would explain to me that these had been real people that lived their lives and had lives like ours requiring the same needs and desires during their lifetime. She would make up stories about this particular name on a gravestone and turn it into a story about the person's life explaining how they could have lived in those times.

At the main entrance of the church there is a small porch with a roof and some old wooden benches before opening the main door. The main door itself is quite small since the people in those days were much smaller in height than today. The door was made of solid oak and also very thick. The door was about six inches thick. As the door opens into the church if you looked carefully and you can see some very old deep nail holes in the oak door itself. History relates that about the period of the 9th century the Vikings would sweep down from the north burning, killing and pillaging the villages. When the villagers of Thundersley heard the news of oncoming Vikings, they sought sanctuary in the stone church of St. Peters which gave them safety to those that had the time and were able to get into the church. Those that did not, were treated very badly by the Vikings. They were skinned alive and their skins were hung on that door by nails. Their ships were named dragon ships because of the dragon's head carved on its bowsprit.

Whenever I was in the church I would be looking around and was always interested in some of the articles that decorated the church. I remember hanging on the west wall was the original spear and helmet of King Henry V. These items had been hanging on that wall for centuries. Unfortunately, they were stolen and are no longer there. I could not imagine anyone in the 13th century even considering stealing something from within the church walls.

I can still recall the lessons during the church service that was read by the Reverend Maily from a high pulpit. Reading the bible from a podium that had at its top an open spread-eagle wing spread out where the large bible rested. The vicar read the bible to his parishioners to give his sermon. The spread-eagle podium was still there when I last visited the church.

The walls were made of solid flagstone. The arches that supported the roof were curved, almost rounded. A steeple that was pointed indicated that it was a Saxon church as well as the tall steeple that was of Saxon design. The steeple of the church held bells that tolled for different reasons such as death or marriages. St. Peters Church had three bells that tolled every Sunday morning suggesting that all should attend the Sunday morning services.

The churches that were built after the Saxons were the Normans from French Normandy. They built their churches with square towers and also the arches of the support of the church were much squarer in their architecture. The early Christians were very sign conscious. They believed that the reason for bells in churches is that the early Christians believed that church bells kept the devil away. Just like when you spilt salt you threw it over your left shoulder to get it into the devil's eye. To the early Christians, the salt went straight into the eyes of the devil who was always looking over your left shoulder whispering bad things into your ear. When we clink wine glasses it makes a sound of a bell ringing which also keeps the devil away, sometimes!

My Auntie Ellie was a great historian and would tell me stories of the old days of kings and princes where large battles were fought near-by and especially of castles and knights in armor. She impressed me with the thoughts of being a knight and keeping my honor, honor to be fought and won, to always do the right thing. She read stories to me as if I myself rode a white horse seeking honor and justice for all. She also told me all about St. Peter being the bedrock of the Christian church and followed his teachings. She also loved to tell me about King Arthur and the Knights of the Round Table when he pulled out the sword Excalibur that was imbedded in the rock by the wizard Merlin. How he originated the Round Table for his knights. To prevent any trouble regarding the seating with King Arthur's table they built a round table so there was no special chair in place for him or any of the knights. This prevented jealousy among them since all were equal around the round table. To this day during many political conferences, they use the concept of the round table where everyone is seated equally. She also told me about Sir Lancelot and other knights that made up the council around the round table in the court of King Arthur. It must have been interesting to be living in those days.

One of the historical stories she told was about the huge oak timbers that held up the steeple and the belfry of the church of St. Peter. During the period when England was at war with Spain in the year 1588, Queen Elizabeth I, daughter of King Henry VIII of the house of Tudor, was on the throne of England. King Henry was not blessed by his present wife Queen Anne Boleyn with any children that would create an heir to the throne so he wanted to divorce her in favor of another lady at court. The Catholic Church in the Vatican would not allow any Catholic king to divorce so Henry being a resourceful man said that he was King of England. That he decided he should be the head of the church and decided to break away from the Catholic Church and make himself head of the Church of England, which in many ways was still very close to Catholic theology but was still really of Catholic designation.

England at that time was being threatened by King Phillip of Spain who was instructed by the Pope to invade England and return England back into a Catholic country. After being blessed by high members of the Catholic clergy prior to sailing, the invasion ships set sail but encountered a very bad storm at the southern tip of Ireland whereby most ships were wrecked. The English believed that this was a divine intervention on their behalf to prevent an invasion of Catholic armies landing on Protestant English shores. Since Thundersley was not far from the sea many of the huge ships timbers of the wrecked ships were washed up on the beaches and fell into the hands of the villagers of Thundersley. The villagers of Thundersley dragged those huge ship timbers ten miles all the way back to Thundersley to St. Peters Church. They used the wooden oak timbers to build the present belfry and steeple to support the bells which had rung out to warn of the oncoming Spanish galleons during the war with Spain.

They also had another reason to bring home the Spanish ship's timbers, which to some maybe quite amusing. All of Spain's ships when they were built and ready for sea were blessed by high Catholic priests or bishops prior to starting their ill-fated invasion of England. They believed that they had God on their side and that their religion would prevail over Protestant heretics of the Church of England. The people of Thundersley thought that it was quite a joke to have these Catholic blessed timbers now captured to be built in a church to support the belfry in a Protestant church of St. Peters of Thundersley. If you were to enter the church today and look up at the belfry you can see those same blacken ships timbers are still holding up the steeple and the bells, blackened by time and are still there to touch.

I thought at the time that as a small boy when attending church services, the church appeared to be large, but when I returned as an adult for the first time, I was surprised to find that it was quite small. The church was completely made of stone with stone arches and pillars for support. At the far end of the church were beautiful windows of stained glass and depicted St. Peter with Jesus and apostles. To think that this artistry was done so long ago just amazed me with their artistry and beauty and realizing the hardships the people had to endure during the time it took to build such a beautiful building. This was their church, their sanctuary in time of invasion. Under these stained windows was located the church alter and I was told that they had put the bones of one of the many saints under this alter. I was fascinated by that and wondered who and what saint ended up in a box under the altar. I remember asking my auntie this and she said that every church in England had some bones of a saint resting in the church altar.

During the years I attended St. Peters there were many festivities. We had many church activities both inside and outside the church. During the winter months when it was too cold to go outside, we had magic lantern shows (slide projectors) shown on a projector that in to-day's world would seem definitely quite antique. The pictures were of the Holy Land shown by some person that had at one time been in that part of the world. St. Peters had a church choir although I was never a singer in the choir. My auntie was part conductor of the choir so I was brought along to attend when she did her weekly practice with the choir.

During each summer we would have outside events that we called a garden fete. These were held on the large lawn of the church vicarage next to the church. The vicarage was the house provided for the current vicar to live in but was owned by the church council. The fete was an old English fair where they set up tents and tables and flags were flying and looking almost medieval. There were some small swings and tables of food cooked by the ladies of the congregation. There were also some tents put up for showing various handcrafts for sale. One of the most popular games of chance was a huge twenty foot by twenty-foot-high board with the painted face of Hitler, at that time the current chancellor of our current enemy, the Germans. His individual teeth were painted on the board around his mouth. Each tooth was made to swing in and out on hinges so that when struck by a heavy cricket ball you could, if your aim was right, knock out his teeth. Some times when thrown accurately you could knock out all of his teeth. It was called a Hitler shy. The word shy was used for throwing the ball and trying to knock down an object. It was a favorite game for everybody to pay a penny and try and break all of Hitler's teeth. A small prize was given when you achieved that capability. All of the events that the fair attendees participated in you would pay as much as a penny for the swings and the buying of cake and handcrafts. The money generated by this was given to the church fund.

The church garden was quite large and the vicarage house was painted a yellow color. I believe it was built during the 18th century and it looked quite a nice home to live in. The gardens were kept up by volunteer gardeners as all of the maintenance of the church was. In Thundersley everything surrounded the church. The church was the center of everything especially for me during wartime period from 1940-1945.

During this time in winter the scouts and cubs did many Christmas pageants and other special event shows. The theater sketches were arranged by the scouts and directed by my auntie. She was a great stage director and rehearsed relentlessly prior to show time. We did this at the church hall which was located about a half mile up the road from the church. There was a stage at one end of the hall and could seat about a hundred people. We did sketches which are best described to be like in Vaudeville Theater.

Most of the songs that we sang as scouts were traditional songs that came out of the Hackney Scout Song Book. Songs like Back to Gilwall, Happy Land. We entertained the audience with sketches about Uncle Tom Cobley which included a two-man horse. To become a horse for the sketch one scout had to grasp the scout in the front around his waist and bend forward and become the body of the horse and the first scout would stand upright with horse's head positioned over his head. A horse-colored blanket covered the rest of the scout's bodies. We then clip clopped around the stage as the scout choir sang about Uncle Tom Cobley who wanted to go to Wydicombe Fair. Referring to a medieval village fair located in that town that actually still exists. Being very small and squeaky in voice I had to say the last name on my own in the list of names in the song Harry Hawk to everyone's merriment.

It began like this:

*Tom Pierce, Tom Pierce lend me your grey mare, all along down
along out along lea, for I want to go to Wydicombe Fair, with
Bill Brewer, Daniel Stuart, Peter Gurney, Daniel Widen, Harry
Hawk... Then on my own at the end I would sing with a squeaky
child's voice Harry Hawk and finish up with Uncle Tom Cobley
and all, Uncle Tom Cobley and all!*

Everyone laughed at that. We had many curtains calls for that sketch.
There were other sketches in the show like the one called Aunt Jemima.
It went like this:

*O' Jemima look at your Uncle Jim?
He's in the duck pond learning how to swim,
First, he does the breast stroke and then he's doing the side
Now he's under the water swimming against the tide, O' Jemima!*

Many other songs have been used out of the Scout Song Book which
had a green book cover.

Living deep in the country there wasn't too much to do for entertainment but we made up our own entertainment listening to the radio.
No modern music was allowed by my auntie such as swing band music.
She always listened to the BBC programs and classical music. She got
me interested in classical music which she called serious music that
was played by the old masters.

My mother was only able to visit me about three times during the
five years that I was evacuated because there was a restriction for any
travel especially on trains since seats on a train were reserved for traveling military personnel. The trains were always stopping in between
stations where government officials would board the train and would
check each passenger's documents one by one to ensure that there were
no spies on board. I think I remember seeing my father only two or
three times during that period since he was in the Army training for the
Normandy invasion.

It was 1944 when I was seven years old when my mother came to Thundersley to take me on a short family holiday. We were going to meet up with my dad for a week in the county of Norfolk so we would have some time together and had managed to get a week's leave. We did not know at the time he had been training for the invasion of Europe and he managed to get leave prior to the departure to D Day when the invasion date was decided. He was just waiting like other soldiers for the actual date of the invasion.

My mother arrived at our bungalow to pack some of my things for the trip and I said my goodbyes to auntie and we boarded the bus to Benfleet station to take a train to London's train terminal. Upon arrival in London, I remember riding the bus with all the blast netting pasted on the bus windows, passing through the streets of huge bomb damage rubble of London to get to the railway terminal at St. Pancras train terminal where we would meet up with my dad to board a train to Hunstanton, Norfolk. As we passed through London on the bus to St. Pancras train terminal, I could see the terrible damage done to the city. There were blocks and blocks of collapsed houses, piles of rubble everywhere and people digging into the rubble hoping to find some of their possessions that bombs and fires had not destroyed. From a recent air raid, I could see the ambulances parked at those houses that had been hit by bombs the night before. The ambulance crews were carrying stretchers of dead and injured people that were caught inside the house as the bombers were dropping their bomb loads.

It was strange to see a row of houses looking as though they had survived, but then a wide gap in between where there was no house. I could see the sides of houses where the previous house once stood. The sides of the walls had marks where the stairs used to be. Not only homes but offices and factories were practically leveled. Passing by St. Paul's Cathedral it seemed that the cathedral was not destined to be destroyed since there it was proudly standing like a monument untouched, while all around was nothing but total devastation. Not only could I see the crushed buildings but fires were still burning from the previous night's bombing. It might seem at first glance that it was not the best of times to take a young boy into the city that had just been bombed, but in those days people went about their business in a normal way. This was essential since Londoners had to get back to their lives and jobs to keep the country operating to end the war as quickly as possible.

We arrived at St. Pancras train terminal and there was my dad waiting under the large clock where everybody meets. There he was in uniform and I remember him picking me up as he had done before and flying me around in the air. He looked so great in his uniform covered in all kind of badges and suddenly we heard a whistle and knew it was time for us to get on the train. When we arrived at Hunstanton, Norfolk we had to catch a bus to where my aunt had her bungalow.

We finally found the house of my old aunt and after the hugs of everyone when we arrived and I had to listen to grownups talk I asked if we could walk along the sea front and look out to sea. The house was a small bungalow along the coast of the North Sea on the corner of coastline called by a quaint name, the Wash. The coastline curved into a large indenture into the underbelly of England like a huge bay. There is a story in history that King John of Robin Hood fame was fleeing from another king, King Richard III. He was escaping in a sailing ship heading out to sea carrying in his hand the crown of England. A storm came blowing in and the ship sunk with King John's crown. King John survived but it has been speculated that the crown is still on the bottom of the sea waiting to be found.

Because of the threat of German invasion nobody was allowed on any of the beaches because they were mined with defensive explosives and along the beach front were huge blocks of cement about fifteen feet by fifteen feet. These tank traps would make it almost impossible to land tanks and drive them across this barrier off of the beach to get inland. The beaches were mined with high explosives and more than likely there were soldiers inside the tank traps waiting, watching the horizon for enemy ships to appear. If this German invasion did occur that would be the first time for over nine hundred years that England had been attacked by a successful invasion which was in 1066 by William the Conqueror.

This part of England lies very low, practically at sea level, so when the tide comes in it comes in fast so you had to be quick on the feet to out run the tide or be caught high and dry on a sand bank and washed away when the tide comes in. The whole area is covered with small creeks full of mud and wild life such as crabs by the thousand. We could see thousands of crabs scuttling along the muddy streams and hear the sea birds crying out.

For the first time in my life I was really happy. I was with my parents, especially with my dad who I had not seen in over four years since he was in the Army moving around with his regiment. He would carry me on his shoulders and tell me about some of the wildlife that was teaming around us and he would throw me up in the air to my delight. We would go down at night to the pub with my family, which in England is a traditional place to go. I could not go in the pub because I was too young but I waited outside while my mum and dad would be inside having a drink. For the first time in my life, I felt complete with both parents being with me together.

At night my uncle and aunt would invite their neighbors in for some partying, having what they called a knee's up. Someone would play the piano and everyone would be singing some of the old songs. First, they always checked the blackout curtains in case any chinks of light would show. We were only a short distance across the North Sea from Europe and the German Army.

However, something comes along to change such happiness and soon we were back to wartime events that probably again changed my life's direction. After only a few days of holiday we were riding on a local bus going into town when a motor cyclist with a military uniform and police driver came past us on the bus and began to indicate to the bus driver to pull the bus over and to stop immediately. The driver of the bus stopped, opened the bus door and I could see it was a military policeman. He climbed up the three steps to be inside the bus and called out to all the passengers in a loud voice, is there a Sapper Phelps on board? Sapper in the Royal engineers was a rank which dealt in explosives and chemicals. My dad stood up in his seat and replied yes sir, here. The policeman said that he had a message for my father. His unit had sent out telegrams that his leave had been cancelled and he was to return to base as quickly as possible. Although we did not know it at the time but D Day was being prepared and all units were cancelling furloughs. He had been trained to go out on D Day and was on his way to be part of the invasion of Europe. It was May 1944 one month before the invasion of Europe.

We got off the bus, crossed the road and had to wait for the returning bus back to Hunstanton. When we got back to my aunt's house in Norfolk my dad quickly packed up his Army travel bag and we headed together back to the bus stop to take us to the train station back to London. We had to pass again through the streets of the bombed out city of London to get to the other train terminus on the other side of the city to take the train back to Thundersley. It didn't seem fair to me at the time but we had to head back to Thundersley and my auntie. Before he left us to catch his train to his base, he picked me up and gave me a kiss and a hug and said do not worry son, I will see you soon after the war is over and then we will back together again. He said good bye to my mum, gave her a kiss and he was gone. I was at that moment a very unhappy seven year old boy. Finally, after five years, I was spending some quality time with my dad only to have it snatched away from me by the war again.

London was still under bombing conditions with additional collapsed buildings and smoldering fires. There was an air raid going on while we were on the bus, but nobody seemed to mind. The houses were in flames and there was lots of smoke and lots of destruction. Some streets were impassable due to houses that had collapsed leaving rubble all over the streets making it sometimes impassable to drive straight through. The bus was continually diverted around the damage to another street. Arriving back in Thundersley my mother felt the need to stay for the rest of the day.

Before she left back to London, she decided to take me to the movies on that Sunday afternoon. She announced her intensions to my auntie that she was taking me to the movies. Auntie did not approve that since it was Sunday. My auntie being religious as an Anglican Church member whose creed was not to attend movies or other entertainment on Sundays. She would go to church three times on a Sunday and here she was being told that her almost adopted son was going to the movies on a Sunday afternoon with his mother. My auntie was quite firm and said no, absolutely no. Roy is not going to see the films on a Sunday. We could all go up to the church together but not to the movies. Then came the arguing and I was told to go outside to play. Apparently, there was quite a lot of argument and my mother in later years told me what had happened. My mother told my auntie in no uncertain terms that I was her son and she could take me anywhere she damn well wanted. My mother could really fight, even when she was in her later years she would get into arguments and usually won.

Well of course the word damn was not used in my aunties home and the discussion went on and finally it was resolved and my mother took me on a bus to the nearby town of Hadleigh where there was a Ritz Cinema. That was the first time I had ever seen a real movie. I even remember the movie which was called State Fair and the song that was in the movie was called It Might as Well Be Spring. I still remember the words to the song and enjoy it whenever it is played and remember that dark day when all was not quiet at Standish Villa, Rhoda Road. When we returned back to my auntie's the tension was still high, but slowly everything seemed to settle down. My mother left soon after to return back to her home in London and her job at Batches store the following morning.

It was during the summer of 1944, a few months after my return to Thundersley, when I was walking to school, I heard a very strange sound coming from the sky. It sounded like a motorcycle with its motor making a spattering sound as if the engine was not firing in sequence. I remember looking up and seeing a strange looking flying tube with stubby wings and rocket exhaust flying above me. It was a doodle bug, the first new weapon the Germans had invented to only kill civilians. The Germans launched it usually from France and Holland which they had occupied and launched it with just enough fuel to fly it to London. When its fuel ran out as it did due to headwinds or other reasons it would then fall to the ground and the explosives in the nose cone would explode on contact doing terrible damage.

The doodle bug was officially called the V1 flying bomb. It was a weapon something equivalent to the present-day cruise missile without modern electronic controls, but much slower. The Germans sent thousands of these doodle bugs across the channel to put fear into the British civilian population. It was a psychological weapon because when the fuel was spent it was unknown just how the aircraft would come down.

Sometimes, due to its short stubby wings it might glide down to the ground to impact and explode. Or it might glide down for a few miles or just drop twisting and turning to the ground. It was unpredictable until it ran out of fuel. We only knew that when the engine stopped it was out of fuel that we had to take cover or at least drop to the ground and wait for the explosion. After the explosion we just went on our way. On my way to school every day I would see many of these flying bombs in the air and as soon as I heard the engine stop, I would drop to the ground and wait for the explosion. I was seven years old. They flew so slowly that they were easy to shoot down and the RAF had a field day in shooting them down in their Spitfire fighter aircraft.

It was explained after the war that it was like shooting fish in a barrel. The only danger was that the explosion would damage the attacking aircraft. Every day as I walked to school, I could hear the chattering of aircraft guns from aircraft high in the sky trying to shoot down these flying bombs. There would be the sound of the guns from the attacking planes and the explosion of the bomb as it was hit. When it exploded, we had to be careful of shrapnel which might fall on top of us from the bomb. At times there were so many of these doodle bugs in the sky that it looked like a swarm of birds. The Germans knew that D Day was coming and wanted to slow down the advance of the armies being prepared for D Day. The designation for the doodle bugs by the Germans was the V1 for vengeance.

This first flying bomb model, the one we called the doodle bug was called the V1 however what was soon to come later was by far the worst that could be done by one civilized nation to another and that was the launching of their V2 rocket. This was just totally devastating since it flew so fast that we did know it was coming, just a whoosh of air and an explosion. No time to take cover. Its speed was over a 5,000 mph. The booster rocket was not much difference to the rockets we use in space exploration today or for intercontinental nuclear missiles but it was devastating to the civilian population. They were also usually launched from France and Holland, but in this case there was no defense. People could be waiting in line at the market shopping on the high street and without any warning and because of its speed V2 would hit a shopping area and hundreds of civilians and would be killed instantly in the street. It could not be shot down since its speed was too fast. It was not guided in any way, but like the V1 doodle bug it was fueled to fly just so far and drop down to the ground.

Fortunately for all of us compared to the amount of doodle bugs they sent over there were fewer of these rockets. The devastation was more severe since there were much more explosives packed in the war-head and many people were killed because of this terrible weapon. These V2 rockets had no guidance systems and were quite crude, but wherever they landed was a disaster. Whenever its fuel ran out is where they landed.

One Saturday morning around 7:00 am, having just woken up, I heard a sound like a whoosh over the roof of our bungalow. I then heard the sound of an explosion which threw me out of bed onto the floor. I heard people shouting and all the local dogs barking. I put on some clothes and looked outside but everything was the same, no damage that I could see. My auntie came into the room and asked me if I was alright. My auntie then took me to the top of Rhoda Road and looked across to the golf course and there was a huge smoking pit where this V2 rocket had landed. It had flown right over the roof of our house about 100 feet high and over the top of the hill on to the golf course on the other side of the hill doing no damage other than shattering many nerves.

The war was still very active in the skies over England even in the first few months of 1944 when we were waiting to hear when the inva-sion of Europe had begun. We still had to run across the lane to Mrs. Willis's air raid shelter when the air raid siren wailed. I would still hear the coastal guns firing off as the German bombers tried to get through to bomb London but these raids were getting less and we knew that the war would soon end. Even with the protection of the coastal guns and anti-aircraft guns called ack-ack guns some got through. The German bombers were usually escorted by fighter aircraft. One Saturday morn-ing when people were doing their shopping in a town not too far away called Southend there was an attack that defied all description. Running down the center of the market place is High Street where the shoppers would do their Saturday shopping. At about noon a lone German fighter pilot flew down the length of High Street, about two miles, machine gunning all the shoppers on the street. Hundreds were killed and that just showed the type of German pilot he was and would do to unarmed civilians.

Sometimes we would hear the sound of an airplane with its engine coughing, starting and restarting the engine of the plane and we knew that a German aircraft was going to crash nearby. After the air raid and the siren sang out the all clear we would run out and look for a spiral of smoke which would indicate where the aircraft had crashed. By the time we had reached the area we could see the police already there with the fire department putting out the flames. Most cases we were pleased to see it was a German bomber that had been shot down and we could see some bodies. On one occasion we saw a German pilot standing by the aircraft casually smoking a cigarette waiting to be captured.

1944 was upon us. The pending invasion of Europe by the allied forces was very nearby. The military traffic in convoys were all heading to the southern coasts of England. There were soldiers everywhere from all different countries especially from America and Canada. For a pedestrian trying to cross the road was sometimes not easy because there was so much military traffic in 1944 because of the military buildup for the impending D day operations. We sometimes could not cross the road while a convoy of military hardware was loaded on huge trucks and we would have to wait. There were constant convoys of military trucks with tanks on their flatbeds and trailing heavy artillery guns. Flatbeds were loaded with tanks and smaller halftracks on each truck with large artillery guns.

The convoy began first with a Jeep with radio antenna. The Jeep with its officer and driver would be flying a green flag on its roof and long radio antenna which stretched the length of the Jeep. If the convoy was American the jeep had a great white star painted on the side of the Jeep and a large green flag flying from the masthead. This indicated that a convoy was following and no civilians were allowed to break the convoy and cross the road until the convoy had passed. When the last truck passed it carried a red flag indicating that the convoy had ended.

There were also many hundreds of soldiers marching down the road towards the coast, sometimes taking more than a half an hour to march past. We would always wave to the men who waved back and sometimes the soldiers threw sweets (candy). If they were American troops, they would throw chewing gum as they marched past. We would call out hey Joe, got any gum chum? It was impossible to describe in detail what these convoys escorted,

It seemed that all of England was covered with trucks full of soldiers, loaded with tanks and artillery guns. Every kind of armament was carried by these trucks and thousands of soldiers from all countries mostly American and British and some other allied countries. They were marching south towards British ports ready to sail across the English Channel to France. Sometimes it would take an hour for the convoy to pass and I will never forget watching this armada of equipment. In the sky, aircraft were flying in from America and Canada and landing on many American Airforce airfields that been hastily built long runways for B17 and British Lancaster's in Essex County. It now appeared that the invasion of France was coming soon and we were all excited about this major war effort. We would soon start, but history will note that America paid a severe price for that landing in France at a place called Normandy on Omaha Beach.

Across the lane opposite our bungalow there was an old rotted gate that said no trespassing. It appeared to sag a little, but over the gate stood a huge old oak tree that to my joy had a bough that overhung the road with accessibility to climb from the top of the gate. I found some old rope about half an inch thick and threw the end over the bough of the tree looped it tight and let the rope hang down. I knotted the bottom end of the rope into a huge knot where I could wrap my legs around it. After testing my weight on the rope, I began my first flight. Carrying the end of the rope over my shoulder I carefully climbed up on the rickety old gate, wrapped my legs around the knot at the end of the rope and swung out across the lane like I was the ape man Tarzan. It was a great feeling flying out and then back towards the tree trunk. Unfortunately, I had not realized that I would return back to hit the tree trunk. The first time I did swing back I landed hard against the tree. The second time I was a little more careful by taking off at a different angle and solved the problem of a softer landing having the swing of the rope do a small circle.

I loved to climb trees and I thought at that time I was part ape. In the future when I played golf with my sales manager in America, he told me that I putted like an ape. That was probably the correct description of my putting! I had seen many Tarzan films and imagined myself in Africa swinging from tree to tree. Since nobody was around to hear me, I would even use the Tarzan yell. Although I did not have any friends to play with, I found that I was quite happy being by myself and was not troubled by not having any other boys to play with. I felt independent when alone. I was seven years old now during 1944 and was left alone by my auntie who was really taking care of her husband who was now an invalid and rarely moved from his rocking chair. Most of the time he was in front of the fireside in the living room of the three-room bungalow.

About a mile into the woods was my favorite fishing hole. It was totally surrounded by woods but there was a small opening in the hedge heading into the woods. There was this beautiful body of water, a pond that had reeds surrounding it and nice thick mud as you put your bare feet into the water and have the mud swish through your toes. Who cares if my feet got muddy, it felt good! There all kinds of residents in my pond. There were frogs and frog spawn in the spring. Then there were tadpoles, which I would put into a jam jar to take home and watch them hatch into toads and frogs.

I had a fishing pole that had a net at the end and as I slowly walked into the water, I looked for my favorite fish to catch. They were called red throats, very small fish about five inches long and very quick to sense danger. They moved out of the way when a small boy came along with fishing pole and net. Other residents of my fishing pond were called newts which were a lizard kind of life form. They were easy to catch. I brought along a long bamboo stick about five feet long. At one end I had tied a long piece of string which dangled down to about ten feet. I did not have a father to show me how to fish so I brought with me an ordinary embroidery pin that is used by women in their sewing basket. I bent the pin to half it size creating a hook and found a worm and stuck it on the pin still wriggling. I dangled the line with the worm on the end of it hoping to hook a fish, but no luck. Any fish that had any sense could see that it was a pin with a worm on the end and ignored it. Although I tried, I never caught a fish.

It was wonderful growing up in those days for a young boy playing in the woods with no supervision since it gave me a sense of independence that I could take care of myself. Although my auntie was a strict disciplinarian in bringing me up during my formative years, I respected her for teaching me that type of self-discipline. When I was only slightly older, I could easily take care of myself and knew what to do when the time came. She gave me a great education and showed me some of the beautiful things in this world that I might normally pass by. Most important of all she gave me self confidence in myself. I will always remember her kindness in teaching me history, geography and astronomy in such a way that she brought many stories to life and made them real for me.

I heard many years later that the tradition of our modern military to salute officers came from the olden days when knights who wore a large heavy helmet on their heads and could not been seen through their face slits in the helmet. They then raised the right hand to lift up the helmet so that the opposite oncoming person could see the identity of the knight riding past them. That is why in the military we salute to show our face, we raised our right hand to our forehead to show that we had no weapon in that right hand that we respected the opposing knight and meant no harm to him.

My auntie was an artist, a painter who painted flowers on vellum paper. She was a very good artist and painted for people who wanted work done, especially flowers. The painting was done in oils and she was so good at flowers they stood out from the vellum in 3D dimension. She gave me one to keep and I still have it hanging on the wall of my home.

Looking up at the stars she showed me where the constellations were and how to guide you in the darkness by looking for Stella Polaris, the great North Star glowing in the north sky. She would then explain some of the rudiments of then known physics and about the periodic table that gives names of all the elements in nature and brings physics to life. So, to a point I can talk relatively easily to anyone about general physics and quantum mechanics.

My auntie had a brother by the name of Alfred Heath who was a real-life Indiana Jones, the fictitious antiquities explorer of movie fame.

She had told me many stories about her brother Alfred who was working during the 1920's as chief engineer building the Trans-Peruvian Railroad that went all the way south down the west coast of South America through to Peru. Sometimes when money to build the railroad and Peruvian funds ran low, he would supplement his income and take on a safari trek with wealthy Europeans to look for the Lacus Solis, which in Inca words meant Lake of the Sun. Apparently when the Spanish conquered Peru the native Incas collected all of their gold to hide before the invading Spanish conquistadors arrived to steal it. To hide it they threw it all into a great lake in the Andes Mountains of Peru. Nobody has yet found this gold and it is still a mystery. My auntie also told me that her brother Alfred had married a native Peruvian woman named Carta, an indigenous native of Peru, who had a dark brown complexion and had a gold tooth in the front of her mouth that flashed when she spoke.

Alfred was also an explorer who travelled well into the Andes Mountains to explore visiting the existing indigenous tribes of South America who hunted with poisoned darts blown through a blow pipe. One day Alfred and his wife Carta came to visit his sister and I did see that she had a brown complexion and also, I saw the big gold tooth in the front of her mouth. He told me many stories of his exploits while he was there. I did not think of it at the time but now I look back and wonder how he got permission to travel across the Atlantic Ocean during wartime which was filled with German U boats looking for targets on their way to England. The more I think of it I began to believe that he may have been working undercover for the British government and came across the Atlantic in a British submarine to meet with the British government in Westminster. He was an interesting man to talk with and I listened to what he described to me like I was reading a book.

D Day, Invasion of Europe

WE BEGAN HEARING on the radio about the D Day landings in France which to all of us on the home front was great news. We also heard of the horrific number of casualties that had incurred while trying to hold the early footholds on the beaches of Omaha and other landing areas. I received a letter from my mother that my dad did not go on the D Day landings even though he had been trained to do so. He was lucky that some officer had checked and found out that he was slightly too old to go on that operation and he was held back for other duties. I was very happy to hear that great news. He was already there in Guernsey and the British were rounding up the German soldiers. He was on the landings there, but the German Army that occupied those islands were starving for food and had been left behind by the retreating German Army and were happy to be relieved

Time was passing and the air raids got less and less. We heard on the radio that Hitler had been assassinated but that was untrue. The Allied troops were closing in on Germany and we all began to feel that the war was coming to an end soon. The end of year 1944 was coming to an end and optimism was running high that the war would soon be over.

Soon I would be leaving my country home and returning to London but not quite yet. I was told that it would be late in the year of 1945 before I would actually return to my London home to my mother. I was not in any hurry to go back to London so we just stayed there listening to the radio for the announcement that the war had finally ended. Even though the war was over, there were still the celebrations coming up in Thundersley. I did not want to go home where my streets were filled with rubble from some of the bombed-out houses and factories.

1945, The War is Over

THERE WAS A letter in the mail addressed to me from my mother who said that she was going into the hospital soon to have a baby and that it was arranged that I would stay where I was until my dad was discharged from the Army which would be in late September 1945. I would not be returning to London until then when she could take care of the baby after its arrival and things would settle down. I was quite happy with this arrangement since Thundersley was still my home and I did not want to leave it.

During the early part of May 6, 1945 there was great excitement because on the radio we heard that Hitler had committed suicide and the war in Europe would soon come to a final end and all the troops would be coming home soon including my dad. I remember the night of May 7th the day before the end of the war, the day we now called VE Day (Victory over Europe Day) when we all were waiting for the formal cessation of hostilities.

It was hard to believe that it was really over. The night before the announcement I was asleep in my bed and woke up to a powerful thunderstorm which was unusual in that part of England. I thought it was the bombs again and ran to my auntie's bedroom to get to the shelter, but soon realized that it was just a violent storm. As soon as victory was confirmed and hostilities had ended there were parties everywhere.

Bonfires were lit all over the country and all the lights went back on again. There were stands where you could play games. There were flags stretched across the pathways in the field and also stretched across where colored lights lit up the whole area. Music was being played over the public address system. I remember hearing Bing Crosby singing Don't Fence Me In being played. It was amazing to me because all of these festivities seemed to come out of nowhere. One minute we were in darkness, the next there was light and music. It was a great evening for me, an eight year old kid who had never seen an outdoor party before. The war was over and I would soon be going back to my mother in London.

However even though the war was over in Europe there was still Japan to contend with so with the fighting still continued in the far east of the Pacific. There were concerns that there would have to be a massive invasion of the mainland of Japan, which because of the terrain and geography of Japan the allies could sustain over a million casualties. On August 6, 1945 the first atomic bomb was dropped on Hiroshima and a second atomic bomb dropped Nagasaki on August 9th which brought the Japanese to their knees and the war ended in all theaters of the world. The most devastating war known in the history of mankind had ended and I was wondering now that it was all over, when I was to go back to London and my family.

As the festivities played out, I found a whole new freedom that an eight year old boy could have. My auntie let me ride the bus on my own to a nearby seaside resort called Southend, which was only about six miles away on a bus, but it was a sense of freedom that I had never experienced before. Summer and fall of 1945 came and went and before we knew it, it was Christmas and I was still in Thundersley. I did not care because I really did not want to go back to London. I had heard of the terrible damage done to the buildings during the bombing of London and its suburbs so I was quite happy to stay in the country doing what I had been doing.

My auntie and I would take trips to Canvey Island which was a small island off the mouth of the river Thames. It was nearby and by taking the bus to Benfleet station we could take another bus across the small creek onto the island. The island at the time consisted mainly of tidal flats. Off in the distance were the mushrooms, which were large guns that were used as the first defense of London located at the mouth of the river Thames. These guns were mounted on platforms and were standing in the water about two miles off shore and looked like very large mushrooms sticking out of the water. These were the guns that we would hear when the bombers from Germany where entering British airspace on their way to bomb London.

One day my auntie said that I could go with a friend out for the day by ourselves and we decided to go by bus to Southend. This was a small city which is a seaside resort and had a mile-long pier sticking out into the three-mile-wide river. I remember I was so excited to be allowed to go on a bus by myself at eight years old. My new found friend David Winfield, who lived at the bottom of Rhoda Road, and I waited at the bus stop to take the number 2A bus to Southend. We arrived at a city that had been bombed many times but was now in a recovery mode and getting back to a near normal. We still could not go on the beach because it had not yet been cleared of mines. All along the sea front was large cement blocks called tank traps. These had been built prior to the beginning of the war to prevent invasion of England and would not allow any tanks to get through off the beach.

We walked along the front of the beach and saw that some enterprising person had liberated a large boat and was now offering tourists boat rides. This was the first time I was on a boat so we paid our fare and sailed off. I was quite nervous because I had read in books that storms would come up fast and tip over a boat. The captain of the boat had an old gramophone working with a phonograph record playing into a loud speaker like a public address system. After the initial fear of being in a boat I began to enjoy it and we sailed past the end of the pier into open water for my first time at sea.

When we got back, we continued to walk along the sea front and came across another enterprising person who had opened up his small carnival. It was called Peter Pans Playground. In later years up to the present I saw that it was is still there under the same name. It had small rides for children so I climbed aboard an airplane that actually had a propeller turning fast and we started to move around in a giant swing. As we speeded up, we were flying way outwards away from the center of the ride and it was so thrilling. Strangely enough fifty years later when I came from America on a vacation, we visited the town of Southend and there was Peter Pans Playground with the same airplanes going around. I wondered how many children had taken the ride since that day we had visited in Southend in 1945.

We then went onto the famous Southend Pier. At that time since it was a long pier it had a small railway train operating. This was an old train that operated from the seafront to the end of the pier. It just had just carriages with benches. I remember that if you sat on either side of the carriage you had to hook a small chain to prevent riders from sliding off. The train ran alongside of the pier and the other side was for pedestrians who just wanted to walk to the end of the pier. It was very strange walking over the top of the sea. At the end of the pier were all kinds of amusements which had been shuttered up during the war and immediately reopened when the war ended. I was so happy to be on my own and I will always remember that first day of my independence. I was finally free of adult supervision.

My auntie and I would take trips to where the cockle sheds were located at Leigh on Sea. One of the delicacies of the British people was seafood and one that was easily available was the cockle. The cockle is a small relative of the American clam. All along a mile-long stretch of beach were the cockle sheds where they brought in the fished cockles from the cockle beds in the estuary of the river Thames. They would display the cockles on the small counters and for a penny or so you could buy a cup. To get to the meat of the cockle you had to have a pin that you would stick inside the shell and twist the meat out. Once you had the cockle out of the shell you put vinegar on it and popped it into your mouth. I did that only once and nearly choked on it. Its food inside was rubbery in texture and had to be swallowed whole since it was impossible to chew. People were eating these things and once they were finished eating, they would throw the shell away where they eventually landed on a huge pile of shells.

I thought I would go fishing. I found some string and a pole and fishing line with a real hook and float colored in red. I remember taking the bus to a small town about ten miles away, which for me that was a real trip, to a nearby town called Corringham. I had heard that there was a large lake there that had plenty of fish to catch. I found the lake and sad to say I did not catch any fish, not even one. I did enjoy the days outing and was really glad that I did not kill anything. I have always been against unnecessary killing of any kinds of wild life and still believe that to this day.

The winter of 1945-1946 came and went and in the spring my auntie told me that I would be going home to London during that summer. I loved the Essex countryside and did not want to leave it for the bombed streets of London. I was not looking forward to going back to London. I was told that because of the time it took for my father to be discharged from the Army I would not be going home until the summer of 1946 which was when he was due to be discharged. The dates of his discharge kept changing.

My baby brother Colin had just been born in the city of Hitching, England on April 1, 1945 in the county of Hertfordshire. My mother needed time to get rested and organized in the house with a new born baby before I could return home. She also was preparing for my father to return home after his discharge from the Army in the fall. He had been away from home and his wife since 1939, over seven years.

While I was waiting to go home there was a scout camping trip arranged for our scout troop headed up by my auntie. We would be sleeping under canvas in a large bell-shaped tent called a Bell tent. We had to erect the tents and we slept on ground sheets. It was cold at night. From then on into this day I do not like camping out. It was so cold and I was always afraid of catching a cold and it would then go into bronchitis since they had told me I was born with that disease.

We camped in a farmer's field for over a week near a town called Pitsea, about ten miles from our home in Thundersley. We piled all of our gear in what they called a trek cart. It was a type of cart with two very large wheels that the Boar trekkers in Africa used to move their belongings. The Boar War in the late 1880's was when scouting began with Lord Baden Powell as the founder of the Boy Scouts. Scouting began when the Army sent messengers out during a battle to get information from battalion to battalion. They were usually older boys in those days. During the week we did our scouting jobs, handicraft and tying knots, but on Sunday morning of the week we had to go to church.

In those days my auntie was a staunch Church of England Episcopal lady and did not get along too well with the very few people near us of the Catholic faith. At ten o clock in the morning that Sunday we marched into the church of Pitsea which, like our own St. Peters was over twelve hundred years old and we each slid into each empty pew in the church. The service began as normal but suddenly the priest came down the isle of the church and began swinging a chain which at the bottom a container was sending out smoke that smelled like incense. The Church of England is really very close in beliefs to the Catholic Church so there is a high Church of England and a Low Church of England. The high church is almost being Catholic. As soon as my auntie smelled incense from the swinging lamp, she jumped out of her pew in her scout uniform and called in a loud voice this is Popery and she ordered all the boys in their scout uniforms to stand up in their pews and we slowly marched out of the church row by row. That caused a great scandal in the village.

We had a great week at camp but I still could not really fit into a camping environment and to this day do not like to camp out. The ground was cold underneath the ground sheet and the insects came into the tent. The farmer's field was full of cow flops so one had to be careful where one would step.

The weather was cold and wet all that week that we were out and were soon very glad to be back in my little bungalow in which I had spent my formative years as a young boy. When we returned to the bungalow there was still no news when I would be going back to London. It was fine with me so I stayed where I was until the spring of 1946 when I finally received a letter from my mum to come home. I was destined to be the eternal gypsy. Later in life this proved to be correct when I would travel to many places in the world from America to Tokyo and Europe as an American business man. It was decided that I would travel alone and take the train to Leyton station on June 1. So quickly the day came to leave and I remember the morning of the day I left to go home and for the first time I could really see my surrogate mother becoming very emotional. After six years she was losing her surrogate son. On the morning of my departure from Thundersley I began to have emotion overwhelming me. She started to pack up my belongings in a small suitcase and I could see tears in her eyes that after all this time I was really leaving and going back to my real mother. Auntie was not usually an emotional person but this time it was really hard on her to see me leave. She packed my small suitcase and put the toys that I had in another bag. After six long years she was losing her surrogate son.

I said goodbye to my best friend, my dog Tess, and we walked down to the bus stop at the bottom of the hill at Kent's Hill Road where I would catch the bus to Benfleet station to catch my train back to London. The bus arrived and we said goodbye with hugs and kisses. I promised I would come back and visit her. The bus pulled up to the curb and I boarded the bus and I was on my way to Benfleet station. The London train pulled into Benfleet station and I boarded the train. I was on my way back to Leyton station where my mother would be waiting for me. As the train moved along the tracks, I felt that I was going the wrong way. I should be going back to auntie. I should be going back to Thundersley to my real life and real home, but I knew that it would be impossible. I must go home to a mother that had been deprived of her first born for so many years.

I was leaving one life and entering another. I watched the station slowly pass by as the steam train slowly picked up speed and watched as the Benfleet creek slowly disappeared behind me and the train chugged up the track towards the city of London. The train continued on towards London passing through Barking station where I remember as a three year old my mother had stayed too long on the train and we had to climb down on to the tracks to change trains so long ago.

A great period of my life was over although I would continue to visit my auntie during the years after I left. Thundersley was still my home in my mind and still is. But that did not help my mother who was waiting to receive her son back who had been raised by another woman. I reasoned to myself that I would only be 23 miles away and could always go and visit my surrogate mother whenever I wanted. I promised myself that I would return as soon as I could.

With the lessons and knowledge, she had given to me I was able to overcome many of my formative year problems that any eight year old would face in a world that was partially destroyed by fire and endured long years of destruction. She taught me that hard work would ensure success, be kind to people as you would want them to be kind to you. Remember that and you will be a success in life. Her voice continues to this day and came back to me in my mind.

Be kind to animals and help them, not to hurt them in any way. Not to kill animals just for the fun of it, not even a fly because the fly was put there for a purpose and that eventually would become some other animal's dinner for the day.

June 1946, I am Back Home

MY MUM WAS there waiting on the platform for me and as soon as the train stopped and I stepped off of the train. We did the hugging and kissing as parents do and that is when for the first time, I saw my new baby brother, Colin, in his baby carriage. Mum told me as an introduction that this is your new baby brother, Colin, say hello to him. I took a look at him and said hello Colin, how you doing? Colin gave me a scrawny face look and I was not too experienced in dealing with babies so I must have said something like hello Colin and began folding up Colin's baby carriage as we boarded the bus from the station to our home.

My brother Colin was born on April 1, 1945 in a town in England called Hitching, in the county of Hertfordshire on Easter Sunday, April Fool's Day. Our mother had been ordered by the British government to go there and have her baby because London was still unsafe during that time because of the V2 rockets that were being launched during early 1945. The law was that any children or pregnant women were to be evacuated out of England's large cities into small country towns like Hitching to escape the German rockets that were still raining down on the large cities of England. Soon after Colin was born there was great rejoicing in the streets of England because Germany had been defeated and there would be no more bombings over London. Our mum returned home to our flat in Leyton.

I arrived home after six years and started to get acquainted with mum after our long separation. We talked about all the things I did and how nice auntie was. We were preparing the flat for my dad to arrive home from the war the following week and my mother was cleaning the floors, walls and furniture to make it gleaming for his return to his family.

I looked around the neighborhood and all I could see were concrete streets and houses everywhere. There were more concrete and more houses and I thought does this ever stop? There were a few trees, fields and no countryside like Thundersley. I could only see damaged shops and houses and nothing that I could relate to. It seemed to me that my new brother during the short time we knew him he was always taking in food. He was always hungry. In later years when he was in his teens that was so true! It was a family joke whenever we passed a Howard Johnson hamburger restaurant, he wanted me to stop the car and buy him a hamburger.

Mum received a telegram from the Army that my dad would be arriving home very soon, being discharged just a week later so we were really excited that he would be coming home in a very short time. We put together a banner to say Welcome Home Dad and hung it on the upstairs window. We did not own a phone in the house so we just waited and suddenly there was a knock on the front door. It was our next-door neighbor who did have a phone and she said she had received a phone call and message from my dad saying that he was on his way home and would be home that day about lunch time.

We waited at the window to see who would be the first to see him coming along the street. The street was covered with flags and huge homemade signs with welcome home painted on them. All the neighbors seem to be on the street at the same time.

1946, My Dad Has Come Home

SUDDENLY AT THE corner I saw him. I knew it was him even though I had not seen him for such a long time, I saw my dad and now he was almost home. I was beside myself with joy! We called out to him from the front room open window, waved and I screamed out to him dad! To see him walking along the sidewalk carrying his kit bag over his shoulder I felt so happy and proud, relieved that he was at last at home and that we were a family again. I had my dad, my mother and my baby brother Colin and I felt that I was filled with happiness that I had never felt before. My dad was home from the war, safe and sound together again and home at last.

I felt so proud of him even though I barely recognized him. Although I had not had much contact with him during the time, he and I were apart for the past six years. I knew he was my dad and it was not a dream and he was safely home. We were all one family again and it felt good. He was still in his Army uniform and he looked good, tall and strong to an eight year old boy who had not seen him for so long. I remember him picking me up in his arms and held me over his head and he was laughing and I was screaming with delight and as young as I was, I knew that the future looked bright. He then gently picked up his new baby son Colin who was tucked up in his crib and held him for the first time. He picked up Colin in his arms and rocked him a few times gently supporting Colin's head with his hands he placed a kiss on Colin's forehead. After a while he slowly put him back into his crib.

As soon as dad was settled in and changed into civilian clothes, we all sat down and had a long talk about our experiences. Mum had saved a bottle of champagne for this special occasion and they had a drink for celebration. They gave me a sip and said not to tell anyone because I was too young. After a few hours of talking, he went over to his Army kitbag, which carried all his personal gear and brought out some souvenirs for me. He gave me some German Army items he had managed to smuggle into the country. The prized item was a real German helmet with the German regimental colors on its side. There was a small hole in one side of the helmet, but I did not ask him how it got there. I assumed that the soldier who had worn it was now dead. He brought me a belt buckle with the swastika and engraved items on the buckle and a cigarette lighter built into the top of a ten-inch shell casing. There was also an officer's pair of binoculars which really thrilled me. He also had some gifts for mum but I do not recall what they were.

After a few days he went and spent some time visiting his family in Walthamstow. He visited with his mother, father and his two sisters and some of my cousins. All together we also visited my maternal part of the family in Clapton, my grandmother and grandfather. All of the men that had been called up for duty had returned so we visited them all. My grandmother, who I called Nan, was my mother's mother.

My Aunt Rose suggested we should have a family party one month from this weekend when everyone could be together again and celebrate their homecoming. Everybody agreed to that suggestion because by then everybody would have returned from the military. We knew it would take a while for dad to settle in and ease back into civilian life. They talked of what they wanted to do and when dad was going to go back to work. He had separation pay from the Army, but he was anxious to get back into civilian life and pick up where he had left off in 1939.

The following weekend our neighbors along Clementina Road had a meeting and decided that we should have a street party with a street bonfire. The street party went off fine and everyone had a great time. By this time most of the soldiers, sailors and airmen had been discharged from the military and were back at home with their families.

Bunting flags hung from each house, crisscrossing the street from one house on one side of the street to the other side and photos of each soldier were in the window of his house. The wives of the soldiers had huge Welcome Home banners hand painted across each door with the name of the soldier written on the banner. May 8th was designated VE Day (Victory Over Europe Day).

Everybody became part of a great big street party. They built a huge bonfire in the middle of the road and found some sort of fireworks left over from the war. Some were actual live small explosives. Somebody brought out into the street a piano that was loaded on a long barrow with a chair and someone climbed up on the barrow and began playing all the old songs.

Everyone was singing along and dancing around the piano player. We danced the old dances like Hokie Kokie, and the song Knees up Mother Brown, all along the street. There was lots of hugging and kissing and I felt very strange seeing all these people that I did not know so full of happiness after living in the country for such a long time. I was nine years old.

Although there was not much food, all the housewives suddenly found lots of food and put it on long tables. They played records from a record player attached to a PA system or as we called it a loud speaker system which played all the wartime songs. As would be expected lots of beer was available and gin for the ladies and was being consumed with a healthy thirst by all.

Most of the children that had been sent away on evacuation, the ones that could be found, were home by this time so I had suddenly lots of children of my own age to talk to and play with.

The street lights were turned back on having been off since 1939 because of the blackout restrictions. Most of the children that had been sent away on evacuation, the ones that could be found, were home by this time so I had suddenly lots of children of my own age to talk to and play with. There were some children that never did return to the neighborhood. They were either killed in the bombing or just simply were lost. Some had lost mothers killed in their homes and lost their fathers to the war. Others were just lost and no one could locate them until sometime in later years when they turned up in some village or drifted back to London hoping to find their parents or their home that they left so long ago.

The war was now over and it was the time to clear away the rubble from the destroyed homes and factories around the neighborhood and try somehow to return to our previous lives. That however was not to be since an era had come and gone and nothing would ever be the same again for England. England, that great democracy that began the Magna Carter in 1215, was going socialist in its government.

A few weeks later we had another party at my grandmother's house for all of my mother's family. As usual the party began over at the local pub and when the pub closed, we moved over to my grandmother's house. They rolled up the carpet in the front room of my grandmother's house for dancing. My Uncle Tom played the piano and everybody began to sing all of the old songs that were remembered sung before the war.

I was now back home living in a flat that I did not know much about. Our flat consisted of two front doors. One flat downstairs led directly into the apartment itself and the other went upstairs that was number 53. To reach the upstairs flat you entered a small hallway and then had to climb up a stairway to the upper level. At the top of the stairs, you could make a U turn and on the right was mum and dads bedroom. This room was a larger room in the flat like a master bedroom with an open fireplace. Above the fireplace was a large picture of our dad looking down from over the mantle shelf. In the corner was one window that looked down to the path leading to the back-yard garden. Next to their bedroom was the front living room. This room was only used on Sundays or for special activities since all the best furniture was kept there. It was a very large room with two lights hanging from the ceiling and an open fireplace located at the far end. At the far end of the room was a black lacquered piano that mum played at various times when visitors called. The couch and two armchairs that completed a suite were brown leather with velvet pillows. The glass cabinet with crystal glasses and other special treasures was standing over in the corner away from any traffic, so that there was no way an accident could happen to harm these china and silver plates or precious glassware. At the top of the stairs there was a long hallway. All of the rooms were off on the left side of the passage. The first door was Roy's room and it was small but comfortable enough for me.

The next door led to the small scullery or kitchen where all the cooking was done. This was also where the clothes washing was done. In the corner of this kitchen was a large pot enclosed by bricking. Underneath the pot was a small fireplace which after you filled up the tub with cold water the fire was lit and boiled up to wash the clothes. There weren't any washing machines in those days and if there were, we could never have afforded one. The water had to be boiled to wash clothes. There was no hot running water and to boil anything either for cooking or washing it all had to be done by hand. All cooking in the area was fueled by gas piped in so we had a gas cooking stove in the kitchen. Next to the gas stove was a stairway which led down into the back of the house where we shared with our downstairs neighbor a small garden. At the end of the hallway was the back-living room which was the main family room. This room was used for everyday living and there was cooking also done in this room on a black cooking hob stove. It was a coal burning stove and in the center was the place for the fireplace.

On the left of the fireplace was a black iron oven with a grate for opening the fireplace to heat the room, and it was also good to get a slice of bread and a long fork to toast bread for our meals. On the right side of the fireplace was a flat surface where you could put kettles or pots on the flat surface to cook and boil water. This living room had the most windows. The two windows looked down on the backyard garden. In the corner of the room was a large larder or cupboard to store food because there was no such thing as a refrigerator. Since there was no central heating in the house there was a fireplace in every room. Needless to say, sometimes it was cold in the rooms that did not have a fire going, since it would be a waste of heat to have a fire going all the time. When it did get cold as it did most of the time in England's winters, we lit a kerosene oil stove in the center of the room called a Calor brand stove which generated a lot of heat by burning kerosene early on a cold frosty morning.

The flat was considered to be a cold water flat. Since there was no heat except from the fireplace, leaving the room made you feel very cold. When it was time to go to bed we all had a hot water bottle. Made of tough rubber we filled it with boiled water wrapped in a towel and put it in between the sheets for a short while before it was time to go to bed. By that time the bed was nice and warm and when you were ready for bed and undressed, I would jump into bed as quickly as possible. It was so nice to put your feet on the hot water bottle. Some people used an old brick and put it in the oven to warm up first then when it was time to go to bed, they would wrap a towel around a brick, and there were plenty of those around. They seemed to have the heat capacity to hold their heat more than a hot water bottle.

I had a letter from Auntie Ellie in Thundersley. I found out that just after I had left Thundersley, Jack Heath, her husband had died and was buried in St. Peters churchyard among the other old graves of history in the shadow of that old church.

It was now 1946 and my dad had got a job working for British Railways as a platform porter at a nearby railroad station called Blackhorse Lane. I waved to the station when he was on duty and stayed with him since I was going to school soon. I needed to enroll in a junior school that was ages 8-11 and then a senior school from 11 to fifteen years. That was the final age to leave school. As a station porter dad's job was when a train had pulled into the station, he would ensure that everyone had got on board then blew his whistle to the guard that was on the train who then waved a lighted green lantern and the train then pulled out of the station. In between arrivals of a train my dad and his partner Johnnie would retire to the porter's room on one of the platforms. Inside the room was a central potbellied coal stove that used coal/coke for fuel.

There was a passenger bridge crossing over to the other platforms between the uptown track and the downtown track. These platforms separated the eastbound and westbound tracks. At the top of the bridge was the ticket office where you paid your fare. The railroads in those days were dirty and gritty with the smoke pouring out of the top of the locomotive and blowing a high-pitched whistle when approaching the train station. If while traveling on the train you put your head outside the window you were liable to get a piece of coal grit that came from the locomotive into your eye.

To cross the station bridge at Blackhorse Lane station there was a long slope instead of stairs up to the bridge that was level across to the tracks and then a down slope to come down on the other side of the tracks and station platform. After dinner when my dad was working at the station, I would board a trolley bus for the twenty minute ride to the station and go visit dad at work. After the train had left the station and there was a period of time when there were no trains scheduled and we used to play a game.

In America the railway passenger trains are called railroad cars, in England they were called carriages, so to avoid confusion I will call them railroad cars. They retained the company colors such as green cars for southern railways (SR) and brown for the London Midland and Scottish railways (LMS). The trains that came into London were of two types depending on the distance travelled. Most local railway cars had one compartment for each door so the cars were like a single compartment with a single door to leave the compartment.

Any long distance train in England had a corridor running down the side and length of the car with a connecting leather enclosure to the next car. My dad and the other porter and I would race up and over the bridge for a prize of a tennis ball. Although my dad was working full time at the railroad station it was still not enough to buy food as it was so very expensive and we were still on ration coupons. Mum had to go to work to earn enough money to help feed her family so she started to work at W. H. Smith and Sons, a printer and box maker located within walking distance of our home near Lea Bridge Road.

I was going to school but Colin was too young to go to school yet, so each morning I took Colin to Aunt Mary in Walthamstow where most of my dad's family was living. After making arrangements for me to start school in September, which was just a few months away, I had time get myself together to start school. However, there was one question in the arrangements, and that was who was who going to take care of my brother Colin who was now one year old while I was at school? Well, guess who? Yes, you are correct it was to be me.

Mrs. Findon was not a blood relative, but at that time anyone that was connected to the family as a close friend we called them aunt or uncle. She knew mum from when she used to work in the war years at Batches, the grocery store not too far from them in the High Street. Colin played most of the time with a boy who lived just down the street. Sometimes he played in Aunt Mary's back yard where her husband did a lot of woodwork. Aunt Mary's husband had chickens in his back yard and Colin always wanted to chase them around.

It was an end of an era on both social and political sides of the spectrum. The lifeblood of a nation had been bled dry by the cost of the war not only in money but in the lives that had been lost. There was nothing left. Families had lost most of their young men on both sides of the battlefield and would never see them again. Great Britain was almost in bankruptcy and in debt to America for the war loans that Great Britain could not repay

The First World War had sucked out of the country the young manhood and killed them off for future generations. Because of that the old moneyed families of England would pass away penniless. Throughout the depression of the 1930's the old rich families would fade away. It took only the outbreak of the Second World War that broke the financial depression and generated a new rich society in both England and Europe.

With new money to spend for armaments, it gave the opportunity to begin another war. Slowly the families regained what was left of their sons and fathers and managed to evade war. There was a general feeling in England that began to sweep the country that never again would the people of Great Britain have to endure this firestorm again. So, giving in to the will of the people the political parties changed to something called socialism. It gave the people what they wanted, but at a high cost to their lifestyle although they did not admit or understand at the time. They just did not want any more wars in their lifetime.

After World War II, England became a socialistic country. The country was devastated by war and basically was bankrupt. Six long years had taken its toll and the people were ready for a complete change. A whole generation of her young men killed in the war and the people were restless for a change. Families uprooted and lost children were taken away from their parents to escape the London bombing and sometimes were never found after the war was over.

The damage by the bombing and the lack of food and uprooting of their children told them that enough was enough. The whole country was sick of war from the First World War in 1914-1918 through the last war ending in 1945. They had enough of war and just wanted to settle for peace regardless of the consequences. The nation felt that it needed a political change right there and then. In the 1946 elections the people voted out of office as Prime Minister the man that saved the country, Winston Churchill, and voted in the socialists and they took the country down the road to socialism.

The national election of 1946 to everybody's surprise brought into power the Labor government. The conservatives that were headed up by Winston Churchill the Prime Minister that had held the country together during the war was defeated and the socialists were in power and were determined to change the whole country. The conservatives led by Churchill who led the country to victory were out of government and a new regime was in and would change the country forever. It sent a shock wave throughout the country when Mr. Churchill was defeated in the 1946 elections and the Labor Party took over the country and changed the country forever.

The country became nationalized and the unions took control of most of the major industries. There were continuous labor disputes all over the country with strikes of most industries such as steel, transportation and the coal industries leading to many labor problems. In the first election of 1946 they dismissed the hero of World War II, Winston Churchill as prime minister, and chose Mr. Attlee who was a true socialist leaning almost to some people to the communistic side of the political center. This feeling of anti-war generated a whole new political concept which changed the way government during the next generation of the nineteen fifties to leading to the rage of the decade of the1960's where everything changed and civil violence became the normal way of protest.

This ends the chapter of my life as a child evacuee. The country of England would never be the same. That would be proven later. Although no one would admit it, the sun had begun to set on the British Empire. Britain had been bled dry by two World Wars. The last one had just ended the most destructive conflict in modern history.

I went to school during the war but never really learned anything. I had no real education, but I did learn not by a school teacher but by listening to the stories of that wonderful woman, my auntie. She opened up a whole world of knowledge for me to carry on the learning she had taught me. To extend that knowledge she had taught me at her small cottage and among the graves of St. Peters Church. In the scouts they always taught me to do the right thing in those wonderful woods and fields of old England. I remember the old songs we used to sing together and the camping out in the farm's fields. The church parades on a Sunday morning, hearing the church bells pealing from St. Peters Church as it had done so for hundreds of years. I was taught to remember past history because history always seems to repeat itself. Mrs. Heath showed me how to take care of myself, not to rely on other people but to handle a problem myself because I was the only person that can be confident in me, was me.

Fifty years after her death I still miss her and I believe that she was a very special person put on this earth and I will always appreciate the things that she taught me. I was very lucky to have had her as a surrogate mother. In May of 1946 I was now 9 years old.

1947, An American Care Packages Arrives

THE YEAR OF 1947 was not a good year for the Phelps family. Although there was no violence on the ground or in the air, we were still on a wartime footing. We still had rationing on food, clothes and any other items that had to brought into England from far across the ocean. One day there was a knock on the door and standing at the door was the postman. He handed us a large cardboard box. It was a care package from an American organization that sent help to England from America. The box was filled with cans of beans, fruit and so many other strange brand names items that I did know what they really were. There were also blocks of chocolate which I had never tasted before and other types of candy.

My mum was so pleased and we all thought how nice it was for some country called America to take the time to help us when food was in such short supply. Everyone was talking about it since it was not only us but many of the other families on the street had received these care parcels. I had seen America through the films that had been sent over to keep everybody's mind off the war. The buildings were so high in America that it was difficult for me to understand how they managed to keep the buildings from falling down and the people spoke with a strange English language. It was the same as ours, but with a drawl.

I had seen many American soldiers during the war and many English girls that had married the soldiers. They were called GI brides and were leaving England after their American husbands had been discharged and first returned home. As soon as the soldiers left the military they sent for their brides and there were photos of hundreds of young women waving from the ocean ships that were taking them away from a grey, cold and partially destroyed country like England to a new world of promise and plenty.

I was ten years old now, back living in the house that I had left when I was three years old. I felt like the world had turned upside down on me because I was so confused. I had two mothers who were totally different in their personalities, two homes totally different and a two year old brother to take care of while my mother was at work.

There were signs of a small beginning since they were building some types of housing now that the soldiers were coming home and they needed housing. The Town of Hackney and its political council built what they called pre-fabricated housing on public lands. One group of housing was in Clapton Municipal Park where they built the pre-fabs as they were now called, on government lands. It would not be correct to call us poor because we were really the middle class of England but there was such a general shortage of housing of just about everything. Food was still a problem that we could not eat right because the food selection just was not just there.

1947, I Started School

I NEEDED TO enroll in a junior school that was ages 8-11 and then a senior school from 11 to fifteen years that was then the final school leaving age. My mother took me to the local junior school called Sybourne Street School, to attend during the day. Most schools in England at that time were named by the street that it was located. School in England started at 9:15 in the morning so after making arrangements for me to start school in September, which was a few months away, I had time get myself together to start school.

My mother had a problem because who was going to babysit my brother during the day? My father's family lived in the next town over in Walthamstow which was where I was born nine years before. It was not too far away but it took two bus changes to get there and back. So, it was my responsibility to take Colin to Mrs. Finden his daily baby sitter before I left for school.

My mother had found herself a job in a folding carton, printing factory as a gluer in a factory that made folded boxes so she started work at 8:00 am each morning. She did not have too far to go, just a few streets away. The name of the printing plant was W. H. Smith and Sons. Apparently, there was a pre-war family tradition on my mother's side of the family since most of the women of my family worked there at some time or another and eventually, I would work there myself a few years later when I finished school at age fifteen.

My brother Colin was now two years old and needed care while my mother was at work. So, I was elected to bring him to Mrs. Finden in the morning for the day and bring him back after I had finished school in the late afternoon so it made a long day for me and a lot of bus changes.

Mrs. Finden lived on the same block of flats that all of my father's family had lived on for many years. She was just a few flats away from my paternal grandparent's home on South Grove Road and she was agreeable to take in my baby brother for day care while I was at school.

We were still on ration books and food was very scarce. The shortage was on everything from eggs to petroleum gasoline. There was also a shortage of housing since there were so many apartments and houses that had been totally destroyed or were others that were unlivable. It has since been estimated that over one million homes had been destroyed during the German air raids.

Although my dad was not discharged from the Army until middle of 1946, he was just in time to see his father John Ambrose Phelps pass away that year. I do not remember my Grandfather Phelps too much except my mother prior to the war spent time over with my dad's family. Mum, Colin and I did catch a bus sometime to visit them on South Grove Avenue in Walthamstow. I remember him as a very large portly man with an old-fashioned suit and a gold watch and watch chain sticking out of his vest pocket. I also remember him as being very jolly and told jokes. In contrast my paternal grandmother was very different. She wore old fashioned clothes that made her look very old. Her dress was dowdy and she wore an overdress that was black. She had high buttoned black shoes and a floppy hat that did indeed look like a hat turned upside down. I do not remember his funeral or where he is buried, but I am sure I was there with all my aunts, uncles and cousins from my father's side of the family.

As often happens in families his wife, my grandmother Phelps, passed away just a few months after her husband John. This time my dad was home from the Army and he was able to attend that funeral as we all did. After the funeral we went back to their place and had high tea which consisted of cookies, scones, watercress sandwiches that were cut into small square pieces the size of one mouthful. There was beer for the men and gin and orange for the ladies. If a lady did not want gin, she would have a shandy, which was two thirds beer and one third lemonade. It was not really a wild wake but just a family gathering for a funeral. All my aunts on my father's side were there, Aunt Mag

(Margaret), Aunt Hilda, Aunt Matilda and of course my dad Eddie who was the only brother in that family group.

My Aunt Mag lost her only son to the war. He was my Uncle Cyril, who at the age of 19 joined the Royal Air Force as a rear tail gunner on a Lancaster bomber and was shot down over Germany around 1942. For many years I was told that the plane crashed and his body was never found. Recently I have been told that the plane managed to land in Holland, but the tail gunner was always the first target of a German fighter. Since that was the rear line of defense of an aircraft and without the rear gun turret operating, the aircraft was almost basically defenseless from behind. Uncle Cyril died at the age of 21 when his rear turret was shot away somewhere over Germany and his body was never found. I have seen photos of him recently and he looked so young.

Our blocks of flats were occupied by some interesting families. Mr. and Mrs. Binstead lived downstairs with kids about the same age as me. Next door was Mr. and Mrs. Cutmore. Mr. Cutmore would lift up my German binoculars and said that he could see angels in the clouds. Mr. and Mrs. Watts also lived next door.

My mum loved to work in the garden and grew roses. Dad built a square shaped lawn in the middle of the area that we could call a garden. He measured it out and poured the concrete for the paving around the lawn. We had to share the garden with the family that lived downstairs from us. We had the left side of the garden area and the other family had the right side. Mum loved roses and she grew some beauties and you could say she had a rose thumb. She had rambling roses down the left side of the fence. Mrs. Straw lived on the left side of the garden and she had the habit of hanging out her laundry on a rope line propped up by a large pole. Hanging on the line of laundry for all to see were her underwear with long legs and elastic and at the middle of each leg and were always the color of pink or blue. She must have been 55 years old or older but in those days 55 was quite old.

It was a happy time for me because I now had a family. I had a dad, a mother, a brother, uncles and aunts on both sides of the family. The war was over so no more air raids, bombs or being separated from my parents. But like anything else it was not to last for too long.

It was now September 1946 and I was to start school at Sybourne Street Primary School located about a mile from the house. I had to walk to school wearing my short pants since I was not allowed to wear long pants until reaching the age of 14. I had to walk along Lea Bridge Road which was a very busy road. There was lots of traffic using this main road. There were cars, trucks and buses by electric, with overhead wires connected to the bus or the newer diesel buses that were motorized. All the buses by now had taken off the sticky netting on the windows that had been on them during the war to prevent bomb blast and breaking glass.

Getting up early for school on a frosty morning was more than anyone could endure. There was no central heating. The rooms of the house were very frosty cold and to just lift the bedclothes off of my body was torture. Just poking your nose away from the covers made your nose cold, but by the morning it was stone cold. We also had a rubber hot water bottle that we put in the bed but by the morning that too had been pushed down to the bottom of the bed and was of no use. The very thought of having to get out of bed and put your feet on the cold bare linoleum floor covering which we called lino, short for linoleum, that made you want to climb back into bed. We sometimes wore woolen socks and heavy flannel pajamas.

I remember my first look at the school building as I turned around the corner on to Sybourne Street. My first impression was that it looked like an orphanage out of a Charles Dickens novel. The building was brick but was built about 100 years before. It was a two storied building that had been partially bomb damaged and had been temporally repaired. The building had lots of tall windows and it was surrounded by an asphalt playground with a ten foot high iron railing with posts shaped like spears. In the place where there were no railings there just was high brick walls. There was no way out except through the gateway.

I started school in September of 1947 and was assigned to Miss. Howells' class. This would be the equivalent to a junior high school in America. There were both boys and girls in the class and we never left the classrooms to change classes. It was the teacher that came to each classroom for each subject change so we each kept our own desks all the time. There were no lockers to put our personal belongings in so we had a long board down the side of the room with coat hooks where we hung our coats up and left our belongings on the floor under the hook and coat. There were no inside toilets. Alongside of the railings of the playground there was a lower building that served as a toilet for boys and one for the girl's. If we wished to use the toilets, we would have to hold up our hand and ask the teacher for permission to put on our coats and go outside to visit the toilets.

Miss. Howell was my favorite teacher and we discovered that she came from Wales. She was a good teacher of social studies and we learned that Great Britain had an empire that stretched across the world. I remember the map of the world where the British colonies and Commonwealth countries were located and were colored on the map in pink. It seemed that looking at that map most of the entire world was colored in pink. We were told that English was spoken in most countries and it amazed me that there were so many parts that were covered in pink. We had an Empire Day which was a national holiday.

I remember our school books were very old and run down which had obviously been used many times over many years. I cannot recall too much about this middle school except that it filled in a time that was very important to me. Since I had been brought up from a very young age by mostly women I was never really into sports. I was in the Boy Scouts in Thundersley where we would play football (soccer) and cricket, which I preferred over football and played quite often.

Later in years when I was in school, I would play for my school team. I remember my dad was an ardent supporter of the local football club called the Leyton Orient Football team. The stadium we had was quite nearby our flat so each Saturday afternoon during the winter months we would go over to the game and cheer on the local team.

As soon as the war had ended there came that ritual that all British men did and still do and that is to play the football pools every Saturday night. I never really did understand it but it seems that prior to Saturday's game you would take a cutting from the newspaper and actually bet on what team in England was going to win on that day and by how many goals. There was quite a lot of money if you won but everybody had that dream to get rich but never did. This weekly operation was operated by a kind of legalized book making firm called Littlewoods. It was like the present day lottery.

My mum and dad had a very good marriage but every now and then they would have a tiff. My father was not one that agreed on arguments or any other family dysfunction so as soon as the argument between my mother got strong, he would say Hey love, I have to go over to the off license to get some cigarettes and he would leave. An off license was usually a corner store that sold beer and liquor. There was no drinking on the premises and there they did not have to have any kind of government license to sell their beer. It was similar in America to what is called a package store. My mother would tell me later that she really got steamed when he did that because she liked a little argument now and then, but he spoiled it all by leaving to go buy some cigarettes thereby eliminating any unpleasantness. By the time he got back she had forgotten what it was all about.

An off license was like a corner take-out building, but it looked like a pub from the outside. To own and operate a real public house, which is why it is called a pub, you had to get a special license to run that kind of business which was very hard to get and cost a lot of money to obtain a license. An off license is just how the word means. You could sell beer and liquor but could not consume it on the premises. They also sold cigarettes, cigars and soft drinks.

As soon as all of the men who had survived the war took off their uniforms and went back to civilian life the family would gradually get together for a party. Fortunately, all of my uncles survived and arrived back to continue their lives. In those days most families got together about once a month for a real party, usually at my grandmother's house. We would all get together on a Saturday night at my maternal grandmother's house in nearby Clapton. There would be my Uncle Tom and Aunt Ivy, my Uncle Charlie and Aunt Maud, my Uncle Harry and Aunt Ida, my Aunt Rose and Uncle Alf and of course my grandmother Rose and grandfather William Went. Then came their children which were Maureen, like me she had a baby brother Roger, Uncle Tom's son, Aunt Rosie's son Malcolm and Aunt Ivy who was my mother.

With the carpet rolled up and crates of beer and gin the party would get going and keep on going. There were a lot of participation dances that we all enjoyed. One was the Hokie Kokie where were all joined hands and went in a circle and at a given part of the song, we would all stop and move to the center and call out Hokie Kokie. By the end of the evening most were close to being drunk. Being under age we cousins were not allowed to drink but we managed to get a sip of beer in when nobody was watching. There was no problem with driving because nobody had a car to drive.

I had joined the local scouting group meeting once a week at their club house that they had built. I was glad to be back in the scouts because it gave me the opportunity meet the other returning evacuees that were coming home to what was left of their city. I still had to take care of my brother Colin but had some time for myself. My dad was still working at the railroad station and mum still worked at W. H. Smith and Sons Printing Company.

Our favorite playground was on the site of bombed out buildings where there were piles of debris that been left over from the ruins of the houses and factories that had been bombed. To put it all in perspective, try and imagine the damage that was done by hurricane Katrina just in one city of New Orleans. Then imagine that kind of terrible damage done to every major city in the country from Philadelphia, New York and Boston. Thousands of houses and factories were either obliterated or partially damaged. That was London in 1940-1945.

It has since been estimated that over a million houses were destroyed in the war in England and it was time to rebuild. Rebuilding was beginning since most of the war veterans had come home bringing their old trades with them. They were tearing down the old buildings and piling up all the bricks and wood that had been half burned. Since there was a severe shortage of building materials, they reused the bricks. Blocks of burned out homes, factories and streets filled with debris where workmen were trying to clear the street so that traffic could drive on the roads and get the city back to a reasonable level of becoming normalcy. It was also a morale booster when all of the bombed out buildings were gradually being torn down and removed. It was an eyesore to grownups but a treasure trove for a ten year old to climb up on to the debris and play with all kinds of treasure such as lost jewelry and other items that were buried in the rubble of someone's previous home.

Prior to the cleanup, the debris had to be put somewhere so they put it all on a dump that was about two stories high for blocks and blocks. The rows of houses looked like they had lost their teeth since one half a block of homes were gone and the others were left standing untouched. The dumps were our playground. I still wore short trousers, usually grey flannel. My trousers were held up by an elastic belt with a snakelike clip around the waist.

While in the Army dad was stationed on the island of Guernsey moving out the captured Germans who had surrendered at wars end in 1945. He lived in a cottage of one of the islanders. He was very friendly with the family of Hugh's. The father of the Hugh's family happened to be the chief of police for the island of Guernsey and had a large family. While my father was stationed in Guernsey, he sent back to our house by Army transport a huge box of unused German tools. These tools were totally unused since they still had the grease protection lathered on each tool which had to be wiped off. He also had sent lots of grapes that grew on the island.

1947, My Dad Becomes Very Ill

MUM AND DAD were planning their first family vacation in Guernsey in the Channel Islands which would be booked for the last week of June and first week in July 1947. Dad seemed to be in good health for the first month of the year but after January 1947 he began to have serious pain in his back. He went to see our family doctor, Dr. Burns, and our dad was diagnosed as having lumbago, a back ailment and was given some ointment and liniment to help ease the pain.

All of the month of February and March he seems to get worse and he went back to the doctor again. The doctor checked him out again and it was recommended that he take some other medicine in addition to the ointment to rub on his back. In today's world he would already have been in the hospital but in those days, people were not ready to be taken to a hospital. I believe that x-rays were not recommended by his doctor because of the radiation it emitted.

Since dad worked for British Railways, he managed to get free tickets and reservations for the train and boat to travel to Guernsey. To get to Guernsey which is one of the Channel Islands lying off the coast of France, we had to take the boat train from Waterloo station in London bound for the port of Southampton. We would then take the British Railways six-hour voyage across the channel in a British Railways freighter ship to St. Peter's Port, Guernsey. Being a railroad porter for British Railways dad had free tickets for him and his family to use the train and ferry but there were no cots for the overnight six hour journey, just sleeping on the deck chairs. The weather across the channel was very bad with gales and cold choppy waters of the English Channel so we had to put rope lounge chairs together with blankets for the cold overnight journey and sleep on the deck.

Dad was terribly sick with pain in his back and he should have cancelled the trip but he was a strong family man and wanted to take his family on their first family vacation after the war. I also believe that he knew that this might be the only time that we could all be together as a family on such a vacation. Maybe he also had an intuition that he might not be able to do this trip in the future. He planned this trip to be with his wife and boys as soon as it was safe to do so. He was in terrible pain and I believe that he also had a high fever. He was coughing a lot and bringing up blood and mucus. He should have been in bed, not on a ships deck. While we were on deck, he called over one of the seamen that was working on the boat and took him aside. I did not know it at the time but he was negotiating with the sailor over some cigarettes to bribe the seaman to let me to go down to his cabin and sleep there in this seaman's warm, dry cabin instead of me being up on a cold and windy open deck. My dad was that kind of man, taking care of his family and neglecting his own serious illness. Mum was wrapped up warm and so was Colin, who was wrapped up asleep in a heavy blanket on mum's lap.

My dad arranged for me to go down into this seaman's cabin for the night so that I would not be so cold. In fact, it should have been my dad himself that should have gone down in the cabin while he was in so much pain and so sick with a high temperature and very ill. But that was the kind of man he was, thinking of everybody else except himself. I remember that cabin and how warm and cozy it was. Soon I was a sleep. Dad came down and woke me up to go to breakfast in the ships dining room. I remember him in his beige raincoat that he always wore as most men did in those days. He did not look well at all. The English Channel is one of the roughest stretches of sea in the world and the ship was tossing around like a cork in a wild stream. I remember in the cabin the lanterns from the ceiling were swinging wildly from side to side and articles in the cabin were not as secured as they should have been. England is not known for fine weather. Most experienced sea captains despise the English Channel because to the north is the North Sea and to the south is the Atlantic Ocean. Stuck in the middle is the English Channel, the sea churning ships around like they were in a washing machine. On most days it can be very calm but if a storm comes down from the North Sea there are usually a lot of sea sick people on their ships.

As soon as dawn arrived, I could see that the weather had changed suddenly from heavy cloud cover to a sky of blue and a promise of a fine day for the beginning of our very first family vacation. I was so excited because at dawn we had sighted land and would soon be disembarking at the dock in St. Peter's Port in Guernsey. For a ten year old boy this was the most exciting voyage I had taken. Little did I know that eleven years later I would be going on a much longer voyage. I sailed in style like I could never have imagined on a huge ocean liner the Queen Elizabeth I to New York for other unbelievable adventures I had ahead of me in America.

We slowly entered the port and passed a huge castle that had been guarding that port for hundreds of years and slowly docked. I was fascinated by how the men on shore grabbed hold of the huge thick lines and tied them to round barrel shaped blocks on the dock. We had arrived at our destination, but one look at my dad and I could see that he was worse.

The Pugh family was waiting for us as the ship docked. They had a taxi to take us to our hotel which was located in the capital town of St. Peter's Port on a cobblestoned street in town. I forget the name of the hotel but it was quite old and very French in design. We had two single rooms one for my mum and dad and one for me and Colin, who was now two years old. The first day after we had rested in the hotel we were invited to visit the Mr. and Mrs. Pugh at their cottage named Surprise Cottage for dinner. This cottage was about 200 years old and had no inside running water.

For the first few days we took the bus to the many beaches that the island had to offer but dad was in serious pain. He was told to go and see a doctor but politely refused said that when he gets back home he will visit the doctor, but not until then. We went down to the hotel dining for breakfast. I could see that my dad was still not well with pain showing all over his face.

They decided that they would hire a taxi for us to travel around the island because my dad could not ride on a bus in his condition. Mr. Pugh, being the island chief of police, pulled some strings to get a taxi for the balance of our visit. The next few days we would travel all over the island which was quite small. St. Peter's Port was the only town on the island at that time with quaint small streets with cobblestones. One of the places we visited was the Little Church which was completely made out of sea shells and was built small enough for visitors to able to bend down and walk through this tiny church. We went to all of the beaches around the island which were different. One side of the island was on cliffs that you had to walk down steps to get to the beach while the other sides were located on flat beaches. One of the photos taken was a group photo siting around a base of a tall monument and would show dad sitting with us and it can be seen how grey and ill his face looked.

The weather was very good since we were now away from the cool and variable weather of England. Guernsey is quite close to France so on a clear day we could see the French coast line. On the horizon there were two other islands one was called Herm and the other Sark.

We spent most evenings for dinner at the Pugh's home which was on a street that had a pub called the Red Lion. Each night we stopped in and had a drink. Dad tried to keep up with us but the pain was too much and stayed behind in the hotel room. I could not drink because I was too young, but they let us in to listen to everybody singing around the piano since most pubs had a piano.

We did some more sightseeing visiting some big, old German gun emplacements that the Germans had left behind with huge guns pointing out to sea towards England. They also had left behind a huge underground German hospital for military troops. This was still 1947 and most of the beaches were still closed to the public because of the land mines that were still in the sand and still had not been deactivated.

One day Mr. Pugh arranged for a local fisherman to take us over to the island of Herm which was famous for its seashells that lie on the beach ready to be picked up. It only took about half an hour to get there but to me that was the first time that I was on a small boat and I was nervous.

By this time dad was so ill he finally went to a local doctor who examined him and the doctor told him in his own words and I quote, "that if you value your life you should immediately go back home and see a lung specialist". This was the first time that any doctor had indicated the problem was his lungs. We were all very disappointed to cut short our holiday but prepared to leave immediately. When my mum and dad told me that we had to go home I said a terrible thing to my dad that still haunts me to this day, which I regret saying to him very much. I asked my dad "Why can't you go back home and we all stay here?" I know I was only ten years old but I think it hurt him. My mother was very angry with me. She took me aside and said that I should not have said such a thing to my dad when he was so ill. This comment has stayed with me all these years so I am still paying the price for that comment to our dad and I continually regret it. Especially since he was in the war while I was growing up and we had not seen each other at all for such a long time.

Somehow, he managed to get return tickets rescheduled to get back on the ship for an early return voyage to England. It took a few more days to do this, but we finally left Guernsey and came home back to London. This time the voyage was not so bad being on deck since the ship left Guernsey in the morning and the sun was shining all day, but I still remember him being so painfully sick. His back was hurting and his face was grey and he looked to me to be very ill. As soon as we arrived home, he went to visit the doctor who should have put him in the hospital long before we went away to Guernsey. The doctor immediately sent him to Whips Cross Hospital which was about fifteen minute's bus rides. They immediately admitted him on or around June 30, 1947. They did some tests and still could not diagnose his illness other than it was a lung problem. They did an x-ray and found a dark spot on his lung, but in those days they did not know if it was cancer.

1947, My Dad Dies of Lung Cancer

I REMEMBER BEING allowed in to see him and can still remember seeing him in bed with all kinds of tubes in his mouth and bottles hanging around his bed. In those days they did not have private rooms, just one long hospital ward with probably about twenty to thirty beds in the ward. I could see a face mask on him and that he was on oxygen that bubbled in a glass bottle with tubes running out of his mouth.

He was able to talk a little and he told me that if anything happened to him, I was to take care of my mum and my brother Colin. He insisted I promised him right then so I promised this to him and vowed that I would do that. His head fell back to the pillow in utter exhaustion. I promised him that I would take care of mum and Colin and I believe I fulfilled that promise. I also told him that I was so sorry I had said that mean and bad comment about staying on Guernsey, but I am not sure that he heard me. At that time the nurse came in and I was told to leave and wait outside. After a while my mum came out of the ward and said that we had to go home.

That was the last time that I saw my dad alive. That night I had a bad dream. I dreamed that I was carrying my dad's coffin on my shoulder going down some concrete stairs of an old building. I woke up with a start and heard my brother making a lot of crying noises across the room. I checked the time and it showed the time was 3:00 am.

I found nothing unusual except that mum was not in the house. I could not imagine where she could be at this early hour, but I went back to sleep. About six in the morning, I was woken up by my mum and I could see that she was crying. She told me that your dad died at three o'clock this morning. That was about the same time that I awoke from that awful dream that I had about carrying my dad's coffin down some stairs. She said that he died at just after three in the morning on July 5th. Coincidently, taking into consideration the five hours time difference between England and America, he actually passed away on the 4th of July, American time. That is a major celebration of the American of the Declaration of Independence. A strange coincidence, since years later I would take part in many happy 4th of July parties that Americans celebrated when I lived in America some years later. The timing was so very coincidental on those two events. Many years later my mother told me that minutes before he passed away, my dad said that he was looking in a mirror and my face reflected was not his face but the face of me, his son Roy. Mum said those were the last words he uttered before he passed away.

When my dad died in 1947, I was ten years old and Colin was two. It is sad to know that he did not have the joy of enjoying his two young sons. After he died my mother was devastated. There were not too many photos of him and I understand mum was so unhappy when he died that my grandmother Rose told her that the only way she would get over this traumatic part of her life was to destroy any photos she had of him, even the one that was hanging over the fire mantle in their bedroom. She did what my grandmother told her to do and she destroyed all the photos she could find. After my dad died my mum had to go back to work to earn enough money to feed her family so she started back at work at W. H. Smith and Sons located within walking distance of our home on Lea Bridge Road.

The cause of his death was still unknown. They would not issue a death certificate until they could do a postmortem (which in America is called an autopsy) so the doctor could not issue a death certificate until that was completed. After the autopsy his death certificate would determine that he had died of cancer of the right lung, but in those days doctors did not know much about what cancer was and I heard it was untreatable at that time.

My mother discovered later that during the war he had been working on projects that included chemical warfare and that probably caused his cancer. He did smoke but not very much. Mum had contacted the

Army and applied for a widow's pension but that application was turned down. She also tried to obtain a widows pension, but she was turned down again because the cancer case was not proven since they did not know much about cancer. More likely the truth was that the government probably did not want to admit that the British Army was working on chemical warfare programs during the war. My mother applied for a pension from the government, but that was turned down on the basis that cancer was not a proven illness at that time. She just received a social security pension and now had to go out to work full time to support her family.

The financial preparations for the funeral were taken care of by my grandmother on my mother's side of the family. I think that caused a rift between the two families Phelps and Went which lasted for a long time. It should have been paid for and cared for by the Phelps side of the family. That is the traditional side of the family which was my dad's side but they did not seem to care. Being just children we did not know this was going on at that time, but later on in years I did hear my mum tell me about this seemingly lack of interest in my dad's side of the family after he died.

In England in those days prior to the funeral, the funeral director picked up the body from the hospital and brought it to the home of the deceased. The undertaker built a coffin for my dad, put him inside and it was then driven home in a hearse. Then they it carried up the stairs and brought it into the front room of our home. He was laid on two sawhorse type stands in the front room of the house. There was no such thing as a funeral home in those days to the best of my knowledge. The funeral directors were Johns and Sons.

I remember seeing this light brown pine wood coffin with four simple handles on the sides. The coffin lid was closed. It was not the kind of coffin that is made in America which is an ornate casket with large handles on each side. I remember coming into the front room when nobody was around and take a look at the coffin and suddenly I had the memory of my dream. The coffin looked the same as the one I saw in my dream before he died. It was like a premonition.

In England at that time there was no such things as a funeral home. The cemetery had an office on site so my mother had to deal with what we would call a funeral director. He did all the planning for the funeral, the service and any monuments that need to be arranged. It was also the custom in England that a funeral line of cars following the funeral lead car, which was a black Rolls Royce, carried the coffin. All the flowers delivered from family members were on the coffin inside and on the roof of the car. Following behind in another car were family members. It was also the tradition in England that as the funeral procession passed along the road people would stop walking and remove their hats or caps with respect for the dead until the procession had passed by.

My dad was going to be buried in Chingford Mount Cemetery which was about fifteen miles from Leyton. It was planned that the procession would pass along High Street, Walthamstow passing Bache's and the store where my dad had worked for many years prior to going into the Army. As we entered the High Street the road had been cleared of traffic and as we passed Bache's store and I remember seeing all the people in each store standing up at their counters in respect for my dad as we passed by. He was well liked by them all.

Chingford Cemetery is a very old and large cemetery which had large gates to enter through from the outside main road. Dad was going to be buried in the new part of the cemetery, so the procession of black cars wound its way through the old part and then into the new field, which was the new part of Chingford cemetery. We slowly reached the grave site where the newly dug grave was open and everyone gathered around with the vicar of the local church in his robes. Alongside of the grave was a pile of soil that was to be put back into the ground after the coffin had been lowered into the grave.

All of my relatives were gathered around the grave site from both sides of the family. I do not remember the actual service but after the vicar had finished the religious part, they started to lower the coffin in the grave. As the coffin was at ground level, they stopped lowering the coffin. I remember mum telling me to go and pick up a handful of soil and drop it on the coffin lid. She also had three red roses, one for me, one for Colin and one for her. We both stepped up to the grave site and dropped the roses on top of the coffin. Mum first, then me and since Colin was only two years old my mum and myself put his on top of the coffin as they lowered it into the grave. She then whispered to me these words that I have never forgotten. She whispered to me and said "Say goodbye to daddy". I was looking at that coffin with my dad in it, suspended now almost at the bottom, being slowly lowered into the open grave. I broke down at that point in tears. I was ten years old.

After the service was over and people were ready to leave the burial site my Uncles Tom, Harry and Alfred called me over to them saying that they wanted to speak to me. They took me aside and my Uncle Harry told me that from now on I was the man of the house and that it was my duty to take care of my mother and brother. They asked me if I understood what that meant. I told them that I understood what they said and promised them that I would now take care of them in every way I could.

I remember now thinking back that I was very angry that not only had the war taken me away from a normal childhood, but had now taken from me my dad. I was also confused since I did not really know my mum since I only saw her maybe two or three times in six years and my dad maybe the same amount of time. Now I had just watched him being lowered down into the ground and I would never again see him.

Now the service was completed and people started to drift away for the grave area. We all made out way home for the small funeral luncheon that my mother and her sisters had prepared. Being a small apartment, it was crowded with relatives and friends. I remember my mother was dressed in black and the men wore black armbands around their sleeves of their suit jackets. They served a typical English tea meal with small water cress sandwiches cut in small triangles from a loaf of bread. There was beer for the men to drink and gin and orange juice for the ladies. It was not like an Irish wake. The mood was somber and quiet as they remembered my dad before the war in their conversations about him.

I was a troubled ten year old boy who could not understand why this was happening to me. What I wanted was to be back in Thundersley away from all this confusion and sadness. My behavior was very bad during and after tea. I had a catapult which in America is called a sling shot. There was a large bowl of cherries that was put out for the guests. I was eating the cherries down to the pit and putting the pit into my catapult and shooting it at everybody. I was running around the apartment yelling and screaming that I wanted my dad back. It was not fair that I had been away all those years, reunited with my dad and having to lose him so quickly. Everyone was totally disgusted with me, so much that one of my uncles took me aside and gave me a real paddling on my backside and then also gave me a tongue lashing about how I must behave like a man. He said that I was not respecting my father by my bad behavior and was hurting my mum.

After that burst of anger from my uncles and paddling my backside I began to realize that I now had a heavy responsibility for my mother and brother and that all this bad behavior had to stop. I was no longer in the country growing up wild in the woods as I had done for so many years and that I had to readjust, but I missed that country life so badly which put me into confusion in the future growing years. After a short while I stood up and apologized to my family for my bad behavior and they pulled me close to them and said that all will be ok. They each gave me a hug and in the case of the ladies a kiss on the forehead and told me that I would soon learn my responsibilities and that episode had ended.

It was now late October 1947, three months after my dad died, when I suddenly got very sick. I was told in later years I nearly died. Mum had taken me and Colin to the travelling circus at Leyton's Coronation Gardens. The circus came to town under a large tent with seats rising up from the circus floor. Before I we went to the circus that day, I had developed a very sore throat. I told mum that my throat hurt badly so she looked into my mouth and told me to drink some vinegar and that would clear out the infection. They believed in those days that a shot glass of vinegar would cure all. I tried to eat a slice of tomato that we had inside a cheese sandwich which we had brought along with us for a snack. I suddenly felt nauseous, dizzy and I knew that I was really sick. She took me home right away and took me to the doctor who said that I should be put in hospital right away.

They sent me to Children's Hospital in London into a ward of at least thirty beds. I am not sure what I had but it was very serious. They said at first it was diphtheria. They kept me isolated for about a week and I finally came around and got better and was discharged from the hospital. The diagnosis was not very clear. The doctor said that it had been a severe emotional episode caused when I had held back all my emotions when my dad died. I had kept my emotions inside of my mind and it had caused a breakdown in my immune system causing me to be very sick ending up in the hospital for two weeks. I have never gone to see a circus since and have no interest in watching the animals perform and the acrobats swinging over the circus ring. After two weeks in the hospital, I came home and never did feel any effects of what was wrong with me.

Christmas of 1947 had arrived and although the adults did not have any money for toys for us kids, they did decide to spend Christmas at my Aunt Maud's home in Clapton. My Nan (grandmother) only lived a few blocks away and Aunt Ida and Uncle Harry was also close by. We arrived there early on Christmas Eve at the Abrahall's and put up decorations and balloons for a festive atmosphere. In England at that time, they did not decorate the outside of the house but decorated only in the inside the house. We made daisy chains of colored paper loops that we strung across the room from corner to corner and across the room. We had homemade paper bells that dangled from the ceiling and had a small Christmas tree in the corner. Nobody had any money for toys at that time but the grown-ups did their best for us.

There were toys being sold in the city market but they were of such bad manufacture that they usually broke after a few hours. Christmas Eve came and we did hang our pillow cases (not stockings) at the end of our beds. I know it sounds strange since in America we hang up our stockings, but pillowcases were used in England in those days. Instead of toys, grown-ups put presents that they had already had before Christmas so there was something in each pillow case for all six of us cousins. Now comes the part that again I deeply regret to this day. My mother had no money and barely enough to keep us fed. She bought me at considerable cost a small cutting tool saw that we called a fret-saw set that permitted a ten year old boy to safely saw through wood. Because it was so badly manufactured, I tried it out and the saw broke away in my hand. I ran to my mother, angry at her, telling her that she bought me bad toys that always broke when I played with them. She was very upset and began crying and two of my aunts took her to one of the other rooms away from me. I knew I was wrong to say such a thing and immediately regretted it. She had just lost her husband but I also lost a father and was beginning to feel that loss. I was still not a good boy, but I knew now that I had to get over this problem I seem to have.

Well of course I got into trouble with my uncles again who did everything except give me a whacking on the behind. They told me that I was an ungrateful boy and deserved nothing for Christmas. After that episode I began to realize that I was not doing what I was previously told to do by my uncles, my uncles had told me that I was to be the man of the house. I think at that moment I began to feel that I must now take serious responsibility for mum and Colin and from that time forward things began to change regarding my attitudes.

She decided that she should apply on appeal again at Leyton Town Hall for a war widow's pension which was the largest and most important financial pension from the British government War Office to apply for a war widow's pension. This is given to all that died during and after the war from a related disease caused by the war. She applied for her pension and received a letter back from the British government that she must appear at a hearing in the city of Leyton Town Hall. I remember that day as mum, myself with Colin sitting in his push chair, called a baby carriage in America. We walked about two miles over to the town hall of Leyton. We passed through total devastation of destroyed streets and bombed out factories. People were rummaging through the rubble to see if they could find anything of value. The town hall appeared as we passed across Coronation Gardens in Leyton. I was pushing Colin in the baby carriage and my mother had a face which was drawn and frightened because of such an uncertain future. She needed to get that pension to survive the next few years until I could get a legal job at fifteen years old. After she appeared at the hearing, they told her that her application would be considered and she would be notified of the decision by mail. A few weeks later a letter came denying her those benefits because, although my dad died of lung cancer and had worked during the war with explosives and chemical warfare materials, it had not yet been proven that that was the cause of his cancer. It was also discovered that he smoked as most men did in those days. Since they knew very little about the cause of cancer the application was once again denied.

Mum had to find money very quickly and she had already started work in a printing company at W. H. Smith and Sons. This was located just a few blocks away from our flat so she did not have too far to travel so with getting as much of overtime she managed to bring up two boys in very difficult times. Her wages for this job was half of what a man would get paid doing the same job.

Now she had to make plans for a baby sitter for Colin while I was at school and she was at work. My mother contacted Mrs. Finden again that lived in Walthamstow. She had two boys about my age and she agreed to take in and look after Colin early in the morning until I got out of school in the late afternoon. I started school at 9:00 am each morning so I had to get up at 6:00 am each morning get Colin ready for school while mum was getting ready for work. She would make breakfast for us before we all left for work or school.

Each morning Colin and I bundled up against the cold and frost and we would board a bus to ride to the top of the hill on Lea Bridge Road, we would then change buses to an electric bus called a trolleybus that had poles attached to the overhead wires and ride for about three miles. We would then get off the bus at South Grove Avenue because I would have to make sure Colin arrived at Mrs. Finden's home safely.

I would retrace my steps and use the same buses and go back to the bus stop and ride the public bus to my school which started at 9:15 am and continued until 4:00 pm. As soon as my school finished at 4:00 pm when school was let out, I would then reverse my journey on the bus back to pick up Colin from Mrs. Finden's home then return home. After taking care of Colin and cleaning him up when we arrived home, I would set the table ready for tea/dinner for when mum got home from work at 6:15 pm. I would get the food ready and sometimes I would cook sausages in the frying pan and fry some eggs ready for us to have dinner.

I would also boil water in the tea kettle then put tea leaves into the tea pot, one spoonful of tea per person, one for the pot. That was the recipe. To make an excellent cup of tea you must warm the pot first with hot water and use both a tea strainer and a knitted cover called a tea cozy to keep it warm. When the tea kettle water was boiled, I would then pour the hot water into the tea pot and leave it with a hand woven tea cozy. One thing I learned when preparing tea in the teapot is to pour hot water into the tea pot first to warm up the tea pot, swish the small amount of hot water around in the teapot, then to pour it out ready for the real hot water to go into the teapot. This was done by loose tea leaves since in those days there were no tea bags to put into the cup as there is today. The tea leaves were strained by a tea strainer.

During the first three years of my return to Leyton I attended Sybourne Street School and Colin was being minded at Mrs. Finden. Each day I did the journey on the busses to take Colin to and from Mrs. Finden while I was at school. During the school holidays June through September, it was much easier since all I had to do was to mind Colin at home and make him breakfast and lunch until mum came home at 6:30 pm from work. We had a three-month summer break from school from June until early September.

1948, I was 11 Years Old

ONE OF MY teachers at Sybourne Street School was my favorite. Her name was Miss. Howell and I felt that I was deeply in love with her. She was about 20 years old and came from Cardiff in Wales. She taught history and geography and deeply impressed me with her knowledge of the world. She was also very pretty and did not dress like the usual teachers who dressed very severely both in clothes and hairstyle.

Our school building was not a pleasant sight to see. It looked like a prison with the main building in the center of a large asphalt playground. Not like my school in Thundersley where there were green fields and pleasant surroundings. This was a severe looking building that offered a no-nonsense education and I was not beginning to be happy in my new environment.

I believe I was also becoming a problem for my mother who had enough problems without her eldest son yearning to return back into the country. I felt that was my real home not in this crowded bombed out shell of a city. I believe at this time I was becoming a problem not only for my mum but for myself. I just had this feeling that I did not know where I really belonged. I belonged in two different worlds that were worlds apart. I was in fact finding myself never feeling satisfied where I lived and was becoming a wanderer in my mind which was determining my future wanderings on another continent thousands of miles away in America.

The British movies in theaters in those days were censored. The movies were rated as good or bad for children and had a code to determine at what age a child should see an adult movie. The way they rated movies was by a code. For a movie to be rated for all to see was rated as a U as in universal and everyone could get in to see it. People over 16 years were rated an A as in adult and no minor could get in the theater unless accompanied by an adult. For movies that were rated as adult only were rated as an X where everybody over 18 could get in. As long as you were accompanied by an adult you could get into see all movies.

The way to get around the censors was to wait outside the theater and look for a likely person that would help you and take you in with them. To do this we would wait outside and look for a kindly face and ask them if they would allow us to go in with them to watch the movie. In most cases they would take us in although it was considered a bad thing to do. The object was to walk in with a person that would be seen as a relative, thereby being allowed into the theater. There were only three movie theaters locally that we liked to visit and we always preferred to see American movies. Nobody wanted to watch a British movie in those days. America ruled the silver screen. It was the year of 1948. I was now becoming of an age that began to make me feel the freedom of being a semi adult. One night when I was waiting at the Gaumont movie theater for someone to take me into a movie I saw my school teacher Miss. Howell walking towards the box office of the movie theater. She was obviously going to the movies. Here I was at eleven years old walking up boldly asking my school teacher, who I felt I was in love with, to take me in to a movie that eleven year old people like me was not allowed to go. I asked her please Miss. would you take in to see this movie so that it appeared that I was accompanied by an adult. I remember when I asked her, she smiled at me and my heart melted right there and then. She hesitated a moment then said she would and we both walked up to the box office together and I paid my money for the ticket and she walked on into the movies alone and disappeared into the darkness of the theater.

The previous national election of 1946 to everybody's surprise brought in the Labor government. The conservative party was still headed up by Winston Churchill the Prime Minister that held the country together during the war but was defeated and the socialists were in power and were determined to change the whole country. The conservatives led by Churchill, who led the country to a war time victory, were out of government and a new regime was in and would change the country forever. It sent a shock wave throughout the country when Mr. Churchill was defeated in the 1946 elections and the Labor Party took over the country and changed the country forever. The country became nationalized in heavy industry and transportation and the unions took control of all the major industries. We had labor disputes all across the country with strikes of most industries such as steel, transportation and coal industries leading to many labor problems.

I listened on the radio to the Children's Hour which began at 5:00 pm on the wireless (radio) and they had plays like Sherlock Holmes and many others, sometimes classical music. Usually it was often a radio play such as Seven White Gates. After Children's Hour ended there was at 6:00 pm a very special program for young boys called Dick Barton, Special Agent and it was a program for young boys. It was a continuing nightly miniseries broadcast on the radio about three ex-Army characters that were led by special agent Dick Barton and his comrades Jock the Scottish one and Snowy, the one who had white hair and was called that name for obvious reasons. They were a take on an older James Bond group except James Bond went on single and they went as a group in their adventures around the world in their fight for democracy. I listened to the radio every night at 6:00 pm and any time that I did something that mum did not approve of, I was punished by not being able to listen to Dick Barton, Special Agent, on the radio that night.

We would only listen to the radio, since there were very few television sets in those days. Some of the radio plays were really good and we would listen to the stories of the classics of Charles Dickens put on as a radio play. There was also classical music available on the BBC which I enjoyed. The BBC (British Broadcasting Corporation) was a Government supported radio station and had only two channel frequencies. They were the only legal radio station in England. There was the major frequency on the BBC called the British Home Service which was somewhat very high-brow as we used to call it and quite boring. It centered it programs on serious classical music and to the old plays. Then there was another radio frequency, also by the BBC but a little lighter in attitude, which was the BBC Light Program which had all the funny shows and band music of the day. We would listen to Billy Cotton and his band at noon time on Sunday. He would start his shoe with a raucous loud voice calling out wakey! wakey! while mum dished up our Sunday dinner of roast beef, roasted potatoes and Yorkshire pudding. They played music just like Spike Jones did in the US, which had washboards, whistles for instruments and rattles, pistol shots and walking footsteps. On this station we would also listen to the big band shows that Britain had to offer such as Ted Heath and his band. There were variety shows such as Arthur Askey known as Big Hearted Arthur, and one particular show that was called Educating Archie. Archie was a wooden dummy and was worked by a ventriloquist. In America this show was also shown, but under a different name. This show lasted for only one-half hour but in the intermission, there was a little girl about twelve years old that sang every week between the first and second half of the show. She had a beautiful voice and she would go on to be a famous Broadway show actor, film artist and performer. Her name was Julie Andrews who was about 12 years old at that time. We also had Richard Murdock and his show called Much Binding in the Marsh. I never could figure out what that name was all about. Max Bygraves, the radio comedian, then became a film actor who would come along later. Most of these artists were originally from pre-war vaudeville and really had their tried-and-true theatrical talent.

Now I was eleven years old and getting ready for the greatest educational test of my life. It would determine what I was going to be in my position in life and would be according to the government and what kind of education I would get. The British Government at that time was very socialist and they had an educational plan built through the Ministry of Education. Their test plan was to have this important separate examination as to what kind of education pupils would have for the future. The best education was given to professionals such as doctors, lawyers and scientists if you passed. If you failed this examination you would become factory workers who would have no real education. You would become the workers of the country; the plumbers, electricians, printers and other union dominated trades. The unions were smart because this restricted the number of apprentices to only a few in each company. This resulted in a shortage of tradesman in later years and they were then sure of continued employment and were controlled by the trade unions. It was the most despicable experiment that any government could do to the future of the youth.

This educational plan was called the Eleven Plus Examination. The plan meant the age of the child was eleven years old at the time when the examination was completed. It was in fact a very bad educational plan to separate the working class from the professional class, to determine who would be the workers of the nation and who would be the professional people of Great Britain, the movers and the shakers of the nation. The doctors, dentists, politicians and all the professional people would run the country. We would be the workers, the carpenters, builders and plumbers to service the rich class if we failed the Eleven Plus Examination. This is how it was planned by the educators of England, to isolate the working class from the rest of the country's population. The record shown was that 90% failed and 10% passed the exam. Every child was to take a one day long school examination which would determine how far their education would go in their lives. 90% failed the examination and they became the workers of the country and the 10% that passed this examination would move on to Junior College and then on to University to become the professional class. 90% finished school at age 15 and went to work in the factories and trades.

All children attended the same school every day prior to the examination feeling comfortable working in their own classrooms with their own teachers. On the day of the Eleven Plus Examination they had to move to a different school for one day away from their districts to take this life altering test. This gave them only one chance to get out of the working class of England. My mother was notified that I should attend another school on the other side of town for that one day. I remember during the testing that the questions were about nothing we had ever been taught at my age level in my school so most failed the exam. I had never been taught about algebra or science. Those questions were way above my head in my scholastic aptitude since we were never taught those subjects with many important other subjects such as science in any advanced area. We were not taught that high kind of lessons that would prepare us for this very important scholastic examination. In other words, we were screwed.

I was one of the 90% that failed the test and was then transferred in the next school year to a different school, a Secondary Modern School. We had a basic education until we were fifteen and then were sent out into the work force. There was no second chance to take the examination again if you failed the first test. I was destined to be a tradesman for the rest of my life if I stayed in England. Fortunately, I did not stay in England as my story continues. I have heard since that this system had been discontinued.

We all looked forward to the Saturday morning movies for kids at either the Gaumont Theater or the Ritz Movie Theater. It started at 9:00 am and to get a good seat in the theater you had to get up front of the long line waiting to buy their tickets which were about sixpence. There was always a lot of shoving at the beginning of the line and inside of the theater. Some fights erupted at the beginning of the show, but eventually everyone got into the theater and found their seats and settled down. The kids were rowdy and talked all the time during the films. We usually had a first reel of a Bugs Bunny cartoon which was either Sylvester and Tweety Pie or Elmer Fudd, and the kids screamed when that started. Then came an interest film which was like a history lesson in film which nobody wanted to watch, so the kids would walk around the theater looking for their friends. Then they showed a cowboy short film with Tom Mix or Roy Rogers and his horse Trigger taking care of the bad guys. The crowd erupted with shouting and whistling on the good guys and boos and hisses to the black hatted cowboys.

Before the feature film started the house lights went on and there in the glow of a spotlight stood the ice cream lady with a small tray with straps over her shoulders giving out Walls's ice cream sticks and cartons of ice cream for a few pennies. All the kids would come down with their pocket money and buy an ice cream, either a sandwich or a cornet ice cream cone. After the ice cream was finished and everybody had the empty cartons handy, the ice cream lady with the strapped tray around her shoulders who was still in the spotlight was suddenly bombarded with empty cartons until she had to drop her tray and run for her life. After everyone had their ice cream the interval came and then the feature film. Suddenly there was silence as we were all entranced by Tom Mix and Roy Rogers chasing down bad bandits in the far west of America. When we saw a bad cowboy get shot, we cheered. On the way home from the Saturday morning movies, I would run down the hill towards my home pretending I was a cowboy on a horse and would slap my sides like a whip to make the horse go faster after the bad guys. Even at that early age I had that American dream inside of me that just would not go away.

When I was eleven years old my interest looked towards the opposite sex. In the newspaper cartoon section, there was a comic strip that was called Jane who was a cartoon stripper. One evening as I was reading the newspaper, I saw that she was appearing at the local Hackney Empire Theater which was originally a vaudeville theater. It was advertised that this young woman would perform nude on the stage so I slipped out of the house one Saturday afternoon to go and see Jane in the nude. I managed to sneak inside the theater and sat in my seat in anticipation. The stage curtain went up and there she was. Not on an open stage, but by light in silhouette inside a paper enclosed box that showed off her figure in silhouette. The Hackney Empire was a theater that was basically left over from the old Vaudeville days prior to the war, but it lingered on in some theaters and offered some very good programs at that time. They had all kinds of entertainments that allowed the best artists to move on to higher theater and became famous for their experience in making people laugh both in movies and in legitimate theater.

I was a radio enthusiast and liked to listen to the various radio stations coming not only from England but also from Europe. To do this I had to adjust the dial on our old radio. I would tune in to one of many American military radio frequencies run by the American Army of occupation in Europe. A few were AFN (American Forces Network) Stuttgart and AFN Munich. I was so excited when I heard American music anywhere, but it gave me my first experience of listening to America that would one day be my future home. I liked to listen to the radio station Hilversum in Holland where they played much of the latest music, but to reach that frequency on the radio it took a lot of delicate frequency maneuvering on the radio dial on my old radio set.

This year was the time we had the great floods which covered most of the area that we lived in. We had a very unusual snowfall in February and it warmed up very suddenly and the river Lea began to flood in our area, which was like a coastal flood plain flat and vulnerable to flooding. The playing fields were covered in water right up to the end of our road. At the back of the gas works was a network of railway lines that connected all the commuter lines to get people to London to work. They were all under water and traffic was bypassed to get around this huge amount of flood water.

After the floods had subsided everything seemed to be back to normal and we were allowed to go back to the fields and play. The back of the fields was not allowed because of caustic pollution. Alongside the gas works was a dirty stream which eventually flowed into the river Lea then into the river Thames. This is where we used to paddle in our bare feet to look for tadpoles and frog spawn. The stream was the color of bright green. Little did we know at that time this stream was highly polluted with chemicals that came down from the factories up stream. At times it had a slight green sheen on the surface and there we were paddling around in this dirty muddy stream in our bare feet. There was a factory nearby that made Thermos flasks. One day we were looking for some discarded flasks outside of the factory in a wooded area and along came a policeman on his bicycle. He took us aside and talked to us. He took down our names and addresses and said that he was going to inform our parents about our trespassing on the factory lands and stealing flasks that had been thrown away. We thought we were really in trouble when we got home, but nothing ever came of it and he was just taking our names down in fun and teaching us a lesson which we learned very quickly.

I used my fishing pole with a net at the end and found lots of frog spawn and brought them home to my mother's horror. I put them in a large jam jar and watched them grow into frogs. I had come back from fishing one day with a whole bunch of fly larva I had used for bait. I had decided not to let them fly away but to put them in a flat tin box where I had punched holes for air to get into the tin. I put them in the drawer and then forgot them. One day within a week I heard a noise coming from the draw like a buzzing sound. It seems to be coming from the tin and to my horror the larva had turned into flies and they were putting their heads through the breathing holes that I had made for them. I opened the tin lid and out flew a hundred or more black flies flying around the room and the house was buzzing. Less than an hour later my mother came home and saw all the flies in the house and I think she almost lost her mind.

I loved to read my comic books. My favorite comic book was Beano and Boy's Own magazine. There was also a new type of comic or magazine for boys called The Eagle which was printed on shiny paper, not like the comics which were printed on newsprint paper. There were others that I forget the names of but they were precious to me. One of my favorites was Dan Dare who was a captain of a space ship that went all over the galaxy searching for adventures in deep space, which at the time few people knew what deep space was.

My mother wanted me to learn to play the piano. We had a small piano in the front room where we entertained guests and where all our best china was displayed in a glass cabinet. Mum made an arrangement with a piano teacher who was blind and lived just a few blocks away from my school. So, once a week mum would give me a shilling, which she could not afford, to pay the piano teacher for my lesson at my appointed time after school had finished. I did not like taking piano lessons. I just was not very musical. I was busy taking care of my brother who was now three years old and I never found the time to practice. On the day of my lesson, I was at school and I put my hand in my pocket and felt a coin. Taking it out of my pocket I saw that it was a shilling. I thought to myself where did I get all this money from not realizing that it was my piano lesson money. I had forgotten that I had a piano lesson after school. Thinking it was my lucky day I left school and headed over to the news agents shop that sold newspapers, magazines and new comic books. I bought a shilling worth of comics and happily took them home.

I was never given a key for the front door, but we had a key system that was to hang a piece of string inside the front door letter box, inside the front door. Attached to the door was the key dangling through the letter box inside the door. We would reach with our hands through the letterbox and pull out the string with the key attached, which we would then open up the door to get in our house. My mother arrived home earlier that night after work and asked me why I was home so early and how did I like my piano lesson. I was devastated when I realized that I had forgotten about the piano lesson and spent the piano lesson money on comic books. Mum was furious and she wacked me over the head and shoulders and my bottom, then took away my comics and hid them telling me to go straight to bed for the night. We never had homework so I had to turn off the light in my room that I shared with my brother.

I still had to take him every day to Mrs. Finden to be day-cared while I went to school and mum went to work and I then had to pick him up in the late afternoon. We really had no money. Sometimes mum was so short of cash that she could not find money to buy loose tea at the grocers. She would give me a few pennies and a worker's thermos flask and send me to the local tea café to buy ready-made tea out of their giant tea urn for about three pence to fill up the Thermos flask with brewed tea.

Mum would wait every month for the gas man to come around to check the gas meter in the house. Every house had gas to cook food. There was a coin meter at the top of the stairs and when the gas got low on the dial you had to put a shilling in the gas meter to keep the gas flowing, like a parking meter. The gas meter had to be fed pennies to get cooking gas. Every month a man from the gas company would come and he would take out the coin box and check to see if we had paid enough or had overpaid. Sometimes after checking the meter he found that mum had overpaid he would give her back a few shillings which made her very happy.

She did not have a very nice life during these years. After the war ended many people were quiet and depressed. It showed everywhere. It showed in the dark clothes that we wore which were drab and had very little color or style. No colors were worn to cheer up the wearer and we were still using ration books since food was still in short supply.

During the summer of 1948 we had two visitors staying with us from Guernsey who were friends of my dad when he was in the Army and based in Guernsey. The sisters were from the family of Pugh, Helen and Dolly, and they wanted to visit us only for two weeks holiday. Although we were cramped for living space in our flat, my mother wrote and said they would be welcome to come visit us for two weeks, since their mother and father, Mr. and Mrs. Pugh, had welcomed our dad when he was billeted by the Army to stay at their house in Guernsey. When they arrived, they were put into my room so I had to sleep on the couch. That was agreeable because I was up early in the morning anyhow to take Colin to be day-cared by Mrs. Finden and then I went off to school. During the time they were at our house I took them into the West End of London where all the theaters were located. They loved the glitzy lights of London, however, they did not pay anything to my mother for food or bus fare or their stay at our flat. The weeks went by and they still did not show signs of leaving.

My mother was running out of ready cash. They kept saying that they loved London and all the things that it offered even though there were many places still bombed out and huge vacant areas where the workers had pulled down the partially destroyed buildings. The city was ready to rebuild when they had enough money. The country was in a terrible condition at that time in both financial and mental areas since the people still had not had not recovered over the terrible bombing and destruction. But everybody's attitude was just to push on and get on with it.

Our home on Clementina Road was quite different from the quaint town of St. Peter's Port in Guernsey where the two sisters were from. They just stayed visiting us and were eating us out of house and home. My mum did not have the money to feed these two people and after over a month of staying with us my mum always the diplomat asked them when they were planning to go back to Guernsey. They just did not seem to have a date in mind and my mum was getting desperate to either tell them to leave or ask them to pay for some of the food. It got so bad that my mum had to have a talk with my grandmother who was kind enough to give mum a quick loan to buy some food for us all. Finally, after two months at our home my mum had to tell the sisters that by the end of the month they had to go back to Guernsey. However, it left my mum in severe financial distress so much that she would again send me down to the café with a workman's thermos type of container to buy three pennyworths of tea. The tea was already brewed at the café in a large urn but it was not the same as brewing it yourself. The two sisters finally left and returned to Guernsey and my mum had a bad time about the whole situation. Of course, the elder Pugh's did not know of this situation since over there they had a large family and my mother did not tell Mr. Pugh that it was a severe inconvenience to her that the two sisters were such a financial burden while they were with us.

I was eleven years old and still wearing short pants. There was this general rite of passage that young boys must wear short trousers until they are fourteen years old. When they reach that age, long trousers were permitted and you knew you were on your way to becoming a man. Before then I looked the typical English schoolboy with short flannel pants with a button fly. I had a belt to keep my trousers up that was narrow, with colored bands running around the belt. The clasp was decorated with two snake's heads which allowed the head and the tail to hook into each other as a clasp. I wore a squared off tie with stripes across the tie and a blazer jacket that had an emblem on the pocket. I wore a peaked hat with round roundels around the ball of the cap, knee socks that turned down at the top held up by an elastic garter and polished shoes. In fact, whenever I see the Harry Potter movies, I see myself, except without the glasses.

The availability of buying food now was easing a little and what my mother could buy would be perishables like butter, cheese and milk on a daily basis because we had no refrigeration and it would only last for a day or so. She would walk down one of the connecting roads in the development to one of the corner shops to buy these foods. The other nonperishable items she did so only on a weekly basis or when she had the money to buy them. She would love to make an iced cake ready for the weekend. The cake would usually be a fruit cake. She would start by making the bottom layer called marzipan by hand mixing the ingredients. I would wait until the bowl was empty and then run my clean fingers around the bowl to pick up the leftovers of the marzipan. She then mixed up the ingredients for the icing. Again, using the same mixing bowl after it was cleaned, she would mix up the icing and pour it over the whole cake and let it sit for a few hours.

1949, My First Real Job

I HAD MY first real job at age twelve and I was so proud to be able to give my mother a full shilling of my wages to put towards the family budget. I was now paying my way and helping to keep the family in a better financial condition. Jewish families were not allowed to do any manual labor in the house after sundown, so I had to visit this family before sundown and bank up their fireplaces with coke so that the fire would not go out during the night. The family was named Cinnamon who ran the news agency shop on the main street. I had this job every Friday evening and would have to go over to their house around 5:00 pm in winter before it got dark and load up their fireplace with enough coke so that the fire did not go out during the night.

A few months later the Cinnamon's asked me if I would like a job as a newspaper boy to deliver their newspapers on an assigned route. They gave me a neighborhood to deliver papers like a sales territory. I managed to get the paper route for my local neighborhood, both the morning papers and the evenings, so I had to juggle my time in between picking up Colin from Mrs. Finden. My job was to write the house number on the top of the newspaper to match the accounting book. In this book was what name newspaper the person wanted delivered. There were no computers to work out the delivery schedule in those days. There were many newspapers to choose to read such as The Evening News or The Evening Standard.

I would lay out all the newspapers on the shop table, write out their street and each house number in order, and then load them on a sling sack that I had over my shoulder. I would then start the route on each street that gave out each newspaper to each indicated house number. It was really easy but the pay was not that great. I still needed money to help mum pay the bills that sometimes did not balance very well.

One day I spoke to our local milkman about a job helping him. I really was not supposed to do this kind of work since I was too young to get a work permit, but he wanted to get home at the end of the day early so he needed some help. Bill was the name of the milkman that delivered milk in our neighborhood so he agreed that he would pay me half a crown (two shillings and six pence) per day to help him deliver the milk. It was not much but gave me some pocket money and I gave the rest to my mother to pay the bills. I had to get up out of bed early at six am on cold Saturdays and Sunday mornings to meet Bill and his milk cart as he came out of the milk depot. He was not really allowed to do this since his company did not approve of having a young boy deliver their milk, so we had to meet on the street around the corner of the milk depot. First, we would have breakfast in a café where I had hot tea and toast. It was warm in the café and outside it was so cold that the cafe windows were condensing and freezing droplets on the front windows. I recall it so warm and cozy in the café and I did not want to leave and do work.

Bill would tell me the house number that owed him five shillings for the week's milk. I would knock on the door and call out like a yodel milkman and the ladies would come down with their purse, pay me and also give me a few pennies tip. Bill did not like this since he had worked all of the week delivering the milk while I was not there helping him and he felt that he should have had the tip. But he did not say anything and was a really good man and did not complain and he and I got along well. The horse that pulled the milk cart's name was Ginger and she was a mean old nag. She definitely did not like me since every time I would pass by her head she would try and bite me. Whenever we would stop and the horse would poop on the street, ladies would come dashing out to the street with their buckets and shovels to scrape up the poop and used it as fertilizer for their tomato plants in their back gardens.

We had a long route which took about five hours to complete and it was tiring work getting off and on the cart. I would meet him at 6:30 am the cart was full of milk bottles. Each part of the milk cart was assigned to hold a certain grade of milk. The milk was in a milk bottle made of glass and at the top of the neck of the bottle was covered in a topped colored foil seal. The white seal was for general Grade A milk, the blue foil was for a better grade of milk and the top bottle had a gold seal, which cost much more than the Grade A milk. The milk bottles were in pints but there were also half pints of milk bottles, so the delivery could be a mix of one pint of Grade A milk with a half pint of gold. There was no refrigeration on the cart but the weather was usually very cold so there was no need for refrigeration.

Very few of our milk customers had a refrigerator in their kitchen so the milkman delivered to each customer their daily milk on their requirements each day for our customers. It was a cash transaction so on a Saturday when the money from the housewife was due, I would be told by Bill how much the customer owed for their milk from the week and she would pay me in cash. Bill had a cash changing bag around his shoulder which hung down to his waist. He would give me change. There were three sections inside the bag for different coin denominations and in his pocket was held the paper money so we were able to make change while we were delivering the milk. Except for the summer months most days were bitterly cold to deliver cold bottles of milk. Sometimes the tops of the milk in the bottle would become frozen and push up the seal wrapper about an inch above the bottle top and the milk bottle would crack spilling the milk. The milk cart was open on three sides so most of the milk was almost frozen as we pulled out the bottles from the milk crates.

After we had finished the route on a Sunday, which was about noon we would start to ride back towards the milk depot. The horse would do a leisurely walk knowing that it was the end of the run. Sometimes Bill would let me take the reins of the horse and the horse would seem to know this her being so mean. Knowing it was me driving she would start to trot and almost gallop down the road with the cart behind swaying from side to side. Bill would have to take over the reins and slow her down back to a walk. At this point as we got near the depot Bill would pay me my weekend money which was seven shillings and six pence for my two days of work. I was now about 12 years old. I would give five shillings of my wages to mum and then I had two shillings and sixpence for myself.

During and after the war civilians were encouraged to grow their own vegetables. Most people lived in flats or apartments with little or no gardens to use. The government allowed the civilians to use public lands or what was called Lamas Land, which for hundreds of years were given by the monarchy for the people to use. These lands were really parkland prior to the war for everybody to enjoy a Sunday afternoon stroll, but also came in useful to be turned into victory gardens when food became short during and after the war.

During this food emergency the uncertainty of any kind of food that could be transported across the ocean for the people of England was very uncertain and was much less than was provided by the government. It was encouraged by the government for anyone that wanted to grow food on this parkland to do so. It was arranged for these lands to be dug up and divided into small measured allotments for anyone to make a garden and keep their vegetables for their family. They were measured very carefully into official lots allowed only according to the council regulation. The allotments were about 1/16 of an acre given on Lamas Land to grow food. They were willing to grow vegetables and build a small shed at the end of the strip to keep gardening tools. There was also another opportunity to make some money. As previously described, we had the gas works at the end of our road that sucked out the gas from coal and transformed it into coke. The gas works would sell some of the leftover coke to anyone that had a cart to haul away the coke. The gas that was in the coal was piped away leaving this desiccated cinder, which was coke, for sale to anyone that had a cart to haul it away. People in our neighborhood needed access to this leftover coke to use in their home fireplaces for heat with little to no pollution.

I built a four-wheel trolley with the wheels from my brother's baby carriage and found a six-foot plank from one of the bombed-out buildings. There was plenty of material to use from the bombed-out buildings of both houses and shops which had been destroyed and not yet cleared away. I attached the four wheels of the baby carriage to the plank to make a cart to carry the sacks of coke to my customers. I built a seat like box at the other end of the wooden plank to hold a heavy bag of coke. People in our neighborhood needed access to this leftover coke to use in their fireplaces. I would go to each front door and knock to see if the lady of the house wanted any coke from the gas works. I would spend weekends and days when there was no school doing coking and asking the ladies if they wanted a 30-pound sack of coke. If they said yes, for the price of sixpence I would go over to the gas works and wait in line for the man who would load up on a scale then tipped the coke into my sack and then I then paid him. I dragged the cart with a long piece of rope with the sack sitting in the box at the end of the plank back to the lady waiting for her coke to arrive and put it onto her fire for cooking. It was a dirty job because the desiccated coal was full of small holes and broke away easily causing the dust of this dirty coal to rise up from my cart and into my nose eyes and mouth.

The man at the weighing machine at the gas works shoveled the coke with a large shovel on to a tip scale. When it balanced at 30 pounds weight, I had to open the mouth of the sack so that he could pour the coke into the sack loaded it onto my cart from the weighing scale. A cloud of dust would rise up as it was poured into the sack. I would then pull my cart out of the gas works yard for the mile trek back to deliver the sack of coke to my customer. She would then give me sixpence plus a penny or two in tips. After that I would knock on another door and ask the lady if she would like some coke and do the same thing again. I only did this on a Saturday morning when I was ten years old up until I got a real job helping the milkman deliver milk and do my paper route.

There was a cricket field nearby where I would watch a game weather permitting on a summer Sunday afternoon. All of the players wore white trousers and white shirt with a white sweater. The shoes were white duck shoes. At one end of the cricket ground was a large building made of wood painted white called a pavilion where the players and spectators went to enjoy their tea during the middle of the game at half time. It was a serious game and was very traditional. The rules of the game are very complicated and although I watched and sometimes played cricket at school it would take a while to explain the finer details of the game. There is no shouting of encouragement by the spectators, just a polite applause when the batsman hit the ball or the outfielder caught the ball making the batting team all out.

1949, The Great Fogs of London

DURING THE WINTER London would experience pollution fogs that literally would shut the city down. Everything was stopped because of zero visibility. Now I do not mean some misty fog that American's experience during the autumn seasons. I mean a fog that you could literally not see a hand in front of your face. It usually occurred in the month of November. It was explained to me once that this fog came down from the central industrial parts of England on the prevailing winds and was really bad smog of the heavy kind of industrial pollution. In the Midland counties of England there were located the great industrial cities of Sheffield that manufactured steel and Birmingham that made pottery such as china cups and saucers. The great chimneys of industry would belch out smoke that would pollute the air with smoke and smog. The prevailing winds would carry this smoke and sulfur down into the southern counties and cause a massive transportation disruption in the London area.

Most houses had open fire places in each room of the house so they built up their fires with coal and coke. Thousands of chimneys were also belching out smoke and sulfurs from these burning home fires, which contributed also to the pollution of the air causing these great fogs. This smog shut down all transportation such as the busses, since the driver could not see in front of him to drive the bus. Schools also were shut down and trains were delayed. This smog seeped into the houses and also into the movie theaters. It was so bad that sometimes you could not see the movie screen showing the film.

I was about twelve or thirteen years old when I got the idea of lighting a roll of newspaper and standing in front of a slow moving bus. The driver of the bus would follow me, I was his guiding light. The driver would give me a few pennies to get him past the worst patch of fog, while I would return and do the same assistance with the following bus.

Sometimes these fogs or what we called them pea-soupers would last for two or more days. Then the wind would shift in another direction blowing away the smoke and sulfur gasses that were suspended into the air which we were all breathing into our lungs.

1950

A NEW DECADE had just begun that would give me some big decisions. I would have to consider my future, especially the one towards the end of the decade, a decision that would change my whole life. I realized by this time that I seriously wanted to first visit and then live in America and become an American citizen.

It was a decade of Rock and Roll music and the demise of the big bands. I was now thirteen years old and free to go out where ever I wanted to go without my mother's permission. I was approaching that very special 14th birthday for a young man. Then I could wear long trousers. The Korean War had just started and many young men were being called up for duty in the Army.

The 1940's decade had come to an end, with its many war casualties and destruction. Millions of young men from Britain were dead from World War II. The dying embers of a once great British Empire were slowly going cold. The sun had set on the British Empire and was moving towards a new socialistic form of government. England was beginning to endure instability in its colonies around the world who were demanding freedom from British Colonialism. We were still enduring food shortages since many types of food came from British Colonies around the world.

That old bull dog Winston Churchill the leader of the Second World War, who had brought his people through the hell of modern civilian warfare, had been voted out of office by a socialist prime minister. The reason for the great change was that the people of Great Britain were weary of war having been through two great world wars sustaining terrible damage to the cities. The coming decade would show the decline of our colonies, giving independence to Britain's Commonwealth of large countries such as India, as well as African colonies such as South Africa, Kenya and Rhodesia.

A once great empire would be forced, primarily for financial reasons to break up, to return these colonies back to their previous citizens. During the next twenty years some of the smaller ex-colonies left to be independent, they would be racked in conquest by civil wars as soon as Great Britain marched their troops out of the colonies. The vacuum left behind many colonies which were soon filled by one dictator after another. Some of the former colonies voted to go back to the British Crown colonies for financial and safety reasons.

The trade unions became powerful and dictated who and what should be produced on the factory floor and what the pay should be to each individual industry. The British people who stood alone in the 1940's facing the enemy now were happy to have someone else take military responsibility for the peace of Europe, which would eventually be America and the United Nations Internationally active in 1946.

A great sigh of relief swept over the British people as a sense of normalcy replaced fear and death to a period of time when ordinary people could look forward to a time of peace. They could start rebuilding their country that had withstood so much pain, misery and loss to families and the loss of a whole generation of young men to war.

However, it was not to be for there were other forces at work in Eastern Europe where another force was being forged, communism. The Soviet Union had gained the ability of using nuclear weapons and fear once more overshadowed peace and prosperity. But that was to come in the coming decade that would change all of the concepts of modern civilization and that challenged everything that had been accepted in the past few hundred years. That was the attitude between the new generation of the so-called baby boomers who, when growing up, wanted to change the world with new ideas that rocked civilization as we knew it, both in music, public display and behavior against the old ideas of the previous generation.

My brother Colin spent a lot of his time playing on the dumps with his friends and if I need to find him to get him cleaned up ready for his tea before mum came home from work, I would go over to the dump. I would find him playing around in the rubble with holes in the knee of his trousers resulting from climbing over piles of old bricks and concrete.

Guy Fawkes Day on November 5th is an important day for the British people. In the 1600's England, there was hatched a large conspiracy to blow up the Houses of Parliament and kill King James and take over the government. The plot was discovered. The leader of the plot was a person by the name of Guy Fawkes, who was eventually captured, tortured and finally killed. Since tradition is so important to the British people, every year on the anniversary of that day boys and girls of all ages would build and stuff an effigy with straw simulating Guy Fawkes.

Colin and I would build a dummy wearing old clothes old left over clothes and put him in a wheelbarrow and we would go around the neighborhood asking everybody if they would like to give a penny for the guy. We would then pin a large paper board reading Penny for the Guy on the chest of the dummy. The money we received would go to pay for fireworks that would be displayed in everybody's garden, together with a large bonfire on that evening of the fifth of November.

However, because of the past war and lack of just about everything, most money was used for food and there was not much left over for any fireworks if there were any fireworks to be found at all. Somehow our mum had managed to find some fireworks for us and we set them off in celebration of Guy Fawkes Day. Luxuries such as fireworks were hard to come by. Normally it would be easy to go to a store that sold fireworks and buy what you wanted, but times being what they were it was like going on the black market. Rumors would run wild when we he heard that a store had acquired some fireworks and some people would line up even before the shop had opened to get in line to buy a few crackers, rockets or Catherine wheels for their children. Our mum had heard a rumor that a shop not too far away was selling fireworks but limiting the purchase to seven shillings and sixpence per person. Our mum found the shop and stood on line for over two hours on a weekend just to buy seven shillings and sixpence worth of fireworks for her two sons. Our mother was that kind of mother who wanted to make her boys happy. When her turn came at the front of the line, she picked out the fireworks that she thought would create the largest bang and put them in a grocery bag to bring home.

As soon as I got out of school after picking up Colin from Mrs. Finden, we had time to go over to the bombed out buildings to look for some old lumber and any combustibles that could be used for the big bonfire that I would build in the back yard to celebrate Guy Fawkes Day. The bonfire would get started as soon as it got dark and then the fireworks would fly all over the neighborhood and what a sight that was to see. We surely did celebrate the fifth of November and Guy Fawkes Day with a loud bang and a great bonfire in the back garden of our house.

Mum still worked over at the box company where they printed soap detergent boxes, chocolate and cigarette boxes, cereal and other boxes. They first printed them and then stripped the excess cardboard away from the box itself ready to be glued. Our mother was a gluer who worked on the machines that glued the boxes as were processed through the factory. She was in a group of friends that worked on the work line and they called themselves The Glorious, Glamorous, Gluer Girls.

Each Friday Colin and I would go over to the factory to meet mum when she finished work and the night watchman and guard would let Colin have a temporary time card and allowed him to clock out when everyone else clocked out at the end of the day. Every Christmas season the management would have a Christmas party for all the employees' children and had their party during the afternoon so all the kids got a gift from Santa Clause. In the evening the party was for the adults only and we had to leave and go home.

Each Wednesday evening there was a dance where they had a social evening for employees and families. Once during one of these Wednesday evening events at the factory canteen I won a prize that was a five pound box of chocolates. Before I could even taste them, the young teenage girls came over and started to eat all of my chocolates. This was my one and only prize I ever won and the girls ate all my hard won chocolates during that evening.

One Saturday each year during the summer mum and her coworkers would go on a bus trip, to the seashore on the southern beaches of

England. They would go off for the day on a trip to one of the resorts located on the southern coast of England. I would take Colin by the hand and go with mum over to the factory gate where mum would board the bus. They called these factory day trips beano's. I do not know why they called it that but that was what they called it at that time. In the rear compartment of the bus was filled with crates of bottled beer for the passengers to consume while they were on their way to the sea shore. They rented about six busses to carry everybody to the destination. In later years as I got older and worked at the factory as a printer, I went on one of these trips and I can say for sure it was a lot of fun for all that attended with a whole lot of alcohol consumed in a few short hours.

As each bus would leave to start their trip we would wait until the last bus left and then both Colin and I would walk home for the day until they returned. Most everybody except our mum was totally drunk and they staggered home. I remember mum saying that they should all be ashamed of themselves, but I noticed that she herself had a good day with her follow workers.

In a few years I myself would be working there also as an assistant printer. In those days women were only paid half pay of what a man doing the same work would earn but it was barely enough to get through. Because of the war the government was getting as much money back to pay for the post war budget for reconstruction so taxes were very high. By now we were in the fifties and things were beginning to become a little more normal, depending on how you would describe normal.

Food rationing had ended and most people were feeling that their country was getting back to normal. By 1950 Colin was five years old and was ready to attend first grade school. His first school was Perth Road School located not far from home so he was able to travel on his own. I took him for the first few weeks and then I would go on to school in the opposite direction which was much further away. Colin's first school was an old school with a fireplace in each classroom. This was called an Infant School or as it was generally known Perth Street School the same school I started earlier on. He started when he was 5 years old and stayed till he was 8 years old. His school was the equivalent to America's primary school system.

To show that life was returning somewhat to normal, travelling country fairs were making their rounds during the summer months and my grandmother loved to take us to the fair. One of the traveling fun fairs was located for a week or so over what we called the fields which was a large area of open land that was covered in some areas with war trenches. These trenches were built for the Army as a defense of London if the country was invaded by Germany, which at the time seemed quite a good possibility. The trenches were not filled in yet. During the years of heavy rains, the trenches had filled with water and fish had somehow made their home in the water in the trench. As I got older, I would go fishing in those trenches for red throats and frog spawn, jellied frog babies ready for hatching.

When the fair came into town everyone had a great time especially my grandmother. The fair was quite large with many rides for kids and also for older people. They had some games of chance. They had the usual side show games and my grandmother was an expert in rolling the penny down a slotted slide. I remember her taking us over to the fair and played the game of rolling the penny down onto a numbered board with squares. My Nan would roll the penny down the slot onto the board and when the barker was not looking, she would quickly push the penny on to a square exactly within the four-side winner box. The coin must not touch any of the four sides of the square. She explained it was not really cheating, just beating the system. She was a very enterprising woman. She was very good at it and won all the time.

There were also roundabouts, carousels and boat swings where you climbed on to a small rowboat that was hanging on ropes. To get the swing going you had to start pulling on the overhead ropes to pull down and gradually the swing began to go back and forward until it really got high. There was also a ride called the Helter Skelter which was a slide ride. At the bottom of the tower a man would give you an ordinary door mat to sit on as you came down the slide. To get to the top of the tower of Helter Skelter you had to climb a circular stairway around the sides of the tower and when you reached the top sit on your mat and slide all the way down. It was built around a tower-like structure or a lighthouse with a beacon on top spinning light which attracted fairgoers. Thirty years later a group of boys from the city of Liverpool started a band calling themselves the Beetles who made a music album. One of the songs would be called Helter Skelter referring to the ride that they themselves had visited as children.

In 1950 I was 13 years old and was slowly being given a lot more freedom by mum to be on my own. I had left the scouts by this time and was beginning to start a new school for the next two years in the coming month of September, but my Nan had held out a great treat for us. Although she never had much money, she always tried to make things easy for us. She had made arrangements for us to have our first holiday together since my dad died and we went to Thorpe Bay. It is located on the east coast of England slightly north of Southend which is still a seaside resort. We went with Nan who I believed paid for the cost of the week's holiday. She rented two rooms in a house that was located on the sea front. It was just a normal house that had been built as a residential home but was now turned into a rooming house. Nan rented two rooms with a communal bathroom on the same floor.

We were going on vacation and we were also very excited about enjoying the week at Thorpe Bay. Although it was called a seaside resort, Southend is really at the mouth of the river Thames joining the North Sea across from Holland on the European continent. There were very little beaches of the kind that we think of such as a sandy beach. It was a sandy beach, but more river mud than sand including probably sewage that flowed on the outbound tide from the slums of London. In those days we never knew what we were eating or drinking or stepping on or swimming in. There was a promenade that was like a boardwalk. It ran along the sea front alongside of the houses that lined the front of the seaside and beach rented as sea cottages. The road on the land side was covered with shops, penny arcades, moving picture machines and fairground barkers that wanted you to pay to throw a ring from a distance over a short stick to win a cheap prize worth less than what you paid to play.

It was noisy with the sound of the machines all being played at once. The record companies were making recordings of all the favorite songs and singers of the time. Rock and Roll had just been created in America and was becoming popular in England, but all of the music of the big bands was still being played on records. Glenn Miller, Guy Mitchell and Doris Day were very popular.

Southend was a very popular seaside resort that had a very long pier. At the end of the pier were some buildings like a dance hall and a carousel and other entertainment arcades. To get to the end of the pier, which was said to be the longest pier in the world, it was about two miles long. To reach the end of the pier you could either walk out on a boardwalk right to the end of the pier, or you could take a rickety old railway train with open air cars. There were bench seats on the cars running across each car and it went quite slow. For safety reasons there was a small link chain to prevent you from falling over the side of the car into the water below.

I wanted desperately to be on my own for the first time and not be supervised so I asked my mother if I could go off on my own and meet up at the front of the pier at a given time. She agreed, and for the first time in my life I was really on my own.

Colin liked to play some of the machines in the penny arcade, especially the ones that were moving pictures. To operate the machine you just turned the handle crank and see the movies that were considered dirty, showing naked women. Mum caught him once watching one machine which was like a short movie. It was called What the Butler Saw and it was somewhat racy for a five year old boy. When nobody was looking, Colin put a penny in the slot and he did get to see what the butler saw. Before I could stop him, he came running to his mother and grandmother saying in a loud voice I saw it, I saw it, I saw what the butler had seen, and he called out loudly that had seen a naked lady. My mother was appalled and almost fainted away. My grandmother was a little more relaxed and did not make a fuss. There was a reason for that because Colin was always her favorite grandson and as far as we were concerned he could do nothing wrong.

So off I went on my own for the first time walking ahead of everybody along the shops and along the sea front and was soon walking far ahead of them. It was indeed a great feeling of being free and taking responsibility for only myself. I stopped in stores that had items for sale of seaside cards and gifts. Looking at the suggestive post cards displayed, if had been with my mother I would not have gone anywhere near any of these sexy post cards.

There was a great amusement park nearby called the Kursall which was similar Coney Island in Brooklyn, New York. It had wooden roller coaster rides and all kinds of fast and furious rides. There was no entrance fee just pay to ride whatever ride you wanted to ride so I had the opportunity to go on many of the rides. I also walked around and take a look at the games of chance. There was the great ride, which after climbing up for about a hundred feet you then sat on a mat and slid down a slide to soft land in a pile of soft pile of material that broke your speed. There was a huge wooden rollercoaster called the Comet and I was too scared to go on that, but watched it as it went up the climbing track and down the other side with everyone screaming with delight. There also was a huge water chute, a ride about a hundred feet high and being that high you came down sliding with the rushing water to an abrupt stop at the end of the slide.

I headed for the entrance to the pier and paid my three pence for the ride on the train to the end of the two mile long pier. As the train rattled towards the end of the pier a pleasure motor boat sailed nearby filled with people taking their first boat ride since the end of the war with a blaring record player which was playing a Les Paul and Mary Ford hit record called Little Rock Getaway. I was truly free and I felt good. I walked around the end of the pier and looking out to sea I could see the huge gun emplacements sprouting out of the mouth of the river. These were concrete platforms that were the main defenses at the mouth of the river Thames as it wound its way to London. It got me thinking again back to when bombers from Germany would be guided by the river to destroy London and the guns from these gun emplacements were the guns, I would hear prior to an air raid. It was so good to be free of any grownups and I did not want to go back to the front entrance of the pier, but at the appointed time I climbed back on the rackety old train back to the shore where my mother, Colin and grandmother would be waiting for me at the entrance of the Southend Pier.

The year of 1950 was very good for me since I became an age when my mother let me go off to do much of anything I pleased. I was thirteen and began to take notice of the news of the day. I found myself listening to the news at six in the evening and I began to read newspapers and became interest in World Affairs, including politics and other news.

I had bought some great items which unfortunately I left behind when I came to America. I had a box of lead soldiers, hand painted with a large khaki-painted cannon that shot real lead shells. This was the time when there was the flying saucer scare where a person in America claimed he was abducted and described the alien's the same way they are described today. Early Rock and Roll was beginning to become more popular such as Teresa Brewer's song Put Another Nickel In.

I was really beginning to get restless at that age. I felt like I needed to get away so I wrote to my auntie in Thundersley and asked if I could visit her for a few days. She said of course, and I was soon back in Thundersley where I stayed for a long weekend with Auntie Ellie. She was so pleased to see me. Later as I grew older, I would ride my bike to see her on a Sunday afternoon, after the noontime meal, and returned after dark around ten in the evening. That meant biking was about 23 miles each way and by the time I got back home I was really tired. I remember laying down exhausted in the front room of the house.

In the city of London in the 50's there were parks for children to play either on a round-about or a swing. Some of the swings had names. One was a pointed hat with bars going down the sides. It would be pushed by kids to make it go around, but it also tilted to each side, so we had a great time on that one. There was the usual slide where you climbed up the iron steps to the top and slid down the slide. There was also, after all the bombed out material was pulled away, playing fields for the kids to play football and set up a cricket pitch with some pieces of wood for the wickets and bails and using a tennis ball to throw at the batsman defending the wicket.

Our home playing field was still part dump and part field and to get to school we had to cross this large park. I found a new friend that summer by the name of Brian Bowden. He lived across the street from my house and we became great friends for the rest of our lives. We would walk together on the way to school and cross the fields where they had dumped bomb damage material. At some of these playgrounds there were water fountains in the shape of a round stone monument. There were water fountain spigots running out of shaped stone lion heads. Attached to the water fountain was a metal drinking cup that was on a chain attached to the lion's head to prevent anyone taking the cup. The cup was used by every child that wanted water but was never cleaned. There were at the time many childhood diseases at that time such as diphtheria, mumps and chicken pox, so there was a huge chance when using these cups, you could catch any of these ailments and probably did. Everyone used these metal cups.

1950, My New School

IT WAS LATE September 1950 and I began my senior school years at Farmer Road Secondary School. I was assigned by the board of education to attend a new school system since I had failed my Eleven Plus Examination. It was called Farmer Road Secondary Modern School and was for boys only. Its location was at least two miles from my home. In later years it changed its name to the George Mitchel School. We had to walk to school since there were no school buses that were used to get us to school. Just before school was to begin a long line of boys would be walking along local sidewalks on their way to school. We just hoped that we did not run into any of the school bullies that if you looked at them in the wrong way, they would punch the students and get you into a fight.

This new system was an experiment in education that was doomed to fail from its first day. I had previously mentioned that I had failed the Eleven Plus Examination and I was about to pay the price for that failure to now go to a school that was a failure in itself. It was a new school day and the beginning of a new term and away from my previous school and all of my friends that I had made. It was located about two miles from my home and I had to walk across the fields that used to be allotments during and after the war. After passing through the parks, I then walked on residential streets that held the same kind of flats or apartments that I live in and as I reached the end of the street, I beheld my new school.

At first I thought I was in the wrong place, but there it was waiting for me. I had read most of Charles Dickens books of the 1840's showing work houses and orphanages and when I saw for the first time my new school, I felt like I was back in that time period. The building was made of old brick and was probably built during the early 1850's. The building was built like an old work house and to a thirteen year old boy and it was very daunting. It looked bleak. This old building was surrounded by iron fencing that looked like spears lined up in rows ready for battle. The playground was built of asphalt with outside open-air toilets located away from the main building across the playground with no roof. Students had to work their way up in this new school system which was a basically socialist system that encouraged the student to fail. This school system was as bare-bones as it possibly could be. Mr. Applebee was my class teacher for social studies, but he also stepped in as a music teacher. We called him, behind his back as school boys do, the mad Russian because his hair was wired like he had just stuck his finger up a live electric wall outlet. However, looking back I really feel that he was a good teacher and he was quite a character.

The system was not an organized education since it was so disorganized within itself. One day a week we would be assigned to a trade shop located on each ground floor corner of the school. On one corner would be a classroom converted into a woodworking class with all the equipment for making wooden items such as chairs and stools. On the other corner of the school was the metalworking classroom which also was a converted classroom where we made things of metal such as lamps. Another corner of was the science classroom which is where we were taught about biology (no dissecting of frogs). Each bench would have a Bunsen burner and glass retort containers. The teacher would briefly teach us the basics about general science, but nothing of real consequence that would help us when we left school at the age of 15 which would be in two years' time.

We had a teacher who was a fill-in gardening teacher. Each Monday afternoon we would all walk the two miles to another school which had a small field converted to a garden plot, owned by the ministry of education. This area was laid out as like a field that included various plots of vegetables growing. We were shown how to plant and dig up potatoes, carrots and other garden vegetables in case there was another war. He also showed how to graft an apple tree twig to another kind of apple to create a new kind of apple. I hated that class at the time and we found ourselves being brought down to this garden to work as laborers digging up turnips. We never knew who benefited from these vegetables. Maybe this was like slave labor and he may have taken home the vegetables that we had grown. I only know that nobody in my class ever took home the fruits of their labor and sold them off as profit.

The school was probably made up of about 500 boys. No girls were at this school. We were segregated since this was an all boys' school. About a mile away was another school called Chatsworth Street School, which was for girls only where they had their classes designed for them to be housewives. The government was slowly separating people to do certain jobs and they would stay in those jobs as workers for the rest of their lives.

After reporting to our first class of the day in Mr. Applebee's classroom for attendance roll call, we all had to congregate on the lower main floor of the school for assembly. We marched in pairs as in a military parade and lined up in front of the podium where the head master was going to address his school of pupils. The headmaster was Mr. Hunt and he wore the cap and gown of a master of the arts. He also carried a small cane which he was not averse to use when he felt it necessary. Our headmaster, Mr. Hunt, was a tall slender man that carried himself well. He had a grey and white small mustache under his nose. He was a no-nonsense teacher and acted like he was the warden of a prison each day welcoming an incoming class like an incoming group of inmates in a prison. We sang songs that were religious and he read a chapter from the bible. We then sang God Save the King, which is the national anthem of Britain, and then we were dismissed to return to our studies in our classroom.

Attached to the wall behind Mr. Hunt's lectern was a huge colored map of the world which showed each country colored in pink that was part of the British Empire. All the nations of the world that belonged to Britain and spoke English were colored in pink. It looked like most of the world was in pink. We were told that at that time one third of the world spoke English and was part of the British Empire.

After we started school in September during one of our morning assemblies we were introduced to a real American. He was on an exchange teacher program between America and Britain. He had a strange accent that sounded like good English but had a twang or drawl to it. I was most interested in this teacher's accent and I had the opportunity to speak to him and ask him why he spoke so different. He said that he was from America where English was spoken but with a different accent. He made a very good impression on me and I was very impressed by his clothes. He wore a fine suit with a dashing colored tie.

On my first day at this school Mr. Appleby introduced me to the class as a new boy and that I was an evacuee and he asked the class to welcome this new boy to their school. There were two rough boys in the class that were trouble makers and they eventually went to a boy's prison called Borstal Institution, which was a reform school in America. One of their crimes was that they managed to climb over the school fence into a private garden and killed some chickens. The names I remember of these boys were Bobby and Tony. I wonder if they are still alive now. They both were very rough and willing to start a fight at anything and we were very careful what we said to them.

To make things more interesting we had a visiting school nurse who would be responsible for all the cuts and scrapes young boys have when horsing around on a concrete playground. If a dispute appeared between two boys during class the two boys would threaten each other and then arrange to duke it out after school in the school playground. There were many bloodied noses and bruises. The nurse was a short, full figured woman who I believe did not like small boys. She went from school to school in the south district checking all the things that nurse's check such as lice in the hair. At least twice a year the whole class, which was called a form, would have to go as a class to visit the nurse upstairs near the head master's office to be checked out. She gave inoculations and shots plus checked out other personal areas of the body. Then we would all have to line up in single line and await our turn. Usually, we would have our hair checked for nits and lice first, and then came the shots and then we would have to go into a line. Everyone seem to know what was coming and the boys started to giggle and laugh since they knew what was coming. She would tell each boy when his turn came to drop his trousers, she then said bend over and she would put a shot into your back side. Looking back at those innocent days I believe that she got a good charge at doing that and I also thought it very funny at the time.

I met for the first time my friend Brian Bowden in class at Farmer Road School in 1950 in Mr. Appleby's class. He lived on Clementina Road just a few doors down from me. Brian turned out to be my lifelong friend and we had many good times together as the years went by. We would leave for school at the same time and walked the two or three miles to school in all kinds of weather.

We discovered that we had many of the same interests such as traditional jazz and Dixieland jazz. He owned a radiogram in a cabinet that was called in America a record player with a turntable to play music LP records, which at that time the music was in its infancy in the country. Phonograph records were made at that time of vinyl and had a speed of 72 then 78 revolutions per minute. I did not have such luxury as others did, only an old radio that I converted. I could listen to the American Armed Forces Network in AFN Frankfurt and AFN Munich in Germany, which was part of the American occupational forces at the time for American soldiers to listen. To get this American program you had to slowly move the tuner knob back and forth to reach each frequency to leave out the static and to hear the music. They had great programs for the American Armed Forces to listen to but you had to get your ear to the set. Because of the distance from England to Germany we only could hear the background static in between the songs being played. We also listened to radio Hilversum in Holland for great music.

We would each take turns to go over to each other's house, but I did not have that kind of record player that he had. I somehow managed to find just the record player itself and after many attempts hooked up with some old wiring for the record player to the old wireless so I had the right frequency. It somehow worked. My mother suffered listening to this music that Brian and I loved to hear.

After a few months at our new school, we soon found out that our headmaster Mr. Hunt was very stern in his ability to head up his school of unruly schoolboys. He believed in capital punishment and dealt out his punishment for any infractions of his laws with great enthusiasm. Whenever one of his teachers needed to send his pupils to the headmaster for some breakdown of classroom rules, the classroom teacher gave the instruction to the student to go to the headmaster's study and get the stick and book. The teacher had the authority to call out the name of the student and order him to go to the headmaster's study and bring back the stick and book to the classroom to complete the punishment. This was done on a daily basis. After receiving his orders from the teacher, the student would then leave the classroom and climb the small, short staircase up to the headmaster's study.

There was only one female in the school and that was Mr. Hunt's secretary. She was a very serious looking elderly woman and we all believed that she came to school on a broomstick and parked it in her parking space in front of the school entrance. The headmaster of the school had the authority to punish any infractions of school laws. He had in his office a cane to punish the pupil and also a very old book that he would write down the boy's name, date of punishment and the type of infraction of the school law. So, it was recorded in the book for posterity. I believe that the book was very old and recorded many punishments.

When a student was sent by his teacher for an infraction of class rules the student would be sent to the headmaster's office to ask for the stick and book. She would summon the headmaster with glee asking him to come to the front desk. He came out with his cap and gown and asked what the student wanted and why are you not in class. The student was forced to tell the headmaster that his teacher had told him to go and pick up the stick and book. The headmaster would stare at the student for a moment and then asked what you did to make the teacher send him to his office for punishment. Upon hearing the answer, he then gave him the stick and book to return to the classroom. He also reminded the student he must make sure to see him before he returned the stick and book and returned to his classroom. Upon reaching the door to his classroom the student had to knock on the classroom door, was told to enter and there was the rest of the class waiting in happy anticipation to view the punishment. The teacher would then tell the misbehaved student to hold out his hand, palm up and look the other way and down would come the cane on his hand, which caused a swelling on the student's hand. Sometimes the student had to have the other hand caned also which would really hurt. After the punishment was completed the teacher opened up the punishment book which was about one hundred years old and entered into the book the name of the student, the date and the reason for the punishment. Then he was instructed to return to the headmaster's office and return the stick and book. However, that was not the end because the headmaster would then ask the boy which hand had been caned. He would tell what hand had been caned then he was asked to raise the other hand and down would come the cane on the hand one more time. After the punishment had been accomplished the boy would be told to return to his classroom.

It was now late 1950 and I was given still more leeway to go and do more things on my own. I still had to take care of Colin who had just started school. He went into first grade and now during school times I did not have to take the early morning buses to take him to Mrs. Finden anymore. He started school early in the morning so before I went to school, I had to deliver him to his school gate and make sure he got to school. Mum worked now from 7:30 am until 6:00 pm. After dropping Colin off at school, I had to walk the other direction meeting up usually with Brian to walk to school. Right after school I had to get home at 4:30 pm and pick him up at his school and take him home. I would then have to clean him up and then set the table for tea ready for when mum came home at 6:15 pm. Mum was very tired in those days, since she was on her feet most of the day.

During the summer I was still in charge of Colin since we had school summer break and we both did not go to school from June until August. Even at five or six years old he and his friends would go over to the fields and play on the dumps. If I had to look for him first place, I would look over the war damaged dump and there he and his friends were at the top of a pile of bricks and wood playing king of the castle. He always had cuts or bruises on his knees and look like a ragamuffin. His clothes were always torn and mum would have to repair them.

This park was located in Clapton, not far away, just a short bus ride and was quite large. It had lots of swings and rides for kids and it also had a large round concrete pool filled with water about two feet deep. So, Colin and I would take the bus and go over to Clapton Park and I would set the sails on my sailboat and push it out into the middle of the pool. Sometimes the wind would drop and it stalled in the middle of the pool. Colin would then jump into the water and wade out to the center whenever the boat got stuck because of no wind and return it to shore.

I just loved to sail my model boat and I promised myself at the time that when I grew up and had some real money, I would buy a large sail boat and go sailing. I almost did while I lived in America, but I never did own a boat. I found myself so busy in business work and travelling across America I had no time. It is now a great disappointment to me that I did not buy a boat.

Near Clapton park ran a river called the River Lea. Not a wide river, but wide enough to have coal barges filled with coal or other materials pulled by large horses plodding along the banks. As the River Lea passed through Leyton the river was quite narrow and from the river's edge for about five miles it was mostly open country, just grassland, then it emptied into the river Thames that flowed through central London.

I bought a rubber dinghy left over from a store that sold war surplus. After the war was over there were plenty of war surplus and the government wanted to get sell and maybe get back money they had spent on the war. The inventory in some of these shops selling this merchandise I found to be quite interesting, but I settled on buying a rubber boat which was an Air Force rubber lifeboat if the pilot got shot down over the sea. It was yellow and had hand bellows that blew up the rounded cells inside the rubber dinghy. The rubber dinghy was a left over from war surplus and I had bought it with the intention to go boating on the Hollow Pond. It was easy to carry on a bus since the air was taken out it and folded up and was quite small. It had two paddles so when we had inflated it up to its full size it was easy to push it into the water and paddle around the large pond. I would row the boat and Colin would steer by pulling with his hands on two ropes attached to the rudder of the rowboat. We would row all over the lake for a couple of hours and we would talk about everything. He was about six and really was a good brother and friend.

Once or twice, we would go for a weekend trip to visit our Nan's bungalow which was located in Laindon, not too far from where I was evacuated. It was a nice bungalow with two bedrooms and a living room. Her bungalow was built on top of a hill with a nice lawn overlooking the fields and hedgerows that covered the farmland. It was near a town called Basildon, which is now a concrete jungle of houses and factories, a high-tech manufacturing area.

After the war all of my mother's family would spend the weekends there and there were lots of fun playing with my cousins and uncles and aunts. They used to play cards in the evening and still did at home in London when they were all together again after the war. We were able to visit the bungalow now without any travel papers and many restrictions had been lifted. We played a game that was called Newmarket after the famous horse racing town. I do not remember how we really played it except you put the four kings of each suit in the middle of the table and put loose change of money on each of the kings after being given a hand of seven cards. Then a player would start to put down on the table their cards which would start a run of the suit of cards up to the jack and queen and then when reaching the king would scoop up the change that was put on top of the king card.

We also went picking blackberries along the hedgerows of the fields. We each would carry a large bowl to put the blackberries in. After about an hour the bowls would be full and another bowl would appear to fill with this delicious fruit. My grandmother would make blackberry pie with the berries that we had picked. She was a great cook and we all enjoyed her meals.

I had always wanted a small two man pitch tent. My mum gave me a Prudential store catalog to save green stamps so that I was able to buy a two men tent. I enjoyed setting up the tent on the lawn of my grandmother's bungalow whenever we spent a weekend there. Although it rained, I still erected the tent on my grandmother's lawn so that I could camp out. It was really good to hear the rain pattering on the canvas of the waterproofed tent and I stayed out all night camping. Because my dad was not there, I never really had anyone to give me advice on how to do things, including do not to take a tent down when it is wet. I should have left it up after I had finished using it because it had to dry before folding the tent up. I did not do that, I folded it up wet and put it into the tent bag while it was still wet. The next time I opened up the tent bag and looked inside I saw my tent was ruined because it had turned moldy with the dampness. When I arrived home, I pulled the tent out of the bag and hung the damp tent on the clothes line in our garden to it dry off. It was too late to repair because the next time I erected the tent it also rained, but now the rain came in through the canvas and the tent was no longer waterproof. I was getting wet.

Most of my early life I had very few male people to advise me and to explain to me how to do things. If I had asked them, they could show me how to do it. I did learn how to do it only by trial and error and there were more errors that I somehow had to correct. In example when I was old enough to have to shave my face. I used a normal bar of soap to lather up my face prior to shaving. My face turned red and sore after my shave because I should have used real shaving cream. Little things like that made my growing up difficult.

The bungalow was without running water so it was my job to carry a bucket down the hill for about half a mile where there was a spigot sticking out of the ground with a small faucet handle. The pathway down to the spigot was all mud, but covered over the pathway were slatted duck boards. Climbing up the hill with a bucket of water was quite challenging, but I got used to it and it was not so bad. The view from my grandmother's bungalow was incredible and looked all the way over to the marshes and finally seeing the river Thames in the far distance. The main Southend-London railway line I could see far down the hill and across the fields and I could see the trains go by with the smoke from the locomotive and the carriages being pulled. on its way back to Fenchurch St. terminal in London.

On the same pathway which ran along by the bungalow was Laindon church which was almost as old as St. Peters Church in Thundersley. Along this pathway were hedges covered with blackberries mixed in with some strawberries near the ground. At the back of the bungalow as if you were going back to the main road there was a small pathway which went down a small hill that was not paved to the lower street. At the corner was a general store run by a family by the name of the Cooper. They sold everything that you needed and Mr. and Mrs. Cooper would pick out the food for you while you waited. I would walk down there before everyone was up and pick up the newspaper.

1951, I Am Age 14

IT IS NOW 1951, a year that was very important to me as a teenager. I had passed the age of 14 years, a milestone in my life. I could now wear long flannel trousers. Prior to the age of 14 years boys wore only short trousers. My mother bought me my first long flannel trousers for my birthday. I was so proud. I reached age of fourteen, a very special age in my life.

England had at that time three special years in a boy's life. They were 7, 14 and 21 years. From birth to the age of seven years you were considered an infant even at the age of six. Upon reaching the age of seven I would be addressed on an ordinary mail postal envelope to Mr. Roy Phelps, Esquire. At the age of 21 years, I was given the key to the front door which allows you to come and go at will. (I really had a key for a long time before I was fourteen.)

I could hardly wait until I was able to wear my new long grey flannel trousers, I had become of age. Such a great day! I was also given a very special gift for my fourteenth birthday. At age 14 my mum bought me a ten-speed bicycle with drop handlebars. She managed to buy it new from our next door neighbor who worked in a bicycle factory so she got it at a big discount employee price. I knew that she could not afford this bike and how she got the money I do not know, but she did and she always managed to give us boys what was due and always kept her promises. I loved that bike because it gave me added freedom to go anywhere, I wanted. I did just that. Now I could go anywhere, I became liberated. I rode my bike just about everywhere.

I loved to travel and still do. It is in my genes and when I get the chance, off I would go. We would have our Sunday dinner at home at midday and as soon as I had finished, I would climb on my bike while mum was taking care of Colin and off, I would go following my map. I could pedal the 23 miles to Thundersley and visit my auntie. I would spend a few hours and enjoy a nice visit and ride back home by evening. About half way to my aunties, there was a large traffic circle at the junction of a pub called the Jolly Cricketers. Inside I would buy a pastry sprinkled with coconut shreds on the top, washed down with some lemonade. After visiting my auntie in Thundersley I would head back and arrive home exhausted from the long ride. Biking in Essex County was very easy because the county is generally flat. They built these bike paths alongside the main road especially for bikes, but completely off the main road it was quite safe to ride following the main road to Southend and Thundersley.

In 1951 there was the great Festival of Britain. It was a type of World's Fair and they built many venues over the old bombs sites that still littered across London. Many times, during this period the Army still found many unexploded bombs which when found the road would be cornered off to the public and the Army engineers blew up the bomb to make it now harmless. The first thing they built was the Royal Festival Hall on the south side of the Thames at the London Bridge crossing. This was a huge concert hall. It held many concerts of famous singers and operatic performances. Also built for the festival was Battersea Park Amusement Park which was a carnival or as we called it a fun fair which was used during the four months of the Festival of Britain. They had the latest of high roller coasters and other entertainment venues. There was every kind of ride that a teenager could prove his lack of fear to face the high drops of that wooden roller coaster. There was also a radar research station at the main festival venue. Up until that time they knew nothing about the moon only what they could see through the telescope. Some still thought that it was made of green cheese. However, they set up the radar signal so that everyone that came to the park would be able to shoot a radar beam at the moon and receive its signals back. I tried it and got a solid return signal back so that dispelled the idea that the moon was made of green cheese, that it really was a solid body up there.

I was a train spotter which was another hobby for young boys. I was always fascinated by trains. During the summer evenings after dinner,

I would ride my bike into the city of London and do some train spotting. To do this I had to buy a special train directory book that had all of the identifying locomotives numbers, its features and names and numbers on the side of the locomotive. I would find an old train bridge just outside one of the five main train terminals in London and sit on the edge waiting for the trains to come rolling through the tunnel. The train would come chugging slowly out of the terminal in just enough time to see the train number. The type of locomotive observed would be placed in my train spotting book and register that I had seen it. In those days the locomotives were driven by coal so the engine would be belching black smoke. As the train approached the bridge parapet that I was precariously sitting on, smoke and soot would come up from under the bridge right into my face and I would be covered in soot. When I got home, mum was angry at me for getting so dirty and pulled down the tin bath tub that was nailed to the fence in the garden and told me to take a bath.

One day during my ride through London I went into Waterloo Train Station where all the boat trains departed from. I was off school that day so I decided to buy a platform ticket for one penny to be allowed to go on the passenger platform where the boat train always left to go to Southampton docks to board the great ocean liners. The passenger carriages were painted with long ornamented boards running down at rooftop height on each carriage and spelling out its eventual destination saying for instance London to Southampton to New York. It would read, RMS Queen Elizabeth-Southampton-New York or RMS Queen Mary-Southampton-New York.

The baggage handlers were beginning to load up passengers' luggage to be put into the luggage car compartment before the passengers were ready to begin to see the train. I went over to a very primitive ironed casted machine located on the terminal walls and paid one penny to buy a special ticket for this platform. It allowed me to go out onto the platform to board the boat train for America at departure time. I sat on one of the luggage trolleys not being used that was located on the platform and I watched. I looked at this marvelous train that was going first to Southampton and then to unload the passengers to the dockside ready to board the ship going to New York

City in America. That great country and city I had dreamed about all these long years.

The passengers began to board the train. In between the hustle and bustle of people boarding that train I captured a happy and busy scene in my mind. I saw porters helping wealthy American passengers walk across the distance between platform and train door with their colorful baggage. Their baggage had labels of all the places they had been. I saw people inside the railway car moving to their seats in the bar car and sitting at tables drinking their cocktails, ladies with hats and gentlemen in their fine American made suits or in their American military uniforms. On each of the white cloth tables there was centered a vase of flowers and the waiter was going through the carriage taking orders for their cocktails prior to departure. This train was only reserved for passengers with tickets going to board that great ocean liner boarding the ship at the docks of Southampton and crossing the Atlantic to New York, USA. It made no stops before reaching the Southampton docks since this was the train used only to go from Waterloo Station nonstop to the Southampton docks and then only passengers boarded the ship and on to New York.

In those days only heads of state and movie stars usually travelled in such luxury. Air travel was hardly ever used since it was a long tedious journey with many refueling stops. I believe that TWA had limited trans-Atlantic service, but it was nothing like boarding a ship for a five glorious day's crossing the Atlantic Ocean. The giant ship weighed over 83,000 tons. I made a promised to myself that one day I too would be on that train, sipping a cocktail and going on an ocean liner to New York and visit the United States of America.

As a hobby I collected used cigarette cartons or packs if it was an American brand of cigarette. As I rode my bike through the streets of London, I would keep looking down in the gutter to see if I could find some discarded cigarette boxes. I also collected match boxes for my collection, which originally had been given to me by a family friend in the form of an album. I liked to collect things so I was particularly happy when I was given by a family friend a collection of match boxes and cigarette boxes from around the world. I am not sure who gave it to me but all of the samples were pasted in each large page album and came from all over the world. It was quite an extensive collection that somebody had taken a lot of time to put into an album. The matchboxes were from all over the Far East and different parts of the world. I was very proud of it and showed everybody that cared to take a look at it.

One day I made a bad error of judgment by taking the album to school to show the class on a show and tell day. The class seemed to enjoy looking at all the cigarette boxes and match stick boxes. When it came time to go to lunch, I put the book collection into my desk and pulled the lid down, never thinking that someone would steal and destroy my collection during the short lunch break. When I returned, I found my desk lid open and my collection shredded and thrown on the floor. The teacher was furious and had great difficulty trying to find out who would do such a thing. It was suspected that the two bullies of the class, Bobby A. and Tony R. were the culprits, but of course it was never proven. I did manage to salvage some of the damaged collection, but I never took anything to school again.

While I am writing about cigarette boxes, there was another phase that was for boys to collect which cigarette cards. During this time cigarette boxes included a card inside the box. Within the cigarette box was a small picture card. The size of the card was about two inches by four inches and each box contained a different theme to collect. Sometimes it was a picture of soldier's uniforms of various regiments at different periods of time. Others were of sports personalities such as in cricket or football, or of different animals or birds and put into albums like a stamp album. The main game to play with these cards was to play ciggies against a friendly opponent. To do that you get a friend to compete with you who also had his collection of cards in his pocket. Then both of you would find a wall and begin taking turns in flicking one card against the wall and watch it bounce back. If your card fell back and landed across your opponent's card then you swept in and picked up all of the cards that were lying on the sidewalk.

Another game we played was Gobs and Bonsers. There would be five small square shaped cubes called Gobs with one different cube called a Bonser. You had to put the five squares on the ground and then throw up in the air the Bonser and try and pick up all of the five squares off of the sidewalk before catching the falling cubes. If you did not pick up the gobs quick enough the ones that were left were counted out and put against your final score.

We also had street skates and I managed to trade for some used skates and we would skate everywhere we could. The skate had metal wheels and you put the skate onto your regular shoes by tying a strap around your ankle. Then there were grip clasps over the end of the shoe and with a key and you could tighten up the clamps to fit over each side of the toe of the shoe. After a while the wheels would wear out and develop what we called windows in the wheels. We would race down the street and sometimes hang onto the back of a moving van until the driver would stop and chase us away.

There was a lot of bullying going on in my school. My school was quite rough with a lot of tough boys beating up other boys. Disputes were often and fights were always breaking out to settle imaginary disputes. I was lucky in one respect because I kept myself to myself most of the time and tried not to get into any kind of physical dispute. It was at times inevitable and I was threatened many times to meet my opponent outside after school with one the boys who wanted to show his strength and beat me up in the playground to duke it out. I was called many harsh names on many occasions. I was small in stature so they picked on me for being weedy Phelps like a thin weed, but If could take that I could take anything.

After school there was a rush to go to the sweet shop nearby the school to pick up an ice pop. It was really nothing more than an ice cube of watery strawberry juice or other fruit juice with a stick frozen in the middle. It was great to have one of those before heading back before I had to pick up Colin from his school and get him cleaned up for tea before mum came home from work.

I was 14 years old when mum suggested that we visit Guernsey again on a family vacation. Mum, Colin and I visited Guernsey again and travelled on the same boat ferry from Southampton as we did before my dad passed away four years before. We had a real family vacation this time staying at the Pugh's Surprise Cottage and discovering that the cottage was about two hundred years old with no running hot water in the house. In each room we had a water pitcher for washing our face filled with hot water.

We visited all the same places that we had been before, Mullen Bay and La'Ancresse Bay. While we were on Muellen Bay beach Colin and I rented out a pontoon paddle boat, when he was about eight years old, and we paddled around the beach. I have a photo of Colin sitting on the cross piece on the small pontoon boat and we had many good times together on that small boat. We visited the little shell church, which was built by a very patient builder who built the little church from collected sea shells. Guernsey is a very beautiful island with cliffs leading down to beautiful beaches. We used public transportation which was an old rickety bus to travel around the whole island. This time our visit to Guernsey was much better than the last time. We travelled around the island visiting the cove beaches on one side of the island and the flat end beaches at the other end. Each evening we always ended the evening in the local pub called the Red Lion, which was a very happy place to spend the evening with all of the Pugh family. There was always someone there that could play the piano and after the first song slowly people would drift towards the piano and beginning to sing along.

One of our favorite inter-islands trips we would make was to take a fishing boat out of St. Peters Port and sail over to three separate islands that were quite nearby. One was the Island of Herm which was famous for its beaches and its beautiful sea shells. The shells ranged from every color to every size. The water is warmer in the Channel Islands because the Gulf Stream passed by warming that part of the English Channel bringing along a different sea fish or mollusk. Nearby was also the island of Jetou which is where the writer Victor Hugo lived. He wrote many of his books there including Les Miserable, which was not only portrayed in a movie but was on a Broadway stage in New York and in London for many years. The largest of this collection of islands is the island of Sark, which has been owned for centuries by a single family affiliated with the English crown. There was at this time an elderly lady who ruled the island and was titled by the royal title of Dame. She had absolute power and owned the whole island. She allowed no visitors near her home and banned any kind of motor vehicles on the island. Everybody in her family traveled in pony and trap which I thought was really nice. We had a great holiday with mum and Colin but after a week we returned home to England. Mum had to go back to work at the printing plant and Colin and myself had to go back to school.

It was about this time that Brian and I joined up with another two friends at school. Their names were Roger Norden and Malcolm. Roger was the son of a reasonably wealthy family that lived on the other side of town, living in a posh semi-detached house and wore sharkskin dress shirts. He showed us one evening his shirts that were hung up in his bedroom closet hanging from a horizontal long pole. There were at least a dozen sharkskin shirts matched up with rows of ties and other expensive clothes. Neither I nor my friend Brian had anything like that in our clothes closet. He also wore an imported American high school red jacket with stripes down the sleeves and a high school number embroidered on the side. His father was a London taxi driver. His father used to boast to us some of the cheatings he did to tourists. Because of the difficulty of a foreigner to understand the British coin system and currency, the cabbies used to take advantage of them. He would tell us that whenever he saw any tourist hailing his cab, he would drive them to their destination in London and when it came time to pay the fare the tourists were unable to decipher the British types of coinage. When the tourist just opened his hand with a lot of coins inviting the taxi driver to pick out the correct fare, Roger's father would say that the big coins were less value than the smaller coins which worth more. The opposite was the truth and they were being cheated.

Roger's family had a pool table in their front room where Brian, Malcolm, Roger and I played snooker or eight ball as it is called in America. We began a tradition in competing with each other to win an old silver plated cup. Snooker is something like pool but with no numbers on the balls just. Sometimes it got rough when we would throw the billiard balls at each other until Roger's mother put a stop to that and told us all to leave the house.

By this time as far as my mother was concerned, I was old enough to go out with the boys for the day so we decided to take the train to Southend, which was and still is a very popular seaside resort. We all wore a very colored Hawaiian print shirts and red neon-colored socks. This was frowned upon by the older British generation, but it was very colorful for sure. The week before we had gone into London to Austin's clothing store. This was an American style clothing store. I had bought my Hawaiian style shirt and hot neon red socks there and Brian and Roger bought the same type of colored shirts. We also had a red sweater that had a white stripe down each arm.

We took the train to Southend again and spent the day at the Kursall which was a great amusement park. We were riding the giant roller coasters and the water slide. As I got off of the coaster Brian said to me that I had a hole in my trousers. We went over to the lost and found shop to find someone that could repair my trousers. There was a nice lady there that was the park's seamstress so she told me to take off my pants. I really did not want to do that because I was shy, but she said sonny I have a son older than you so do not be embarrassed. I had to drop my pants in front of this lady while she sewed up the hole in my trousers. We had a great time at Southend that day. I have photos of the four of us sitting in the park at the Kursall after my brief encounter with the lady seamstress waiting for my trousers to be fixed.

We had a neighbor who liked to play cards. This was the Watts family and they had a daughter called Pauline. I think she was sweet on me because she asked her parents if I could come play cards with them every Thursday evening. We played gin rummy and it was the first time that I had played cards and been treated as an adult and was doing things that adults do.

At about this time there was a great discovery in the city of London. While they were tearing down one of the old bombed out buildings and digging deeper into the ground, they found the remains of a 2000 year old Roman house. Inside was a statue of one of their Roman gods. Digging was immediately stopped and this discovery turned over to the archaeologists and it seemed to wake up the still dazed war torn people of London. It was in the newspapers and there was so much interest that the government told the demolition people to stop working until the archeologists could take a look. They even installed a stepped-up fence around the statue so that members of the public could line up and take a look at it for themselves. I was one of the first to take a look and to me it was like a trip back in time because I was most interested in the history of the city of London.

London is well over 2,000 years old and at its very beginning it was just a small village settlement on the banks of a large river which was later to be named the river Thames. The Romans made the first permanent settlement and called it Londinium and built a large defensive wall around the city. After a while they also found a small courtyard of a Roman house with a path made of tiles as a walkway to the actual living quarters. During their occupation of Britain, named by Romans as Britannia, they built roads from rocks and bricks. The Romans were road builders and spread out in all directions from London. These roads radiated out from London mostly to the north where the Romans were fighting the Celts, the Welsh and Scots of Scotland, trying to push them back into their mountains. These Celts were the original people of England and are now called the Welsh, Scottish and Irish. The Romans had pushed them all back behind their mountains. The Irish were pushed back to a very large island now called Ireland.

During my school holidays I would take the bus into the city of London and spend many hours each day at the British Museum. I walked those halls of history and was fascinated by what had accrued in my city during the past two thousand years. I would also visit the Science Museum in Kensington learning things that would help me hold a decent science conversation in the future. I visited all of the museums of London including the National War Museum and all of the museums in Kensington, a neighborhood of west London. The largest was the well-known British Museum and I spent many days of my school holidays looking at the Egyptian exhibits and mummies in the huge Egyptian galleries that were located there.

1952

DURING THE LATTER part of this year my cousin Pauline invited me over to their house because they had visitors from America. The party was scheduled at my cousin Pauline's house in Walthamstow which was not too far away. Apparently, her aunt had married an American serviceman after the war which made her a GI war bride. They both had performance jobs in the Sonja Heine Traveling Ice Show European tour. This European tour was visiting many countries and was now visiting London. I was invited by Pauline to visit their house since she said that their American visitors were staying at their house for that night and were leaving London the next day to return to America. I did visit them that night and I remember that after the party they threw packages of Lucky Strike cigarettes as presents for everyone to catch. American cigarettes were very hard to find and was considered a great gift.

They did a film slide show about America that they had visited that also perked my interest. In fact, it was such a great influence on me, it made me decide to go to America as soon as I had finished up my military obligations that were soon coming up. I was ready to spread my wings and go to work and make money to go to America.

I was in my last year at school and I was now allowed to go out at night and enjoy my new found freedom. Colin was now old enough to be with his friends and stayed home with mum. One day each year was my school's sports day which was held on the open fields near the school. Everyone had to participate so as soon as we arrived at school that morning the whole school had to walk about two miles to the sports field. We were escorted by our class teacher and it looked like an army of kids marching along the road to the sports field.

I was not interested in sports at all and my friend Brian did not care either so we plotted to break away from the other kids when the teacher was not looking and take the day off. We thought we should have a day off of school. Finally, the break out that we were waiting for came along and we slowly moved towards the edge of the sports field where there was a long high hedge and behind was a fence. We quickly dodged behind the hedge and walked slowly along the inside fence to find an opening to get away from the sports field. I suddenly turned around to say something to Brian and as I did so I caught my trousers on a rusty nail that was sticking out of the fence. It tore my trousers badly plus it penetrated the cloth and I felt the nail stick into my bottom. We both then went home and played records all day until the late afternoon. I should have got a tetanus shot. My mother was not pleased at the news of my accident with the rusty nail.

During the first period of the next day, we were all told that we would be meeting an American exchange teacher. This would be the second American teacher to visit our school and he would be telling us all about American schools. We all assembled in the main hall to see this new teacher from another country. He told us how the school system was in America, but he had a strange accent to his words. We were all excited because he sounded just like a movie star. After his talk to us he asked us if we had any questions about America and many boys did ask but I was too shy to put up my hand to ask any questions that I would have loved to ask. I was fascinated to be in contact with another American teacher and I was thrilled to have the opportunity to meet for the second time a person from the country that I would ultimately become a citizen.

Located at one end of the area that we still called the fields there was a shed that contained all of the mowing and cutting machines to maintain the park area during the summer. Being something of an adventurer Brian and I climbed up the trees alongside of the shed to get onto the shed's roof. We made our way across the roof just for fun and decided to slip down the slope of the roof to the ground. I reached the edge of the gutter and began to slowly slide down over the side of the wall when suddenly I was caught on a hook of some sort. There I was almost hanging upside down. Suddenly the hook gave way and down I crashed onto some of the machinery. I was not seriously hurt but I had hit my nose on the lawn mower and my nose started to bleed. Brian helped me home and the bleeding stopped. When my mother came home from work, she was not pleased to hear about the escapade. Again, she had sewing to do.

My other friend Roger Norden had a BSA motor cycle as some rich kids did. We were both fans of the motorcycle speedway at West Ham, which was another part of London located not far away on the dockside river Thames docks in the city of West Ham. We rode his motorcycle from Leyton to West Ham with me riding on the back pillion to West Ham Speedway dirt track where our team, the West Ham Hammers, raced around a circled dirt track in a real stadium. The stadium was located at the East London docks. I could see from high up on the stadium stands all the smoke stacks and company insignia painted on the funnels of the large ships that were docked ready to leave. Each smokestack showed its colors and design of the ship's owner. My mind kept wandering as to where their last port of call was and where they would be going next voyage. I would also hear the ships horns as they pulled out on to the river. I think at that time my mind was beginning to want to go to those faraway places.

The dirt track speedway was open for racing every Tuesday night so Roger and I went to West Ham Speedway to cheer on our champion, Jack Young, the champion bike rider of West Ham Speedway. It was a stadium with a circular, banked up track of cinder material, but if you were seated too near the track you usually got some cinders in your eyes drifting up from the track. The bikes went racing around with their re-engineered mufflers making such a noise and the people cheered them on to victory. I also loved the smell of the high octane fuel they used. There were many crashes and the meat wagon, otherwise known as the ambulance, was always standing by ready to take a rider to the hospital. Although I was not a sport's enthusiast, I did enjoy this racing at the West Ham Speedway. I wonder if it is still in operation. I doubt it since time changes everything often a stadium becomes a large housing track.

There was a favorite song of mine that was played over and over again on the radio sung by Rosemary Clooney called Those Faraway

Places and whenever I heard it played, I wanted to go to those far-away places myself and see the world, especially to America, my dream country. Another song that influenced my life was See the Ocean in a Silver Plane, See the Jungle When it Was Wet with Rain. Eventually when I lived in America, I did fly in a silver plane many times and looking out the window and I saw the jungle far below in various parts of America and the Caribbean Islands.

I was working now at Bache's, the grocery store in Walthamstow High Street where my father and mother had worked before the war. My mother still worked there during the wartime bombing, but she was now working at W. H. Smith and Sons that was a folding carton printer. I worked at Bache's on Saturdays all day until closing time and did the same job as my father had worked prior to him being called up going into the Army in 1939. Each Saturday morning I worked the wheelbarrow stall located outside the store. My job was to take a paper bag and fill it with eggs and work the sidewalk trade calling out to the ladies as they walked by that they should buy my dozen eggs which I held out in the brown paper bag. I worked with my uncle Bill who was not my real uncle but he had known my family for many years so I always called him Uncle Bill. I enjoyed the day working, selling groceries and talking to the people as they walked by the market. I sometimes spoke to some of the regular shoppers that remembered my dad when he worked there. Jack Lyons was still the manager together with his wife Beryl. We also sold canned goods as well as sliced bacon from inside the store. We started at 8:00 am until 6:00 pm and after we had put everything from the curb back into the shop and we had finished closing it up we were done.

After work on a Saturday night, it was party time for us boys. That was the time when Brian and I would climb onto a bus and go into the West End of London on Oxford Street and spend Saturday night at Club 300. It was located in the basement underneath a store and was the location Club 300 called Humphrey Littleton's Jazz Club. Oxford Street in London is a very upscale shopping area with very expensive shops for every kind of item. Under each of these shops were basements where there was either a restaurant or other types of entertainment in the basement of the store. The basement of 300 Oxford Street was our

Mecca since that was the place where on a Saturday night we met and listened to Humph and his band playing Dixieland jazz. Humphrey Littleton was said to come from a very wealthy family. Rumor had it that his family did not want him to become a musician playing a trumpet so they only way he could practice was in the bathroom of his house.

His band consisted of himself playing the trumpet, Mickey Ashman on bass and two others completing his jazz group. His music was great and although there were no chairs to sit on, we stood and stomped our feet as he played his jazz. The favorite was When the Saints Go Marching In. It was rumored, although I did not see her, that Princess Margaret of the Royal family visited there often, taking off her shoes and dressed in jeans, danced to the jazz music in bare feet. No alcohol drinks were served there, but during the bands half hour interval we would all go over to the pub across the street for a pint of beer before returning to the next session of jazz. On other Saturday nights we would take a bus all the way outside of London to a pub called the Fishmongers Arms where there was also jazz played to a packed crowd on a Saturday night.

May 1953, I was Age 16

IT ALL BEGAN in Roger's dad's taxi. We were all riding one Saturday evening with my four friends Brian, Roger and Malcolm in Roger's father's taxicab. Roger's father was going off to work so he dropped us off at the Harringay Arena to see the Roller Derby and we all saw the action on the skating track for the first time. I was fascinated by the skaters that were roller skating on and around a banked-up track, each skater racing around the track trying to knock each other down to gain points. I liked the colors that were displayed on their jerseys and the track itself was all different colors. This was all very impressive action to a teenager living in a drab almost colorless city of postwar London.

The Roller Derby came to London to race at the Harringay Arena which would change the direction of my life. I could not have known then how much the influence of the Roller Derby would change my life and in turn changed the life of others in my family. Not many British people knew much about the Roller Derby including me, but I loved it. Roller Derby competition came to London with experienced American Roller Derby skaters. To make it more exciting the skaters were all American Roller Derby professionals and they split the skaters into two teams and called it America versus European skaters. We all knew that they were all American professional skaters from real American leagues. They had men and women skaters and the crowd roared with delight when little Joe in a squatting position slipped between the legs of one of the leading skaters of the pack and scored points. He scored points of each skater that he passed until he put his hands on their hips, which indicated that they no longer wanted to play that round. They had passed the leader of the pack and scored their points. The track they used was what they called a banked-up track at each end.

I also discovered that they had organized leagues in America so I decided to find out more about this sport. I talked to my friends in the taxi cab on the way home and told them that I was going to find a pen pal to write in America to tell me all about the Roller Derby in America. They all laughed at me saying you don't know anyone in America to even ask. Who do you know in America that you could write to? I told them I would find a pen pal somewhere to find out more about this sport from an American. To do this I decided I would write to the Mayor of New York and ask him to find me a pen pal that knew the roller derby and could explain all of the rules of this new sport. I looked at my map of New York that I had located in my encyclopedia and found the location in New York City where the Mayor's office was located. I looked further and discovered the name of the present Mayor of New York City was Mayor Robert Wagner.

I sent off a letter and after waiting for a long time I did not receive any response. I thought that it had just got thrown away and possibly I would not get a return letter from the Mayor. To my surprise I received a reply from the office of the Mayor of New York's private secretary who had a daughter of my age by the name of Joan Mary Mason, living in Flushing, a town in Queens County, New York. This was a close suburb to Manhattan, New York on Long Island. I really was not that excited after reading this letter since now I had to write as a pen pal to a sixteen year old girl. I was more interested in a male pen pal who would be more likely to know everything about the Roller Derby. I also discovered in her first letter that she did not know anything about the roller derby at all. She wrote that she would like to write to someone living in England and get to know more about my country and the British people. We wrote to each another for over six years sending letters, birthday and Christmas gifts. One gift I treasured was a real cowboy shirt. She wrote to me about her school work and where she and her girlfriends went out to picnics and the beach.

This continued for six years even when I was in the Air Force. I told her I would like to come over to America and maybe visit her. She responded that that would be a very nice thing to do. I wanted to be an

American so bad and began to believe that something was driving me to do this for a reason. It was a Y in the fork of the road and I had to choose the best fork to turn into.

It was so much in my mind that one night I had a dream that I was an American with an American accent. I awoke in the morning finding myself to be very depressed that I was not an American and did not have an American accent. I went to Austin's that stocked American clothes and I bought sports jackets and trousers made in America. I also subscribed to the newspaper New York Herald Tribune and read it on the subway on my way to work so that in my crazy mind people on the train might think that since I was reading an American newspaper therefore logic dictated, I must be an American. In those days America was very highly respected and anything that was built or made in America was expensive and therefor had to be of good value. America had a great deal of world respect.

One evening I was in Waterloo Station at the ticket window lining up to buy a platform ticket. In front of me was an American airman who was also buying a ticket. He looked so smart in his gabardine uniform and badges of rank and other decorations on his uniform. I looked down at his military suitcase and saw the stickers on his bag. They read where he had been. The stickers said Charlotte, North Carolina, and Texas and I thought that was absolutely fabulous to be able to walk about the world as an American citizen.

1953, Graduated from School

IN JANUARY OF 1953 I was fifteen and had graduated out of school, received my Testimonial and began thinking about my future as a tradesman and finding a job. Since most on my mother's side of the family were all in the printing trade it was assumed that I would also be a printer. All of my family at one time or another worked in the printing industry. It was not surprising I was going to be a printer and that would be my trade for life, but fate had something else up its sleeve. All of the young men in England at that time were in a sort of a limbo because we all knew that we would soon be inducted into the military, conscripted into the armed forces at the age of 18. This was called National Service and we had to register at age of 18. It was a couple of years away from that and I did still have to find a fulltime job.

My Uncle Tom was my mother's twin brother who worked as a monotype caster for one of the daily newspapers in London and worked the night shift. He lived with his family in Chelmsford about 20 miles away but he talked my mother into letting him sleep in my bed during the day. He said that it was too far from Chelmsford to commute and he worked the night shift at the newspaper. He never repaid my mother for his board and lodging at a time she needed it most. He would arrive at our house from work early at about 6:30 am so I had to be out of my bed prior to 6:00 am before he arrived. My mother talked to him about helping me get a job, but for some reason or another he could or would not help.

I checked all the help wanted pages in the London newspapers and I found a job in the center of London on Oxford Street at a company called Cleaver-Hume Press. They used small duplicator offset presses they showed me how to operate and they promised my mother that there would be an apprenticeship available for me within a year. It was a company that dealt in home education by sending out lessons on paper in the mail giving the person an opportunity to learn while he worked. It was interesting work but the machines were really duplicator machines called a Roto-Print. The people that worked there were quite decent and treated me well. It took about one and half hours to get to work leaving at 6:00 am. I had to take a trolley bus to one point, change to take the underground subway to Marble Arch Station then walk into the back streets of the West End to the office and printing plant. I worked there for about a year and quit.

Now I was over 16 and I began to figure out in my mind where my life was heading. I decided that I would sit in a quiet park and try figure out where was I going in life and what was I going to do with it. I needed a good paying job and needed to get into the printing union where the pay was about ten pounds a week, which in those days was an enormous amount of money. It was basically impossible to get into the printer's union and become a pressman. The system was like a father to son job. If you knew someone in a print shop who would be able to get you in as an apprentice you were lucky. The union's theory was to ensure that the fewer apprentices would ensure a shortage of pressman in the future which ensured job security. I managed to find a list of printers in the city of London and started every day, walking to every address and knocking on each printer's door. I went all day door to door and I finally after about a week of worn out shoe leather I found a printer that must have taken a second look at me and gave me a chance.

I met the foreman, his name was Ernie and he seemed a nice person. It was a small printing company and he asked what my experience was and I told him. He told me that for the first month of employment I would be given odd jobs around the presses and if worked out well they would put me as an assistant on the press and teach me how to hand feed the paper through the machine. I worked there for about a year first clearing paper up off the floor and cleaning up the bathrooms and then gradually Ernie put me on a press and showed me how to help the pressman make ready the machine prior to printing. This was my first step, but I had other ideas.

There was a very large printing college on the south side of the river Thames across the river. The London School of Printing and Graphic Arts was operated and basically owned by the printing union. To enroll for classes to start college in September the applicant had to be employed by a printing company that belonged to the union that operated the college and be able to prove it. I had to be employed by a union printing company and have that union company sponsor me. I had heard that there had been instances when an applicant sometimes fell between the cracks and got in through the back door during the rush of registration.

September 1953 was the registration deadline time to enroll into this union run school. I thought that it would be very busy and chaotic since everybody was checking in for their classes and when people are busy, they just rubber stamp applicants and do not check. I got in line and registered for the classes crossing my fingers that I would get through and not be challenged. My theory was correct, since it was chaos in the registration hall and everyone was busy. Nobody asked me for any identification and I was quickly signed in and paid my tuition fee in full and received all the necessary confirmation papers. I could not believe my good fortune. I answered the questions correctly as to where I was employed. I started classes three evenings a week at this union school for union members only I was not a member yet. I was told that if you could get passed through the registration door and start classes you were considered registered. Being in a socialist society as Britain was the union would come down hard on any union official that admitted a person into the union school and found out he was not a qualified applicant union apprentice.

After about two months of attending classes I approached the teacher of the class who happened to be the head union representative for the Associated Press one of the largest printers in London. I asked him very casually as class ended for the evening if he could find me a job in a union printing plant that would be able to get me a union card and be apprenticed. After I said those words to him, he went red in the face and started to stutter asking me with a question about are you not already in the union? I explained to him that I had been promised by my employer that I would get my card but I was not yet a member of the union. He started to ask me how I managed to get into his class in a union run school and I truthfully said that I just walked into the school and had my application accepted and paid my tuition. He implied that he could get into serious trouble with his own union by letting me into his class in the first place. He asked me the name of the company I worked for and said that he would find me a company that would take me on and make me a full apprentice as long as I could do the job. He did find me a printing company that he was very well known and they said they would take me on as an apprentice beginning as soon as possible. Everything was covered up quickly. Once I started work and had some instruction, they would have some union people come over to the printing plant and test me on the machine and if I checked out, I would get my union card very quickly. I believe he wanted to clear the error up as soon as possible. They did as they promised and I finally got my card as a union printing press apprentice.

At that time unions ran the country. The system was really quite good since the union trained and organized the whole industry ensuring the owners of printing company that they would have a qualified pressman guaranteed experienced sent over from union headquarters. The hardest thing was to get started and that was up to the employer when a space opened up in his company for an apprentice. I made some very good friends with this company and there was some nice benefit's such as a weekly dance night at the company canteen, playing pool and other games with social gatherings.

We could play Russian pool after work and listened to jazz records and all the top of the chart's music from the early fifties. At about that time the big band lead singers went solo in their careers at the time when the big band era ended. We would listen to Doris Day and Frank Sinatra. I even joined the Doris Day fan club and they sent me a large glossy photograph with her autograph which I treasured. The big song of the time was music from the musical South Pacific such as Some Enchanted Evening.

All I had at home was a small record player which I hooked up at the back of the old radio set by connections located on the back of the record player. I had a friend next door whose name was Tony Ferguson who had the latest model of a radiogram in his house so we would take our records and played music on his radiogram. We played a lot of Percy Faith music such as the theme from Moulin Rouge and the theme from Charlie Chaplin's film called Lime Light. The music was so pleasant to listen to in those days. Rosemary Clooney was my favorite and so was Frankie Lane singing Mule Train and Lucky Old Sun.

I now had a steady day job and also worked on weekends at the grocery store so I decided to buy myself a real record player instead of this setup I owned and I could play my music in my own home. After visiting my grandmother one Saturday afternoon I made my way to the outside street market in Hackney and noticed that there was a small shop that sold these record players and other magical electronic gadgets that I did not understand at all. I asked to see the owner of the store and he showed me some of the wonderful record players that he had in his front window. I asked him about the price and I could see that it was a lot more money that I intended to pay. It was just a record player as stereo had not been invented yet, just a straight player but with a new and different kind of needle that made the music so much clearer that the old voice box devices that I had been using. I really wanted that record player so much but I did not have the money to buy one. I kept looking in at the shop front window gazing at that record player that I wanted so much. I decided to go inside the shop and again speak to the owner of the store. I felt that I could bargain with him and arrive at a plan for the both of us to come out pleased with the transaction. After being inside the shop and talking to the owner of the store I came up with a plan. I asked him if he would agree for me to pay him an agreeable cash amount each month for the record player. There were no credit cards used at that time, they had not yet been invented. Everything was cash if you wanted to buy anything. Retail stores had only just started using a new system called hire purchase which really was a private credit arrangement with the owner and buyer. In my case I got lucky since I had no credit and no money, the owner of the store agreed with my suggestion of payment for a year payable each month in cash and I left with my record player tucked under my arm. I now had my own record player thinking I could not wait to get it home and set it up. I went to the store faithfully every month with cash in hand and paid my monthly bill as promised. I seem to remember that the term of payment was for six months just the total cost divided by six. There was nothing in writing that I can remember and I was under eighteen so he took a chance on me but I did the right thing and had paid him in full when the term was concluded.

We used that record player every evening we could and I soon began to buy records at Rollo's record shop located on the corner of Lea Bridge Road and Mark House Road opposite the Savoy movie theater where we used to line up as kids for the Saturday morning picture show. Rollo Records located on one of the corners of this intersection always had music playing through a loud speaker out front on the sidewalk to play music outside their store to encourage buyers to come into the store. The music playing outside on the street brought customers into the store to listen and buy records. This was the beginning of the record mania for music on vinyl records.

I sometimes took my new bike to work, but if it was raining I would take the bus and subway train into London to get to work. It was not far and I was young and strong and it was great exercise. I could still bicycle easily to Thundersley on a Sunday and now that mum had her son back, she did not challenge my determination to return and visit my auntie in Thundersley.

My mother had bought a bike for me at the age of 14 at great expense to her. It was apple red in color, but after I had saved up some money, I had a local bike shop paint it blue. It had a Simplex ten speed gear changer and it became part of me when I would pedal the 23 miles to and from Thundersley visiting my Auntie Ellie. The last time I had visited my dog Tess, who had become such a part of my life as a child, was sick and was near death. She was quite old by this time and my auntie said she had a tumor in her stomach so my good friend Tess died. The following weekend she was buried in St. Peters Church cemetery alongside my Uncle Jack. In England it was illegal to bury a dog alongside or in a human grave, but somehow in the dead of night Tess was buried alongside Uncle Jack. My Auntie Ellie would lie there twenty years in the future when she herself would pass on.

I was still making plans to sail on the Queen Elizabeth to New York, although I still had to have my military service for England completed before I could leave the country. There were many other countries that were looking for young British immigrants. Australia, New Zealand, Canada and other Commonwealth nations would compete and even offer to pay the travel fare to their country and find them a job. It was a time when Britain called immigration to another country the brain drain as many young men left England to go overseas to live in other British countries and colonies. In Africa, the colony of Rhodesia and Kenya were asking for people and would pay their fare on a steamship to Cape Town, South Africa. There were long lines of young people waiting to get official papers to live in these countries at the colonial offices in London.

When I was about seventeen I happened to look out of the window from the upstairs part of the bus. I had noticed that we passed a large window in a building at upper bus level that showed printing presses being operated and the name of the company was on the name of a large clock hanging from the wall. I got off the bus at the next bus stop and entered the building of this printing company. I asked to see the shop foreman who gave me time to explain that I wanted to upgrade my job and would he be interested in my services. I was now fully trained to operate a printing press and had my union card so I was thinking I could better myself financially for my trip to America. He invited me into his office and we had a long talk about the fact that he was looking for an additional pressman but had just put it off for a while. He asked if I was a member of the union and I showed him my union card. I started work there the following week with extra money and a promise of overtime, as much as I wanted each week. I moved up to a larger machine which paid a higher pay grade. My saving at the bank began to grow.

I felt lucky again since it was only by accident that I looked into that window from the top of the bus and noticed that there was a printer in that building and they were looking for a pressman. Destiny again was calling me and directing me to my distant future in America. I was still receiving letters from Joan in New York and she sent me a beautiful American style cowboy shirt for my birthday and a real leather wallet. Inside the wallet was an American one dollar bill. I had never seen American money before and it was fascinating to hold it in my hand. She had also sent me a photo of her in her back garden and she was very attractive.

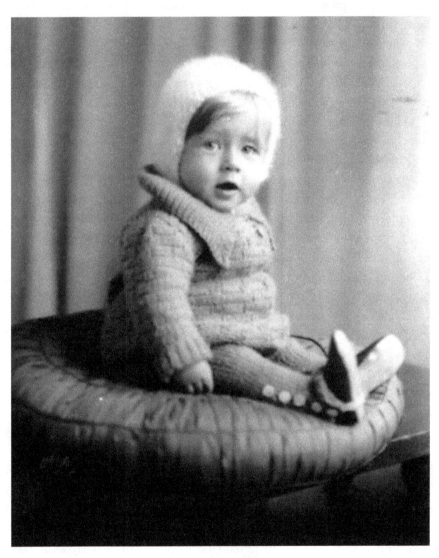

1939 Roy age 2

1940 Bread & Cheese Hill, Thundersley

1940 Eddie Phelps, Roy age 3 years

1941 Mrs. Ellie Heath, Mr. Jack Heath, Roy age 4

1947 Roy age 10, Eddie Phelps, Colin Phelps, Ivy Phelps,
Guernsey, Channel Islands

1955 RAF Induction

1958 Roy, Queen Elizabeth

1960 Roy and Ivy Phelps, Arrival at London Airport

1961 Ivy Phelps, Rose Went, Colin Phelps

1994 Carolyn, Roy, Patty in Front of Bungalow in Thundersley

1953-1954, I am Now 17

BRIAN AND I would occasionally take a bus into the city of London's West End where all the theaters and movie theaters were located. In England at that time top rated movies were released first in the plush movie theaters located in the West End first before they were released in general to the rest of the surrounding suburban areas. These theaters were very plush with nice velvet seats and we paid extra money to go see a pre-released film and then be able to tell our friends and relatives all about it. We sometimes would take my brother Colin with us. On one of those evenings, we would take the double decker bus into the city. We usually went upstairs because we liked to smoke and that was the only part of the bus that allowed smoking.

One Saturday evening we took Colin along to see a movie in London, he was then about nine years old. To go to the movies in Leicester Square we caught a bus and went upstairs as usual. We were riding the bus with Brian and I sitting together while my brother Colin wanted to sit on his own in the seat in front of us. The bus had an isle in between seats in the center of the bus with seats on either side and there was a young couple sitting in front of us apparently out on a date for a Saturday night event. The man was seated on the aisle seat while his lady friend was seated at the window seat. The man put his hand in his pocket to pull out his handkerchief and as he did so he accidently pulled out a small shiny package of three Durex's condoms, otherwise known as French letters. Colin noticed that the man had pulled something out of his pocket that fell on the bus floor. Colin left his seat and went to the object that had fallen out of the man's pocket and picked it up thinking he was being helpful he said to the man and his date in a very loud voice mister you dropped this out of your pocket. The man took a look at what it was and his lady friend looked horrified and was very embarrassed. The man immediately denied it was his and Colin said yes mister, I saw it fall out of your pocket. The female companion was so embarrassed that she hid her face in her scarf and pretended to look out of the window.

In those days if you needed to buy a condom the only place a man could buy any was at the men's barber shop. After cutting your hair, Conrad who was my barber, would ask each customer if you would like something extra for the weekend. Whereby, if we said yes, he would pull open a drawer and pull out a small brown paper package to give to you and you paid him for its contents. That was the only place you could get condoms in those days.

We also would go out to the West End quite often to see a show at the Palladium Theater where many of the American performers did their acts. Johnny Ray, Bob Hope and Tennessee Ernie Ford, they all came to the London Palladium which was a mecca for all the entertainers of the day. We used to love to go into the West End of London to see first run movies and also live entertainment.

I would also at times spend a whole day in each of the museums of London. My favorite was the British Museum where I would wander the halls of these magnificent exhibitions all day and be home ready for tea. I was most interested seeing in large cabinets of Egyptian mummies embalmed thousands of years ago. The dinosaur halls were also on my list to explore. There also was the British War Museum where there were mementos of the various wars that Britain had been involved during past years.

The Kensington Science Museum was located in the district of Kensington. I would catch a double decker bus from home and spend the day there looking at the various floors that had its own subject. I remember there was a giant floor to ceiling pendulum that slowly swung from side to side showing how the earth was revolving on its axis. The pendulum slowly began to swing at a different angle showing that the earth had also moved off center. There was a center mark on the floor at the bottom under the slowly swinging pendulum showing that the pendulum was swinging off center as the earth moved in its orbit. This museum showed just about everything about science that they knew at that time and now they have learned so much more. Since then, the exhibits have probably been modernized to present day science. So much has been learned in today's world in science especially after they went to the moon in 1969, twenty years later. We understand so much more about science than we did in those days when I visited the South Kensington Science Museum.

Just before it was time to march off for national service at age 18, I wanted to go on a special railway excursion that they were advertising on billboards. I saw an advertisement that showed that there was a special day trip offered as a day excursion to the city of Teignmouth which was a seaside town in the county of Devon in the southwest part of England. This was a long day trip since it took about four hours on a train ride get to the southwestern part of England about 200 miles away. I had never been to the southwest part of England especially the county of Devon. Being close the port of Bristol it has a long history of British seafaring about the Royal Navy and Caribbean pirates, privateers and Freebooters of the time of Queen Elizabeth I in 1588. That was about the time when the Spanish Armada was approaching the English coast. Queen Elizabeth the First had some great ship captains such as Sir Richard Grenville, Sir Francis Drake and many more that were from the county of Devon that were great historic sea captains.

My train left Paddington railroad station at eight in the morning scheduled to return to Paddington station by midnight the same day. My mother had gone to work that day so I caught a bus to London's Paddington station and boarded a day excursion train to the city of Teignmouth, Devon. It was a cheap day trip ticket which the railroads offered from time to time. It took about half an hour on the bus to reach Paddington station in central London and I just managed to buy a ticket and get on the train before it left the station and I found an empty window seat looking out the window as the English countryside passed by.

It was a great train to ride. The distinctive colors of the railroad cars were cream and brown which were the company colors of the now defunct Great Western Railway. We rolled along passing some beautiful countryside, the kind I that I had never seen before. After a while there appeared at the western end of the English Channel the beginning of the blue Atlantic Ocean and there were the beaches of Devon. I got off the train and went into the station to make sure the time of the return train to London was correct so that I had plenty of time to explore the beaches and town. To my horror, I had misunderstood the timing of when the return train left Teignmouth to go back to London. They told me that the train actually left Teignmouth station to return to London at midnight and would not get back into Paddington station in London until after 6:00 am the following morning. It was a night train. I would have to stay in Teignmouth for a whole day from my arrival time to midnight to get home.

I was really shocked at my misunderstanding because somehow, I had to call my mother that I would not be home until the next morning. My problem was how to contact my mother, to tell her when I would be arriving home since she did not know where I had gone for the day. Looking back, I realized that I should have left a note for her. The only person that I knew who did have a house phone was my friend Roger so I counted my coin change for the pay phone and I had just enough change for a long distance phone call to Roger, asking him to bike over to my home and tell my mother what had happened and that I would not be home until the next day. I was not sure how she would understand it, but I told myself I was seventeen and almost an adult. I was able to contact Roger on the phone and he passed along the message. He would ride his motor bike over to my home and tell my mother or leave a note on the front door.

I began to explore the seaside town. I would buy some lunch first and then to do a lot of walking around this large bay. Teignmouth is a very old seaside town and at that time quite small. I looked into the seaside shops and there was a small seaside carnival with a fairground and a small pier. I bought some picture postcards and then walked back to near the station to have some sort of dinner prior to waiting for the midnight train back to London. There were some pubs near the station to have some liquid refreshment while I waited for the train. There is always a pub nearby in England to spend some time while waiting for a train. I finally did get back to London and found an early six am bus that was beginning to operate that early in the morning and I arrived home. Needless to say, it did not go over too well with my mother who was frantic when I arrived home. Although she knew I was quite capable to travel, it was my fault that I did not tell her where I was going. Her eldest son, who has wandering shoes, did not return home when expected at the end of the day.

1954

IT WAS NOW time to take a vacation before entering the military. Brian and I talked it over. One evening we talked about going on vacation to Guernsey for a week before we both had to enter military service. Brian had not been there before and I thought it would be a fun trip. We bought our tickets and made lodging reservations in a small bed and breakfast cottage on the cliff side overlooking the bay. The weather was so much different than it was in London. We left Waterloo Station which was one of five railroad terminals in London and caught the channel ferry for the night voyage to Saint Peter's Port, Guernsey.

We stayed at a small rooming house bed and breakfast cottage where there were other guests taking a holiday. Being in the middle of summer there were lots of activities going on. There was a lot of car racing on the island that coincided with our time during our stay. The drivers did not use a special track. They used the streets of the island that had been blocked off during the racing time with spectators kept behind police barriers as protection from crashes.

While we were watching the cars racing around the streets of St. Peter's Port, we sat on the sea wall where I got so sunburned that I was taken ill. In those days we had never knew much about sunblock and I was so sunburned that I had fainted and almost fell off the high wall down to the rocks to the beach at the bottom. We took the next bus back to the small cottage where we were staying. We called the visiting doctor who diagnosed that I had received third degree burns all over my body and had developed heat stroke. In those days some doctors made house calls. He prescribed some ointment and instructed me to stay out of the sun for a day or so. I soon felt better and back we went to the car racing the next day and continued our vacation. While we stayed at the cottage one of the other guests were a Mr. and Mrs. Martin who lived in the city of Bristol in southwest England. They were a very nice couple and when our holiday was over, we agreed to keep in touch and see each other again.

Soon our vacation had come to an end and we sailed on the day ferry back to Southampton to go home. While crossing the English Channel the sea was usually rough since it is considered to be one of the roughest channels to sail in the world. The English Channel is narrow but is squeezed at north end by the North Sea and to its south by the Atlantic Ocean. The sea acted like a washing machine which was how so many people described it over the many years of naval history.

As we finished our crossing, while entering Southampton docks something happened to me that was so coincidental that almost seemed like it was an omen. As we approached the port of Southampton and were heading to our docking pier, I saw a large ocean liner docked further along the dock. This ship was huge with a black hull, its upper decks were painted white and the two funnels were painted black and red. It was the Cunard White Star Ocean Liner the Queen Elizabeth. As we drew closer to our docking pier, I saw for the first time that great ship that I planned to sail one day to New York and see all of America. It took my breath away and I was so excited to see her. It was the Queen Elizabeth of the Cunard Line backing out of her pier and turning to face the Atlantic Ocean on her way to New York and America. I knew for sure after seeing that beautiful ship with her red funnels and black funnels being positioned to sail by tugboat. I had seen my destiny knowing that one day I would be on that ship heading out to sea for America and New York. I could see the passengers on deck waving and throwing paper streamers back on the dock where friends and relatives were waving Bon Voyage.

During the summer of 1954 after we returned from Guernsey, Brian and I went on a jazz festival cruise on a ship called the Royal Daffodil. We got up early to catch the bus to the Tower of London dock where we would embark from London on our way to the French coast. It was a great day leaving the pier from the Tower of London on the river Thames as we headed down river into the English Channel. For the next hundred miles from the mouth of the river Thames the sight of France was on our left port side. We could move around the ship sampling the many types of Dixieland jazz playing from each of the different bands. The 1950's was the decade of innocence and freedom for young men and women because life was getting better for the people of England. The ship was full of happy people and the sound of jazz was all around us. We could move from deck to deck and in every nook and cranny there was some small band playing Dixieland music. It was a great cruise and it was a tired group of teenagers that walked down the gang plank to go home after a great day of music across the Channel.

The rubble of the bombed out houses and factories were gradually being removed and new buildings were being built. There was a new type of music being played. Not real rock and roll yet because that had not arrived in England, but softer and more poetic songs that were being sung by Doris Day, Rosemary Clooney and many others. It was like a song in poetry. At our young age we were at the peak of our optimism, we felt that the future looked good and we were very confident that those bad old days of the war were gone and were now just bad memories.

The music being played was also just instrumental to a link to the past of the big band era. The British commentators were suggesting that England was now entering in a new Elizabethan era and England was going to be strong again as it was in the first Elizabeth days of exploration with the Spanish Armada and great sea captains in the 1500's. We would be exploring worlds of unknown places. We were going to the moon and the stars but unhappily that was not to be. The British Empire was soon to be dismantled around the world into socialism and sunk into the dark abyss of uncertainly. Countries that were of the Commonwealth demanded their independence and many used violence to obtain their independence, others negotiated their independence peacefully.

The world was beginning to wake up and begin to enjoy life once more after that terrible war of death and destruction. There were still many open spaces of buildings that once were people's homes, but it was too soon for any full recovery which would take years to rebuild the city. We were beginning to hear many different kinds of music coming from the radio and it seemed that everyone was trying out new types of music but not finding the right one yet. This was also a time when commentators were saying that the record business was a dying business since the era of the big bands had come and gone with nothing to replace Glenn Miller, Artie Shaw and many other famous bands that had occupied the radio during the pre-war days, during and after the war. Home TV was becoming more accessible to the people.

There had to be some sort of a bridge to carry over the style of music that would become popular for the next generation. When the big bands were so popular their bands usually had a lead singer or group singers like the Andrew Sisters or the Modern Aires to sing the songs that the band leaders would compose. There on the bandstand would be the whole band but alongside of the stage was a chair that was usually occupied by the lead singer. As the big bands slowly disbanded and left the music scene, these lead band singers went off on their own making careers in single records singing songs that would bridge the music gap that lasted for about fifteen years prior to the arrival of a different kind of music called Rock and Roll.

These singers had great voices like Doris Day who I immediately fell in love with when I saw her photos. Then others took the lead and made records of their music and as they said went single away from the band era. These records were not always made by ex-big band singers. There were other performers like Tennessee Ernie Ford singing his Sixteen Tons in his twangy Tennessee accented voice which everybody loved to hear. He became an entertainer and rose to the top of the entertainment industry. There arrived on the scene two entertainers, one was a singer and the other a comedian who quickly became very popular called Dean Martin and Jerry Lewis.

The record industry was suddenly reborn and was really becoming a very large industry in the music business. Every Saturday night on the radio at 11:00 pm there was a music program named Jack Jackson's record roundup, which although aired late at night it was enormously popular and just about every teenager listened to songs like The Green Door. Suddenly the top of the charts became so popular that every week there would be a competition as to who would be voted number one on the charts. This was not only for singers but for the Dixieland jazz bands that were popping up all over England playing all kinds of jazz. They played music singing a song that would be become a classic called the Rock Island Line, which was kind of jazzy, a little bit of early Rock and Roll. Even the masters like Duke Ellington and Lionel Hampton made their singles. Record music was everywhere and a generation of young people had been born.

These were not the so-called baby boomers; they would come later. It was the kids that were born a few years prior to the war and wanted to come away from the wartime depression, the time of acute unhappiness, the drabness of the clothes that people wore, to just have fun. Something exciting and new, this music fitted their expectations and they loved it. Some joined gangs and caused violence in the streets others and wore clothes that were styled as Teddy boys. These were young men who wore clothes of the Edwardian times causing trouble with their signature clothes of dark jackets with velvet collars.

If you went to an open air market like the Walthamstow High Street you would see and hear from a street side stall that had a record player turntable hooked up to a loud speaker and was playing all the latest vinyl records kids were dancing to. They were selling records including inside music stores with speakers centered outside for pedestrian and or just passersby. One store nearby was on Lea Bridge Road and Markhouse Road which was located at an important four way intersection. There you could go inside and browse through the racks of records like a library. It had silent booths with headphones where you could try out a song and if you liked it you would buy it. It became an explosion of music in just a year or so during the first half of the 1950's.

In many homes there was a radiogram radio which included a record turntable in a section of the furniture console. By changing over to phono, you could play records as well as listen to the radio. This was the early beginnings of what is called today an electronics store. Records up until then only played at one speed which was 45 revolutions per minute, then it upped its speed to 78 revolutions per minute. Coming up on the music horizon were the albums which now had speeds much slower and contained more songs by the artists.

I did not have a radiogram to play records. We could not afford such a luxury at that time. The music industry was quite smart because it introduced the 45 speed single record of an artist with a flip side so for the price of one artist's song you could listen to it and turn over the record and you would get a bonus of another song. Keep in mind that the music business was not anyway as sophisticated as is today and all electronic goods such as TV and music players were sold in England by small stores that were usually located on the corner of the street.

Some of my favorites in long playing records were an album that I bought from Rollo Records that I brought with me to America. I have been playing it so much that it now sounds like frying eggs in the background. It was Lionel Hampton's 1954 concert at the Apollo Hall concert in Amsterdam, Holland. I have tried to find a replacement of this LP on either vinyl or CD but have not been successful. The other record that I brought was a Louis Armstrong 1927 record which is amazing to hear that it is that old. I believe that old record is worth much more than I paid for it. Other long known entertainers still recording were the well-known artists like Frank Sinatra and the new singers like Perry Como, Frankie Lane and many others that had crossed the bridge from the big band's era to the singles and the new Rock and Roll era. That began in 1954 with the song called the Great Pretender. This song is now considered by many the very first Rock and Roll song on national media.

With my three friends Brian, Roger and Malcom and I decided that we would get tickets to see a show at the theater in London named the Palladium which was a theater that brought in all the famous American and British show people. It was very elaborate theater and we decided to really splurge and get tickets for seats in the royal box which was located along side of the wall of the theater with cane chairs. Below our box seats hanging on the side wall was a huge royal motto with the mounting of two lions. We were going to see Tennessee Ernie Ford singing his famous song Sixteen Tons and we were going to see him from the royal box at the famous London Palladium Theater.

We were growing up fast. We could now drink legally at a pub so whenever we went into the west end of London we would always stop in a pub and have a drink before and after a performance. Our group of three boys and me had been together for many years and were now growing up, but we were also beginning to break up. Roger had his motor bike and took weekend rides and Malcolm was trying to get out of the pending military service. His parents had connections and Brian and I did not approve of Malcom trying to ignore his duty to his country. Brian and I just went out on Saturday nights alone to a dance and then soon after he was going steady with a girlfriend in the town of Reading, which was not far from London.

I joined the YMCA which was located in the town of Leyton and went to their Saturday night dances. One night Brian and I went to a dance that was promoted as the greatest dance of all time. We attended this dance and it turned out to be in a church hall. That was fine by us since we met two nice ladies at the dance who apparently was turned on by us two lads.

I have always been interested in science fiction and rockets to the moon which in those days was considered then to be close to sheer lunacy. There had been reported sightings since 1947 of flying saucers and I yearned to be one of those that had seen the actual sightings of one of these discs. I had read many of these paperback books of flying off in a rocket ship to the ends of the galaxy. I was constantly drawing plans of rocket ships on pieces of paper with different designs. I also went to see grade B movies of science fiction where there was speculation that we were being watched by alien eyes. It made my blood run cold to think of running into an alien.

I was getting more and more interested in stories of flying saucers being sighted. There were stories from America about a man named George Adamski who claimed to have been abducted by aliens in a flying saucer which landed in 1952. This brought on a storm of controversy which still continues to today. It was about this time that I joined the British Astronomical Society which had its meeting rooms in the west end of London near the center of the theater district. Our meetings were held in some very distinctive rooms of a large hotel. The club was very exclusive and gave membership mostly to professional astronomers and also amateur astronomers.

Many of the famous scientists of the world at some time would be there at a meeting once a month to lecture. We would first have a general meeting and then we all broke up into various departments of our special interest. My interest was always about the planet Mars so I would go into the meeting where a professor of astronomy would be lecturing about the planet Mars giving all the new information and theories about that planet. He was at that time the most informative professor on the latest information about the planet Mars, but in those days, it was pure speculation not on fact or on ideals like it is today. They had no idea what was on Mars. They had no real proof of what they were discussing other than what they saw in their telescopes and speculated in their minds. It was only speculation in scientific theory that an object could be sent into space at a certain speed and because of the earth's gravity it would orbit and it would not fall back to earth, but circle the Earth for every 90 minutes and keep circling. If the orbiting item fell below that speed the object would start to fall back to the Earth and burn up in the earth's atmosphere. At that time, we knew very little about Mars and most of the discussions were of unknown speculation of the science that we knew at that time and what we saw at the end of the telescope. It was impossible to conceive of what we have today as tools in astronomy such as the Hubble space telescope that allows us to peer into the cosmos and see the planets and stars so clear in detail.

One special October evening at the British Astronomical Association we were having our general meeting prior to us departing to our various departments when there was a flurry of activity at the door to the room. The door burst open and everyone stopped what they were doing and looked in the direction of the door. It was one of the society's officers that had brought some astounding news that seemed to turn the room upside down. There was a loud sound of everyone talking at once and finally the president of the society tapped his gavel and the meeting came to order. The room became quiet and from a tape recorder operated by the society president we heard the sound of beep, beep, beep, of an object that had been put into earth orbit by humans. They again brought the meeting to order and with a great flourish announced that the Russian Soviets had actually launched a satellite into orbit for the first time called Sputnik. The result was absolute pandemonium in the meeting. Members were cheering and jumping on to their tables and stamping their feet with joy. They were not just happy that the Soviets had beaten Britain and America into Earth orbit but they were professional scientists that it had now been proven that what goes up does not necessary what will come down. It had been done when others said it was impossible. The physics of all the astronomers in the past needed proof that their theories of what goes up does not necessarily need to come down if the right speed of the object was slightly faster than that the earth's rotation it was in free fall. This proved it that it can be done. Prior to that moment the idea to put an object into Earth orbit was just pure speculation and now it had been proven that it could be done and opened a whole new world for the future.

I was deeply involved from a personal point of view into future space flight that now it could be done and the knowledge on how to do it had been proven. We now knew that we could go into space as long as we could fly faster than the planets orbit and with able speed, we could fly into space forever. I felt giddy with pride that the impossible had been proven. We could soon be headed to the stars. I had read books on this subject and had discussions with astronomers at our meetings each month on what it would be like to walk on the moon. We did not even know for sure if the surface of the moon would be strong enough to support a human body to walk on the moon let alone a heavy vehicle to land on its surface. There were of course at that time many movies that depicted futuristic space activity, including an alien messenger warning us, arriving on a flying saucer like in the movie The Day the Earth Stood Still, Rocket Ship XM and many more. I believed that it was possible one day to travel in space and that I would be able to see it in my lifetime. Nineteen years later I would watch Neil Armstrong climb down the ladder on to the surface of the moon on live television in real time to see that it was such an historic moment.

I became very friendly with one of the officers of the British Planetary Association by the name of Patrick Moore who would go on to be in later years a main contributor to space flight with a program on British TV. An expert on the stars and planets, he wrote many books on the subject many of which I personal own. He invited me to his house in the country where he would set up a large telescope in his garden. I took a bus into London and boarded a Green Line bus to his country home in the county of Kent and was invited into his house. There, for the first time because of the high power of his telescope I looked through the telescope eyepieces at the moon and could see for the first time the craters on the moon, even looking into the inside of the craters showing rocky terracing of the sides of the crater. He showed me Mars and Saturn and its many moons. We talked a long time in his garden with the telescope and I learned from him about the cosmos by peering through his telescope into our solar system from his garden. I promised myself that one day I also would own such a large telescope.

March 1955, RAF Induction

THE DAY HAD arrived when I was to be inducted into the Royal Air Force (RAF). I had received my letter from the government who advised that according to an act of the War Office all able persons at the age of eighteen must be inducted into the armed forces for a period of no less than two years which sounded to me like a prison sentence, which to some it was. Most of my friends were called up and did their duty, but unfortunately others did not do their duty to their country and claimed all sorts of personal medical ailments to prevent them from serving for two years in the military. I was given a time to appear before a medical board to be given an overall medical examination and a letter followed that said I was fit for military duty.

My friend Roger whose parents were quite wealthy somehow managed to get him a permanent deferment and so did Malcolm, but Brian and I did what we thought was to do the right thing and I went for the initial interview with the service of choice. I wanted to go into the Royal Navy but I was turned down because they wanted me to sign up for four years of service. They said that it would take two years to train me and then I would end my enlistment and be discharged so they would never get their in-training investment back from me.

My second choice was the Royal Air Force. I went through the interview for that, but again initially was turned down for that same reason which was two years and was not enough time for them to recoup their training investment. The interviewer noticed my disappointment so he called me back to his desk as I was leaving and asked me if I ever had a close blood family member who served and died in the Royal Air Force during the Second World War. I quickly turned around and said, yes, I did have a family member who lost his life in the RAF. My uncle Cyril was a tail gunner in a Lancaster bomber during the war that flew many missions over Germany. He did not survive when his rear turret was blown away with him in it and they never did find his body. The interviewer explained that there was a tradition in the RAF that they would recruit any person that had such a family fatal death in combat during the war. I could then apply after initial training to the same position in air crew as my uncle, in the rear turret of a large bomber. He said I must show proof by sending in his Air Force serial number with my application. I got it from his mother my Aunt Margaret, found other factors of my Uncle Cyril's service and reapplied to the RAF recruiters. They accepted it and I was told to wait for further instructions.

I agreed to do this and since I had already passed the medical testing, and now through the interview it was settled that I would join the RAF during the month of March 1955. They would send me a letter outlining the time to join up and get on the train to do basic training prior to being sent to my active station. Sure enough I did get the letter which told me that I should report to a London train station at a certain time and certain train number to be transported to my outfitting base and begin my service in the Royal Air Force.

I began my service on March 14, 1955 and said goodbye to my mother and brother and I went off to serve my country. I was told to take one change of clothing for one night and all of my bathroom items. When I arrived at the station there were thousands of young men waiting to board the troop train. I had asked my mother and Colin not to come and see me off since I do not like long goodbyes. Finally, I was on my own, ready for whatever came my way in the British military having joined the famous and prestigious Royal Air Force.

After I found my platform number at the station with all the other recruits, I found lots of uniformed sergeants with a clip boards checking off the names as we boarded the troop train. I boarded the train with hundreds of other recruits from Waterloo station and found a seat. I did not have much in the way of possessions with me other than the clothes we were told to bring. Everyone was about my age. Some wore their hair long since we had entered the age of long hair as being fashionable. Some of them were tough looking like Teddy Boys. I tried to find out where we were going since this was a train that had one destination and someone said that we were going to a RAF outfitting station called RAF Cardington. There were lots of Air Force uniformed sergeants on board to accompany us to our destination. There must have been over a thousand of us on the train all wondering where we were going and what it would be like to be in a military recruit training camp.

The boys were all nice enough on the train. It pulled out of Waterloo station in London heading for somewhere but nobody knew where. It is always pictured in movies of young men in civilian clothing heading for a military boot camp installation that usually included a game of cards being played but I do not remember that we did that. Everybody was pleasant and apprehensive. We were really a bunch of scared 18 year olds who did not know what the future held for us. There was the usual know it all people who told everybody that they knew where we were going. Their older brothers went there a year before and told them stories of how bad it was and what the Air Force was going to put us through during the induction process.

The train continued on for about two hours before it began to slow down to a crawl then to a stop in the middle of nowhere. Suddenly, it started up again and looking out the window I could see that we were being switched off onto a single track going off in another direction so obvious to me now that the train had entered its last phase and we were almost at our destination. Suddenly the train stopped again at a small railway station that was outside the base front gate. The sergeants came down the aisle of the train and started bellowing that everyone had two minutes to get off of the train, so there was a dash for the exit doors of the train to get on to the station platform. Waiting alongside there were parked light blue painted trucks with the rear gates dropped open. We were all pushed into the trucks that had been lined up ready for us to climb into. Gradually all the trucks began to move with the recruits standing up in the bed of the truck and we were slowly moved in con-voy towards the base front gate, which was waiting for us. As we neared the camp we passed through a welcome sign. The sign read Welcome to RAF Cardington. That was nice of them I thought.

The sergeant told everyone to stand alongside a post that had an alphabetic sign on the top. Then the sergeant told us to stand by each sign that was the first letter of our last name and wait until told to move away. Soon a corporal came up to us standing under the letter P and called out our names. He told us that we were in RAF Cardington to be outfitted before we went to another airfield for basic training. For now, we were to go into one of the barracks, pick out a bed space and wait for further orders from the corporal that was in charge of that barracks.

We were marched rag tag into each one of the barracks since most did not know how to march. Since I was in the Boy Scouts most of my life, I had done plenty of marching, but the others in my group were sloppy and we stumbled our way into our numbered barracks where we were to stay for one week. We were told to select our bed for the week and then after we would be taken by train to a basic training camp. This was only a fitting out facility where a uniform was given to us. The corporal told us to leave our belongings on our selected bed space and told everyone to get in a marching line three across and march with him to receive the necessary bedding for the night. After being given our overnight needs we went off duty for the evening, but were ordered that we would be woken up at 5:00 am the next day to march to the mess hall for breakfast.

At exactly 5:00 am the hut sergeant woke us up and we were ordered to use the bathrooms and then go to breakfast. Marching up to the mess hall we were given our breakfast buffet style and then returned to our quarters and were told to form up and follow the sergeant to get outfitted. We marched to a large building where one by one in single file we stopped at various openings along the wall where there was a corporal who would be giving out various items that we would need during our two years. The first stop to be outfitted was when I was given a large canvas kit bag with a long number that was stenciled on it as we waited. The corporal asked for my name and serial number and stenciled it on the kit bag and told me to move on.

Moving on to the squadron office we received our dog tags to put around our neck. Each dog tag gave personal serial number, blood group and religious information. We put them around our necks and were told to never take them off until you are discharged. I realized that this was going to be my military number for the time I was going to serve my Queen and England and I would be forced to remember this number for the rest of my life. I still do remember that serial number. For the next two years or so I would be constantly called out to confirm my number saying at the end of each order to say your last three numbers.

We stopped at each opening of each building with a table attached where we would be given our uniform which included two pairs of blue boxer shorts and two tee shirts, Air Force blue of course. The outer uniform was made of a type of blue colored wool trousers and jackets and seemed to feel quite heavy especially if it got wet. The blue woolen trousers were well creased, two pair of blue socks, one pair of hard hob nailed boots and one pair of shined dress shoes. One battle dress blouse with the flying eagle on each shoulder, a belt with the RAF emblem on the buckle and over all that came a large blue overcoat with large lapels, all having the RAF emblem on the shoulder pads. They gave us two hats to wear. One was a blue beret with a brass insignia on the beret which was our working beret. For formal events there was a blue cap with the RAF badge above the peek. Behind the brass RAF insignia, they gave us a round yellow temporary disc that went behind the brass RAF insignia. This showed that we were only recruits, that our rank was only ACC2 the lowest form of human life on this planet, as they kept reminding us. They said that they would soon be giving us a short haircut.

Then came the time when they gave us our permanent equipment such as our mess kits and other necessary items. We were told that we must fill up our kit bag with all of our stuff and go to our barracks for the rest of the day. We would be at RAF Cardington for one week. It was a fitting out base and during that week we would go to classes to be acquainted with Air Force protocol. We would have classes and see Air Force movies showing medical and various military films on life in the RAF. We would be there for one week and the following Monday we would take another train to our basic training camp 200 miles north.

As we all began to introduce ourselves, we made friends together in the barracks. The barracks sergeant came and gave us information as to what was expected of us while we were in the RAF being outfitted. He showed us how to make up our beds and keep our bed space clean. The barracks would be inspected by an officer every day while we were there. He told us to remove our civilian clothes and put on our uniforms right then. We then had to pack up our civilian clothes in a cardboard box and take them over to the squadron office to be mailed home. He told us also that he lived in a room of his own at the end of the barracks, which was private for his use only and we must knock on the door first if needed. This base was a place where they just gave us supplies and explained Air Force procedure. It seemed to us that this was very easy going.

Some of us went over to the camp canteen where they served our personal extra cost food and there were chairs and tables to use. I likened it to the Salvation Army. There were also pool tables to use and dartboards, something like a place to be used for recreation. I could not believe that this was so nice. The sergeants did not shout and we were assigned as a team of 12 recruits with various names and numbers. We were given the title of Intake 12 relating I suppose to the jet engine air intake and we had the yellow discs behind our beret badges to show we were recruits. We were also put into groups that were called Flight Group 12.

I became friendly with some of the other men and we agreed that we would all stick together while we were in this camp not knowing for sure that we would all be separated at the end of the week to go on to different camps. We would all be separated after taking some educational tests to determine if we were qualified for the various jobs of being an airman. This would determine what type of job we would be assigned to and what basic training camp we would be sent to. Each training camp was a basic training camp, but had different outlets for our jobs while we were in the service. Lights out was at 10:00 pm and rise and shine at 5:00 am. It appeared that we had survived our first day in the RAF after being pushed and pulled from one office to another.

The following morning at 5:00 am we were loudly awakened by the banging of pots and pans by the barracks sergeant who told us to shower, shave and dress in our working uniform and to line up outside in fifteen minutes in a line of three columns, which he then marched us to the mess hall for breakfast. I remember the meal was great and was very surprised that this second day would be as good as the first. Things were looking up and it was not so bad after all. It might even be fun. However, time would tell but we were really being misled which we would soon find out. After breakfast we were given fifteen minutes to clean up bed spaces and be ready for a haircut. We were on the end of a long line that started outside of the long hut. The line of recruits went in with hair on their head and everyone came out with almost no hair. We all looked like shorn sheep! The orders throughout my time in the Air Force would be that hair can be as long as you want as long as it is under your blue beret and out or sight from any officers.

We had classes each day outlining how the RAF military operates. We had classes on how to salute an officer and when not to salute an officer. We were shown films of all the venereal diseases that an airman can get if he is not careful. We were given a full medical examination top to toe and out came the needles for our bombardment of shots on our behind. Some of the men were scared to get shots and some of the larger men boasted that it was nothing. When it came time when the needles started to stick in your arm and butt it was the larger men that rolled their eyes backward and collapsed on to the floor. We all had a great laugh over that.

We had classes for typing and were shown movies of how firearms are put together. The was also some history films of how the Air Force became the RAF showing some of the old films of biplane aircraft during the first World War. We were beginning to come to the end of the week of pre-induction training and were then told that the following day we would be loaded on to a troop train that would take us to our destination for basic training.

We had discovered that the RAF had four different types of basic training camps throughout the country and we did not know as yet where we would be going. It appeared that when we took the classes, each class was of a different kind that was related to what our work would be for the next two years. We were inducted people and not volunteers so we had no choice as to what we would be doing while we were in the service. I was told that because of my Uncle Cyril had been an air gunner I was destined eventually to take his position as flight crew. I would be trained for flight crew. There were many other jobs as aircrew, as an example there was the was the radar operator and wireless operator and gunnery so we did not know what we would be assigned to and to where we would be going that was specializing in that type of job. They indicated that during our twelve weeks of basic training all tests would be completed we would know what our duties would be for our active duty in the RAF when we had completed boot camp.

On the last full day at RAF Cardington, we were all told to put on our best uniforms and be ready to have our photo taken before we were to leave for basic training. We gathered together leaving our kit bags out of the camera field of view and the group photo was taken. I still have this photo and often wonder where all of my comrades are now.

On the last day at RAF Cardington at the crack of dawn we had a rude awakening from our pampered first week in the RAF. Somebody bellowed get up now. Do your ablutions shouted the hut sergeant, which meant we had to clean up, shower and be ready for breakfast in fifteen minutes then line up outside of our hut in work uniform ready for embarking on the train. This was the time when we found out where our basic training camp would be. It was to be RAF West Kirby located in the north of England on its west coast near Manchester. So now the first good week was past and the real training was 200 miles away. We got ready as fast as possible and returned to our hut. We were instructed to fill up our kitbags with all of our possessions and leave the kit bags in front of the hut. Each kit bag had our name and serial number marked in large letters on the kit bag. We were ordered to line up again in double file of two men across and then marched to the mess hall and given a package lunch that would be eaten when told to do so when on the train. The trucks that brought us to the camp were waiting to take us to the railroad station and then on to our basic training camp. We had a few minutes to say cheerio and good luck to some of the friends we had made who themselves were going to three other basic camps. We arrived at the same railway station that we had arrived a week before and loaded onto the train to carry us off for a full twelve weeks of basic training to learn to be a soldier in the RAF. I thought to myself, wait a minute we are in the RAF and were not supposed to be soldiering but they had other ideas. If an airfield had to be defended then we would be prepared to defend it by this training. They had loaded all of our kit bags into the luggage car each identified by name, rank and number and would be waiting for us upon our arrival.

We were going to West Kirby for twelve weeks to be trained as soldiers. The train was fairly comfortable for us. The railway car had four seats across in rows down the railway car. There were about forty airman recruits loaded into each car and since we did not carry our kit bags, we did not have much baggage. Some of the boys played cards while others sang in groups of the songs that had been sung for the past twenty years since the end of the First and Second World War. While others like me just looked out the window at the fields and meadows that the train was passing through wondering just what lay in wait for us at the end of the line at West Kirby.

After about four hours of travel the train began to slow down deep in the countryside. The train stopped and everyone was wondering why it had stopped. Suddenly, it started up again and soon we could see why we had stopped. They had turned a switch directing the train onto a branch line with a single track that took us off of the main line through some country that looked very different from the place we had just left. We could see a wide stretch of water which was a large river. We crossed over this wide river that we found out later was the river Mersey. We were passing through some rough country, which appeared to be bleak with very little habitation. We pulled into a large siding that had many railway cars. Suddenly, the train stopped. We had arrived at our final destination for our basic training camp. There was loud shouting of the sergeants screaming directions to us to get off of the train and get into line ready to pick up your kit bags. Get off! Get off! Now they were screaming. We all scrambled off the train on to the platform and started looking around to see what we were getting into. I soon found out.

We had arrived at the gates of hell and were being marched through the open door of the basic training camp called West Kirby where I would be living for the next twelve weeks. What was even worse was that of all my friends that I had made at camp Cardington had all been sent to other camps and I did not know anyone here in our group, so I needed to make friends here quickly. After the train had stopped and the NCOs now were called drill instructors had now taken over our lives that the full intent was to somehow replace our civilian lives and turn us into airmen. Over a loud speaker we were told to get off the train in two minutes and assemble alongside the railroad track in formation. We were then told to step forward when our names were called. Slowly it went from an orderly bunch of eighteen year olds to a disorderly bunch of eighteen year olds that did not know what to do and were a very confused and scared bunch of recruits. However, the drill instructors took no time at all to tell us what we had to do and do it quickly in between bellowing out orders and cussing us out to all of us and quickly we were in an orderly line.

He got us into line to recover our kit bags that had been put into the baggage cars of the train. He screamed to us that we had to reclaim our kit bags in less than ten minutes and then to get back in line with our kit bags. We looked across this large parade ground or square and there were our kitbags piled at least 10 feet high on one large pile. The drill instructors screamed at us that we had ten minutes to find our kit bag and get back in line. He gave a count of 1 to 10 and said now! Two hundred scared eighteen year olds rushed towards the pile of kit bags looking for their serial number that was printed on the kitbag hoping that theirs were on the edge of the pile and not underneath the huge central pile. There was absolute chaos as we all dove into the mass of kit bags looking for our number. I supposed looking at it from the outside it must have looked funny, but I was lucky as I found my kitbag was on the outside of the perimeter of bags. I soon got my bag hooked over my shoulder and found my way back to the line that was forming for those who were also lucky enough to find their kitbag quickly. The poor guys who were still scratching their heads trying to find their bag were still hunting and finally did find their bags but in much longer time than was allowed by the DIs (drill instructors). They were going to be late and will pay for that tardiness. They slowly made their way back to the line. The DI's slowly walked along the line picking out the last dozen or so of the late comers who could not find their kitbags and told them to report to the squadron office after evening meal for jankers punishment for not being quick enough. Jankers was slang for extra work in the kitchen after meals which took about an extra two hours. We did not know what that term jankers meant but we were soon about to find out. It was a punishing kitchen work after hours, scrubbing the pots and pans and counters.

We were then marched in line to our new quarters which were similar to the ones at RAF Cardington. Each recruit airman had his own bed space which was an area that covered a bed and bedside table. Each airman was responsible for his own bed space for spot inspections. There was also a footlocker at the end of the bed to put all of our personal belongings. The bedside table had shelves where we were told to put our clean underwear neatly folded. There was a small closet to hang up our two kinds of uniforms. One uniform was for work and other for only official events such as ceremonies and outside camp travel. There were about thirty men living in each hut and in the center of the hut was a pot-bellied wood stove to keep the barracks warm since it was March and still cold in northern England. The hut had no ceiling but a pointed raftered roof. The end of each hut was connected to the communal bath house, such as toilets, washbasins and showers and it was all located in the open for all to see.

The drill sergeant had his own small room at the end for himself and he became our drill instructor for the twelve weeks that we would be living and working there during our training. After the initial confusion while settling in we were given the order to stand by our beds for inspection. The sergeant's name was Callahan and he was huge man with a small waist which we quickly called him wasp waist. He yelled and screamed at us, pushing and shoving any recruit that was too slow to move at his command until we got into some degree of order. As we settled down the sergeant gave us a welcome talk. He described that we were to get up at 5:00 am each morning. He said he would be our alarm clock. We soon found out what that alarm clock was to be.

He described our first four weeks of training would be marching, drilling, marching in perfect drill order and learning to use our weapons. We would after 12 weeks become a military group which he would personally be held responsible during the 12 weeks of training. He said that we would not be allowed outside the base until the first six weeks of training had been completed and then maybe, just maybe, we would be issued a weekend pass.

I remember that a few of the men asked some questions which were immediately rebuffed by the Sargent who told them not to not speak unless spoken to. I began to wonder what this had to do with being in the Air Force. It was more like being in the Army. We would have to learn and be shown the military courtesies of saluting to all officers. Since he was a Sargent, we were not to call him sir because he was a non-commissioned officer. We were to call him sergeant whenever we discussed anything with him. We would wear our blue berets all the time except in a building. Our uniforms were the color of medium blue. He then said that we had the rest of the afternoon to get acquainted with each other and were given the evening free. Training would start at 5:00 am the next morning.

The first four weeks were learning how to march in groups. Some were small groups of about fifty men. Some were as many as a small Army marching in time to the clicking of boots on parade grounds and others to turn left wheel, turn right wheel, right turn of left, all orchestrated by the drill instructor. Every day was the same routine but gradually we found out that practice did work well and after about a week or so we were marching in almost perfect precision to the tune of various songs to keep us into step. The Sargent was never satisfied and called us all the bad names that we were lower than sub-human, lower than whale feces, the usual insulting remarks. Like he had never seen such a bunch of losers to train, but all in all by the end of the fourth week we were fairly good at marching in unison together working as one unit.

We had other jobs to do also during that first four weeks. The men who did not respond quickly enough would be punished and go on jankers like latrine cleaning duty, cook house chores like cleaning dirty barrels or potato pealing of mountains of potatoes. Everyone wanted to skive off which was slang to take it easy or do assigned duty except marching and drilling and make sure everyone could see you doing something for the day's work. We were ordered to do the most senseless work anyone could imagine. Outside our barracks hut that we lived in we were told to paint the grass surrounding our hut green. They actually gave us a can of green paint. Other times we were told to paint the coal pile that we used for the potbellied stove at night white. There were some really crazy jobs we were told to do and as is in any military base they had to keep us busy. We had no time on our hands to complain. Nobody thought that the painted coal burning in the stove might be a hazard to our health. One day we were told to pick up trash around the camp so my friend and I picked up a large empty garbage can, each one holding the handle on each side of the can and walked around the camp doing nothing. Any officer that saw us thought we were collecting trash up on the camp roads but all we were doing was walking around with an empty garbage can. Another skive was to have a manila file tucked under our arms and would march around the camp all day and nobody stopped us. We did that many times to while away the time.

We had many unscheduled barrack inspections by the officer in charge of a large number of huts. We would not be told about the pending hut inspection until the last minute that there would be a complete inspection of the barracks within a half an hour and everything had to be white glove clean. We went into a panic because we were looking forward to moving on to the next phase of basic training which would be gunnery and rifle training, both small arms and light machine gun (LMG). The inspection consisted not only of the barracks to be spotlessly clean but our personal belongs were to be put into the correct order. We had at our bedside table a display of our underwear folded in perfect inches apart. We had a small piece of cardboard the size and the width of a tee shirt. It was two inches high and eight inches wide. We had to fold our tee shirts in half with the width wrapped around the tee shirt and the height exactly two inches high. Our foot locker would be left open so that the officer would see in side. All of our clothes were to be in regulation order and he even had a measuring stick to ensure that the regulations were met. We had to clean all windows and windowsills of any dust. The floor had to be swept perfectly clean. The bedroll mattress had to be rolled back exposing the springs of the bed. Even the bed springs would have to be cleaned.

When all was ready the sergeant would enter the hut with a loud voice calling attention, officer in the barracks. Our barracks sergeant would then announce inspection ready and we would all stand at attention at the end of our beds as the officer would come into the barracks. He would examine the barracks like under a microscope and even put his white gloved finger up into the springs under the mattress looking for any dust. He ran his finger along the windowsills to check for dust. Each airman's uniform had to be clean and the brasses on his belt and other items on his uniform were bright and shiny. He checked inside the clothes closet to see our best uniforms were hanging. He checked to see that our boots were shiny. He would check the potbellied stove to see that it was blackened by special polish with the coal bin and coal nuggets all in order and piled in regulation order. The officer walked down one side of the bed spaces looking at each airman, checking his uniform while we were at attention. We stared straight ahead and held our pant seams by our fingers, forefinger and thumb and then he walked down the other side pausing and checking how clean the bed space of each was. He ordered us to hold out our hands to check dirt under the fingernails. He wore the uniform of a squadron commander with a swagger stick under his arm. He would gaze at each airman eye ball to eye ball as he paused at each airman asking if there were any complaints. No one ever complained.

I had not been outside of the camp in the real world for over four weeks and was getting to the point where I just had to get out. Somehow, I felt like I was in prison. They posted on the bill board of the barracks that if any airman wanted to go to Sunday services at the local church for the upcoming Sunday, permission would be given and transportation would be provided for us to do so. I volunteered just to get out of the camp and see the real world. That Sunday evening, we boarded a blue Air Force bus that took us to the local church which was Church of England (Episcopal). It felt just great to pass through the gates into the real world for just a while, in fact on reflection it seemed strange to be free for a few hours.

We had a good group of boys in our hut although a few were of the exception. They all played jokes on each other and everyone got their turn and my turn came just before one of the largest important inspections that had been scheduled within a half an hour. I had cleaned my bed space like it was sparkling clean and we had about a half an hour before the scheduled hut inspection. My bed was made so good that I could bounce a coin on the blankets and it would bounce back. I went out back to the bathrooms at the end of the hut and returned back to my bed space and to my horror there was nothing there. My bed, my bedside table all had gone, including my closet and its clothes hanging inside there ready for the important hut inspection and here I was with nothing for the officer to inspect. There was just an empty space where I had lived for four weeks and now coming up in a few minutes there was a big important barracks inspection. They all laughed at my discomfort and my panic then they very quickly pointed up to the rafters in the hut.

There balancing perilously on the two cross beams were my furniture, my bed and bedroll mattress. With barely ten minutes to spare the boys all chipped in climbing up to the rafters and brought down the furniture and placed it in its rightful space. We all got it together just in time before inspection began and the inspection luckily was a quick one. The officer had some other place to go and went through the motions of an inspection leaving quickly to go to another hut. The officer said that he was going on leave himself that evening so he was not so particular in his inspection on that day. I was sure I was going to be put on jankers for that and probably lose my first weekend pass issued after six weeks had been completed in the twelve-week basic training course. All went well and we passed the inspection and a pass was issued to our barracks to go outside the camp the following weekend.

RAF West Kirby was about fifteen miles from Manchester, a port city on the Mersey River. At noon on the first Saturday of the sixth week we were given a 48 hour pass or leave of absence. This was the second time that we had been outside of the main gate of the camp in over six weeks and we could not wait to get out of this place. There was a bus service from West Kirby to Manchester with the bus stop at the main gate. A nearby RAF airbase was quite a good thing for the local shopkeepers although they did not like the idea of a military base in their home town. The economy was very good for them and many civilians were employed and worked inside the base and made the local economy strong.

The bus pulled up to the bus stop and we all piled in and went into the city of Manchester. We all were looking for bars and dancehalls to have the opportunity to pick up some girls where most of the local girls also went to pick up some RAF recruits. After arriving in Manchester, we all broke up into small groups to check out the city and each went their separate way to see firsthand what it had to offer young eighteen year olds in the ways of entertainment. We had found out that there was a large dance hall in the city and soon we found out what was going on. The dance hall was just great and they had one of the last of the big band era bands playing to crowds of uniformed men from nearby Army and Air Force bases. The evening came to a close and we had to make sure we caught the last Air Force bus back to the West Kirby airbase to be through the main gate by 23:59 hours, Sunday midnight.

The next phase of our training was much more interesting. The first area was learning how to assemble and disassemble a light machine gun. We practiced for hours until we were able to do it blindfolded in the dark. We then had to learn how to fire the weapon. I felt very good about this weapon. It could be fired as a single shot weapon or a rapid firing machine gun when you spray the target with rounds.

Next came the assault course where we had to climb over and under objects that had barbed wire covering the top and bottom carrying a rifle in our arms, walking on our elbows. As we were creeping under the cover of barbed wire eight inches above our head, they were firing live ammunition over our heads. It was a great incentive to keep our head down while live ammunition was passing eight inches above over our heads. We went through heavy swamp like ground and over brick walls with the sergeants screaming at us urging us on as fast as we could. Swinging on ropes and falling down into the filthy, muddy water, we got soaked to the skin. I do remember asking myself why we had to do this since we joined the Air Force not the Marines. We finally finished the assault course and was pleased with myself that I had passed through. Some did not make it and had to do it all over again. I was skinny and could crawl through very low fences but still remembered to keep my butt down.

The next course was the rifle range where we would be handling a 303 Enfield rifle, which for the past fifty years was the mainstay of the British armed forces. We would all be told to lay down with our legs at an angle and aim for the targets which were about 500 yards down the range. We had to get a two inch grouping, which was a set of rounds on the target, to pass this phase of active target activity. Behind offside to the targets, the NCOs had put an airman in a position and was placed there to show if the shooter managed to get the two inch grouping that was required. When the shooter missed the target as well as the two inch grouping the airman at the target waived a large red flag from side to side, it was called out as a Maggie's drawers. That meant that the shooter had not got his two inch grouping and then it had to be done again until all the grouping was completed. I just could not get this tight grouping and tried many times and I was the last one in our group to still be trying to get it. I got Maggie's drawers so many times and the NCO was getting fed up with these results. We could not officially complete the target training unless we all manage to get the two-inch grouping. My drill instructor was anxious for me to get the grouping. He snatched my rifle away from me with a disgusted grunt and fired the rounds into a perfect two inch grouping within seconds. His passing remark to me was son, you need to get more practice. He then shoved my rifle back to me and told me to join the others. He had shot a perfect grouping on the target which went to my credit and strangely enough a few days later I was approached by one of the officers who complemented me on my great shooting on the rifle range with such precision. He invited me to join the squadron gun club. I respectfully declined his suggestion not wishing to get anyone into trouble, but I sure appreciated the help of my drill instructor because it would be a discredit to him if his group did not complete grouping on the target range.

We were coming to the last part of our twelve week basic training. Since we were in the Air Force, we might get shot down over enemy territory we would have to fend for ourselves. We began training in survival tactics mostly in theory in one of the huts. Many of these non-commissioned training officers were experienced airman who had survived the Second World War. Sometimes I thought that in their minds they were still fighting that war. In fact, we were in a cold war with Soviet Russia in a different kind of war, when aircraft was said to actually carry nuclear weapons on the B52 bombers that constantly circled Europe.

We spent many hours in special classes being lectured on how to survive on different terrains and finally the day came when we were sent out into the north Welsh mountains for a week on a survival course. Each of us was given our rifle and six rounds and extra ammo and I filled up my backpack with some of the items we would need. We also were given a ground sheet which is a canvas waterproof sheet which we rolled up and wrapped around our shoulders. We were kept in our original flight group of 11. It was the equivalent of a bomber air crew. We were then trucked out 30 miles away from the base and ordered to return to base within eight days. We were to be driven by truck up into the Welsh mountains in early April where there was still snow on the ground. I was going into those mountains and ridges where there was snow on the ground with little food or shelter in bitter cold conditions. We carried our ground sheets which were rolled up and wrapped around our shoulders. These waterproofed ground sheets could also be used as tents that when put together would make enough room for a tent for two men. We had to live off the land for the next week. As the truck climbed up the steep mountains of Wales we considered just where we were going. For now, we were a quiet bunch of recruits contemplating our next few days in a cold wilderness in Wales.

First, we voted for a leader to act as the captain of this fictitious airplane crew that had been shot down and crashed. We voted for one of the men to be the pilot. We were given a compass so at least we knew which direction to get back to base. In a few hours in the truck we had reached the top of the ridge of some mountains of Wales where suddenly the truck stopped and we were told to get out and start walking. The Sargent rechecked our names on his list to ensure that we were all there and said that we had one week to walk the 30 miles back to West Kirby. He confirmed that we had some rations. The sergeant gave us a simple map to show where to head and he wished us good luck and climbed up into the cab of the truck and off it went out of sight down the mountainside.

The first decision we made was to get together and check out the map and find the quickest way down the mountains towards the coast where our base was. We were alone all eleven of us, cold, feeling miserable and looking to start our way down the hills into the fields where there might be a farmer's fields of potatoes and turnips available to steal. In our back pack each of us had been given some matches to light a fire and our mess kits to fill with water to boil tea, potatoes and turnips if we managed to liberate from the farmer's fields. It began to snow and we were getting wet. Looking across the mountain ranges we could see the highest mountain in Wales named Mount Snowden. Checking our compass, we started heading north towards where we came from and headed across the snowy land and started our long trek back.

We each had a ground sheet that had been issued to us at the beginning of our induction. This was like a waterproof poncho with eyelets sewed in the side, so after we had walked about five miles we decided that we should make camp for the first night and regroup ourselves. We tried to keep out of sight that nobody could see us but all we could find was lots of sheep, mutton on the hoof. We divided ourselves at night into two groups, which gave us a two man teams. With five tents we put our ponchos together by stringing each eyelet together to make a tent for each two men. One lucky airman was the odd man out since he would have a tent all for himself. We stood watch every two hours, but it was so cold we never really saw anybody most of the time.

We needed ridge poles for each tent so we did find some fairly straight pieces of tree branches that did the job. We then found two strong four foot high Y sticks for the ridgepole to rest. We managed to build a tent which would shelter us from the snow and rain that was coming down, but the bare ground that we had to lay on was wet ground. We had nothing to cover the ground of snow inside the tent. We therefore had to sleep on the wet snow with at least a roof of waterproof poncho to keep off the snow.

The next day we came across a farm that had turnips still in the field with some potatoes in a barn. We scouted out the fields and carried on walking back towards the north in the direction back to the camp. We were wet and miserable by the third day and we had only covered 15 miles. We lit a fire from some dry branches that we found inside some farmers barn and boiled some potatoes and carrots in a pan. We continued to walk back to the base. Each day of that week was just cold and wet but we were progressing towards our destination.

By now as the days passed by we were nearing some sort of civilization where there would be roads and maybe trucks. We were in the fifth day of returning back to base with about ten miles to go when we came across a busy road that one of us recognized. It was the main trucking highway from London. We thought that this would be a good location to be picked up by a large truck. We all were very tired and wet so one of the groups had what we thought a brilliant idea. He suggested that why not try and get a ride on a truck back to base, no more walking in the rain. There were some houses now appearing and we knew that we would be able to find some sort of truck that would give us a lift close to the West Kirby base especially since we were in military uniform. We were dirty, cold, and unshaven but still in our RAF uniforms with the blue beret on our heads. One of our group decided that he had had enough and said that he was going to raise his thumb to try and get a lift from a truck for all of us. We were in such a state of suffering that we agreed, so as soon as we arrived at a main road that was going towards Manchester, we would start hitch hiking. In those days a uniformed military man could easily get a ride when hitch hiking.

We stood on the curbside holding out our thumbs for a ride when a spiffy small sports car came along and began to slow down and stop at our location. But we had made a serious mistake to thumb a ride at this vehicle. Driving inside this small car was an RAF officer in uniform. He asked us where we were from and where we were going. Someone told him RAF West Kirby which made him angrier because if you were in enemy country you never disclosed where you came from. He said you men are on a survival course and should not tell anyone where you are from. He intoned as per the Geneva Convention you are only required to give your name, rank, and serial number. At this time, I thought he was actually going to put his hand inside his blue jacket pocket and produce the actual document of the Geneva Convention. He said you never tell an enemy if you're captured, what base you came from or where you are going. He then asked us if we knew who he was and we said that we did not know. To our discomfort he identified himself as the commandant of the West Kirby RAF base and that he thought it was just disgraceful that a dirty bunch of recruits were standing on the main highway in the Queens Air Force uniform begging for a lift. He ordered us to continue back to base and ordered not to continue any more hitch hiking in the uniform of his Queen Elizabeth. He wrote down in a small book all of our names and serial numbers. He said he considered this a major offence and he ordered us to report to the Squadron office at 8:00 hours the following morning to receive punishment for this crime. He had an absolutely disgusted look on his face and his mustache twitched with anger or supposed anger. But I notice a twinkle in his eye before he drove off disappearing around the corner of the road never to be seen again. We were all devastated by this turn of events and started arguing between ourselves as to whose idea this was in the first place to hitch hike and now, we would probably lose our coming up weekend pass. We decided that we would not try hitch hiking again and we did finally arrive back at the base late the next day very tired, cold and very unhappy bunch of recruits.

The next morning, we all went to the squadron office at 8:00 am by order of the commanding officer. The squadron office clerk asked us what we wanted and we told him that we were told by the base commander to report there at 8:00 am. He said that he knew nothing about reporting this incident and to go about our business for the day. I do not know who this officer was in the sports car, but I was very glad it appeared to be a hoax and nothing more came about it. We did not hear anything more, but we did not forget it.

We were nearing the end of our 12 week basic training but we still did not know where we would be eventually be posted to when we returned from our weeks leave after completing our basic training. One of the clerks at the squadron office told one of the men that the list was ready for us to see what our posting would be after graduation and where we would be sent for the second part of our service for queen and country. Everyone by now heard that the list had been posted and we crowded into the squadron office to see the good or bad news. For me it was bad news. I was supposed to be sent to aircrew training after recruit training, but with the Air Force changing over from propeller bombers to the new V jet Delta bombers there would be a cut in air crew, requiring only three air crew members needed by each aircraft instead of eleven. The Air Force had changed in a short time and I kept asking myself what was I doing here!

There were now only three types of operational bombers with a triangle shaped fuselage V airframe. They were called the Victor, Valiant and Vulcan bombers. Each type of aircraft carried only three or four crew members. I was not going to be aircrew since they did not require as many airmen to fly these new V jets. Now I asked myself what I was going to do in the RAF for the next 18 months. I was now being officially described as redundant, meaning not required. I actually felt like I had been laid off from a civilian job.

I did finally find my name on the posting board and yes, it was an OK and almost good news that I would be posted to radio school RAF Compton Bassett in the county of Wiltshire. I was very happy and I would soon be going home on my first leave after our passing out in a parade ceremony which was scheduled for the following Saturday. We had almost come to the end of our training and were ready to graduate. The term they used to pass out meaning to pass out in review and to have completed basic training. The amount of airman completing the course was about four hundred, each broken up into a flight group. We had managed to be very good at marching in a tight line and turning at right angles when the Sargent said to left wheel, we did the maneuver in perfect unison. He told us that he wanted to hear our eyeballs click when he shouted eyes right as we passed the reviewing stand since the base commander stood at the reviewing stand. I did hear eyeballs click. As we marched toward the reviewing stand I saw the base commander saluting us. To my amazement I suddenly recognized him as the officer who had stopped us on the highway and who told us of his disgust of all airmen who hitch hiked in the queen's uniform. It apparently was not a hoax but he was decent enough not to follow up his orders to report to the squadron office and we were now in the clear. Maybe in his early career he also went on a survival course at officers training and hitched a ride somewhere. We stopped in front of the reviewing stand and the camp commander made a speech for about ten minutes and declared that we had completed our twelve weeks of recruit training and that we now could remove the yellow circle of plastic behind the RAF badge in our beret. He now proclaimed us promoted in rank from ACC2 to ACC1 and wished us well and dismissed us. When the commander said that we were no longer recruits we tossed out berets up in the air.

We marched away from the reviewing stand perfectly as one, all together during the parade, marching in time to the base band as one. I remember we were all very proud of what we had accomplished and had been taught to do. We never forgot our last three serial numbers of our personal serial number and never would during our lifetime. The base commander had invited our family members to attend the passing out ceremony and some did attend, but I did not expect my mother to be there since she had to work.

We had all been screamed at, insulted and cursed during training and we all would never be the same person as the young civilian that had been unloaded from the train at the camp 12 weeks before. We had become men with discipline and a direction to go in our lives. The time had come to complete our training which was to form up in columns and pass again in review of the families of the recruits that had watched. Our column was now four abreast and we marched in formation away from the reviewing stand. The band was in the front of our group playing so well.

After the ceremonies were completed, we were ready to pack our kit bags with all our personal belongings and say good bye to friends that I had during this training that made this place unforgettable. Our drill instructor assembled us together now, quite a different man than when we first met him. He congratulated us on being one of the best recruit groups he had trained and wished us well. He shook each airman's hand and he wished him all the best of luck and went back to his room. I suspect he was expecting more recruits coming in on the next train and was preparing their welcome.

I went over to the squadron office to collect my orders and paper work which included our railroad ticket to get home. It was a free round trip train ticket to get home for a week's leave and another train ticket to get me to my new posting in the south of England in Compton Basset, Wiltshire. This was an RAF radio/cypher school where my new assignment as a radio operator in telecommunications would begin in just over two weeks' time.

While taking the train down from Manchester to London I began to think about what I wanted to do when my military time was up and I began thinking it would it be possible that I could plan to go to New York one day when I had completed my service. I was still writing to my pen friend Joan Mason in Flushing, New York, but then I answered my own question by thinking about who was going to take care of mum and Colin if I left the country? I had arranged when I entered the service in the RAF for their accounting department to take out 90% of my pay allotment to my mother which was sent to her each month through the time while I was still in the Air Force. However, I reasoned to myself that this is in the future and I would have to get through the next two years of National Service hoping that there was not going to be a war while I was in the military. I did get home and what a great time it was to see mum and Colin again.

It seemed very strange for me to be away from the airbase and be sleeping in a soft bed. As soon as I settled in, I went around to the family visiting everybody including my grandmother and uncles and aunts in my blue RAF uniform with a blue beret on my head with brass RAF emblem. I was so proud of that and everyone said I looked good, but was a little skinny kid that needed to put on some weight. They asked me with a wink of eye don't they feed you much in the Air Force?

My best friend Brian who lived across the street was also home on leave and had arrived home about the same time as me. He was in the Army entering at about the same time as me so we both had stories to tell and describe our experiences while we were in recruit training.

Mum was really happy and was parading me around the neighborhood as mothers have done for centuries each time their sons went off to join the military and returned home on their first leave. Since many of my friends all got called up for duty at the same time, they all had their leaves at the same time so they were all on leave at the same time.

We decided that the next Saturday night we would go out on a big bash at the Fishmongers Arms. They played great music there and played Dixieland jazz which we all enjoyed. However, we all drank too many strong beers and for the first and last time in my life I really got drunk. I found myself sitting on the curbside with my friends waiting for the last bus to take us home and singing the old songs together on the bus. My friend Brian who lived across the street from me took me to the door of my house and tried to be quiet so as to not wake up my mum but I could not find my key. We had to knock on the door with the door knocker. My mum came downstairs and looked at my condition and grabbed me up the stairs and put me to bed. That was the first time and only time that I got into that condition.

After two great weeks my leave was over, we had to report to our new postings, but we had a problem. As I explained before the country had gone socialist and the government had nationalized most of the previous private companies. The train systems were run and owned by the government and were always at odds with the unions and consistently going on strike. Most branches of industry were now owned by the government which caused travel problems. Over the last few days of my leave the transport workers had gone on strike and there was no way that we could travel. No trains or buses were running so I could not get to my new Air Force base in Wiltshire. We did not own a car or have a phone so we had to listen to the BBC radio announcer who would advise military personnel trying to travel to their stations. This affected every military traveler so on the radio an announcer told all servicemen to report to their nearest military base.

Being in the Air Force I had to locate the nearest RAF airfield which was not too far away at a place called East Horndon. I took the bus on the day I had to report and reported to RAF East Horndon which was about twenty miles away. There had to be over a thousand airmen sitting on the grass alongside of the runways waiting for some kind of transport to get back to home bases airfields. Some airmen had to fly overseas and they could not feed all of these men. Many of the airmen were flown out immediately to bases overseas and some to other airfields. They seemed to have forgotten about us but after a while we were told that we should go home and wait for instructions. I checked in at the air base squadron office to register that I was not AWOL and was taken by Air Force bus to the nearest bus stop and took the bus back home.

After a few days the strike was settled, the trains were running again and I once again said goodbye to mum and Colin. I took the bus to into London's Waterloo Train Station and left again by train for my new posting at the radio school in the southeast of England in a small town of Colne, Compton Basset, in the county of Wiltshire. Since RAF Compton Bassett was near the train station, the RAF trucks were waiting for all of the returning airman after the transport strike. With my kitbag on my shoulder, I found my designated truck, loaded my kit bag onto the bed of the truck with all the others and arrived at my new base with one exception. I now had been promoted to ACC1, one notch above basic training. I was back to being a human being again and somebody else was hearing drill sergeant Callahan at the gates of hell screaming at new recruits they were lower than sub human beings.

June 1955, RAF Compton Bassett

RAF COMPTON BASSETT was one of the many RAF stations that were the second step after basic training for recruits. There were other stations across the country that received recruits from basic training for other schools such as ground crew training or as armorers who loaded bombs and other weapons on to the bomb racks underneath the aircraft. RAF Compton Bassett was a special school for radio and cryptology, intelligence training and was strictly for radio school training for airman starting out into radio communications after basic training.

RAF Compton Bassett was quite large as we entered through the gates of the base strictly guarded by the RAF regiment guards who were really MPs. The truck pulled up outside the squadron office and we all lined up and were addressed by the base commander who welcomed us to RAF Compton Bassett. What a difference from the NCOs welcome of our previous basic training camp at West Kirby. The commander told us that we would be staying at this school training for the next 12 weeks while we learned how to communicate by radio and other electronic sources. After the short speech he turned us over to a Sargent who walked us through the camp to find the barracks hut that was now assigned to us, which would be our home for the next three months.

We were told to stop outside one particular hut and then to select our bed space and he would address us once we had settled in within half an hour. Again, we were taken to get our supplies needed for our stay such as a bed mattress, bed sheets and pillows and we also drew other basics. He outlined what our duties were, where our initial classrooms were located and the times to arrive at class each morning. Then he marched us around the camp showing us where the mess hall was located and other locations that we needed to know. We had a camp recreation room with pool tables and darts, a canteen to buy tea and other mess hall food and it seemed quite good after the past three months at basic training.

We were in the part of the camp that consisted of huts that were classrooms filled with all types of radio transmitters, teletype machines, crypto machines and typewriters. At the end of the first day, we were told by one of the officers to gather around since he had some information for us. He told us what we already knew that some of us had been inducted to train as aircrew. There was some disappointment throughout our group and one airman asked very carefully what we would be doing on this airfield. He replied that we would be trained as radio operatives and some coding and decoding codes and we would be told more at a later date and he left it at that.

I wondered at that time what was we ex-civilians were doing here being drafted to a job that no longer existed. Maybe they would send us back as civilians, but no such luck. They had us and they were going to use us even when there wasn't any war going on at that time. The key word here was that within a year Britain would be in a war in Egypt fighting for the Suez Canal which was owned by Britain and France. Maybe someone in the upper levels knew about that.

After the meeting we all returned back to our quarters and began to get acquainted with each other since we would be living together for the next three months. They seemed to be a nice bunch of boys from all over England and I thought hopefully that we would all get along together. Our first morning started off well enough. The breakfast in the mess hall was quite good compared with what we had at boot camp and we were ready to get started at our new training. The Sargent began by introducing himself and showed us that for the first two weeks we would learn how to type. I was not pleased with that answer since I had never touched a typewriter in my life. To complete this course, we had to be able to type thirty words per minute without any mistakes before we could move on to other classes and other jobs. After a week we all had a good ability to do this and were ready to move on to the next step.

One good thing about this camp was that it was only 60 miles from London, my home town, so after the second week at Compton Bassett we were allowed to have our first weekend pass. I did not have much money since I had requested to the Air Force that I still wanted them to send 90% of my pay to my mother as a monthly allotment. That left me with almost nothing for myself to spend. I knew that in the future the only way I could get home on weekends was to hitchhike along the road and pick up a ride from civilian travelers and truck drivers. We had duty in the classrooms for only eight hours each day and were allowed the evenings either to play pool or study. There was a movie theater on base which was free and in the canteen we could buy various items, but I had no money to indulge in any of these purchases.

The county of Wiltshire is a very beautiful county near Stonehenge and was filled with all kinds of old time ghosts and stories about the Druids who were thought to have built Stonehenge. During the summer evenings sometimes, I would walk for hours by myself along the lanes walking up the hills to where the giant white horse was carved thousands a of years ago on a hillside. This horse had been carved out of the limestone of the hill and was at least the side of the hill in size and could be seen for miles. No one knew who created this carving of a walking horse in white chalk on the side of the green hill. It was considered at least three thousand years old and maybe older than that. Stonehenge itself was one of my memories.

Walking up the lane from the camp entrance to the main road there was a café that had a juke box. I would go there for a cup of tea and a cake and listen to the music from their juke box. My favorite song that was very popular at that time was Unchained Melody sung at the time by Al Hibler. I still enjoy listening to that beautiful song on the radio.

I will not go into our military training too much since I do not think that it has any bearing on my story. Each weekend on a Saturday morning I would keep my uniform on and go up on to the highway and start hitchhiking the sixty miles to London and home to mum and Colin. I was still thinking of going to America when I was discharged from the Air Force but an interesting event occurred. On one of those Saturday mornings while I was standing on the side of the road with my thumb out to all passing cars I was looking for a ride to London. In those days military servicemen in uniform would always be picked up by some civilian cars since civilian drivers still had that wartime good feeling towards the military especially the RAF. While I was standing on the roadside curb with my thumb out, I saw a car coming towards me that began to slow down. I put out my thumb and then I could see that it was an American car, a convertible painted red on the outside with white interior seats on the inside. Driving the car was an American Air Force airman clothed in an American Air Force uniform. He stopped and asked in a definite English accent where was I heading? I told him that I was heading for London and he said to hop in since he was going to London also. He looked like an American Air Force airman in an American Air Force uniform but to my surprise he had an English London accent. At first this did not make any sense to me at all as I opened the car door to get in. He told me that four years before he was discharged from the RAF, he left England and went to America. He stayed in America for a year and joined the US Air Force and was then sent back to a base in southwest England. The car was his and after he joined the US Air Force, he had it shipped over when he was sent overseas by the USAF. It was so great to ride in that beautiful car.

I decided that at the end of my two years in the service I would definitely go to America and maybe do the same. I believe that was one of many deciding coincidental factors that made up my mind to visit America for six months on a working visit.

I had many adventures when I hitchhiked back and forth from home to Compton Basset on most weekends. I left RAF Compton Basset on a Saturday morning, hitchhiked home and spent the weekend visiting my Nan and family of uncles and aunts and then I got ready to leave home about 9:00 pm Sunday to get back to camp by morning at 6:00 am. I would then ride the bus up to the North Circular Road which was a ring road like a beltway around London. I would leave the bus at Heathrow airport entrance and start hitchhiking southwest usually arriving back at the base by the middle of the night. We had to be back through the camp gates before 6:00 am or we would be considered AWOL.

One Sunday late at night in the dark I was returning back to base walking backwards along the side of the road by the curb looking for a ride with my thumb stuck up when I suddenly fell into an open manhole filled with dirty water that had a very bad smell. Someone had left the manhole cover open and I had fallen into it. I was not hurt and I managed to climb out, but was wet up to my waist and I began to smell. Suddenly down the road I saw a truck coming. I stood on the side of the road with my thumb up to catch a ride. The truck stopped and told me to hop in. This trucker was a great guy and we talked for a long time as we travelled along the road. In those days the heater of the truck was inside a central console metal cowling between driver and passenger. He saw I was wet and I explained that I had fallen into an uncovered manhole filled with dirty water that had a very unhealthy smell. He said not to worry, take off your trousers and put them on top of the cowling of the heater and they will dry very quickly. I did that but after a while the heat started to make the trousers smell very bad. The truck driver went quiet for a while and then asked me what is that smell? I explained to him again my fall into the manhole. After a while the truck driver could not take it any longer, he asked me to get out because of the smell of the dirty water I had caused in his cab. He was nice about me getting off the truck, but we had a long night to go and he could not endure that smell any more. I climbed out of the truck and watched his tail lights disappear down the road and here I was without a ride to get back to my military base soaking wet and still waiting for a ride at 2:00 am in the morning.

The road that I had hitchhiked on was the A4 which was one of the main roads at that time leading to the southeast part of England. There were no modern motorways in those days so we had to drive through small villages on narrow roads where barely two trucks could pass each other. Some weekends on my Sunday evening return to base, after leaving home about 9:00 pm, I would take the bus to the nearest underground subway station in Leyton. I would get off the underground train at London Heathrow Airport, although at that time it was just a small airport previously used by the RAF during the war and now just beginning to become a major civilian airport in the future. Today it is one of the largest airports in the world. I would then start to hitchhike on the A4 road and was sometimes lucky when a truck stopped for me that was going most of the way to Compton Bassett. This particular night was a very cold and frosty night and I was glad to be wearing my Air

Force issued great coat that was made of wool. Being I had a lucky night for hitchhiking I arrived at the base around 2:00 am, much earlier than usual. After checking in at the base guard gate showing my ID 1250 identifying card, I made my way back to my barracks.

At first it seemed that I was one of the first to arrive back at the airfield except I did find one other airman who had reached the base before me. That one other person was from our barracks hut and was a friend of mine called Whiffing. We just called him Whiff for short. It was a very cold frosty night, very clear with a bright full moon that made it look like daylight. In the middle of our barracks there was a large pot-bellied fireplace stove and I could see that the fire was almost out and we needed more firewood. So, Whiff and I decided to cross over to the other side of the air base, in the older part of the air field, where there were some abandoned barracks left over from World War II. These barracks were filled with old furniture that was still piled up with old unused items, but we thought at first that the doors were locked and unable to open. There were three huts joined together so we tried to open the doors to all three, but they were nailed shut and we were unable to open up the doors to get the furniture. We then went to the one barrack hut that was on its own and checking it out found that with a little shoving and pushing we were able to open up the front door.

The night was almost bright as day with a full moon high in the sky and heavy frost on the grass. The barracks were designed with a pointed roof with open rafters inside with skylights set in the roof letting inside the hut any glowing moonlight which make the inside of the old barracks hut almost as bright as day. At first Whiff and I seem to have some sort of trouble pushing in the door, but were able to slide in since there was some kind of heavy furniture on the other side of the door. We slowly managed to push the furniture back into the hut and were able to see old broken furniture that could be used to break up for firewood. These huts were on the abandoned side of the airfield so all the furniture in the huts was discarded and would not be missed. The moon was shining so bright through the roof skylight that we could easily see to the far end of the hut and the wash rooms at the end. There was plenty of old furniture so we began to break up enough that we could carry.

Suddenly during a quiet period of us breaking up furniture we heard footsteps coming towards us. The footsteps seem to be coming towards us from the other end of the hut. The footsteps were slow and casual steps as though someone had just come out of the shower and was walking back to his bed space. But of course, there was no bed space anymore, just old broken up furniture. The footsteps were coming towards us but we could not see anybody causing the footsteps. I suddenly felt a cold feeling run up my spine and said to Whiff, do you hear those steps? But he had already heard the footsteps and run out and left me. I saw him running across the field. I looked again to the end of the hut where the footsteps were still walking towards me but I saw nothing. Even to the end of the hut there wasn't anyone walking towards me, but the footsteps still kept walking towards me. I could see right down to the end of the hut, but there was definitely nobody there. I quickly picked up some pieces of furniture and dashed out the open door and ran across the field not too far behind my friend Whiff.

When I arrived back to our barracks, we were still the only ones there and Whiff said to me did you hear those footsteps? I said yes, that I had really heard them so after we calmed down, we began to figure out what those footsteps could have been. We discarded the possibility that someone was on the roof playing a practical joke on us. The roof had a pointed top and would not allow anyone walking evenly and casually along the pointed roof causing the even footstep sound we had heard from inside the hut. We also discarded the idea that it was someone outside the hut, since the hut was surrounded by a grass lawn that had overgrown any pathways that might have been there. Also, that early in the morning we did not think anyone would play tricks so there we were with no explanation except to say that we heard those footsteps coming towards us from inside the hut. There was plenty of light through the windows on the roof that let the light into the hut for us to identify someone if there was anyone walking towards us, so it remains a mystery. We decided that it was probably a harmless ghost of a World War II airman that had just washed up in the wash room and was casually walking back to his bed space, but I do admit it was very scary at the time.

The time that I spent in RAF Compton Bassett radio/crypto school was for another 12 weeks so half way through that period I had a week's leave. I applied for a travel warrant to visit Guernsey in the Channel Islands. Mum and Colin were going to be there at that time so I thought that it would be a break from military life. I applied at the squadron office for a travel warrant and managed to get passage on a British Rail tramp steamer that carried 12 passengers leaving from Southampton docks. A travel warrant was given to all airmen that were traveling on leave and I was using the state railroad which at the time was then called British Railways.

It was great to be with my mum and Colin again and I had a great week in Guernsey with them. While I was there I met a very nice couple. They lived in Bristol, a city in the southwestern part of England, which had a great seafaring history. I was invited to visit them some time after I got back to base and could get another weekend pass. A weekend pass was necessary since Bristol was not too far away from Compton Bassett, Wiltshire, probably about 80 miles. They gave me their address and invited me to visit with them. Just before the end of my 12 week training at Compton Bassett I arranged to visit them.

He drove a motorcycle with a side car so one weekend we planned my visit to Bristol and he offered to pick me up at the Compton Basset Squadron office at the front main gate and take me to their home in Bristol. He arrived one Saturday morning on his motorcycle and side car at the squadron office gate and off we went to Bristol which was about a two-hour drive. They were both so very kind and showed me around town. One place in particular was Cheddar Gorge. This is the Devon County area of England where cheddar cheese is made and the Cheddar Gorge is a large cut in between two large hills. A small pathway runs along the side of the gorge and alongside of the pathway is a small alcove cut into the limestone of the hill. In its history, it is said that a minister took shelter in this small alcove to keep out of the rain during the late 1700's and while he was there, he had an inspiration for a hymn. Because the weather was so bad with wind and rain, he sheltered in this very old limestone alcove. He composed a hymn that is sung around the world in many churches called Rock of Ages. By Sunday afternoon we were headed back to base in the pouring rain on the motorcycle.

The 12 week radio course at Compton Bassett was interesting, working with telecommunications and codes and breaking down codes. It was still only a school for radio reception and not an actual operating facility. Most interesting was listening to the Soviet Russian radio in English. First, we learned how to type, and then we learned how to use the Murray code, which was a punched tape that somehow worked through an oscillating fingertip touch that punched through the holes in the tape. We would send out training messages to all parts of the world. We were also shown how to do crypto investigation such as code breaking from all over the world especially from the Soviet Union, which was considered a serious challenge to world peace.

At RAF Compton Bassett there was not anything really military except once a week we had guard duty around the camp and carried a rifle looking for anyone that should not be there. Although it was a school it did have very sensitive equipment for our training purposes. We had concerns during that time on guard duty about the Irish IRA that had raided some of our military installations and had taken some weapons, but we had no events while I was on duty during our communication school period.

We were at RAF Compton Basset for 12 weeks and as soon as we had finished the course, we would know what our permanent assignments would be. All final assignments were posted on the squadron office bulletin board. I found posted on the bulletin board the posting where I would put all that I had learned to good use. I was promoted to LAC which is a higher airman rank and my next assignment was to RAF Bletchley Heath, Stanford/Bedford. RAF Stanford was at that time a very important intelligence center at that time filled with all kinds of characters called Buffins or the back room boys. They developed small weapons for intelligence officers and their overseas operations. They were called field officers like a James Bond type and they actually existed.

Being not too far away from London, it was at that time one of the most secretive air bases in the country. During the Second World War it was here where they operated the captured Enigma decoding machine that the Germans used to send messages to all their submarine commanders which was intercepted here. I was quite pleased at my assignment, also because it was only about 25 miles from London and I could get home easily on most weekends.

August 1955, RAF Bletchley Park, Bedford

I SPENT ONE week leave at home with mum and Colin and the time went so quickly. Most of my friends were still on duty in the military so they were not home on leave. I visited my grandmother, Uncle Harry and Aunt Ida, but also took the train out to Thundersley to visit my surrogate mother Auntie Ellie.

I received my travel warrant to my new posting at RAF Bletchley Park. I first had to check in at the squadron office to deliver my orders to the orderly there and find my permanent living quarters to settle in on the job. It was quite different here since there were two places. Our housing was on the main Air Force base itself but the area we worked was in a very large mansion. We lived in RAF Bedford which was where the living quarters were and all the camp facilities. We had to take an RAF blue bus, which was called a Gary, using the bus schedule to the actual Bletchley Heath operations area.

When I arrived for the first time at Bletchley, I had to check into the area which was highly secure and had to show my 1250 ID card many times before I arrived at my work area. The place that I would have to work was like an old house or stately home of some aristocrat who was down on his luck. Part of my assignment was to detect messages from unfriendly countries via radio. I had to find a code to decode the message and teletype the final message to a decoded address. They showed me around. I found my work space where I was to work and met some of my new friends that I would be living with for as long as my assignment lasted.

So here I was quite enjoying what I was doing at RAF at Bletchley Park. I was home most weekends whenever I could get a pass. I enjoyed working the job and its duties and the security duties that I was involved with sent out many important messages to many different places. One of which also had a direct bearing on the future of my life in America. I was temporally assigned to the American USAF/RAF combined base at USAF Chicksands which was further north of where I was based. It was there that I had my first American hamburger and I tasted my first popcorn in their movie theater. These were two air bases that had merged on the main base for the two different countries, American and British. We were permitted to merge socially with each other off and on base.

In comparison to our part of the combined base it was quite different. The US servicemen wore smart blue gabardine uniforms of the American Air Force while we had woolen-made uniforms of blue for the RAF. We lived in our barracks on base while the Americans lived mostly off base and arrived back to duty on base next morning in those beautiful American cars. I really enjoyed my transfer to USAF Chicksands and met some nice people that did influence me in visiting America after I was discharged. Many of the American airman suggested to me that I should visit America after my discharge from the RAF. We had complete freedom of movement of the base except the American PX which was for American servicemen only. I attended their movie theater and saw many movies.

After I returned back to my unit at Bletchley Heath, I continued on my duties that were assigned to me checking the codes that were constantly coming in. One morning I was called into the squadron office at the request of the clerk and he informed me that I was being reassigned to RAF station Air Ministry in London. I was assigned to the Air Ministry located in Whitehall, London which was part of London where most all government houses are located. The military of all services in Britain are not located in one huge building like the Pentagon in Washington, DC where all branches of the services are located together. In Britain, each branch has its own building such as the Navy has a building called the Admiralty. The Army had at the time a building called the War Office although I believe it has changed its name since then. The Royal Air Force had its head location at the Air Ministry London. We were located on the embankment of the river Thames near the famous Savoy Hotel and New Scotland Yard metropolitan police headquarters.

This was a cream puff posting for me with only about a year to go before my discharge and I had many interesting experiences in decoding communications while I was there being involved in many areas of interest. We did not have to always wear a uniform while on duty and I was sent many other places. We were located 300 feet down in the war rooms under heavy security which were made famous during World War II. Prime Minister Winston Churchill had this war room there where he lived most of the time. It was considered at the time the safest place in London and most of the war preparations were directed from this location.

At the entrance of the building there was an armed guard who checked our card 1250 ID before we would walk down the stairs to the elevator that took us all the way down to the various departments that we were assigned. Nearby was the building Scotland Yard the famous police department used.

The history of the police in Metropolitan London goes back to the 1840's where a man called Robert Peel began a small security force to try and stop the incredible crime waves that were accruing in London during that period. The industrial revolution arrived about that time and the aristocracy began to use machines to work their farms. They began to evict the families that occupied the rented homes and worked on their farms. The farm families of England once evicted had nowhere to live so they moved their small number of belongings on a horse and cart and moved into the nearest cities of England one of which would be the city of London. As the country people poured into London with no food or shelter, they began to steal or went into prostitution. Murders were rampant and so bad that Robert Peel arranged to begin a group of men that became policeman called by the general public as Bobbies named after Robert Peel. They started out in the Central London area on a street called Scotland Yard.

As the police grew larger, they moved into another location along the embankment of the river Thames now called New Scotland Yard. They wore top hats and were generally called Bobbies, named after Robert Peel and thereafter they were called cops. That was the meaning of constable on patrol or C.O.P. At his time Charles Dickens wrote about the crime and terrible conditions that occurred during this period. He wrote books such as Oliver Twist in the workhouses and streets of London during that period of history. The aristocracy, who owned large farms in the countryside, operated the farms with workers that lived free in the cottages owned by the farmer. They were given free vegetables grown on the farm with occasional meat after the Sunday hunt by these wealthy farmers. This is where the saying eating humble pie came from. The intestines of a killed deer were called the humbles, which was considered the unwanted part of the deer, while the real meat was given to the farmer and his guests on the farm. The farmer would give the unwanted intestines to his workers at no charge. This became a saying that is used even today. If anyone had to lower themselves to ask for a favor or apologize, they would be said to be eating humble pie.

That is also where Yorkshire pudding came into play with leftovers. Lower class people usually had only one day to eat meat and that was on a Sunday. The wife would then put all the left overs of the Sunday dinner in a batter pudding to eat for the rest of the week. The family would be eating leftovers from the Sunday meal called Yorkshire pudding.

1957

MY TIME WAS coming to an end for my service in the RAF although I never did get the opportunity to learn to fly or be a member of the air crew as I was promised at the beginning of my service. I was ready to be de-mobilize from my duties and I was ready to get on with my life. I was 20 years old. The RAF had changed over to large jet bombers which only required fewer occupants to fly the aircraft so that was disappointing to me. As far as I know the Vulcan jet bomber is the only V aircraft still in service.

One of the last courses I had to do before my discharge was to go on a firefighter's civil defense course somewhere up in the north of England. The course was called essential because in a future war the airfield would be bombed and buildings would be burning so every airman would be able to help put out fires. They did not understand that in the nuclear age there would not be any need for firefighters on an airfield because of radiation, since in reality there would not be anyone left to put out any fires. The civil defense course was much more interesting since it was a weeklong classroom activity showing what would happen if a thermonuclear bomb would be dropped on England. It was shocking to me to be told the details about how the civil defense would operate under those conditions. It was too terrible to discuss the plans that would be put in force if and when such a fearful even should take place. Anyway, that was a long time ago and military hardware has changed, but the end result would probably still be the same.

It was now time to be discharged from the RAF and we had to go back to where it all started at RAF Cardington, where over two years before I had been an eighteen year old recruit being fitted out prior to being taken to basic training. We had to return all of our military clothing, weapons, pots and pans both our work and dress uniforms. I was disappointed because I had hoped they would let me take home my dress uniform but no, they had plans to give it to some other poor soul who was to fill in my place. After signing out some paperwork at the squadron office and my official discharge papers I was given my railway travel pass to get back to London and home. I was given two weeks of paid leave and the money I had saved up in the Air Force bank account so I had some money to get back home and find out if my old job was still mine. I remember walking out of the same gate that I had arrived in a truck filled up with civilian kid recruits who were just starting, ready to go to boot camp.

Here I was leaving through the same gates heading for the local railroad station. I remember it was a typical March day and while I was waiting for the bus to take me to the railroad station. I thought about all the things that had happened to me during my service and then I began to realize that I was now living in the future and everything now was in front of me. I was now convinced that I would be going to America the following year, but first I would have to start getting back to civilian life and get myself a job and save up some money to get to New York. I had already planned to leave one year from that time which would give me plenty of time to save up for that adventure I had planned for so long. I was going to board that boat train for Southampton and go to America. When I did arrive home, mum had taken the day off and Colin had taken the day off from school and we were all together again.

1957, I Was Now a Civilian

I HAVE NOW moved on to the second part of my life and I had to find a job. Although my job that I had before was still available to me, I wanted to go on to a larger printing company. By law a returning military airman would be able to take his previous job back upon returning to civilian life. I visited my old company at T. Whitton and J. Mead and they asked me to come back and work for them. My job was still available and they even gave me more money and said there was lots of overtime. I returned to my job in early March of 1957 and began to fit into the flow of the plant. There was plenty of overtime and I began to build up my savings account.

The lifestyle of the military does change one's perspective on life. I was now twenty years old and still living at home with mum and Colin. I had a job with a good salary with money left over to put into the savings bank. Now came the first of many changes as I began my early preparations for my travel plans to New York the following year.

I applied the British Home Office for a passport. After filing all the information required by the government, I soon received in the mail my passport with my photo. The next step was to apply for a visa to live and work in America. I had to apply to the American Embassy at Grosvenor Square in London where they sent me in the mail a very large envelope that carried all the information and forms that I had to fill out and apply for a visa. Fortunately for me they explained that every country at that time had a visa quota. The quota was based upon the type of country the applicant came from, whether they could speak English and their working skills. Most importantly the applicant would not become a financial burden to the American government. Inside the envelope was also an FBI cardboard sheet that included a fingerprint check card. Two cards, one for each hand where there was room in each square for each finger in a large square on the sheet. I had to take that down to my local police department where they would take my fingerprints and sign a document that the fingerprints were legal.

I must have filled in about a dozen different forms that related to my life and I had to get a character reference from my ex-commanding officer in the RAF Air Ministry. I was also obliged to get a letter of reference from a member of my local clergy. The last form was that after my arrival in New York I would agree to register every six months under the US Selective Service Board to be conscripted into the American military which I signed.

I now had all the paperwork together and put them into a large envelope and mailed it off to the US Embassy, Grosvenor Square in London and awaited a call to be interviewed for a visa. The call came in via mail and I was instructed to appear for two days of interviews, including a medical examination, to be cleared for a visa. I reported on a Monday morning for the medical and was told to appear the next day for the interview by member of the Embassy staff. The medical was very thorough and I had to prove that I had my shots for small pox and other diseases. The physical exam was very long and that took most of the first day. The following day was the interview with a consul and it also went well. I completed all of the requirements. It was great news that I had been granted a permanent residency visa, but they asked me if I intended to work while I was in the US. I told him that yes, I wanted to work as soon as possible and that I had permission form my trade union in England to transfer my union documents over to the union in the US. He then said that there had been a slight error. He said to work as a permanent resident in the US that I must pay 20 UK pounds for the extra visa and then it would be approved. He said that it would appear in the mail within a few weeks. I was very happy with that information and now I could make my travel plans.

I was now working at T. Whitton and J. Mead on Old Street, London and was making some good money as a journeyman printer. I did as much overtime as possible to save up money for my trip. I worked about 12 hours per day and on each Friday lunch time I would take a bus across the river Thames to where our union local headquarters was located. I would line up with the other union members for weekend work on the London newspapers for the following Saturday night. We worked on huge newspaper presses that printed the Sunday newspapers. For one nights work I would earn the equivalent of what I earned per week on my day job at my normal printing firm.

In those days the trade unions were strong and each company had installed at the company's pressroom a shop steward paid by the union to supervise the operation of the press room in each company. He was called father of the chapel otherwise known as FOC. This representative of the union settled disputes within the company with the owners. This FOC had an office in each company pressroom.

The newspaper pressroom was located on the 2nd floor of a three floor building. On the ground floor there are the great rolls of paper ready to be fitted on to the press spindle ready to be mounted on the end of the press. The web as it was called is then fed up through the ceiling of the first floor to the second floor where the printing units are located. After the paper has passed through the press and printed it goes on to the next step where it is automatically folded and trimmed to size down to a completed newspaper on the press. The next step is the completed newspaper which is picked up on a high flying wiring system called a creeper up on to the third floor where it is bundled and tied by string. It is also counted into what they call quires of 25 printed newspapers. Each 25th copy is automatically kicked out of line slightly ahead of the line. This gives a real count of newspaper bundles and it's then dropped down a chute to street level and onto a waiting van for delivery to the drop areas around the city and country.

I had to report for duty on the pressroom floor at 6:00 pm. There were seven jobs required on each printed unit. There were two men on the downstairs floor responsible for the rolls of paper to be mounted on the press, two men to mount the heavy lead plates onto the cylinders of the press and one pressman in charge of the whole operation. There were two men to work on the third floor to ensure the bundles of paper were correctly sent down the chute to the waiting van. Although there were seven jobs per printing unit, the union requirements were 14 men to work that same unit, however, the system is that only seven men are working per hour then the second seven men would go off on break for an hour. In fact, the job required only seven men to do the job but the company paid for 14. It was an easy job and the first thing we did when we arrived on the pressroom floor was to pick a number out of a hat from 1-14. The even numbers were part of the first crew that would go on a break before we had even got started. While the odd numbers chosen would plate up the press and wait for the final edition to be completed by the editorial staff, then the curved lead plates would be formed and sent to the press room where we would mount the plates onto the press, which sometimes was not until after 9:00 pm.

We had a fixed number of newspapers to print for our printing unit during the shift and if all went well, we would be finished by three o'clock in the morning and I would be finished for the night. I made the same amount of money for about six hours work as I did in one week's work in a commercial printing plant. By adding the weeks work at a commercial printer and then adding on the two nights for the newspaper weekend job I made a lot of money to be used to finance my travel to America.

1957 was a great year to be a young man in England. I was now free from my military obligation. I would only have to report to the National Reserve once a year. Knowing that I was going to America a year from now, I did not worry except to tell them that I was emigrating and needed their permission to do so. Our group of four friends had broken up prior to going into the military. Roger had somehow got out of his obligation with the help of his father and Malcolm. What was left was my lifelong friend Brian Bowden. He still lived across the street from me and we still spent time listening to jazz records at each other's home during the week time evenings. Other Saturdays we would take a bus out to the suburb town of Finsbury Park where there was a pub called the Fishmongers Arms, where they also had hot jazz and we enjoyed great evenings with Brian and my other friends that we met there. About this time things began to change with Brian who had found himself a girlfriend who lived about thirty miles away, south of London in Reading. He began dating her and suddenly we did not hang out as much as we did before.

I had now finalized my plans to travel to New York City for the following year of 1958. I was now money hungry. I needed over three hundred pounds to pay for my estimated travel expenses to America which were the expenses for the voyage on the Queen Elizabeth, expenses on the ship and other items that I need to have in place before I left. I drew up a list of what I expected to spend for the first three months after arrival in America.

I knew that when the time came to leave for America, I could not leave home without paying mum in advance the money I would have paid her each week. I felt obligated to pay her for at least six months up front and also, I wanted to do the same for my brother Colin since I always gave him a weekly allowance. He got from me six months of allowance. I was working two jobs and not going out much except on a Saturday night to either a jazz club in the West End of London or during the week going over my travel plans. Many times, during the week I would go over to Brian's house and play records and sometimes he would come over to mine to play records.

During the week I would leave the house at about 6:30 am to catch a bus at the bottom of my road to get to work. Usually, the bus was full so I had to either stand or go upstairs in the double decker bus and find a seat. The only place on a bus in those days that you were allowed to smoke was upstairs so when I climbed up the bus stairs to the top deck the smoke was so bad, I could hardly see the end of the bus. I then would get off the bus by just jumping off when I was nearly at my next bus stop. I caught the underground next at Fenchurch Street Station, going down escalators leading to the underground ticket office to buy a ticket to my station where I was supposed to get off. London has one of the best subway systems in the world and consisted of many lines all colored differently on the directory located on the train and in the station. I had to catch the Central Line which was colored red on the directory and I got off at Marble Arch which is at the bottom of Oxford Street.

Marble Arch has quite a history. It was a place called speakers corner where the law allows anyone to get on a box and talk to the crowd of onlookers any subject usually political without anyone to stop you. It sometimes got them into a very lively discussion especially when it was political in nature and the crowd became rowdy and strongly disagreed with the speaker. Marble Arch also was famous in the past for this was where the hanging gibbet was located and they publicly hanged criminals in the eighteenth century. When criminals were arrested and convicted of a crime, they were sent down to be publicly hanged the next morning. No appeals were available and sentence was carried out usually the next morning. There were instances where the judge did not think that hanging was the right sentence so the convicted was given an alternative. Hanging the next day or being transported in chains on a prison ship which was waiting on the river to take those convicts to Botany Bay in Australia. It took about three months to sail to Australia and they were being chained down in the hold of a prison ship before starting their sentence. Usually, their sentence was for life but some were sentenced for seven or ten years. Although they may have finished their sentence, they had no money for such a long voyage to return to England so they stayed in Australia and never returned home.

When I showed my mum my new passport, I could see on her face that she suddenly realized that she would be losing her son again for the third time. That made me feel bad. Since the time I had decided to go to America I had reasoned to myself that I was twenty years old and it was about time to leave home, but I realized now that my mum was not in favor of that at all. Although we had discussed this subject, I had told her that I was only going for six months, but in my mind I knew that I would not be coming back, not to who I was now, and if I did return I would probably be a different person. I am sure that she knew that and I began to have second thoughts to be going on this trip while she was going to work and Colin was growing up without his older brother. Again, the family was splitting up and I started to begin to regret that I should be doing this. Then common sense kicked in and I would argue with myself that this was part of life and that I should do this. I had taken care of the family since I was ten years old.

I was twenty-one years old and a great adventure was approaching. I should not be responsible for everyone in my life, so I had a talk with her and she said that they would be alright while I was gone. I was secretly pleased about this statement because I felt that I should go off on my own and I was beginning to be so obligated that I really wanted to be away from that obligation. It was hard on my conscience and from time to time I wavered as to whether this was the right decision but finally, I got over it and I came to terms with it, I was going for sure.

I walked into the main office of Cunard White Star Lines and I was surrounded by luxury. There were models of the different ships all around the office inside glass boxes showing in detail each ship. I approached the counter and told the woman behind the counter that I was planning a trip to New York and had decided on traveling on the Queen Elizabeth. We went through the sales part and then I told her that I wanted to go cabin class and I told her the date was going to be April 23, 1958. She said that the date was open for buying passage on the Queen Elizabeth. She began to explain to me all about the ship and the ticket cost of a one way one person. I would be bunked in with a stranger and she asked if I did not mind that. I said no and I put down the deposit that was required so now that I had decided on a date I was now fully committed. She told me details regarding the ship and accommodations would be sent to me at my home. The boat train from Waterloo was available so I reserved several seats on that train for my mum, my grandmother, Colin and what kind of seats would I choose since the first train ticket was included in my fare to New York which was two hundred pounds. I told her that some of my family would be going and needed reservations for them. I bought three train tickets with reservations which I would pay on the day when I travelled and each included a small deposit.

1958, April

I WAS NOW committed. I was still writing to my pen pal Joan Mason in Flushing, NY. We exchanged letters about once a month and she seemed to be a very nice girl. I thought it might be a good idea to send her a recording of my voice so I made some inquires and found out that there was a studio that does voice recording. That would last for about twenty minutes so I made a trip to this studio on Oxford Street in the West End of London. I made a script and timed it for twenty minutes and went into the studio. I remember it was very stylish like a TV studio set with a producer who looked over my script and said that I should make some adjustments since it was too long. We did finally get it together and I recorded myself on a record and sent it to her in New York.

By this time, I had received my visa for a six month renewable working permit in the United States and I had already bought my ticket on the Queen Elizabeth leaving from Southampton on March 23, 1958 and time was approaching. I had quit my job and everyone in the printing plant offered me their best wishes. On the last working day, we went out to lunch and then it was the first of many goodbyes.

I had previously bought some new clothes American style in an American store in Piccadilly. I purchased a grey checkered sports jacket, a nice tie and shirt, blue slacks and a red sweater worn under the jacket. I bought brown lace up shoes and other clothes and items. I bought two new suitcases and attached the sticky the labels that the Cunard steamship line had given me in the personal package with my full identification ticket to New York. I stuck one label on one suitcase and another label on the other. The labels were quite large and the Cunard label stood out very well in their picture of the ship that said in bold letters RMS Queen Elizabeth. My name and cabin number were identified on the label and there was a small area for my destination which was New York. My full name was in bold letters so it would not get lost. I felt just great.

Now came the difficult part of my voyage. My mother knew that I probably would not be coming back even though I had insisted that it would only be for six months. I knew myself that I would not be coming back and felt very guilty as the time came to say goodbye to my family. I kept saying to myself that I was 21 years old and it was time to strike out on my own, but I also said to myself that my mother's life had been full of goodbyes. She said goodbye to my dad in 1939 when he went off to war. She said goodbye to me as a three year old when I was evacuated out of London in 1940. She said goodbye to me when I left to join the Air Force and now here, she was again saying goodbye to her eldest son to a country that was 3,000 miles away. I kept feeling guilty again about leaving my family and more than once thought of cancelling the whole thing. But the thought kept consoling me that it was time to break away from that responsibility that I had since I was ten years old and go on my great adventure. If I came back after six months then it was fine, but if I stayed as I was beginning to think I would, then, I thought it was my life to do as I wished and to go to America was what I wanted to do.

My family on my mother's side was very large. I had about five uncles and aunts plus my maternal grandmother. I also had seven cousins all about my own age plus some younger cousins who were very young like my brother Colin, who at that time was 13 years old. My maternal grandfather had died in 1952, but as a family we were very close. They decided to throw me a great farewell party on the last Saturday night I had before I left. Our apartment was not very large, but somehow we managed to fit everybody in. We rolled up the carpet in the front room to the bare linoleum for dancing and as I had said before this room was called the best room used only on special occasions like this. My mother had a piano located in the front room and my Uncle Tom played piano, so on the last Saturday night we had a great party. There was plenty of beer and liquor. The men were drinking beer and the women drank their gin and tonics or gin and orange and before long the party was getting a glow on.

One dance was doing the Hokey Kokey where everyone joined hands in a circle and sang the song that was meant for that dance. It was almost like line dancing except it was in a circle. Then they all did the Conga line and before long nobody was feeling any pain and having a great time. As the time came to do the last song, they all sang together a song especially for me. It was a popular song at the time called the Hawaiian song called now is the hour when we must say goodbye. It was all very touching and my Uncle Harry said a few words of a speech that wished me well. They filled their glasses again and offered a toast to a safe journey and I should write to mother as often as possible. Soon everybody was leaving with calls of good luck and see you soon as they went down the stairs to the front door to catch the last bus home. None of them lived too far away and they did not have a car so being partially drunk did not matter.

I still had those pangs of guilt on leaving my mother and Colin alone and I did not sleep well. I began to wonder if I would ever see my family together again and once more began to wonder if I was doing the right thing by leaving for America. I wrote this thought in my diary which I still have today and sometimes I read it again.

It was springtime in London and the weather was fairly good. My mother had promised me that she would make me a last Sunday dinner of Yorkshire pudding, peas, roasted potatoes and baked beans. I suggested that since it was such a nice spring afternoon, we should take the bus to London and visit Hyde Park and then have tea in one of the café's that would be open in the afternoon. Mum cheered up a little at that idea so with Colin we went by bus to Hyde Park and what a lovely day it was. The sun was shining and the spring flowers were out in the garden beds. There were daffodils, tulips and bluebells in every garden bed in the park. We strolled along side of the Serpentine which was a huge lake that twisted and turned around a very large part of the park. There were boaters on the lake rowing their boats and other people were just wandering through the park. Mum was sad I know and it showed on the photo I took of her.

Hyde Park is just one of the three or more royal parks of London. They used to be private hunting parks owned by the royal monarchs of England where they hunted deer over the last several centuries. It was a serious offence to hunt deer in the park if you were not one of the royal families. Royalty or their guests were only allowed to hunt deer, but the park was turned over to the city of London many years ago and now I believe they are public lands. There are other parks in the same area of London such as Green Park with the same history.

After strolling through the park, we decided to have tea in an open area that had a shop that was a tea shop that had both inside and outside tables. We chose since it was a nice day to sit outside with the striped red and white awnings of a small tent sitting on iron chairs and iron decorated table. I still have those photos that I took of that day. We wandered over to one of the many small bridges across a small part of the lake and I took a photo of mum on her own standing by the bridge with the city of London buildings in the background. She looked so sad. Little did she know that many years later we would return to this spot with my wife Patty and my daughter Carolyn to visit London. Carolyn stood on the same bridge at the exact same place that I took a photo of my mum standing on that last Sunday afternoon on my last weekend with my family so many years before.

I took many photos of that last Sunday together of young Colin and mum and then we caught the bus back home. However, little did I know that in two years I would be back together again in London. I would be back on a vacation visit. Three years later both mum and Colin would be living with me in America so although at the time it was a sad Sunday it would work out well. In the end we stayed together until my mother passed away in 1996. Even she became an American in both mind and spirit. She now was Americanized and happy. It shows in the two photos taken. First when she was sad in Hyde Park and other in America.

It was the following day on the Monday before I left for America that my Uncle Harry invited me to take a ride on his small Italian motor bike called a Vespa to visit my Aunt Rose. It carried the driver and also a seat on the back behind the driver and we drove south through the county of Kent to visit my Aunt Rose who lived in a small town on the south of England called Deal. It was located near Dover and she had lived there for a long time. It was too far for her to come to my going away party so we went to visit her and say my goodbyes. It was an adventurous day for me having never ridden on a small motor bike like a Vespa. I had been on my friend Roger's large motor bike but this was a quite small Italian built motor bike. We visited my Aunt Rose who was a large roly-poly woman who was just great person to me. We had stayed with her one time during the war but things were beginning to change for the better now. She had one son by the name of Malcom who was the same age as me and it was nice to see them all before we returned to London.

The next day Tuesday was a day to start packing and making last minute plans. I had notified my pen friend Joan that I would be arriving on the 29th of April in New York and she had replied that she would be there to meet me at the docks. I had decided to take my two suitcases to Waterloo Station the evening before I left. I would check them in at the ship's baggage center the night before I left so that it would be easier for us the next morning and we would be free to travel better in the morning leaving the house on time. The train was scheduled to leave Waterloo station at 12:00 pm.

My grandmother had arranged a taxi to pick us all up at my house and then went to Nan's house to pick up Uncle Harry and Aunt Ida. We did not want to get stuck waiting for a bus and getting stuck in London traffic, so it was an easy ride to the railway station. We had quite a few people coming with me, my mother, grandmother, Uncle Harry and Aunt Ida. I am not sure why I do not remember if Colin was there. I have asked him many times but he said that he did not go to the ship with us and could not remember why.

As we passed through London, I looked at the landmarks of the city of London that I knew so well as we drove into the Waterloo Train Station to collect my luggage at the luggage center. I had bought all of their train tickets so I picked up my suitcases at baggage claim. We went through that decorated platform gate that had a gold archway that I had passed through many times before with my penny platform ticket. I thought as I had passed through that archway I am really going to get on that train, not just watching others going. For real I was going on that train to New York. There would be no stops for the train along the way. Every passenger and guests on this train was going to board the Queen Elizabeth ocean liner when we arrived at Southampton docks and it was then going to New York. At the platform entrance the large round golden archway had written large boards reading Boat Train-Southampton-New York. We found a porter to take my suitcases to be put into the baggage car. We passed under that archway on to the platform itself and I was walking down that same platform that I had done so many times before.

We then located the doorway in the train that corresponded to our seat numbers on the seat that was assigned to my party. I was so excited I was really going. This time it was me sitting at that table in the boat train carriage on my way to America looking out at the people waiting on the platform seeing their friends off and waving goodbye to them before the train left. I was fulfilling my ambition and now I was boarding the boat train to New York City beckoning me to that great city in America and that huge country that lay beyond to explore.

The difference this time was that I was following my dream and it was me that was sitting at a table with white table cloths and silverware, waiters in white dinner jackets waiting on the seated passengers taking their orders for cocktails before the train left the station. My family who was with me on that train to Southampton will board the ship and visit the great ocean liner that was to carry me three thousand miles to New York will be quite impressed. Just as we were settling in our comfortable seats, we suddenly heard the whistle of the train and gradually the train began to pull out of the station and I was on my way to a new life in America.

It was just as I had previously seen when I sat on that baggage wagon many years ago watching the train pull out wishing that I would be one of those lucky people who were going on a fantastic journey across the sea and now I was really on my way. Everyone was cheering their goodbyes to friends and relatives from the train platform as the railway cars slowly moved out of the station to begin its journey to Southampton. They were calling out Bon Voyage, Bon Voyage! Goodbye, Goodbye! The train whistle blew again and we were on our way. We travelled through the county of Kent and I tried to keep a good face because again felt guilty that I was leaving my mother and Colin for the second time that they had both seen me leave home and this time it would be a long time before I would return.

After about two hours our train began to slow down and very slowly entered the huge dock area of Southampton. I looked out of the window as we made a turn on to the dockside and there was this huge ship that to see its upper structure, I had to look high up. The side of the ship was painted black and the superstructure was pure white. The ship had two funnels painted black on the bottom half and red on the higher part. From the train window I had never seen such a large ship, so big and so beautiful. The train pulled into the docking area right up to the side of this great ocean liner. When we arrived at the station platform slowly slowing down to a halt, we all got off of the train. There was a large Ocean Terminal departure building where there were porters moving passenger's bags from the baggage car of the train into the terminal to be processed by customs and immigration officers.

My family and I got off of the train after being assured that my bags would be transported to the customs hall for loading onto the ship and proceed up an escalator to the departure hall. All my family guests were allowed to pass through this area as a visitor. I had previously arranged with Cunard for visitor's permits to board the ship when I bought my train tickets. We could see the wide cavernous entrance opened in the side of the ship that led into the ship that was to carry me three thousand miles across the Atlantic in five days. We boarded the ship up a wide gangway entering the ship through a very large opening in the side of the ship. We found ourselves in an open area like a large hotel lobby. I checked myself in at the reception desk showing my sailing ticket as well as being issued ship visitors passes. The wide entrance in the side of the ship was leading passengers into the ship that was to carry them three thousand miles across the Atlantic in five days. There were two passenger gangway bridges to board the ship. The right side gangway were those who were boarding the ship and the left gangway was for the people that were leaving the ship or for the ship's crew that were providing carry-on luggage for the passengers. Alongside of the giant dock were high loading cranes that were loading suitcases in large cargo netting, suitcases that eventually would be deposited in the appropriate cabin decks and numbered cabin designated on the label located on each suitcase. We had to board quickly because there were people behind us working their way up towards that giant opening in the side of the ship. Soon we were at the top of the stairs entering the inside of the ship passing through that great opening in its side and suddenly I found myself in another world.

The décor of the ships lobby was overwhelming and just beautiful. The chandeliers where so glamorous and the carpet was so clean and new looking. Mum, Uncle Harry and Aunt Ida were all overwhelmed at the opulence of the glamorous surroundings of the ship. It was like walking into one of the finest hotel lobbies like I had seen on the movies. Everyone was preparing to let go of the giant ropes and hawsers of the ship that was keeping it tied to the shore and the ship seamed anxious to break the bond of the shore and head out into its natural environment, the open Atlantic Ocean. There was such a hustle and bustle of people moving around: bellboy's running around checking luggage names, page boys carrying signs with passenger names on small sticks the boy calling out the name of the wanted passenger with some message to be delivered to them.

The air was filled with excitement everybody getting ready for the departure of this huge vessel. We took one of the many elevators down on to the lower decks where the cabins were and I found my cabin number on C deck as we all crowded into the cabin and found my luggage had been delivered. I had arranged ahead of time for a bottle of champagne and enough glasses for each of my family members. I gave the first glass to my mother and then my grandmother then to everyone else of my family party. It seemed that everybody including me was overwhelmed by the size of this ship. I later discovered that the elevator had eleven deck stops from top to bottom. After we had our bon voyage champagne we had enough time to take a tour of the ship through the dining rooms and along the outer walkway around to the front of the ship. We returned to my cabin and had some time to talk my mother and grandmother. They give me some well-intentioned advice as to being careful in a different land when suddenly the steward came walking down the hallway ringing a bell calling out in a loud voice all ashore that is going ashore, this ship is ready to depart. All visitors must leave by the main gangway. It was time to say our last farewells.

We made our way up to the main deck to the main lobby and that huge open hatch in the side of the ship with a large gang plank where we had previously boarded. A steward stood by with a checklist of visitors to ensure that nobody sailed that should not have sailed and we all hugged each other. My mother was in tears and my grandmother had a tearful look on her face. Mother had previously told me they had planned that after visiting the ship they would leave the ship and return into the Ocean Terminal and up the escalator to the high flat top deck on dockside. They said that they would try and find me among all the waving people from the deck of the ship as it pulled away from the dock. I watched them walk down the gangway to the dock and move across to the terminal doorway that led to the roof of the terminal. I thought that this was the last time I would see them in such a large crowd of well-wishers.

I then found myself a prominent position on the dockside of the ship to see our departure and maybe see my family waving from the rooftop as we had planned, but I did not hold too much hope since there were so many people waving. Luck was with me and I did see them waving to me from the rooftop of the building. I could pick them out one by one. The ships horn began to sound again to announce the departure was imminent and the urgency of visitors hurrying to exit the ship back on to dry land before we left for America. The ship's seaman working with the dock workers were preparing to let go of the giant ropes and hawsers of the ship that was keeping it tied to the shore. The ship seemed anxious to break the bonds of the shore for the open sea and the Atlantic Ocean beyond.

I went up on deck as high as I could possibly go and saw my family again on the roof of the customs building waving to me. I waved back and suddenly I heard the ships horn blow and a band began to play and people were throwing out paper streamers towards the dock and people on the deck of the customers shed were also throwing colored streamers back to the ship. There was cheering and waving and lots of excitement. Slowly the engines of the ship rumbled to life and there was a lot of activity on the dockside with the sailors letting loose the huge lines that held the ship attached to the dock. As these ropes dropped into the harbor the ship was free and broke loose from the dock and the giant ship slowly backed out into the river.

Now I could still see my mum and family waving from the roof of the Ocean Terminal but as we drifted away from the dockside and started to move forward, we went further down the Solent River and soon the Ocean Departure building became lost to my eyes and suddenly I realized that I was finally on my own on this great adventure. Not only had the great ship Queen Elizabeth broken free of its moorings of the dock, I was also broken free from all the family responsibility that I had had for so many years. I was on my way to America. I was on my way to realize my dream in America. As soon as I realized my family was out of sight I returned to my cabin.

I was given a boat station of number 39 as my assigned derrick lifeboat station then walked along to my numbered cabin. I remember thinking to myself how do I find myself around this huge ship. The door of the cabin was opened and in came my companion for the voyage and we introduced ourselves and he seemed a nice elderly gentleman. There was a dresser with drawers for each occupant and a desk with a cabin phone. There were also many pamphlets on the desk top showing information regarding the entertainment while on the voyage and other suggestions. There was my table number assignment for both dinner and breakfast and I was excited about who would be one of the groups of people that would be joining me for my meals during the next five days. I could slightly hear the throb of the powerful twin engines of the ship as it made its slow move down the Solent River towards the English Channel. Then the open sea of the English Channel on our way to the French port of Le Havre where we were told that we would stop and pick up more passengers before heading out into the Atlantic. I had relatives that lived on the Isle of White so I silently wished them well and said a fond farewell to them. Suddenly I heard the ships siren sound out three times in sequence and knew that the anticipated lifeboat drill was in effect. We put on our life preservers and we had to find where all the strings and straps went, but our section steward was there to help guide us and direct us to our boat stations. We climbed up the stairs to the upper deck, which was where all the lifeboats were positioned and we found our assigned boat station number 39 and assembled there with our deck officer in charge. Everyone had their life vests on and on command from the officer the lifeboats were swung out over the side of the ship. It was quite exciting to see this drill being put into operation. After about fifteen minutes each officer in charge of the boat station in sequence blew a whistle and the drill was complete. We were ready now for any event while crossing the great Atlantic Ocean.

While I was up on deck, I could see we were still moving slowly down the Solent River and could see a shore line on each side of the river. As we passed the river traffic the boats blew their horns and whistles as we sailed past them in honor of this great ship. The weather began to get cloudy and I could see that crossing the English Channel was not going to be easy, but I had crossed the English Channel many times in smaller ships and had no trouble with the rolling of the ship. By this time it was tea time, which was about four in the afternoon and the announcement was made that tea would be served on the upper deck lounge which was the curving front of the superstructure with huge windows looking forward. I went with the others moving in that direction and did not have to sit on my assigned dinner table. I met up with some strangers at their table and we were served on silver plates scones, sponge cake and of course tea in a beautiful cup and saucer with the Cunard steamship logo both on the plates, cups and saucers.

I recall at that time attending my first event on the ship and returning to my cabin which was an adventure all of its own since I knew that it was somewhere on C deck, but this time I used the ships elevator map. This showed the cabin numbers and I could then make my way to my cabin. The elevator served eleven decks from the main top deck down into the last level below the ship. This ship was huge and I also read that it weighed over 83,000 tons. It was completely self-contained like a small city and had every function that a city had. There was a movie theater, barber shop, beauty parlor, two dining rooms, five night clubs and even a print shop that printed the daily ships newspaper and its daily dining menu's. All of this was just for Cabin Class passenger's in one section of the ship.

After returning to my cabin which took a while, I put all my clothes away in the dresser and closet and went back up on the top deck since I knew that I was approaching the end of the Solent River and would be passing the great white chalk cliffs of the Isle of Wight. As we came to the mouth of the Solent River heading for open water of the English

Channel, we passed the Isle of Wight with the its tall rocks and needles made of chalk. We slowly passed the island and the needles where many a good ship had been lost and soon they fell far behind us. I took a photo of this event in passing and slowly they fell below the horizon.

I had taken my last look at England and realized in my heart I would never be the same again. I was on my way to a completely new life. I had left Southampton and sailed down the Solent River to the open sea. Passing by the last piece of land I saw the white cliffs of Dover slowly slipping out of sight astern of me. That is when I knew that I was no longer an Englishman. It was the beginning of over sixty years of high adventure and experiences in the new great country of the United States of America.

I thought I would go up on deck and see how the weather was doing. It had started to rain as we passed into the English Channel now the great ship was beginning to pitch and roll in the rough seas of that very violent waterway called the English Channel, sailing first to LeHavre, France to pick up some other passengers then set a new course bearing westwards towards America, five days and three thousand miles away.

It was time for dinner so I put on my evening clothes, suit and tie, and I went to find the main dining room and approached the dining room steward. I gave him my name and cabin number and he asked me to follow him and he escorted me to a large round table and I was introduced to the people that would be my dining friends for the next five days of the voyage.

The ship was fantastic and the services were something I had never experienced before. I had never had a meal before in a real restaurant with waiters dressed in full evening dress. I maybe had a meal in a café, but not in a real waiter style restaurant that everybody was in full evening dress with such gracious style with ladies in their long gowns with pearl necklaces around their necks with lots and lots of jewelry. I had heard that the ships purser arranged this table seating when I had bought my sailing tickets and that they would seat different people with different interesting backgrounds of each member of the table. This helped to make the voyage more interesting and have good conversations and make new friends. The first night I did not know who these people I was to have dinner with.

I looked at the menu and could not understand just what the different parts of the menu were. It was a four course dinner and none of the items listed that I understood. On the first night after serving cocktails, they began serving many kinds of food that I had not been served before and some that I was not used to eating. The waiters all wore white dinner jackets and they served the beautiful dishes with white gloves. The ships orchestra was playing in the background. One of the waiters served me a large bowl of cracked ice that filled the complete bowl. Placed in the middle of the bowl with the cracked ice was a small glass about five inches high filled with some kind of red soupy liquid. I did not know what it was and I did not know how to eat it. Was it some kind of soup? Do you use a spoon or drink it out of the glass? I had a plan. I would wait until I saw what the others were doing with it around the table. I waited and watched others and noticed that they drank it from the small glass like it was a drink and did not use a spoon. After reaching for the glass, I drank the contents and discovered that it was chilled tomato juice, which I had never drank before in England with any kind of meal.

The main course came after that which was a fine piece of beef with some kind of gravy. As the meal went on, we all finally introduced ourselves to each all around the table and I found them to be quite friendly with a mixture of backgrounds. There was one who introduced himself as the president of the triple AAA motor club out of Philadelphia. There was a British doctor and his wife going on a special convention in New York. To my right was a very attractive American lady whose name I remember was Doreen Zimmerman. She confided in me that she was 31 and was returning home to California after serving five years in the State Department in the American Embassy in London. In those days many young women who were highly educated could not get a satisfying job in a general business office so they entered into the American State Department which gave them the opportunity to travel to wherever an embassy was located and they were assigned to go. She had been assigned by the US State Department to work in the London American Embassy and was returning to her home in California after five years of overseas assignment.

When we finished dinner and the servers had cleared away the tables the cabaret entertainment began on the open floor of the dining room. In those days there were not many transatlantic airlines available to fly to Europe. Most famous entertainers used the scheduled transatlantic luxury liners from America to Europe and carried many well-known entertainers of that time. During the voyage famous entertainers would be on board and would perform on the ship for their fellow passengers. Sometimes whenever a popular singer was on board as a passenger he or she would sing to the diners. In this voyage a dance group was on the way to a show on Broadway, New York, and did their dance routines of their show.

I tasted my first bourbon and water cocktail and began having mixed drinks with all of the other people at my table. I usually drank beer and then only maybe an occasional rum and coke, but they did not offer beer in cabin class on the Queen Elizabeth. Being now a newly born American, I ordered bourbon and water. I liked it so much I had another, maybe more than I should have done. Most of the groups around the table were party people and after dinner and dancing they invited me to join them in one of the continuing night clubs on the ship. There were three different night clubs on the ship and when one closed the other opened up so we kept on moving from one club to the other. I surely was in a different world from where I came from.

The first night we did not stay up late but I remembered we were going to stop off at Le Havre in France to bring on board additional passengers and I wanted to be on deck to see the docking. I went up on deck and could see that it was raining but we were heading into port and soon was docked at Le Havre, France. We were only docked for an hour and soon we backed out of the dock and headed out to sea heading west along the English Channel towards the open Atlantic Ocean to New York.

I slept like a log on that first night out except when I did wake up the ship was beginning to roll so I knew we had entered into the Atlantic. On the way to breakfast I had to hang onto the hand rails that ran along the walls of the corridors of the ship. When I arrived at the table for breakfast there was an announcement from the captain who said that we were sailing into a storm and that we should take precautions. As soon as possible we must return to our cabins and secure all personal objects located on dressers and secure any items that would fall off as the ship was going to pitch and roll. The ship was equipped with stabilizers but the sea was pitching from bow to stern and stabilizers would not be effective in those kinds of seas. He also said that no passenger was allowed on the upper outside decks until further notice. We must keep within the confines of the ship or stay in our cabin and be safe.

To cross the North Atlantic at that time of year was usually bad because of the many storms that occurred during April. The first night we were not allowed on deck because of the high waves which were said to be over forty feet high. One wave tore off one of the radar domes at the top of the masthead. The ship pitched and rolled. Down in the ships corridors where the cabins were located, they laid down a string of ropes which passengers could hold on to as they tried to walk the corridor to their cabins. We headed out into the Atlantic Ocean and headed west into the North Atlantic and the ship really began to roll and pitch. The first two nights we were tossed around but slowly as we headed west the sea began to ease off and we could then go up on deck and move around the upper decks in safety. Each night we were told to turn our watches and clocks back one hour to compensate for passing each time zone. New York is five hours behind London. They had a giant size model clock in the main lobby that was manually changed at midnight and every day they announced that there was a time change.

After two days the sea began to become calmer and the sun came out and the deck chairs were laid out on the open deck. It was quite warm and they served tea on the open deck during the afternoon. We had lunch on the forward club lounge which was a wrap-around superstructure of the ship with large forward view looking windows. The service was superb and cocktails were served with lunch. All we had to do was to sign the check to our cabin number.

They had deck games on the sports part of the ship, such as shuffleboard and badminton. As the voyage progressed the ocean turned a deeper blue in color and the air began to get less damp and much warmer from the sunshine. People were now in the deckchairs on the promenade deck taking their tea and scones in the sunshine, although they had a blanket over their laps. Stewards in white uniforms were moving around the passengers on the sun deck making sure that they were comfortable and if they needed another drink of either cocktail or tea.

Since I was a printer, I was eager to see the ships print shop. I was invited to go down into the inside of the ship to visit the print shop. A steward came for me and took me deeper and deeper into the bowels of the ship and I never thought I would ever get there. At last, we arrived to a small print shop with an old press. They printed the menus for dinner, lunch and breakfast.

Every morning people would walk around the deck of the ship for exercise. I walked along the promenade deck and greeted each person. Here I was, the kid from the east end of London, rubbing shoulders with the rich and famous. Every night after dinner our group from our dinner table would go on to an early night club and when that closed, we moved on to the next one that had just opened up. The cabaret in each club was excellent with different dancers and entertainers. It was Las Vegas on steroids. We also had a small movie theater showing latest movies.

As all good things have to come to an end sometime and tomorrow our voyage would end. The captain held a great last night party with after dinner entertainment and the dropping of balloons and we all had a great time. The party lasted into the wee hours of the morning until the last of the party goers slowly and wearily made their way back to their cabins to get some sleep.

After breakfast we repacked our suitcases and got ready to disembark from the ship. At the beginning of our last day shipboard our steward told us that first we must go up to the front desk lobby of the ship and pay our final bar bill that we had charged to our cabin during the voyage. We were also advised very discretely that we should tip our cabin steward before leaving the cabin. This should be done by enclosing cash in a sealed envelope. I did not know how much the tip was expected, but I put an amount in an envelope. I gave him the envelope and he was nice enough not to peek inside the envelope.

Today, our last day, I sensed that there was an air of expectancy on the ship. Our arrival in New York was pending. Preparations were now being made for disembarkation for later in the day. The sailors were attending to their jobs of clearing away the decks and other arrival jobs. The captain announced at breakfast the time we would expect to arrive and we would be disembarking in New York at approximately 7:00

pm that evening. He then gave out information that we were now in American waters and approaching the United States of America. This morning at 10:00 am we would be at anchor in the New York Narrows while the immigration officers boarded and checked everybody's passports and visas. We should line up in the large dining room and start the process of entry into the US as soon as breakfast is completed. He also said that we must completely pack our bags for customs inspection, just have on the clothes that each passenger would be wearing for the day. The cabin should be cleared by that time.

In the early fifties they had closed down Ellis Island, the original disembarkation point of entry into America. Now the immigration boat would come out to meet and board the ship. The immigration officers boarded the ship and set up their portable office desks in our lounge area. Sure enough on the last morning around 10:00 am I looked out from the front of the ship and could see land, which was the coastline of Brooklyn, the actual mainland of the USA. The first structure I could see through the morning fog was the famous parachute jump from Coney Island sticking out of the land with its tall arms ready to carry people down to earth on their parachutes. Slowly the ship came to a shuddering slowdown in speed and was now stopped for the first time since leaving Southampton, England five days before. I heard the rattling of the anchor on its chain being dropped and from a distance I could see the immigration boat slowly approaching the giant ocean liner.

That boat with the immigration officers looked so small against this giant ship. The ship's crew lowered down a companionway down the side of the ship and soon the small ship was close by our ship ready to allow the immigration officers to board our floating home. The public address system then announced and asked would all passengers move into the main dining room where the immigration officers would check every passenger's papers. We had to line up in front of three tables, each occupied by an immigration officer. When it became my turn, the officer looked up at me and smiled and said welcome to the United States of America. I thanked him and gave him the documents he required. He kept my visa and gave me back my British passport. He then gave me an official document that said I was allowed to permanently live in America for six months, but could apply during that time for extra time. That I was allowed to have a job and after five years could apply for citizenship in the United States of America.

As quickly as it arrived, the small boat carried back the officials to New York and suddenly I heard the sound of the ship pulling up its anchor. When that sound of the anchor chain stopped, I could hear the ships engines began to rumble and we were under way again heading for New York harbor. I took photos of the immigration boat arriving and pulling away and in the distance I could see the Brooklyn shoreline as we headed up river towards the city of New York. The ship had stopped in the New York Narrows, still out to sea but I could see the New York skyline up ahead. I did not realize at the time but I was watching for the first time was where I would live for over twelve years in New York City, Greenwich Village and Long Island. I was in America for the first time and the excitement was just sizzling through me. I was nearly there!

As the ship slowly approached the shore of Brooklyn all of the passengers were out on the upper decks watching for the Statue of Liberty slowly appear which would be on the left side of the ship as it approached New York's harbor. Suddenly, there she was standing tall holding the lamp of welcome to all visitors and new Americans to be. She stood tall and looked magnificent as we slowly passed by her. As we passed her, I heard cheering coming from the passengers that were lining the decks and heard some singing the national anthem as we passed the Lady in the Bay. The ships horn blew two blasts. Suddenly the ships band struck up playing the National Anthem and the ships horn began to sound and the excitement of passing the Statue of Liberty was complete.

We began to leave the New York Narrows and began to head slowly up the Hudson River towards the intended ships berth at 59th Street on the west side of Manhattan. It was late afternoon as we passed the skyscrapers of downtown New York that appears just off our right-side bow. A fireboat was hosing water into the sky welcoming the great Queen Elizabeth. It was one of many boats welcoming her into New York with many other ships blowing their horns as we passed by. Other ships were spouting water hoses up into the air as a welcome to this great ocean liner that was fast approaching its scheduled destination. We were now past many of the downtown skyscraper buildings of Manhattan and slowly moving up the Hudson River nearing our ships final berth. Slowly this great ship arrived at the docking area and the river pilot in a tug boat began to turn the ship around. She would be slowly moved into her berth. It started to rain as we arrived at the docking area but that did not stop us from gazing at the huge skyscrapers towering up so high. I could see the Empire State Building and Chrysler Building and cars racing down the West Side Highway. We moved slowly into the docking area and the engines finally shut down.

I had arrived in America! I had arrived at the Cunard Lines dock located at Pier 59 in the City of New York, USA at 7:00 pm. Now came the time when 2,000 passengers would rejoin their luggage. Passengers must disembark this great ship which had finally arrived safely at its destination in America. Holding my personal belongings in a small bag, I slowly made my way up from my cabin on to the upper decks towards our exit area ready to move down the companion way to the pier and find my luggage. The ships band was playing and there was cheering and the excitement of arriving after five days at sea felt very contagious. There were people crowded on the upper decks of the arrival pier calling down to friends and family that had just arrived. There were people crowded on the roof of the dock buildings waving and cheering our arrival. I finally found myself walking down the wide gangway onto the docks and once more looking back directly at this huge ship that had carried me from England to America over 3,000 miles across the mighty Atlantic Ocean. I had finally arrived in America! I was standing on American soil.

1958, I Arrived in America

I ARRIVED IN New York at Pier 59 at 7:00 pm on April 29, 1958 and it was raining. During our arrival the steward of my cabin area had picked up my luggage and put it somewhere ready to be picked by a rope netting which was scooped up and swung across the docks away from the ship and put into a huge pile of other luggage piled on the dock waiting to be claimed. I had been told that we had to go through customs first and that our luggage would again be found under the first letter of the passenger's last name. I looked for the letter P and there under that letter P was my luggage ready to be carried over to the customs table to be examined and released to each passenger for pickup.

I arrived in America with my worldly possessions, two suitcases one in each hand and a lot of hope. I carried each one by its handle to the front of the dock where we would pass through a great arch at the end of the dock. I remember looking back again at that great ship which had been my home for five days and had carried me across 3,000 miles of ocean.

I was getting very excited because now I was going to meet for the first time my pen pal Joan who I had been writing to me for so many years. Now I was going to meet her in person. As I passed through the arch of the dock area into the waiting area crowded with people who were meeting the ships passengers, I began to look for Joan. I passed through the main hall where all the friends and relatives were waiting to greet the passengers after leaving the ship and she was not there. I now began to look around for my friend Joan Mary Mason outside the secondary barriers and was still carrying my suit cases in tow. At first, I could not find her but suddenly I saw her in a corner with another lady which turned out to be her mother. Because of photographs she had sent I recognized her right away and went over to her at once to greet her. I introduced myself and asked if she was Joan and she said yes, I am Joan. She was the right person and I said that I was so happy to meet you after all those years. We chatted a little and they welcomed me to America and told me that their home was a long subway ride away and that they had made arrangements for me to rent a room in the YMCA in Flushing. I was surprised at this kind of reception since we had been acquainted for so long. I thought I would probably stay at their home for a day or so until I found a place for myself. I know if the position was in reverse and they had arrived in London they would have stayed at my house for sure even if it was only a small flat.

They lived in Flushing which was about an hour subway ride from where we were, but we had to walk the streets in the rain to find the subway station first. I offered to get a taxi cab at my expense but no, they wanted to walk in the rain. It was pouring hard with rain so I suggested again that we could take a taxi to the subway, but they again said no we would all walk to the station. There I was, carrying two heavy suitcases in the rain for about six blocks to the subway station.

Over the years many people had asked me what my first impression of America was after landing from the ship. One of the first impressions I had of New York as I walked off of the pier into the street was the noise. Many taxi cab horns, blowing whistles and traffic, lots of traffic. It seemed total chaos, lights and colors lit up everywhere, people hustling everywhere. All the cars I saw had different colors. The taxi's all had different colors. There were reds, blues, two tones, and greens cars that sported high fins on the bodywork and the cars were long and high and some looked like a rocket ship from the film serials of Flash Gordon.

We walked along the street and I felt something very strange between the three of us. I was talking to them but they were not talking much to me. Nobody said a word to me and I thought there was something wrong here. I had been corresponding with Joan Mason for over six years giving gifts to each other. Her father and mother actually sponsored me to come to America. In fact, they as a sponsor were legally responsible to the immigration government for me while I lived in America. There we were walking in the pouring of rain along New

York's west side streets towards the subway station in silence. We finally found the subway station and they had hardly said a word to me while we were walking. We finally walked about six blocks from the dockside and arrived at Grand Central Station to catch a subway train to Flushing. While we sat on the subway seat, I tried to make conversation but had little or no response from either of them. We caught the train and while it was travelling to Flushing Joan's mother was doing some writing on her homework, she was on some evening business course. She was using pen and pad and Joan just sat there did not say a word to me. I tried to chat with her telling her all about the ship. We arrived on the subway at the end of the line which was Flushing subway station and, in the future, I would get to know it very well. We still had to walk about six blocks to the YMCA from the Flushing train station in the rain. I am still carrying my two suitcases one in each hand.

When we did arrive at the YMCA hostel, they walked me into the lobby and front desk. We sat down on one of the sofas in the lobby and Joan's mother said that they lived a short bus ride away and wrote on a piece of paper their phone number and said here is our phone number, give us a call sometime. One of the few other words they said to me was a question which I really thought strange. Joan's mother asked me if I was a Catholic. I hesitated and replied no. I was surprised at such a question at our first meeting and then endured a long silence but had no response to my reply. To this day I do not understand that I received this kind of reception as a visitor to America. They suddenly both got up and left me there.

I walked up to the lobby counter where I was told that there was a room reserved for me. I had to pay $12.00 annual dues for joining the YMCA and pay eight dollars for my room, with one week's rent in advance. The room was small but had no private bathroom. It had a telephone in the room which I thought was quite nice since back in my home in England we did not have a telephone, in fact most people did not have a phone. To take a shower there was a special area that had open showers and the soap was provided. The room was made up every day. It reminded me of the military showers in the huts in the RAF.

I finally had arrived in New York City, but not under the most pleasant circumstances. My mother had asked me to send her a telegram upon my arrival in America to let her know that I had arrived and that the ship had not sunk. I inquired if I could send a telegram by Western Union from the front desk of the YMCA, but he said that he could not do that but he did suggest I go down the street to the Sanford Hotel where they would be able to do that for me. The front desk at the Sanford said that I could do it but I would pay by cash only. After the telegram was sent, I paid the man and asked him if there was some sort of restaurant nearby. He directed me to what they called a diner which I found quickly and had my first meal in America, a burger and fries.

I returned to the YMCA and looked around in the lobby and found a recreation room where there was a TV and coke machine. The price of a bottle of coke was 5 cents from the machine dispenser and finding a seat I began to think things out. I could not understand why they had treated me so strangely on my arrival so I decided that the next day I would get to the bottom of this. I decided to find my way to where Joan worked in Bellevue Hospital in Manhattan and if I could find her office, I would ask her out for lunch. Then maybe I would find out why there was this strange attitude upon my arrival and what was wrong.

The YMCA, Flushing is in the county of Queens and located on Northern Boulevard. To get to Manhattan I had to take a subway ride of about one hour to get into Grand Central Station. The subway cost 10 cents to go anywhere on the system regardless of how far you wanted to go. The very next day I looked out the window of the Y at America for the very first time and I was amazed at the amount of people and traffic. Cars were driving past me painted in all different colors. I was used to only one color in London, black. The cars were very colorful and streamlined with huge fins on the rear end of the car. It was no longer raining and looking out across the street there was a high school. I could see the kids were walking across the road to go into the open courtyard into the school building. It was Flushing High School and I believe it is still there. I took photos of the street from my window that showed the cars and the students entering the high school. They wore the same clothes and jackets that I had seen in many of the movies. The jackets were very colorful with a long white stripe running down the sleeve and a large number on the back of the jacket and smaller one on the front.

I knew that Joan was a secretary in an office in the hospital called Bellevue so I walked down to the Flushing subway station and caught a subway train to Grand Central Station. This subway station is a transfer center which is a land mark railroad terminal station in New York City. I then climbed up the stairs to the surface street level and began walking downtown towards Bellevue Hospital which was on the east side of Manhattan. I did not realize how far it was because it took me about two hours to walk downtown to that hospital. I did not mind the walk or the time it took to walk that far since I was a tourist. I was really anxious to talk to her because the first meeting with Joan and her mother was so tense that I just wanted to know why that would be. If they did not want to sponsor me all they had to do was to say that they could not do that. They need not be obligated to be responsible for me.

Arriving at the Bellevue Hospital I walked up to the information area and asked the receptionist behind the desk where I could find Joan. She made some phone calls and said that she had contacted Joan and that she would come down and meet me in the lobby in a few minutes. I waited in the lobby of the hospital and finally she came down the marble steps. She asked me what was I doing there and I said that I wanted to talk to her and maybe we could have lunch when her lunchtime became available. She explained to me that she could not do that since she had brought her own lunch from home that day. I remember responding saying yes, I understand but what I meant was to really take you to a nice restaurant for lunch. Again, she responded no but compromised by saying that tomorrow she would not bring her lunch and we could have lunch the next day at the same time. She then turned around and returned to her office. I thought afterwards that maybe she could get into trouble by having visitors during the work time. I asked the receptionist and she confirmed that it was not unusual for visitors to stop and ask for certain employees and that there was no problem.

I was walking across streets from east to west to find Broadway and walked back up north towards the central part of Manhattan. I was exploring my new city and discovered that just by walking was the best way to find your way about town. To explain the street system in New York, it is built on a grid system. The beginning of this system began in lower Manhattan which was where the original Dutch/English colony in the 1600's was built at Battery Park at the tip of Manhattan. It is arranged that the streets go east and west and are numbered in that sequence, while the avenues go north and south with each avenue having names. It is quite easy to find your way around the city if you remember the numbers of the streets and the avenues running north and south. Seventh Avenue goes down the center of the city. The numbered streets would go from first street east and west, in example east of Seventh Avenue was E 1st Street and west of Seventh Avenue was W 1st Street and so on up with the street. Easy, right? Numbers moving up higher the further north you go. I walked north until I found a nice cozy restaurant for lunch around 14th Street. On many street corners there was a shop that was usually called a candy store or a luncheonette. Little did I know at that time I would be walking in the future these same Manhattan streets selling printing presses knowing by that time seemingly every square inch of New York City.

I arrived inside Grand Central Station and thought I had time to take a look at the huge station before getting on the subway train to Flushing. I walked up some marble stairs and arrived into a huge train station with all marble railings and restaurants everywhere. This was a main railroad terminal station and this is where long distance trains arrived and departed to mysterious but famous names like Boston, Chicago and all places north of New York. The station was so elegant and the trains were all mostly electrified or had diesel locomotives so there was no smoke or smell of coal like the train terminals in London. There were statues everywhere with wide marble steps taking people up to cocktail lounges while they waited for their train home. I decided that I would return soon and explore this beautiful place. The loud speaker PA system called out the names of the train and its destination and what designation platform numbers it left from.

I thought I had done enough exploring for the day and decided to head back to Flushing and my room at the YMCA. I first I had to figure out how to buy a fare token for the train. It was not like the London underground where you paid for the distance that you travelled. Ten cents took you everywhere on the system. Here for ten cents, you bought a small round brass metal disc token with a hole in the middle from a manned kiosk prior to moving onto the platform. Then down the stairs and with that token you dropped it into the turnstile and went through onto the platform and waited for the train to come in. For ten cents you could go anywhere in the greater New York area with hundreds of miles of tracks to choose from. The train had its destination on the front of the train car so it was easy to get back to Flushing station and a short walk to the YMCA.

The subway system at that time was nothing like the London underground. The trains rattled and rolled on old tracks and as it went around a bend the steel of the wheels and tracks began screaming in protest as it went around a curve. The train cars as they called them were very old and some had seats made of cane and the seats felt hard to sit on. There was no heat in the subway in those days or any air conditioning in the summer. There were fans in the ceiling of each car for moving air around. I was not impressed at all with the New York subway system compared to London's tube, since I had to find a job as soon as possible. I decided to eat a hamburger again at the diner. On the next corner there was a bar and I had a beer then I turned in early after a very difficult day.

I was up early the next morning. The Y as it became to be called was just for sleeping. They had bathrooms but it was communal with toilets all lined up in a row with no privacy. When showering everyone used the same bank of showers and carried a towel to cover yourself up while you dried yourself off in a locker room and dressing before walking back to your room. The dining room was like a hall with tables and white table cloths and a buffet breakfast. There were only men allowed in this place, since it was called the Young Men's Christian Association. I found out later that women had the same kind of arrangement with the Young Women's Christian Association in another location. I finished the day off by staying at the Y and watching American TV for the first time. It was great and so different than the TV in England.

The next morning, I made myself ready to go back into the New York City to have lunch with Joan. Since I had arranged to meet her at the Bellevue Hospital at 12 noon for lunch, I took my time to get down to the subway at Flushing to catch the train to Manhattan and meet her at noon. I arrived well ahead of time and told the guard at the front desk of the hospital I had arrived and to tell Joan that I had arrived. She came down a marble staircase and very pleasantly invited me up to her office before we left for lunch. We walked together into an elevator and came to her floor where she opened one of the many doors in the corridor and I was in her office. There were other ladies in the office that shared the space with Joan and she began to introduce them me to me. The other girls were giggling and said they loved my British accent. The other person said all the introductions and then began to tell me how well dressed I was. She was especially admiring my British brown shoes and she enjoyed looking at them. I did find this strange but thought that I since was in a different country maybe people admired shoes. She also liked my blue raincoat. Joan was very nice and totally different from the day before so she got ready to leave the office to go to lunch. She asked me if I liked pizza. I did not know what that was but I said that I was willing to try it. She said that she knew of a nice pizzeria nearby and we could have lunch there.

We walked across the road mostly in silence and arrived at the restaurant which was a very small local place. We were seated at the table and I tried to start some small talk. I asked about her job and what she liked to do until I asked her casually why both she and her mother were so silent on the evening that they met me at the docks. She really did not answer that question and just avoided it. She asked again, was I Catholic. I said no, I was Church of England. She then said that denomination in America was called Episcopal in the US. She said that her mother did not like her to go out with anyone that is not Catholic. I explained that I did not understand any of her questions since we were just pen friends. I had just corresponded with her for over six years and it was her mother who was secretary to Mayor Wagner. I also told her that since I originally had written to the mayor of New York City the mayor had received my letter and I assumed that my letter was passed to your mother. I also told her that I appreciated very much her father and mother sponsoring me to come to America. It was a nice conversation but was strained. It was not unpleasant, just a question and answer type of meeting. The pizza finally did arrive at the table and for the first time I tasted pizza and I loved it. To this day it is my favorite meal.

We talked a little more and I asked her if it was possible to make some arrangement at work to allow her to take some time off to show me her city. She did say that she would try and eventually she managed to get two days off the following week. She said that she would ask her mother if I could come over to their house for dinner the following Sunday. She arranged for me to meet her father John Mason under the tower clock on Flushing Main Street at a certain time and we would take the bus together to their house. I met her father and we caught the bus to make a connection and then to another bus to the corner of her street. We went into her house which was quite small and met her mother again and they were both very nice to me compared to what it was like when I arrived on the dock. Their house was very small with only two bedrooms and I could now understand and realized that since there were only two bedrooms it would not allow a visitor to stay overnight. There was no room for any overnight visitors in their little house.

She told me that they did not have a car, her father worked on the subway trains in some unknown position. I began to understand that maybe I had misjudged them from the beginning but even that did not really work with me. I believe to this day that if I had not gone to visit her office the day after I had arrived, I would never have contacted her again. I eventually did meet her again later on which I will mention at a later time in this book.

Now after all these 60+ years being in America I can understand that they were probably just embarrassed to have to send an overseas guest to the Y for a room, maybe. After my dinner with them I took the bus back on my own to the Y and had an early night after watching a little TV in the community room. I phoned her and thanked them again for their hospitality which I think made them feel a whole lot better.

One visit I had to make was to go to the British Embassy to register my arrival in the US. The British government at that time encouraged all British subjects to register so that they knew you were in the country and they gave support to their subjects. I now had to start looking to get my union card for work in America. I had previously made plans to transfer my British printing union card before I left England so that I could transfer to the equivalent printing union in New York. They called it a traveler's card. My British union chairman wrote a letter to the president of the New York Printers Union who wrote back saying that I would be welcome to work in America. I must make an appointment to appear before the board of directors to establish my credentials after I arrived. I would then be told when the date of the next board meeting would be. I made a date to appear before the union board and made my way to the address of the union headquarters and went upstairs in an old building to the offices. I first made the mistake of going to the ground floor where the men were waiting for a work call. One man pointed upstairs.

There were a lot of men sitting around playing cards smoking cigars and the smoke was so thick I could hardly see across the room. They were obviously waiting to be called when a job came in. I was quite unhappy about that because I had heard that there was a deep recession in America in 1958 and looking at all these men that were out of work I wondered if I could ever get a chance of getting work with so many Americans out of work.

I climbed up the stairs to the union office and was met by a heavy looking man with a cigar in his mouth that had to be six inches long. His face was ruddy red and he looked like a movie gangster. I told him who I was and he said that he would set up an appointment for me to meet the board of directors of the union and they would decide if I was to be given a union card to work. He indicated that the next board of directors meeting was the following week on Wednesday evening at 7:00 pm and the next important step would be taken then. I would be notified when to attend that meeting

In between time I decided to do some sightseeing so I walked uptown to midtown Manhattan to Times Square. It was a fantastic sight with three roads meeting together like a giant crisscross then parting at the end of the crisscross in a different direction. I thought at the time how busy the area was. There were many cars moving from all directions. All cars with large fins on the back bumpers with lots of chrome all over the car and they were large in size. Horns blew from the cars and there was such a jumble of activity it made me feel that there had to be an accident any second. I walked across into what they called a pedestrian safety zone where pedestrians could be safe from the traffic in the middle of Times Square. I took a lot of photos of Times Square amid the traffic that afternoon and I still have them showing the colors of the cars and how much traffic there was. I really felt at home because here I was in the middle of Manhattan known as the crossroads of the world. The hustle and bustle were really fantastic. I could see all the advertisements showing American products like an Admiral television. There was even a large lighted billboard that had a face smoking a huge cigarette with a huge cigarette puffing out real smoke. All along the sidewalks were shops selling everything from radios and souvenirs and above the shops were dance studios where as I looked up at the glass window where they were teaching dancing. There were nightclubs advertising the show for the night with big names like Dean Martin and Jerry Lewis. There was a kaleidoscope of color, noise and bustle and the smell of food cooking that was exciting. I could not wait to see Times Square all lit up at night. There were also what they called duel toned cars that had two colors painted from the roof to the lower part of the car and the car was at least fifteen feet long. I made way over to the subway station to catch the subway back to Flushing and the YMCA.

Before I left England one of my friends told me that they had a relative in New York and that they would introduce me to them by mail so when I arrived I could contact them. They gave me their phone number so as soon as I arrived I did call them and found to my surprise that they lived just a few blocks away from the Y that I was staying so they were kind enough to invite me over to their home for the evening. Their name I remember was Mr. and Mrs. Shetty. We set a time for me to visit. They lived in a high rise apartment building and the home was very impressive to me. We first had cocktails which I had taken a great liking to on the ship coming over and then they said that they had made reservations at a restaurant for us. They were both professional people and did not usually eat in their home. They preferred to eat out in a restaurant when they returned home from work. They said that they were editors for Time Magazine in New York and that they commuted each day from Flushing subway station into New York to their offices. I remember that they were very proud of their Hi Fi custom made record player that was so big that it stood on the floor. He played some of his favorite records on it and it seem like there was speakers all around the room. I had never heard of a Hi Fi stereo system in England before arriving here.

They kept their car in the garage of the apartment house underneath the ground floor of the building so we took the elevator down to the garage. As we pulled out of the garage, I could see that we were not going into the direction of where the YMCA was located, we were going to a whole different area. We pulled into the parking lot of a very nice restaurant that advertised it being a steak house. I knew then that I was in trouble because I was a vegetarian and did not eat meat. We were seated at the table and the waiter came over and asked what we would like to order. Mr. Shetty ordered a martini for all three of us and then began to recommend what kind of steak would I like. I felt embarrassed because I did not want to tell him that he had brought me into this kind of restaurant so I ordered my steak well done. When it arrived on the plate, I could see that their idea of being well done was quite different to mine. It was still a little bloody, but I decided to eat it and managed to eat half of the steak that was put in front of me. There was nothing else that I could do other than attack and eat it quick. I can definitely say that I did not enjoy that steak although I knew that it must have cost them quite a lot of money. We had good conversation during the meal and after the meal was over and the check was paid, they both said they would like to drive around town and show me the local area although it was dark outside being well past eight o'clock.

He drove us up and down Northern Boulevard where the lights were so bright that it almost seemed to me to be like daylight. I was not used to seeing so many neon flashing lights in stores and restaurants and I didn't know that Northern Boulevard was one of the main shopping areas in that part of Queens County. Suddenly he pulled off of the road up a ramp and we were on a highway called Southern State Parkway, where he speeded up to keep up with the traffic. I had never been driven in a car that went this speed in such comfort before. Suddenly behind us there were flashing lights and I heard a siren. By showing me how fast his car could go he had been caught speeding and the police were going to pull him over. It was just like the movies as the officer came up to the door and asked for his license. Mr. Shetty tried to explain that he had a visitor from England and that he was just showing him his car and the kind of roads America used to drive around. He gave Mr. Shetty a speeding ticket for exceeding 50 mph speed limit on the Southern State Parkway. He was quite upset and it really killed the evening and soon they made their way back to the Y and after I thanked them for such a nice evening, they said that they would call me again and would have dinner at their house. He probably thought that it was safer to do that with me. We did eventually make a dinner date.

Joan Mason and I did eventually did get together again. We did have a good time during those days. We would meet each morning at the subway station at the Flushing subway terminal. She took two days off and we took the subway into New York, into Grand Central Station and then took the downtown train to Battery Park. It was located on the lowest tip of the city where the ferry boats docked and we went to see the Statue of Liberty. The ferry ride was really great since we could then look back at the city and see the high skyscrapers in the business part called Wall Street. Then in the distance were the skyscrapers of mid-town like the Empire State Building and the Chrysler Building. The next day she showed me the mid-town part of the city. We went into the United Nations building and then up into the Empire State Building. We went to a restaurant for dinner on Broadway and walked across Times Square. It was full of theaters, great restaurants and a place that I got to know so well in years to come. Afterwards we went to a movie that was playing on Broadway called South Pacific which was made from an original Broadway musical show. She was turning out to be a nice girl, but unfortunately she had no personality and I just could not get through to her. At times I was beginning to think that all those years of writing to each other I had been writing not to Joan but to her mother who was very nice to me.

I really had to find time to look for a job so the following week was my appointment for the interview at the union office. I presented my-self at the correct time to the board of directors hoping that I would be able to work in the printing trade in Manhattan and make some mon-ey. I arrived at the appointed time of 7:00 pm and was directed into the board room of the union headquarters of Local 13 in New York City. It was a meeting of very strange men. They all dressed and looked like gangsters with the gold jewelry and various colored suits. Mr. Alexander was presiding and they all welcomed me to New York. In fact, they were very nice people and I felt very comfortable with them. They asked me about my printing background then asked me various practical questions on how to operate a printing press. After about ten minutes of questions about the trade the president Mr. Alexander asked how I crossed the Atlantic, by sea or by air and I answered that I had arrived on the Queen Elizabeth. This definitely impressed them and Mr. Alexander then asked me if I saw the Lady in the Bay, thinking quickly I realized that he meant the Statue of Liberty. I said yes, that I had seen her and thought that it was a magnificent statue standing with her arm up reached with the torch light welcoming all those that entered America. He then said some very important words that would get me to stay in America. He said always remember that while you are in America the Lady in the Bay will always take great care of you. I was a little taken back by this and I thanked him. He also said that America and the printing industry in America were going through a recession and jobs were hard to find. He asked me to leave the room for a while and they would discuss my case.

I left the room and could hear the men still in the other room even at this late hour. The door to the conference room opened and I was called back into the meeting room. Cigar smoke was everywhere and I nearly choked on the smoke with ten or more men smoking these long cigars. Mr. Alexander called the meeting to order and then told me that they had agreed for me to have a temporary working union card, but I must find a job in a union shop first. The catch was that nobody would hire me if I did not have a union card.

America in the year 1958 was very different than it is today, both socially and economically. America had large cities but most were surrounded by small communities. The country was vibrant and pulsating with optimism. Everyone talked of the future, of how things were going to make life easier. Most Americans owned their homes with small gardens. They were built for the returning soldiers from WW II. People then had money left over from their paycheck at the end of the week. Taxes were low and few if any other taxes were imposed except Federal wage tax. Many states had no state tax at that time.

During the first month I had great difficulty in finding a job because there was a business recession in America and there were a lot of people out of work. I practically lived downstairs in the union hall with the others waiting for that call that said a job was available for two weeks at some printing company and the hands would go up to be chosen. I did get a couple of night jobs here and there and was able to operate the presses but nothing that was a permanent job. I began to quickly run out of money by mid-June so I decided finally that I would have to go back to England soon, since without a steady job I could not stay for too much longer. I decided to return back to England as soon as I could get a reservation on a ship. It seemed that everything was going wrong and maybe I was not destined to stay in America.

In the meantime, I would ride a Greyhound bus and do some exploring of the country while I was here. The date was June 1958. I had been in America for about two months when something strange happened to change everything. I had called the Cunard shipping lines and found that because summer was approaching the ocean liner ships to Southampton, England were booked full of American tourists going to Europe. I asked the ticket agent if there were any other alternatives he might suggest. He suggested that I book a passage on a United States Lines freighter that was going to London docks on June 6th and a one-way ticket would cost me $200.00. I bought a one-way ticket to London Docks, England on a freighter that carries 12 passengers first class only. Not back to Southampton where I had left on the Queen Elizabeth, but on a United States Lines freighter called the American Harvester. It was ironic to come over on the elegant Queen Elizabeth and I would be returning back to England on a freighter that carried only 12 passengers although it was first class only. Then something happened that was very strange. One evening fate overtook me and changed not only my own life but of other lives that would follow behind me in later years. Now here is a twist in the saga of my story which to me is almost unexplainable.

One evening I decided to go to the movies in downtown Flushing and noticed that they were showing a movie called Clipper Ship which was about a Danish training clipper ship. In the movie the ship was visiting New York and the cadets on board were sightseeing all of the places in New York that I now knew very well. I found myself feeling that this city was still part mine. I went into the movie theater prior to seeing this movie with the attitude of not caring if I went home to England, in fact actually looking forward to going home. When I came out of the theater after seeing that movie it had entirely changed my mind and some sort of voice in my mind began telling me to stay here in the US.

On the way back to the YMCA I passed by the newspaper stand at the Flushing subway station where I decided to buy the New York Times, one last time. I had a strange urge to look one more time to look at the job ads in the newspaper before I left New York. I felt that to go back home to London would be a failure. I had looked at so many jobs in the wanted ads before and found nothing. I wanted to see in the want ads one that said, union shop on the printer listing but it seemed unlikely if impossible. I was not going to look anymore because there were no jobs available for me and it would again just disappoint me to take another look. But fate looked favorably on me that day. I bought the newspaper at the news stand at the subway station and opened up the pages to the want ads and there it was. I could not believe my eyes! I had turned to the want ads and incredibly in the help wanted I saw there was a printer's job listed as a union shop. It is very unusual since normally an employer that is under contract to a union must call up the union first and have them send over an experience member of their union. A company who was under union contract could be heavily fined if they did not first call the union for a pressman if the position became open. The position should be filled by a card-carrying union member. I was so excited I could not sleep wondering what could have happened to have caused that job to be listed and become available to a union shop.

The next morning, I took the subway to the printer's location in downtown Manhattan and met the owner. He was located on Murry Street quite near the Mayor's office that had started my odyssey with my letter years before asking for a pen friend. I arrived at the address and I climbed aboard a rickety elevator that was at least a hundred years old and it creakily wheezed its way up the shaft to the ninth floor where the elevator doors opened up to a printing press room. I could smell the printing ink and the smell of paper, that great smell that I loved. There was a lady in a small alcove typing on a typewriter and asked me who I wanted to see. I told her that I wanted to see the owner. He came out of the press room and asked me what I wanted. I showed him the newspaper ad and that I wanted to apply for the job. First, he looked at me very strangely. He was a small wizened looking man of about 60 years old and told me in a heavy European accent there must be a mistake.

Shaking his head, he called out to his receptionist which turned out to be his wife. Did you place an advertisement in the newspaper for the pressman's job? She shouted out from the alcove, yes, I did. He then began to explain to me that there had been a terrible mistake since his wife had made an error in putting an advertisement in the paper instead of notifying the union. She should have placed the job through the union. After showing her the ad, he started yelling in Yiddish at the woman and told her he would now be in trouble with the union for her not calling the union about the job. He turned to me and said that he was sorry but this was a big mistake that he could not hire me because this was a union shop. I explained to him I had been given permission to work in America by the New York union and if he did not hire me, I would have to return to Europe and abandon my dream of becoming an American. I was guessing that he originally came from Europe, so I looked him in the eye and mentally pleaded with him to give me a job so I would be given my union card and stay in America. He looked me over carefully and finally said he would hire me if I could do the job. I was to call the union and speak with them and if they agreed he would hire me for a six months trial.

I raced back to the union office and looked for Mr. Alexander who I had met during the board meeting and found him in his business of-fice. I explained to him the situation and would he help me so that I could get a job. He explained to me he was in a difficult position since it would not be right to give a non-member a job since there was other Americans out of work in the hiring hall downstairs. He looked at me more intently and said hey, aren't you the Limey boy that came before the board a few weeks ago. I told him yes that was me and I needed help to find a job for me to stay in America. I explained the situation to him and he said that the rules are that you cannot work in a union shop unless you have a card. I decided that this would be my last chance to stay in America so I took a deep breath and went for broke. I said to him, Mr. Alexander, wasn't it you that asked me if I had seen the Lady in the Bay when I passed the Statue of Liberty on the ship? You then said to me always remember that while you are in America and the Lady in the Bay would always take care of you. He replied yes, I do remember saying that to you. I then said to him Mr. Alexander please take care of me because if you don't, I will have to go back to England on a freighter leaving from Brooklyn docks back to England next week. He looked at me in an old-fashioned way and smiled and said ok boy'o tell the printer to call me and I will authorize you to work there and if he hires you and you work out to his satisfaction, in six months you will get our union card.

I was so happy and found a new feeling of being part of something. I did not know what, but I did feel a very different person and a great feeling of accomplishment of belonging. I quickly went back to D&F Printing Company to tell Sam that the union had agreed. He told me that they had already called him and asked me when I could start. I answered very quickly how about tomorrow? He laughed and said tomorrow would be fine and be here at 8:00 am. Fantastic! I now had money coming in each week to pay my bills. The take home pay was only $100.00 dollars per week at that time and time and a half for overtime, but it was like a fortune to me. I will always be very grateful to Sam for giving me this opportunity, he was a good man.

I cancelled the reservation on the freighter at Cunard and received my passage money back and felt like I was a rich man. I started work the following day and stayed there for over two years. I took the subway each day to Manhattan to get to work and returned the same way. Luckily for me the job went well and I worked there for over two years and received my union card and all of its benefits such as medical as promised.

The interesting thing about this event in my life is that it changed everything for me and others. I had gone to the movies that night knowing that I would have probably been going back to England a failure. First, if I had not looked at the help wanted advertisements in the newspaper that evening, I would have not found that job advertised. I had given up even looking for a job at that time. Something told me to look again in the newspaper when I had given up all hope. Secondly, if the employer's printers' wife had not made the mistake by posting the job in the newspaper instead of calling the union I probably would have returned to England as planned on the freighter and carried on my life's plan in England. It was like a fork in the road that changed everything for the future.

My mother and Colin would not have come over to America three years later to live in America. Colin and I would have probably married English girls somewhere in England and our children born here in America would not have been born as they are now. Colin would not have to have gone to Vietnam with the 1st Marine Division and endured the great hardships that he had to endure while he was in the trenches, fighting the Vietcong soldiers. Life for me would have been quite different.

After a few weeks at the YMCA my financial funds became much better so I moved and rented a room in a house that took in gentlemen boarders for ten dollars a week. The landlady's name was May Mallick. She was a delightful elderly Jewish lady who had a son who played trumpet on the cruise ships and came home about three times a year. My landlady told me she gave him everything he wanted. I remember that she even bought him a brand new yellow Ford Sunliner convertible car. That car was beautiful and was huge, at least fifteen feet long with yellow primrose paint.

I was getting lonely after a while and asked around if there were any other English people in the area. I was told there was an organization called the British War Veterans of America. It was located nearby and consisted of British war veterans living in America and as long as I had military service in Britain, I could join this club and enjoy the company that it offered. It was really great. They welcomed me into their club and before long I was part of them. While active in the BWV I met lots of friends and they had many activities during the summer such as picnics and outings to other branches of the organization. I was not so lonely anymore and was beginning to merge into American society. I was also beginning to understand the lifestyle of being an American.

My British background got me into trouble during the first year. We did not have a telephone in the house when I lived in England so if we wanted to visit any member of our family in the same town on a Sunday afternoon, we would take a bus to visit them. The saying which was very innocent meaning to let's go knock up Aunt Ida. Meaning we would physically knock on her door to see if she was in. If she was not in, we would walk down the street to visit another relative. To use the expression of knocking up was an innocent remark that was said every day in England. This did get me into trouble a few times as the incident I will relate actually happened as follows.

During the first few months in New York, I met some interesting people and one lady asked me to join her and her friends at her uptown east side, high rise apartment. The city of New York is an island, Manhattan appears on a map in the shape of a carrot with the point at the bottom called downtown then further north is midtown, as we proceed north the numbers of the streets go higher. As you proceed higher up the neighborhood gets very expensive and very nice. The upper east side of Manhattan that has numbers in the mid-eighties is very upscale with tall residential skyscrapers fifty floors or higher. I had met a young woman one Saturday night at one of the dances I attended and I was invited to her afternoon party on the upper east side of Manhattan the following Sunday afternoon. I accepted and she gave me her address and the suggested time of arrival. Her apartment was located on the 33rd floor of a high rise apartment building overlooking the East River of Manhattan and was very, very upscale.

I rode the elevator up to her numbered floor where the elevator doors opened right into her apartment living room. There were lots of well-dressed people at the party and the talk was a typical New York stand up, Sunday afternoon, subdued cocktail party. They were all drinking different cocktails with different liquors. Looking out of the tall, wide windows overlooking downtown New York the view was fantastic. I could see all of Manhattan to the south to Battery Park. It was a nice party with guests talking very low in their grouped conversations. I had not seen anyone that I could talk with since most all were couples and my friend who had invited me was like a social butterfly moving around the room chatting to everyone. She had a waitress that worked around the room with a tray of cocktail drinks and food. After about an hour or so, after meeting everybody I decided to leave. I went up to my hostess who had invited me to the party and thanked her and I said thank you so much for your invitation and next time I am in the neighborhood I will knock you up again! At that time my British accent was quite prominent and it stood out well in a quiet crowded room. All of the guests were speaking very low between their groups. My voice carried, all around the room, loud and clear to all of the other party attendees.

Upon hearing this everybody stopped talking, there was a silence and they all looked towards me. My hostess was shocked. Unknown to me at the time knocking up was and still is a very bad, improper phrase in America. To me at that time, it was just calling on someone and knocking on their door. Needless to say, I was not invited back to any of her future parties. It was I believe an opportunity lost.

I had been in America now for about six months and I felt myself moving ahead for the first time after the severe bumpy ride I had for the first few months when I almost returned back to England. I was having a great time meeting a lot of new people now both on my own and through the British War Vets. I decided to learn how to drive. I had a friend in the BWV named Frank who agreed to teach me how to drive his car. We went out to Jones Beach on the Atlantic side of Long Island and I learned to drive in the huge open parking lots of Jones Beach State Park when there was nobody there in the winter. He drove a 1956 Chevrolet dual toned in the color green on the bottom and cream color on the top. Week after week I practiced driving around this huge parking lot and finally, he said I was ready to go on the roadway. I was really nervous driving for the first time on the open road driving on the right hand side of the road on the way back to his apartment. We arrived back at his house and I was ready to take my driving test.

I first had to contact the New York Motor Vehicle Bureau to make an appointment for the driving test located at their Nassau County driving test track. We all can remember our first driving license test. My test appointment time came and there I was with the driving instructor sitting alongside of me directing me to drive between the red cones weaving in and out hoping that I did not knock any cones over. He told me to pull up and do a parallel park and I felt like I was shaking I was so scared of failing this driving test. We drove towards a line of cars parked alongside of the curb. There was a space in between a group of cars that seemed to me to be a very small place to do a parallel park. He told me to parallel park and slide the car into this tiny slot without going on the curb. Impossible I thought since there did not seem to be much room to slide in behind the space between two cars. He gave me the first try which did not pass and then he said he would let me try again. I did and this time I parked in between the cars perfectly without going up on the curb. I saw the driving instructor writing on his sheet. He asked me if I had applied before for a license and I said no, that this was my first time. He smiled at me and said that he should not really tell me but I had passed the test and that I would get my license in the mail in a week or so. I was thrilled and so was my friend Frank because I was practicing with his car and I did not have to do that with him in his car any more.

I started looking around for an old car to buy but I had a problem. I was still 21 years old and insurance was very expensive for young men of my age to get car insurance. The system in New York State was that when you applied for insurance you were put into what they called an assigned risk pool where all of the insurance companies pooled funds for the young people into a group insurance policy until they turned the age of 25. After that time the individual driving insurance could be purchased by any insurance company and the insurance rate came down very quickly in price. The interesting part is that I bought a grey 1952 Chevy power glide for $365.00 cash but because the insurance pool was so expensive, I had to finance the insurance.

I finally had wheels and could go anywhere that I wanted to go. I took the car out for a test drive on the parkways of Queens, on the northern and southern parkways. The Long Island Expressway had not been built at that time, but a year later after it had been completed it would be called by the locals the longest parking lot in the world because of traffic jams. My car had an AM radio on the dash board, had automatic transmission, power steering and a real clock. This car, two years later, was destined to carry me across America on the famous Route 66 highway to California, but those adventures will be told in later chapters. It was really great in the spring-summer of 1959. I was young and I was living in a great country and had wheels to go wherever I wanted to go. I played the radio listening to all the rock and roll music while I was driving to anywhere taking a joy ride just so that I could get on the road and go anywhere I wanted to go.

One of my friends was a guy called Ritchie Villani. I often wonder where he is today. He was a very strong guy and I was just the opposite. I was very skinny and could not find a girl to go out with me. When Ritchie and I went down to Jones Beach we no sooner laid down the blanket on the sand when the girls would drift over and chat up Ritchie.

Before long there were three or four great looking girls on our blanket. He also was the manager of a health club called Vic Tanney's over on Manhasset Miracle Mile Shopping Mall. It was one of the first malls in the country. It had a pool and some exercise machines and was the forerunner of a modern day health club. He was going out with a girl who at that time was the hat check girl at a night club on the beach called the Magic Touch.

Long Beach was a town on the southern side of Long Island and was a very nice place to spend an evening. There were many very nice restaurants usually with dinner, dancing and a stand-up comedian included at a very reasonable price. Dinner was offered since it was a restaurant or if you did not want to have dinner there was a band playing with lots of dancing into the wee hours of the morning. Ritchie also introduced me to a German girl named Perkie and she came from Frankfurt, Germany and was here in America to be a student at a nursing school in Virginia in the fall. We were good friends for almost a year until she had to leave and go to a nursing school in Newport News, Virginia.

In those days Long Island was not readily accessible to anyone in the city of New York or Brooklyn because the distance for them to travel and the time it took to get to Jones Beach only allowed them to use the closer beaches such as Coney Island. They began building the Long Island Expressway in 1955 and by the time I arrived the construction had only reached Flushing, Main Street and even then, it was just a wide ditch in the land not even close to being finished. People that wanted to go to Jones Beach from far away in Brooklyn and Manhattan would have to take old Route 27 Sunrise Highway which was a long slow ride out east on Long Island.

I was having a very good time in America by the end of 1958 and was beginning to realize that I was not going back to England but would be staying in America and become an American citizen. I felt happy and feeling at home living on Long Island and in America. I began to think that it would be nice to invite mum and Colin to come to America and see what it was like. I wrote to mum and asked her if she and Colin would like to come over for a three week vacation the following year of 1959. I told her that I would pay for everything. I would pay for the Queen Elizabeth ship cost and for the three weeks that she would be here in the summer of 1959. She wrote back that she would like that very much so I began to make plans for the three of us to be together again the following year of 1959. I saved up my money and worked long hours so that there would be enough money to pay for them to come over here, including the ships fare for two people on the Queen Elizabeth. I reserved the same cabin that I had and clued her in to the social items such as a posh dress for dinner and a suit and tie for Colin. It was settled for July 1959.

During the late summer of 1958 I met a young woman named Charlotte Stone at one of the BWV picnics in Montauk Point which is located at the far eastern end of Long Island. She was the daughter of one of the BWV members. We all had a great picnic there and when it came time to go home, I discovered that Charlotte had taken the train outbound from New York to Montauk Point and would have to do the same for the return trip back to New York. She had an apartment in Manhattan on East 54th Street and Madison Avenue. I decided to ask her if she wanted me to drive her back to New York at the end of the picnic. She gratefully accepted and we did the two hour drive back to New York. We had some dinner on the way. It turned out that she was an advertising executive on Madison Avenue and one of the first women to be able to get such an executive position. In those days' women were not offered a working position like that and she had, as they say today, broke the glass ceiling.

After we arrived in Manhattan, she invited me up to her apartment on East 57th Street. There were expensive stores at street level, but by opening up a small street door there were stairs that led up to various apartments above the stores. Her place was a walk up like a studio apartment more or less one room with a small kitchen in an alcove covered by a curtain. She was a very nice lady about ten years older than me but she had a medical problem. She had contracted a few months before a hepatitis strain which prevented her from going out and partying as all her friends were doing. She could not drink and tired easily. She assured me that the medical problem was not contagious and would take a few months to allow her to do her normal social activities. I could not afford to take her to all the very expensive places where she would previously go with her friends. We went out together quite a lot to the movies and drove out into the country and I felt it would do her good to get out and be with other people. She told me that her doctor had given her a medical note to say that the medical problem with her liver would heal but would take time. Charlotte showed me all the best places to go in New York such as Birdland's night club and Angelo's restaurant. The 1930's song Lullaby of Birdland says it all. We went to jazz clubs on Broadway, Roseland Dance Hall, Greenwich Village night clubs, and other nightspots in the downtown area of New York. It was a mutual arrangement since she needed someone to go out with and I needed someone to show me all these good places to go where it seemed she had been and done it before. Our agreement was that when she felt better and she wanted to return to go out with her wealthy friends again we would part company and she would go back with her friends. A simple arrangement. She told me her family came from one of the surrounding counties of New York City and her family was very politically active in New York.

One Sunday I drove into Manhattan to her flat and she said that we were going to take out a young girl that was her niece. The girl was about six years old and lived downtown New York so we arrived to pick her up and I met her family who's named was Foster. The girls name was Jodie we all drove up into the Bronx to visit the Bronx Zoo. It was really strange for me at 21 to be this domestic walking and holding hands with a little girl like she was one of my own family. We took some sandwiches and drinks to picnic in the park area and it was a wonderful day for me, like I had a family.

One day Charlotte and I drove out to the Pennsylvania Dutch country in Pennsylvania for the day. Not knowing at that time in the far distant future I would be living in that state. We drove around the countryside and saw the Pennsylvania Dutch people driving their buggies around the countryside. I did have some very nice times with her and she did a lot for me to get used to being an American showing me some nice places to visit and just how Americans at that time lived. After about four or so months of going out with each other I began to see a restless in her and asked her what was the problem and she said that some of her friends asked her to go out for an evening just like she did before she got sick. She felt bad that I would be left out of things. I reluctantly said that it was no problem and we parted company as we had agreed to her going off on her own back to her circle of friends. I was wondering what next was around the next corner. I often wondered what happened to Charlotte after we parted company.

Christmas of 1958 arrived, my first Christmas in America and I was still active in the British War Veterans. There was the Christmas party for the BVA and I met another person that came from Britain. Billy Sievright came from Glasgow, Scotland. He came over to America to stay with one of his aunts who had married an American after the war. He was really not my kind of person that I would choose to be friends with but it seemed we were just thrown together. His aunt lived not too far away on Long Island so they invited me for dinner one Sunday afternoon. His uncle went by the name of Mac who also came originally from Scotland. I do not believe that they were really married but just lived together. They were nice enough to me and I was invited a lot to visit them for dinner after that first Christmas holiday. Billy and I went into Manhattan many times and one visit is worth mentioning.

We decided to go to a famous night club on Broadway and 44th Street called Birdland for New Year's Eve. This night club was very well known to New Yorkers and it was a place that you must wear a suit and tie and go for dinner and dance for the evening. It was New Year's Eve 1959. The entertainment was top notch with sometimes having the best entertainers in America doing their show. In those days it was so inexpensive to go out for a nice evening at a famous nightclub. Billy and I had dinner there and during the dance period we were introduced to two Australian girls. Bill picked out his girl and I was left with a very attractive girl by the name of Amelia. We danced the night through until the wee hours of the morning so it came to a point that we could not find Billy and his girlfriend that lived with Amelia. I suggested we take the subway uptown where she and her girlfriends lived in an upstairs apartment on 114th Street west of Broadway and escort her home. In those days it was quite safe to travel on the subway so late at night. We arrived at her subway stop and we walked over to the west side to her apartment. She was on the third floor with no elevator. The staircase was old and dirty as we climbed up to her apartment. She invited me inside to her apartment and put on a pot of coffee. She was a little bit drunk but we did not have a problem.

After a while I told her that it was in the wee hours of the morning and I must be getting back to my place in Queens, about an hour away. She knew where that was but said that it was too late to go home now, but if I promised to behave I could use the sofa until the morning when I could leave when it was daylight. I agreed, so she wished me good night and retired to her room and shut her door. I undressed to my underwear and had a blanket over me and went to sleep. It was about 4:00 am in the morning at that time. About 7:00 am I was awakened by a rough shaking of my shoulder. It was Amelia, a very angry Amelia, shouting what have I done, I have spent the night with a strange man. She pushed me off of the sofa and I tried to find my clothes, get dressed and head for the door. She was shouting that now since she was a good Catholic she must now go to confession right away and then she suddenly threw a book at me. Suddenly, she saw that she had thrown her bible at me as I was carrying my clothes under my arms and trying to dodge whatever more she would throw at me. She pushed me towards the front door and as I went past the door on to the stairwell, I heard a click of her door locking. I was out of the apartment in a cold January morning on the stairway. I found myself locked outside a closed door on a freezing cold apartment stair landing with a big problem. She had thrown my clothes out with me and here I was standing on a cold marble staircase with all my clothes under my arm hoping that nobody would come walking down the stairs. I started to put on my clothes and suddenly my fears become real as I heard multiple footsteps coming down the stairs and suddenly there appeared two adult people with children. It looked like they were walking down the stairs on their way to a church service. I was balancing myself on one leg and trying to put on my trousers, putting one leg in first and trying to balance myself at the same time. I noticed that it was a family with a father, mother and two children. I was horrified since here I was being thrown out of an apartment with only half my clothes on. I was half naked standing on a cold winter's morning on the first few hours of New Year's Day trying to put my clothes on and here come these people. As they became near, they stopped, looked at me first with a facial expression of total distain looking at me hard like only a true New Yorker can do and slowly passed by me and continued on down the stairs without a second look. I was shocked because I had spent the night on a sofa in a girl's apartment at her invitation, and I had been thrown out into the cold. Needless to say, I made no further contact with Amelia and when I did catch up with Billy, he said that he went home after the dinner dance and did not know where his girl had gone.

I was still working for D&F Printing Company after two years with Al Finkelstein, the owner, and had completed my six month trial period of operating a press. One day there was a great commotion on the stairway. I had noticed that they had opened the freight elevator doors that indicated that something large was being delivered. It was a press with new, modern operations. He brought in his brother-in-law to work in my position and I was laid off and out of work. I went over to the union hall and told Mr. Alexander who said that since I had completed my six month trial, I would soon receive my union card in the mail. He told me to go and wait with the other men and who were out of work and wait my turn for the next job to come along.

I only waited at the union hall for about four hours when the hiring boss called out that there was a job opening uptown for a press operator. Nobody seemed to want the job because it was only for two weeks so said I would take it. I took the official note of employment that proved the union had given me. I was to give this to the foreman of my new job at a large printer called Lenz and Richter located in a large building full of printers alongside of the Holland Tunnel. I introduced myself to my new boss Al Richter. Here I thought was a great opportunity because it was a large company with about fifty employees with a higher pay scale, but it was on the night shift from 4:30 pm to 11:30 pm. The machines that I operated on were much newer and to me that was a great step up. I worked the two weeks and was ready to leave when Al Richter the owner of the business came over to me and asked if I could stay on permanently. I immediately agreed and I now had a full-time job in a large company offering more money.

After I had been working there for a few months they bought a brand new machine that had a new technology called offset. It was a lithographic printing press. It was the start of a new printing trend in the printing industry called lithography that would continue through the next forty years. Al who was the owner sent around a note to me that they were prepared to offer an apprenticeship to either me or one other young guy on this new process machine. Before I could really say yes, they decided to give it to an older person with more experience. I had lost again the opportunity for an apprenticeship which I had been after since I left school in England. I was assigned again to a larger machine with more money and was in charge of this machine that needed two men to operate the press.

As pressman I was primarily located at the front end of the press where the printed sheets were stacked and the feeder operator loaded all the paper into the press in a large pile on a skid at the back of the machine. One night I talked with my press operator who worked at the other end of the press who had a heavy accent. I asked him where he was from and he said he was from Germany. I told him I was from London and grew up as a child during the war. I then asked him had he ever been to London and he said with a great big grin said yes, he had visited London but only from the air. I asked him how could that be and he said that he was a Luftwaffe bomber pilot during the war. I was not happy working with him at that time with someone that had been trying to kill me when I was a child, but I thought it was OK and we remained work friends while I worked there.

It was now the day that mum and Colin would be arriving for their three week vacation in America. I went to meet them at the Pier 59 where I had arrived a year before. I was so excited for them to arrive and maybe get the same feeling I did. The ship docked at 7:00 pm and I soon found them coming through the arrival hall and under the great arch. They were so impressed with what they saw from the dock and looking out of the car window as we sped through the city and on to the expressways. I was then living in a single room in Queens at May Mollick's boarding house. I only had one room so I put mum and Colin in my room and I slept in my car in an underground garage to save money on a hotel room.

I drove mum and Colin all over the east coast by car. From New York City to Niagara Falls, down to Virginia, Williamsburg and Jamestown in the short time we were to be together. We drove just about everywhere.

I managed to get three tickets for a Broadway show and we saw the Music Man on the Broadway stage. I took them to Jones Beach to the Atlantic Ocean and I still have pictures of mum and Colin in the ocean surf. I believe Colin then was 14 years old at the time I hope it impressed him and that he would be able to tell all of his friends about this fabulous country called America when they returned home.

One day while we were out doing our touring I had a thought. I asked my mum if she would like to live in the US. I had actually thought long and hard at this idea, considering and asking myself would it be fair to uproot mum and Colin from their friends and family. In the end I decided to at least ask her if she was interested in emigrating. She replied that she did not think so but she would think it over after she got back to England. Soon it became time to say good bye to my family as they boarded the ship to take them back to England. My mother was quite tanned from the hot summer sun and seemed a different happy person. Colin seamed the same and looking forward to returning back to school and his old friends. He was also tanned since he had been at the beach whenever possible.

Their ship left on time from the New York City docks so after the ship had backed out heading downriver, I quickly climbed into my car parked at the dock. I drove as quickly as possible towards Brooklyn to a small park down river where I would be able to park the car off the road and watch their ship slowly move into the Narrows and gradually sail out into the Atlantic on their way back to England with mum and Colin on board. Later I received a letter from mum saying that all was well and that they had an enjoyable sail back home and was back to work and telling the family about her trip to America. I am sure there must have been a lot of envy going around the family after she got home. I think also she was a celebrity at work since no family or fellow workers had such an opportunity to go to America and she told them all about it.

1959-1960

IT WAS A new decade. It seemed that everybody in America was very optimistic about the future because this new decade held a promise of continuing the good feeling left over from the presidential Eisenhower years of the fifties. The 1950's were coming to a close and American's in general were feeling very good about themselves. The fifties in America were one of political calm, new music, with a general upbeat feeling. Although the Soviets had been the first to send up Sputnik into Earth's orbit, the real concern here was most Americans did not believe it. They could not believe that the Russians were able to do such technology. The unions were very strong in the trades so job security was solid and everybody went home at the end of a week with a full paycheck to pay for the luxuries that Americans enjoyed. They thought that they were on an island separated by the Atlantic Ocean in a sea of prosperity and that the peace would never end.

Anybody that wanted to work had a job and at the end of the week their paycheck paid all the bills and there was always a little something left over for the family to indulge. Such as new kitchen appliances or even a new car in the driveway since credit was so easy to get and everything was made in America. We did not have to worry about the strength of the dollar because most everything was made here. The dollar was king and in post war America, Americans felt good. If we had savings to put in a savings account in the bank, we received a 5% interest on our savings. Our clothes were mostly all made in America and if you bought a business suit it always came with an extra pair of pants. There were very few personal taxes to be paid, just Federal tax and in some states no sales tax at all. After paying all the bills there seem to be a little left over for some luxuries such as international travel and a new car and maybe even buy a new house. They bought new houses in modern new townships like Levittown that was made by a builder named Levitt. This builder was known for changing how houses were built simpler and less expensive. With the help of Uncle Sam's money, Levitt created new cities and built small single-family homes called Levitt homes for the returning GI soldiers from the Second World War and the Korean conflict. He actually made new towns of these homes in the open farms and fields that had not been used for building houses. Returning from the war military personnel were part of the GI bill which gave them an opportunity to go to college and be able to become professional in the trades and in business.

Because of that mindset most people considered themselves middle class Americans and some had enough money to travel all over to Europe or visit Cuba (before 1959) for a vacation. The favorite place that they vacationed was Miami Beach for the summer or winter holidays. Interstate highways were just being built connecting states, cities and towns. Small towns were merging with each other and becoming one large city and were literally merging with each other where they soon began to lose their identity.

There was however still plenty of space to build more homes in the years ahead. I paint this picture because this was the feeling I had when I first arrived in America. There was the feeling of complete freedom due to the high amount of open space. Everything seemed so big and roomy. At times you could drive for fifty miles or more without seeing much traffic or houses. Just open farmland and small quaint towns with houses all mostly framed and made of wood. Houses in America are usually made of wood framing, a design left over from the English Colonial period 1600-1776, because house bricks were too expensive to ship from England. Trees were abundant in the large extensive forests that were readily available in the early colonies. At this time about 1960 we all felt that a change was coming. The feel of the good fifties was leaving and the fabulous 1960's was upon us with all of its crazy characters and songs and demonstrations. What a change that decade made to the average American citizen, both good and bad and in just about every way. Life changed from different kinds of music to a different type of lifestyle and even the clothes that we wore were totally different. The baby boomers had arrived.

For me, this was a great period living in New York City as a young man. It portrayed in this song that Frank Sinatra sung the words and they really applied to me living in Greenwich Village in 1959. The song was called It was a Very Good Year. If you hear it played, listen to the words. He sings about the city girls that lived up the stairs. It happened to me exactly like he sang. It was such an exciting place for a young man to live in Greenwich Village at the southern end of Manhattan. I lived in a brownstone walkup apartment that I rented with another person. The parties were really wild, not bad just different, with out of town people moving into the city. They wore different clothes than other New Yorkers and were called Beatniks. I do not remember his name, but he showed me around the village and we went to many parties and attended the coffee houses listening to folk music that was usually being played on an old guitar.

To see what it was really like, rent a movie called Breakfast at Tiffanies. That movie really typifies the early sixties in New York City and relates to my experiences very much when I lived in Greenwich Village. I really had a great time. Guys were wearing goateed beards and they would recite poetry from a small barstool on the stage area at the back of the bar. There were plenty of restaurants and bars that operated two shows and were open all night. The shows were of popular songs by stars of screen and theater. New York City to me was a wonderland of lights, crowds, traffic, taxis, clubs, and music for as long as the night would last. Most places were open until 5:00 am and nothing much happened before 11:00 pm so we started late to begin with.

First class theater people played there as well as jazz musicians. Birdland was on Broadway and 43rd Street they played Dixieland jazz with Louis Armstrong playing his trumpet up on the bandstand with other well-known jazz musicians such as Duke Ellington. All of the well-known entertainers were there at some time or another and sometimes in the audience a person would be spotlighted and recognized and invited up to play a gig with the band for a few numbers. Many film stars visited there for dinner and entertainment.

In America I found that any shyness that I previously had seemed to have mysteriously left me. Everything that I experienced in England being brought up so reserved quickly disappeared and it was as if I was starting a completely new life and was reborn. I surely fitted in and soon became just another New Yorker. Further uptown on Broadway there was Roseland Dance Hall at 49th Street and Broadway and if you could not find a lady friend there you had a serious problem with yourself. Ladies would come up to us and ask to dance with us. They usually came from the mid-western states and from all over the world to seek their fortunes in New York. They were all headed for New York. I had an edge over the competition because of my English accent. Americans seemed to love it. They would say I just love the way you talk, please say something more. Here I was talking English in my best East London accent and they loved it.

Roseland Dance Hall was packed on a Saturday night and had a dance floor that could hold about 500 people dancing at the same time. It was divided up into two kinds of music, two bands with a huge rotating bandstand. The bandstand would revolve after each set of the ballroom dance music had played and as they were playing, they would then revolve and out would come the Latin American band that played the rumba and meringue. This band would be wearing tropical satin shirts while the band that played regular American dances would all wear bow ties and dinner jackets. Usually when the Latin music started there was a mad dash to the bar to chat up some of the girls that were lying in wait to exchange phone numbers and set up for the next Saturday night. I was like a kid in a candy store, also sometimes out of my depth.

I would listen to WABC New York radio station and listen to the disc jockey Wolf Man Jack who was playing the top 100 songs on the charts. Wolf Man Jack was a disc jockey who had a deep raspy voice and sounded like a wolf man. The radio dial must have had about twenty radio stations AM. At midnight I would tune into the radio show called Milkman's Matinee and they would play all the fifties songs and even 1960's.

We would go out on Long Island to one of the towns and cruise down the streets playing rock and roll music with the windows down in the summer and the music playing loud. Everything was going along just fine when calamity came knocking at my door. I had a shift change. They put me on the night shift from 4:30 pm until midnight, which sometimes included Saturday evening overtime until 11:30 pm. My pay jumped high which was fine but the problem was my social life came to a screeching halt and an immediate standstill. I really could not go out late at night after work. I was too tired since the job involved fairly heavy lifting work. My social life was gone and I could not get any female companion to go out with me because I worked nights.

American television in 1960 came with what we called rabbit ears. This consisted of two chrome covered sticks located on the top of the TV that could be rotated and moved any way to improve the picture quality. This was the only way to adjust the picture. At the back of the set were knobs that you could adjust the horizontal or the contrast of the picture. It was a serious undertaking by having to go around the back of the TV set to adjust the knobs. The TV signal was received through the air by the rabbit ears. While watching TV you constantly had to get up out of the arm chair to adjust the black and white picture. There were always great problems trying to watch your favorite shows with a very poor picture quality. At the best of times many arguments began over the controls of the TV. Unless you grew up with that environment and appreciated the TV quality of color TV today, I do not believe anyone would want to watch any kind of TV show under those conditions.

During the early part of the year of 1960 there was a new candidate that was probably going to be elected as president in November of 1960. His name was John Fitzgerald Kennedy. That caused a big problem in America because he was Catholic and there had never before been a Catholic president and so there were lots of discussions and I began to get interested in politics. He was very appealing to the American electorate because he came from a very wealthy and politically motivated family in the state of Massachusetts. But he was Catholic and many people did not like the idea of a Catholic in the White House. The discussions always indicated that if a Catholic was elected as president he would be influenced by the Pope in the Vatican.

1960, My Visit Back to London

AFTER THE SUMMER was over fall and winter had arrived, I decided I would like to return back to England the following year on a vacation for two weeks to see the family and my old friends. I was really happy to go back to England and see everybody. I bought myself a new suit and other clothing and this time I flew back on the Comet jet airliner. This was the first time that I had flown on a commercial jetliner on a newly designed plane called the Comet. It only took six hours to fly to London. I felt at the time that there was an interesting coincidence since it took almost six days to get to America by sea but only six hours by airliner. However, sailing on the Queen Elizabeth might be slower, but those five days on board were well worth it.

I landed at London's Heathrow Airport just west of London and my mum and Colin met me after I disembarked from the aircraft. Heathrow during the war was an RAF fighter air field that was used by spitfire aircraft to attack the oncoming German bombers in the 1940's. It had now been turned into an international airport, very small, not like it is now. It is now one of the major airports in the world. I have a photo of my arrival in London including me, mum and Colin and some other members of my family. I remember I had on a new brown suit and a bow tie so I think I looked quite dapper.

The first Saturday night I was back in London they gave me a welcome back party. We started off at the local pub then after closing time we moved into one of the houses. Just about everybody crammed into my Uncle Bill's house. Uncle Tom played the piano and everyone sang the old songs. We danced the Hokey Kokey and of course that old

London cockney song Knees up Mother Brown. We also began dancing to the new rock and roll music and dancing to the new beat.

It was good to see my grandmother and uncles and aunts but it felt strange to be in an old-world city. I noticed that everything looked so small. The houses and the highways were small and looked old. Not in the way as being old that needed to be repaired and the roads were not wide like it is in America.

I rented a car for a while but all of the cars were a stick shift gears system that I could not get used to. Up shifting and down shifting, then stalling each time I stopped and started up again. Once I was stalled on a busy road in a shopping area called the Bakers Arms and I just could not get the car into gear without stalling. As I was sitting in my car trying to get it started a policeman knocked on my window. Seeing me struggling to get the car in gear he asked me in a very polite voice saying excuse me sir but are you a qualified driver? I explained to him I was from America and not used to driving a stick shift car in heavy traffic. He was a very polite policeman. He responded that if I allowed him to enter my car, he would give me a few lessons. I certainly agreed and he showed me how to combine my foot pedals, one on the clutch and the other the accelerator slowly engaging each in time together. I tried that and after a few more tries it worked. I thanked him for his lesson and successfully drove away. However, after that incident I decided to turn the car in to the car rental and use the buses and trains.

I wanted to visit my surrogate mother Auntie Ellie in Thundersley so I took the train out to Benfleet and the bus to Bread and Cheese Hill. I had sent a message that I was coming to visit for the day and looked forward so much to seeing her again. I stepped off the bus and followed it slowly up Bread and Cheese Hill and walked up that lovely lane that I knew so well. She was in the front garden checking on some of the roses and we hugged each other and she was so pleased to see me. I looked around for my dog Tess but she said that Tess had died a year or so before because she was so old and unhealthy. She told me that Tess was buried alongside of Uncle Jack in St. Peters Church on the hill. She also told me old Mr. and Mrs. Willis had passed away almost at the same time the year before. We walked up Rhoda Road to the church and looked around the church yard. We returned back to the bungalow and talked some more and had tea and it was time for me to go. We each gave each other some very big hugs and the last I saw of her was her waving from the front garden gate as I walked down the lane to catch a bus back to the railway station and back to London.

I hoped that she would stay well until at least to when I would visit again which happily, she did and we did visit her one more time in 1965 after I was married. I noticed that many of the older people were passing on. It seemed that it was a generation change when the older ones passed and the younger ones took their places.

Mum and I visited my father's grave site at Chingford Mount Cemetery taking some flowers to put on his grave. The cemetery looked nothing like when I had visited before I left for America. At that time there were fewer graves but now the new section where my dad was buried was now full of new graves. Most of the graves there looked in poor condition. While I was standing at the grave memories came flooding back to me of that day July 5, 1947 so many years ago at my dad's funeral. I remembered when I put the rose on top of the coffin and some earth and what my uncle had reminded me of my duties to take care of Colin and mum. We laid the bouquet of flowers on the top of the grave. I quietly whispered and told dad that we missed him so very much and that I was now living in America and that I wished that he had been able to have gone with us to America as a family. I said a quiet farewell dad, I will always remember you, stay with me always.

I had a great time in London and now it was nearly time to go back to America. Before I left, they gave me farewell party at my maternal grandmother's house in Clapton. All of the family was there and they rolled up the carpet in the living room and my Uncle Tom played the piano while my grandmother sang her favorite song 'I can't get my winkle out' referring to a small snail like creature in a black shell from the sea called a winkle. The only way to get the winkle out was with a pin and twist out of the shell that was a great delicacy to the British people.

We talked a little more about mum and Colin living with me in America but she said that she was not ready to make that kind of decision. I said OK but if you change your mind let me know and I will find an apartment for us all on Long Island. I knew enough people to get her and Colin a job if she did decide to live here. I was back on English soil but what a difference I found during my visit to the old country. It was so good to see my family, I felt so different and the country seemed so different. It seemed to me after the wide-open spaces of America that the streets were so narrow and the TV had only three channels.

I realized that I could never again fit into British culture. I had been Americanized to a point that I was better fitted in America society rather than in my own birth country. There was something about America that was so special for me. As we were on the way back to the airport, I asked my mum again if she and Colin would consider immigrating to America and come to me in America. I would make all the permanent visa arrangements for her and Colin. She said that she would like to consider this possibility and think it over so on that note I took that as a possible yes. As my jet took off and I saw my old country dropping away I realized England was no longer was my home country. When the captain said over the speaker that we had crossed back into American airspace I realized that I was an American and could not wait to get back into the United States. I was really going home to America rather than leaving home to go to America. I had spent two weeks in London visiting all my relatives and friends including going back to Thundersley and visiting Auntie Ellie. I began now to look forward to returning home to America. I realized that I could never return back to England as an Englishman because I knew now, I was an American for life.

The campaigning was furious during the summer of 1959 through 1960 and we all watched the presidential conventions of both parties on TV. I was becoming quite political in my new country. Kennedy was elected by one of the narrowest margins in American history. It has been said that the voting was somewhat questionable especially in the state of West Virginia. That state put him over the top of the Electoral College giving him the presidency for four years.

They were building the interstate highways that one day in the near future would crisscross the whole country. They were building the Long Island Expressway in 1959-60 which started at the midtown tunnel that crossed under the East River in New York City into the county of Queens. Prior to building that road it was difficult for the people who lived in New York or Brooklyn. They would have to drive along roads that passed through small towns on Long Island. Some of the names of the roads had such quaint names such as Sunrise Highway, which at that time took half a day to get to any of the beaches on Long Island.

By 1960 the Long Island Expressway had been built as far as Plainview. It headed east past the Jones Beach exit which allowed thousands of New Yorkers from Brooklyn to turn off on the beach exit to go to the Jones Beach. It then became an easy trip for New Yorkers to visit Jones Beach with such an easy to drive from the city to the Long Island beaches. People began to move from Brooklyn out to Long Island and build houses. I lived only a few miles from the beaches. Jones Beach was a barrier island state park and after crossing the bay by way of a causeway there was a toll which cost only 75 cents over the short stretch of water on to the state owned beach. The road ended in either a right or left road that led along the ocean front. There were seven different parking areas for beach goers to choose. It was a huge state park with many different locations. One area had a huge swimming pool off of the beach where there were changing rooms with lockers. There was also another parking area where they had an outdoor stage with theatrical shows during the summer equal to any Broadway show were playing and in the summer time the cool air was cool.

1960, My Trip Across Country

THERE WAS A show on TV called Route 66 that I enjoyed watching. It was about two young guys who drove a corvette across the country on that famous road called Route 66 and having all kinds of adventures and meeting all kinds of people along the way. I felt that I was just as adventurous as these two guys were on TV so I decided that I would do the same and pack up just as the old pioneer settlers did in the 1800's. I had no ties in New York and it would give me an opportunity to see the country as the old settlers did before the open land was taken up by more suburbs.

In my first year in America, I had established myself, done what I wanted to do and now in the true pioneer spirit I wanted to see what lies over the next mountain. One of the young men at the British War Veterans who was about my age and came from Ireland about the same time as I arrived in America, we struck up a friendship. He was going to get married in early June and was moving to Los Angles with his bride. He told me before he left to go to California I would be welcome to stay at their apartment when I arrived for a week or so until I could find a place of my own. I thanked him and said I would do that but how about his new wife, would she have any objections? He replied no problem. That is until I arrived at their house and she discovered that I was English and she was Irish. He had forgotten to tell her that.

After the Labor Day holiday in early November 1960, I began to plan my route across country just as the westbound settlers did in the 1800's and to explore a new country in the west. So late in November I began taking out the road maps to plan my route. I needed to travel west on the southern route since at that time of year the heavy snow-falls began in the higher elevations early so the southern route west took me through Texas and Arizona which were warmer. If I took the northern route, I would pass into the northern states which at that time of year would have early snow. Now I had a plan to drive out west on the famous Route 66 by way of the southern route. There was not much for me to do to prepare since I did not own much to load up in my car.

First item I needed a mechanic to check my car since it was a 1952 Chevy with a lot of miles on it. I had kept it serviced and it seemed to still be running well so I took it down to the local garage and had it tuned up. He checked it out and it had a few things to repair and the mechanic said it was good to go and would hold up well for a long trip like the one I was planning.

Since I was on my own I had only myself to worry about regarding my personal comforts and I could stand up to a lot of inconvenience if that happened to come along and no need to complain if I ran into any difficulty. I now felt myself committed to this trip. I quit my job and decided to drive out to Los Angeles in my old Chevy 1952 model power glide and drive across America coast to coast. Now as I think about it, I must have been crazy. I would not have driven that car today more than one trip around a city block let alone across 3,000 miles of rough country, but I was young and did not have a care in the world and I thought it would be a great adventure. After all I came to America to see America and now, I will see America as it really was. I was going to do it!

Between October and November, I began to close up all the loose ends to start my trip the day after Thanksgiving. I paid my rent in full to May Mollick's for my end of month room rent. When I quit my job, they said they were sorry to see me go and wished me luck. They knew I was a good worker and they told me if this trip did not work out and I had to come back I need only to call and they would reinstate me. Which I thought was very nice of them to say that. I decided I would leave the day after Thanksgiving so I loaded up my belongings onto the back seat of the car and into the trunk. It seems that most of my life I was packing up and going somewhere. I had dinner with some friends for Thanksgiving on Thursday so early Friday morning I headed west to the Golden State of California 3,000 miles away.

I began driving along the Long Island Expressway passing New York City and through the Holland Tunnel from New York into New Jersey. I was bound for more of my adventures in America, to cross the mountains and then cross the Great Plains just as the settlers did in the 1840's. It was going to be a great adventure for a young man from East London at the age of 23.

In those days there were very few interstates that had been completed. I could only use state and federal highways. As soon as I reached St. Louis I would drive on Route 66. I applied and received from AAA Auto Club special maps and I had asked this organization to work out my route plan which was called a Trip-Tik. It is obsolete since we now have GPS systems on our cell phones. It was a flip over booklet which planned out my whole route for three thousand miles. As I passed out of NYC through the Holland Tunnel driving under the Hudson River to New Jersey little did I know the adventures that I would encounter as I drove across America. I would be crossing through the eastern states of Pennsylvania and Ohio, across the Mississippi River, which divides the eastern states from the Midwestern states, where I would pick up Route 66 which began actually began in Chicago.

During the first day it was quite easy since I had travelled this road before. I was heading south towards Philadelphia where I turned west on the Pennsylvania Turnpike and would continue west through the countryside of Pennsylvania. Incidentally, Pennsylvania was named by William Penn of London who had obtained a charter from King James to establish a colony on the banks of the Delaware River. Pennsylvania means land of streams and woods which is worth its title because it is a beautiful lush state especially in summertime.

My first stop for the night was in town called New Stanton which was about forty miles south of Pittsburgh. My motel for one night was quite expensive at $10.00. The motel was nice, clean and quite comfortable. They had a small restaurant at the motel for travelers like me that were on a very tight budget. I remember I had only $300 dollars in my wallet but in those days $300 dollars was worth more than today.

The following morning, I began my westward drive along a highway called US Route 40 West. It was just an ordinary double lane road but I was finally on my way out west. The country I remember looked just the same as where I had come from with some small hills and lots of farms. After entering the state of West Virginia there began a change in geography, seeing small mountains, and I appeared to be slowly climbing up from sea level. I crossed into the state of West Virginia into the city of Wheeling. This was coal mining country with short hills where the deep underground coal mines were. I soon passed through West Virginia into the state of Ohio. I then entered the mid-west where the farms were gigantic. The country was quite flat, nothing like the states I left behind. There were giant silos of grain and fields of corn that had already been harvested and just the stalks were left. The roads of Ohio had been not like the old colonial roads of the eastern states but roads that were straight either north or southeast or west so it became quite easy to keep the car going into the western horizon. Before long I was in the state of Indiana where the corn fields that was stripped bare at this time of year were coming into winter. Now only the corn stalks were left sticking up in the air and waiting to cut by one of the great machines that cut the cornstalks down to the ground level, which allowed the combine to gather up the crushed stalks as feed for cattle during the upcoming winter season. I do not recall too much during my crossing of Indiana, but soon I was approaching the great Mississippi River that took me over to the city of St. Louis in the state of Missouri. St. Louis is known as the Gateway to the Golden West.

It must have been difficult to travel west in a Conestoga wagon in the early 1800's because most rivers in America flowed north and south and could not be used as westbound roads. For settlers heading west, engineers built a canal in 1812 named the Erie Canal beginning near Albany, New York. It flowed west towards one of the Great Lakes and Lake Erie connected to the Alleghany River that flowed south to Pittsburgh or Fort Pitt as it was known then. The immigrants who were heading west would have to depart from a dock in New York City and head north up the Hudson River to the city of Albany, board a small canal boat that headed west on the Erie Canal towards the Allegheny River which flows south to Pittsburgh. The family would then build a large raft and have a carpenter build a small shed in the center to take them and all their belongings south on the Alleghany River past the city of Pittsburgh, Pennsylvania. At that point the Allegheny River joined another river called the Monongahela River into one great river called the Ohio River that would carry them down river to access the Mississippi River into the now state of Missouri. West of Pittsburgh was called the Ohio Territory or some called it Indian Territory. It was a difficult journey down river because of high rapids and water falls. River pirates would hide in caves on the bank of the river and when an opportunity would arise, the river pirates would ride out in their birch bark canoes and kill the pioneer families on their raft, take their belongings and the boat would then drift off down the river empty.

It has been said that just outside of St. Louis is where the prairie begins and there are still imprints imbedded and preserved in a small deep rutted wheel ruts in the grasslands made by the great Conestoga wagons that were on their way across the great prairies in the 1840's. Pioneers would sell the wood of their old river raft and sign up with experienced wagon train masters in St. Louis and load up with passengers and their belongings. Here began the great wagon trains that crossed the prairie of maybe up to 25 wagons led by a qualified wagon master who knew the two great trails to the west. They would take the two great travelled trails to either the California Trail or the Oregon Trail to the west coast. The wagon master was the captain of this wagon train journey and he was experienced in the way across west and was its leader.

I had now crossed the Mississippi and was in the state of Missouri and now considered myself in the mid-west since it was generally known that after passing over the Mississippi River that was the boundary between east and west. Still pushing on I crossed into the state of Oklahoma and this is where my imagination became very strong since I remember in the movies Indians chasing the settlers in the 1800's. This was the area of the Oklahoma land rush in the late mid-1800s. The government of the United States was giving away thousands of miles of free Indian country that was to become part of the state of Oklahoma. It became a land rush. At a certain place and time on a special day the settlers in their wagons waited for the race to begin. The signal flag was dropped and thousands of families in their Conestoga wagons began the race to stake out their new homes in what once was Indian land, but was now given to the settlers for free looking for new land to farm and build a home in a previously restricted territory.

As I continued my journey westwards, I imagined hearing the sound of Indians coming up behind me on their painted ponies with arrows whizzing past my head but no, it was quite calm as I crossed the plains. As I proceeded further west, I saw in the distance on the horizon the snow tops of the great Rocky Mountains which seemed a long way off. This was because the land was so flat the grasslands of the prairie created this mirage of beauty on the horizon.

To my surprise I came across a toll road. I thought I had left toll roads behind on the Pennsylvania Turnpike but it was the Will Rogers Turnpike. I then drove across the state of Oklahoma that allowed me to pick up some lost time and I was still looking on the horizon at the great Rocky Mountains. But something seemed to be wrong since as I kept driving, heading west I did not seem to get any closer to the mountains. They always seemed to be just there on the horizon never getting any closer. Many of the old pioneers also experienced the same effect that the mountains of the Rockies never seem to get closer since the horizon was so flat and the Rockies were so far away. I realized however that it was a mirage and I soon felt the feeling of beginning to climb to a higher altitude as I approached the Rocky Mountains. I continued westbound across the Great Plains and the home of the Cheyenne, Arapaho and Apache Indians. I would be soon be leaving Oklahoma slightly changing my course southwest, crossing over the great Rocky Mountains into the great state of Texas where I began to enter the deserts of the Texas Pan Handle.

There now began signs appearing on the roadside that warned of approaching desert country. These signs appeared in many towns warning motorists that when entering the great southwest deserts the law and just plain common sense told travelers that you must buy a two gallon leather bag with long handles at the top. The bag had to be filled with water and hung onto your front bumper in case of emergencies. In those days cars had two chrome spikes one on each side of the bumper and the filled water bag was to be hung in a prominent position so it could be seen by law enforcement. The reason for this is that once a driver entered the desert there were very few rest areas so the water was to ensure drivers safety. If your car became disabled in the desert you would have water to drink or if the radiator leaked water and overheated there was water in the bag to pour into the radiator. The water would be available to get you to the next stopping point.

There now appeared a sign that read that I was now entering Texas and crossed the state line into an interesting situation where I almost got a speeding ticket in Groom, Texas. I was in the state of Texas and the sign on the state line offered a welcome to all. I had been warned before I left New York not to speed in Texas. I made an observation at this point that I noticed that for the past day I had not seen a single car either coming or going my way on this road. I appeared to be the only car on Route 66 going east or west. There were no exit signs to leave the road since there was nowhere to go.

In those days it was just desert but still beautiful in its own kind of way. The beauty of the state in the desert was fantastic with cactus and the tumble weed and lack of people. There was a posted speed limit of 70 mph on the straight open range at that time. I was told before I left New York that if I was stopped for speeding in Texas you would be taken directly by the Texas Highway Patrol to the nearest Justice of the Peace, who was usually a small town judge, and pay your fine right there in cash. With me driving with New York license plates back and front I knew I was real target for a highway patrol officer of the law. I had finally left the east behind me and was now driving forward into the real American west by way of the desert.

Texas is a great state not only by its people but by its vast area of square miles. It has a variety of geographic scenic areas and an interesting history that is not only interesting but comes right out of the movies. Imagine if you will a young impressive man like me who had only been in America for two years, who loved American western movies with Roy Rogers, Tom Mix and Gabby Hayes, now here I was traveling through this great American West. It was really just like it was illustrated in the movies. The tumbling tumbleweed actually was blowing across the road. There really was cactus growing in the desert. My planned route was still to continue on Route 66 West to Los Angeles and I was about three days into my trip. I was in the middle of a desert where there was absolutely nothing to look at but high mesas and buttes. It was a desert, barren but at the same time a beautiful desert that was flowered with plants. In those days cars did not come with air conditioning. To alleviate the heat in your car there was just a small triangular window on each side that you could open which would force some air into the car. You could also open the windows, but that would only let more of the hot air inside the car.

I mentioned the suggestion about not to speed in Texas. There I was in my car with New York license plates on the back and front of the car. I noticed that suddenly the road began to narrow and I went through some small towns that were nothing but a main street and a railroad station building. It also had lots of cattle ramps leading up to the railroad track for cattle to board or leave a cattle train. Each of these towns had a speed limit of 35 mph so each time I came through a town I was very careful not to go over 35 mph. I soon arrived into a small town called Groom. It was just a small town like the others, a main street with a few stores on either side of the road that had no sidewalks or posted speed signs. I felt like I was driving into a trap.

I was driving at 35 mph like the other towns I had just passed. I saw no speed limit sign except one which was 30 mph and so hidden I almost missed it. I slowed to that speed and slowly moved along this dusty town of Groom. To describe the town of Groom would be best to remember it looked like a Hollywood movie set with gun fighters in town as in the movie High Noon. This dusty old town just looked exactly like that town in the movie.

I had just passed through the center of town and I noticed in my rear view mirror to my horror some flashing blue lights behind me in the dust. Was it a local cop or was he a Highway Patrol officer? Was he was looking for a patsy like me that was speeding through his town with New York plates on his car? He pulled me over and I stopped my car. I began to wind down the window expecting to be asked for my registration and driver's license. His car was the color of white that also had a bright shiny Texas star painted on its bodywork. Out stepped from his car was an officer of the state Highway Patrol. To me he was very impressive. I was in America, land of my dreams in the state of Texas, being pulled off the road by a Highway Patrol. He was dressed like he was an actor in the movies and maybe even like the show I used to watch on the TV called Highway Patrol. I even thought that maybe Broderick Crawford would be coming towards me to give me a speeding ticket! I admired the way he was dressed. He was dressed in a big cowboy hat and wearing a beautiful blue shirt cowboy style, buttoned down, chest pockets and on his chest was a silver star. He was also wearing beautiful leather cowboy boots. I was so impressed that I forgot to be nervous, but I knew I was going to get a speeding ticket for going 35 mph when I should have been doing 30 mph. How was I going to talk myself out of this one? He casually sauntered over to me and walked around the car. He checked my rear plate and checked the front and he said to me who are you, what is a New York boy doing in my neck of the woods and speeding through my town on the way to god knows where? He asked me for my vehicle registration card and my driver's license. He kept on saying that being I was from New York I was breaking all of the laws in his state. I tried to explain that there weren't any speed limit signs going through Groom like all of the towns I had passed through on Route 66 and had a speed limit of 35 mph. He disagreed and said no there are plenty of signs that the speed limit in his town was 30 mph. I noticed he emphasized his town.

Then he changed his tone of voice to being much friendlier and he said to me that you do not sound like a New Yorker, that I did not have a New York accent. He then asked 'hey boy where ya'll really from and where are you going?' I explained to him that I was from England on my way to Los Angeles to live. His attitude suddenly changed and his face broke into a grin and said 'well I be danged. I just got out of these United States Air Force and I was stationed in USAF Ruislip just outside of London. I explained to him that I was based temporally at USAF Chick Sands in England. I told him that I had just got out of the Royal Air Force three years before so we had something in common. He then asked me what years was I based in the London area and told him in 1956. He said again gosh darn it that was the time I was there; did you ever go to a dance hall called the Laccano? I replied I went there almost every Saturday night. He said golly, we could have been there together at the same time, maybe passed by each other and had a drink! He grinned again and said something to the effect that you English people were really nice to me while I was in England so git on going to LA and keep an eye on your speed. I thanked him and said good bye and I slowly drove out of his town. I was really lucky because I did not have cash to pay a fine to a Justice of the Peace because I probably would have ended up in the jail for the night. However, just to see a real Highway Patrol officer dressed in traditional clothes like in the movies was fantastic to me and his picture of him will remain in my mind. I regret now that I had not asked him to take his photo. But then again, I might be pushing my luck.

I was still in Texas, but in the panhandle of Texas. If you look at the map of America, Texas resembles a panhandle, the kind they used to find gold in the gold rush days. The bowl was to the southeast, but pointing to the west is this thin handle of the pan. I was passing through and along the panhandle of Texas.

Now I was really in the desert and cattle appeared everywhere with very long horns. These were Texas longhorn cattle and could live in rugged areas of the Texas panhandle area. I had my water bag full of water hanging on my front bumper like we were supposed to do and I began heading into the most desolate country I could ever imagine. There were occasional ranches that appeared in the distance but positioned way off the road. All of the left or right hand turns seemed to go off into nowhere and I was beginning to feel thirsty and decided that I wanted some soda of any sort to quench my thirst. I did not want to use the water in the water bag.

Suddenly seemingly out of nowhere there appeared a road house which had a sign that indicated that they sold Coca Cola. I slowed down and was relieved to find that this was a place to get a drink, but little did I know that I was entering again into American folklore, cowboys with guns. It was such an impressive sight for a boy from the East End of London. I pulled up into the front of the parking area and did not see any cars parked in the lot. There were five horses tied up on a wooden rail with their reigns tied to the rail post by their owners, lariats tied to their saddles and there was the traditional rifle slung in a long holster alongside the saddle.

I noticed that the wooden frame building was a town bar just like you might see in old movie towns and to my delight there was an actual real swinging saloon door behind the old door screen which lay in front of that swinging door. Looking around the whole area I was totally alone in front of this desert saloon, a tenderfoot from the east coast in a western setting. I was in this strange but also familiar scene like I had entered into an old movie set and was ready to open the door of the saloon to find out what really was behind that swinging door. The building was built short across the front but went way back as in a long oblong. I parked the car in front of the saloon doors and pulled opened the screen door and pushed through the swinging doors into a long shadowy long room.

The bar was located at the end of the room about fifteen yards down to the bar at the end of the saloon. At the bar there were five cowboys standing and leaning against the bar each with one foot on the foot bar talking and drinking. There was a bottle of whisky on the bar in front of each cowboy each with a small glass like a one ounce one that we used back east. This was about three pm in the afternoon and I thought a little early for drinking, but it was hot and dusty and I could feel my throat dry and I needed a drink.

I could see that the cowboys were deep in conversation with each other seeming like old friends. The floor was made of old plank worn wood where many boots had walked for many years. As I walked towards the bar at the end of the building, I could hear my footsteps tapping on the wooden floors. I slowly walked towards these five rough looking men. They were dressed in full cowboy western clothes. Stetson hat, various colored shirts and a colored scarf carelessly wound around their necks coming to a triangular point. Around their waists they wore a gun belt holsters and each holster carried a gun. Their faces looked like tough dark leather, walnut in color, probably the result from their long days in the sun. Their eyes were squinted like they had been in the bright sun for many years. I began walking down the length of the saloon towards the bar at the end, the sound of my shoes making footsteps towards the bar and five cowboys. As I began to get nearer to the bar, they heard my footsteps coming towards them and each cowboy began to turn slowly around and stared at me as I approached the bar. It was like being on a movie set where there was going to be a shootout about to come down. I found a space at the bar and the bartender asked me what I wanted and said that I would like a coke. The bartender looked like an old western barkeep wearing a white apron and polishing glasses as he was talking. All of the men turned to look at me and for a minute there was just silence. I wished them good afternoon to these cowboys but I remember they still kept looking at me. One of the cowboys responded and said to me replying to my good afternoon, same to you fella where yo' heading? I told him that I was driving to Los Angeles and I was just passing through. One cowboy noticing that I had an accent asked where was I from. Another asked me if I was from Boston. He said he had been there once and didn't like it and spat into a brass spittoon at his feet on the floor. I asked him why he did not like it. Too crowded, too many people he said. I told him that I was not from New England but from the real England.

Well, that started a great conversation that went on for over two hours. I found during the next few hours you could not find a better bunch of guys at a bar than these five cowboys. We exchanged experiences and they wanted to know what it was like to live in England. I remember one saying to me if I knew the Queen and how were things at the palace. I had to explain that we were not able to know what was going on in the palace. I asked them what they were doing way out here in the desert and they replied that they worked along the fence line to repair fences, just stopping for a drink before they headed back to their line camp which was about twenty miles away. They worked at a ranch about ten miles to the south and they had to repair these fences to keep the cattle enclosed. The fences I found out were wired to stop the cattle from wandering across the main road. I could not understand that since I had not seen another car all day, but dared not question their reasons. They bought me a few whiskies straight up and then I asked the question that I wanted to ask but was hesitant to do so. I asked them why they carried guns on their hips. One of the men told me that while they were fixing fences the guns were used to shoot rattlesnakes which I thought was a fair answer. We said our goodbyes, as I left to get in my car. They were really good company but it was time for me to move on so we all shook hands and they all said they enjoyed my company and I felt that these men were really genuine people and I liked them very much. As I left the saloon, I still saw the horses tied up on the horse rail but now I noticed that by each saddle bag was a rifle holster and inside the holster was a long rifle. I wondered what they were for, too long a rifle for shooting rattlesnakes and wondered what they really did for a living out there in the middle of nowhere, maybe robbing banks? No banks out here in this country.

I can still see in my mind those five cowboys and at the time I was very impressed and enjoyed the experience, buddying up with real cowboys for a few hours. It was getting late and I had to head further west on Route 66 to find lodging for the night, so I headed into the setting sun admiring the huge buttes and mesas of New Mexico. The coloring of these giants standing tall in the desert was an orange red, but as the sun went down those rays of the setting sun turned them into a red hue. Some were hundreds of feet high and had a flat top with trees and bush on the high tops. I did not know then but these beautiful monuments of nature were made millions of years ago when the land rose up higher than it was now. At the top of these mesas was a type of rock called cap rock. As the land began to weather away the soft rock, silt sliding rock down to the desert floor, the hard cap rock stayed in place and was not worn away by rain or wind, cold and frost. What was left was a column of rock with broken rocks falling away at its feet and is still continuing like that even today after millions of years in the making.

It was now getting near sundown so I began to look for a cheap room for the night. I saw a strange site up ahead. It looked like a giant teepee Indian tent but it was made of concrete and had rooms around the edge. I pulled into the front office of this strange looking motel and rented a room for $7.00 per night. It was clean and comfortable and just fine for me. After I finished up dinner I went to bed after a very interesting day passing through six hundred miles of the states of Texas and New Mexico and meeting my cowboy friends and dreaming of rattlesnakes, rifles, six shooters and cowboys.

The next day I headed out after breakfast and continued on Route 66 heading towards the state line of Arizona. At this point the scenery began to change. I was moving into the high desert that had many strange plants and trees. I noticed that beside the tumble weed blowing across the road there appeared these strange three pronged type cactus sticking up out of the ground rising to a height higher than myself. I was fascinated by these strange events and decided to take a look. I stopped the car, got out and walked into the desert to inspect these strange trees. They were quite tall and some were at least fifteen feet high or more and had prickly needles all over the arms of the plant. There were also flowers blooming beside the needles sticking out of the stem making the cactus very attractive in a primitive sort of way. The desert floor was covered as far as the eye could see by these strange cacti with their arms outstretched. I was told later that the reason for so many arms on a tree was for counter balance when the winds blew through.

I had now crossed the state line out of New Mexico into what was now the state of Arizona and my mind was thinking about what it was really like in the great southwest part of America during the 1880s when the settlers were arriving from the east. There were towns springing up and railroads being built from coast to coast bringing in the best and the worst of settlers into the western part of America.

I discovered that the reputed bad, lawless cowboys seen in the movies and on TV were actually drifters that had survived the Civil War twenty years after then moved out into the lawless west where there was no law and where without lawmen they could run wild. In fact in some areas were not even states, just territories, and statehood would come to them in later years. They each gradually gained statehood after these troubles ended, and between fighting off Indians and trying to make a new life in a new town without a town marshal it was not easy to keep the law. It was open season for these lawless gunmen depicted in history.

This was Apache and Comanche Indian country and these were the bad lands of New Mexico. They lived within the area from the state of today's New Mexico through the present state of Arizona and the Apaches were hard to live with. They attacked wagon trains as they were passing through the last part of the journey to California killing usually all of the settlers, setting fire to their wagons. The wagon masters were trained, experienced drivers who had crossed the country many times and had to take great care to travel through Apache country since they were in charge of the wagon train and the people that travelled with them. Some wagon train masters could speak some Indian language which helped.

I was about fifty miles east of Flagstaff, Arizona when for the first time I had car trouble that entered into my planned journey. I was in the most desolate part of Arizona and at that time rarely meeting any other traveler or car for that matter. I saw a beautiful country with fantastic scenery but when I looked at my gas gauge and saw that I needed some gas and there were very few gas stations along this lonesome highway. I saw a small sign that said there was a gas station up ahead so I drove about twenty miles and at one of the rare cross roads there was a gas station. It was a gas station like I had never seen in the mid or eastern part of America. I had no choice so I pulled into the area and saw that there was just one gas pump and it was hand operated by the most grizzled old man I had ever seen. His face was wrinkled by the sun and he came out of a small hut as I pulled in and asked me how much gas I needed. He filled up the tank and I paid the man in cash and as I turned to pull out of the gas station the old man called out and came running out to make me to stop. He asked me if I knew that my car was leaking oil. I walked up to the spot that I had stopped to pump gas and there was a pool of oil where I had stopped. He looked under the car hood and gave me the bad news. I was leaking oil from the main seal of the engine and needed an engine gasket. I asked him if he knew of anyone that could fix it since I was on my way to Los Angeles having to go through the great high desert country and did not want any trouble in that part of my journey. He said no, he did not know of anyone nearby but the city of Flagstaff was fifty miles away which was a decent size city and there I could find a mechanic to fix the problem. In the meantime, he suggested I buy five or six quarts of oil to put in my trunk and he gave me an ordinary beer can opener because in those days motor oil came in a beer can type of lip and had to be opened up by a beer can opener. I had to keep checking the oil by stopping the car, lifting the hood to check the dipstick and dipping the dip stick into the oil level every twenty miles or so. I also had to have to keep filling up my water bag to hang onto the front bumper in case the engine over heated and failed completely, which would leave me stranded in the middle of a hot desert without water.

Finally, I did reach Flagstaff and had some difficulty finding a mechanic to fix the gasket of the engine to stop the leak. One auto repair place I stopped in had a mechanic that came out of the garage, a big heavy built guy wearing a pair of overalls and carrying a large hammer. He asked me if I wanted him to fix my car's engine. Looking at him carefully I decided to decline his offer and drove away leaking oil behind me. I did eventually find a place that was able to temporarily stop the oil from dripping, but was told that I would have to keep on checking the dip stick in the engine for the oil level every fifty miles or so while I crossed the great desert. The Mohave Desert to the north was Death Valley.

Knowing that I would be out of contact for at least two days still travelling on Route 66 through the desert I had to make sure that I had a bag full of water which was still hanging on the front of my front bumper. As I had previously suggested that the reason for the bag of water hanging on the front bumper was that the laws of the three south-western states ordered that a bag of water must be carried at all times. It wouldn't be helpful if the cars radiator broke or one of the hoses leading from the radiator broke causing the engine to overheat and boil over in the middle of nowhere.

It is difficult to describe in these later years how desolate this desert was to drive through in those days 60 years ago. It is easy now to get on an interstate highway and there would be a service station at every exit and entrance and find a service station to fix your car right away.

The mountains were the color of sand and on the horizon were more jagged and high mountains while the dessert floor was covered in a course type of sand. Not the kind you find on a beach but a dirty mixture of dust, sand and small pebbles. Covering the floor of the desert were strange looking trees they were called Joshua trees. These strange looking trees held up their branches like two human arms up to the sky like they were welcoming down the gods. Across the road tumbled the tumble weeds that just keep blowing, tumbling and keep on going as the wind blew them along the desert floor.

This part of America is where the Apache and Comanche's Indian tribes lived. Being so new to this country and also very impressionable I looked around me as being totally alone in this territory. My mind was running wild in my imagination. I could look behind me and see horses then a see a band of Apache Indians chasing after me bareback on their painted ponies. Their war whoops loud and clear, their bows and arrows ready to fly. I could also imagine hearing the sound of the arrows whizzing past my car as I drove across the dessert. But that was pure imagination and then I began to see the pure beauty of the raw desert and the mountains, flat top Mesas, large buttes and draws.

When sundown came and you could see the sun setting in the west which is where the contrast was so prominent. The contrasts of the dark shadows of the mountains covering the bright dessert in a twilight color and the sun setting behind the far mountains caused huge shadows over the valleys. The evening became so different in that part of the desert since it was dark and other parts bright where the sunshine still touched the mountain tops in a glow of orange glory and suddenly it was night-fall so quick and so beautiful. The stars glowed brilliantly in the deep black night sky and it seemed you could see the whole universe above your head and the white belt of stars of the Milky Way was given to me to explore. This was my last night on the road before I arrived in the city of Los Angeles and I had to look again for a cheap motel for the night in western Arizona.

Tomorrow I would cross the great Colorado River into California where the whole geographic of the west would change. This is where the great wagon masters, pioneers and settlers would follow the trail into the lush, sun blessed California valleys. However, before that there were still lots of dessert to cross.

That last evening I remember there was only one restaurant I could find. It was a Mexican restaurant since I was still in a desolate kind of place. At least there were other cars and people that I had not seen for the past day or so crossing the dessert. I remember walking into the restaurant and looking at the menu which was totally Mexican. I also remember that I asked the waitress what item on the menu she might recommended that was only cheese and beans so she recommended a bean and cheese burrito with Mexican hot beans on the side with a Tequila drink or two. I took a first bite and thought I was on fire. I grabbed a glass of water to put out the fire in my mouth and she was laughing at me as I tried to swallow this fiery bean. They played Mexican music for the diners and it was strange since I felt like I was on a movie set with people dressed in western clothes and the Mexican musicians dressed in their national dress. It was a good night to finish my last night on the road for tomorrow I would cross into the state of California. Still heading west my adventures were out there in the future somewhere and what they were I did not know. One of the popular songs of the day which I had heard frequently on my car radio was called Cast My Fate to the Winds which was exactly what I was doing. Next morning after a good breakfast I started to head west still on Route 66. I had a full day's drive in front of me and so far my car had behaved well. Although I had to keep dipping my dipstick into the engine to check the oil level, I was definitely finally on the last leg on my way west to the Pacific Ocean.

As I drove towards the California state line the weather suddenly turned warmer. The Colorado River looked beautiful over warm sunny skies which promised to be a hot day. Checking my map, I could see that I had to proceed west on a downhill slope into the valleys of California. I had not realized it at the time but, since I had left the east coast five days before, I had steadily climbed higher up from east coast sea level to a much higher elevation without noticing that I was doing so. I slowly climbed the Allegheny Mountains of Pennsylvania. I had crossed the flat plains of Kansas and Oklahoma, then climbing up higher into the Rocky Mountains, but now I had to come down from the high desert of Arizona, returning down to the sea level of California on the west coast. As I drove westwards, I saw a sign that warned drivers that there would be a 45 mile downhill slope in the road and that truckers would need to reduce their speed and check their brakes. I started to go downhill rapidly and it was difficult to hold on to the brakes and not burn them out. The brakes in the old cars in those days are not like we have today. If they grew hot as the car kept braking, they could entirely fail and I would be trouble going down this long hill.

Suddenly I came to a sight that made me pull off the road to a truck lay by and stopped the car. I stopped on the side of the mountain looking across the most beautiful sight I have ever seen. Below, about two thousand feet down to the bottom of the mountain was the whole valley of the flat western end of the state of Arizona. In the middle running in the valley was the mighty Colorado River and on the other side of the river was the city of Needles, California. Here lying before me was my promised land, stretching out before me I was entering California, the last state on my journey.

I still had a way to go but I was nearing my destination. I calculated that I would be in Los Angeles by the end of day. Getting back on the road downhill again, I put the car into neutral and coasted over forty-five miles free fall on the road to the bottom of the valley and I crossed the Colorado River over a large bridge into Needles, California.

This was also the time of a great migration of young American youth who like me were leaving their home states to go and live in California and other parts of the country. It was part of a great immigration of young people. I did not know it then, but this part of California was the crossroads of all the young people of America that wanted to move to California. They were crossing from the northern states and from the east, moving together towards their common destinations, Los Angeles. I think I saw every car or truck license plate on cars from the whole country to meet at this point and steer their cars towards the city of angels, Los Angeles.

It was hot as I passed over the Colorado River so I wound down the windows. In those days we did not have car air conditioning so I pulled over to a rest area to change my clothes into summer clothing. I passed through the city of Needles, which was just an ordinary small desert town in those days and continued on towards Los Angeles and my final destination. I still had at least another six hours drive to go and although I was in California the scenery at first did not change much. It was still desert country but slowly there appeared more towns and highway exits. I immediately noticed more traffic and more people and the highway began to get wider with additional lanes. I was now approaching San Bernardino and had lunch where there were plenty of stores and places to eat as I got closer to Los Angeles. Suddenly there appeared a sign that said that a few miles ahead was the San Bernardino freeway pointing southwest towards Los Angeles.

Getting on the freeway now going south was certainly nerve racking since the traffic was so heavy and moving so fast. I slowed and drove down the southbound ramp and merged as quickly as possible into the traffic and now I was on my way to my destination, the City of Angels. One thing I did notice as I entered California that the temperature was warm and it was strange to me that in November it was so mild and sunny so I looked forward to this change of climate. I noticed as I drove southbound that there were many oil refineries and oil pumps moving up and down pumping oil out of the ground. There was a smell of oil everywhere and so much traffic.

It was getting early evening when I eventually entered the city line of Los Angeles and drove into a gas station area to make a phone call to my friend who had agreed to put me up in his apartment for a few days until I could find a place of my own. He had given me directions as to where I would find the exit off the San Bernardino freeway to his apartment in Los Angeles. This was the Irish friend that I had met a year ago at the British War Veterans club who had married and moved to California. He said at the time that if I ever left New York to come west he would put me up for a few days until I found a place of my own. Patrick and his wife, who I had never met, lived on Normandy Avenue outside of downtown Los Angeles.

I did finally find the exit that he directed to me and I quickly found his apartment. It was quite nice and built in a Spanish style with a large fountain in the middle of the driveway to the front part of the apartment building. I found Patrick waiting for me at the front entrance and he guided me to the parking area for guests and I entered into his apartment. It was quite small with a single bedroom and I wondered where I was going to sleep that night. His wife who had long red hair waited until I was in their apartment. She was about the same age as Patrick and her name was Bernadette but she told me that everyone called her Bernie. She had a deep Irish brogue more lilting than harsh but welcomed me into their home and I felt relieved that I had finally had made it to the American West.

They both went to work early but that should not concern me. They said that I could stay there until I could find an apartment for myself. They said I could use the couch for sleeping. Looking around the apartment I wondered what couch I would be sleeping on since the only couch was in the sitting room, but it was explained that there was a small annex alcove of to the side that had a small couch to use as a bed. When everyone retired, I was in bed on the couch in the alcove, but I could not sleep since as I closed my eyes all I could see in my mind was a long white center line of the road that I had been traveling for the past six days. I felt like it was a miracle that I had made it to Los Angeles in the old car that brought me there. I awoke early and I got dressed and cleaned up the sofa before they came out to leave for work. They said their goodbyes and left me there in their apartment.

I stayed at the apartment all day getting myself settled in and they came home about 5:00 pm. It was about dinner time so we had a meal. Then they had some friends over for drinks but soon departed when they saw that they had a guest. I was ready for bed so they said they were going to turn in since they had to get up early and reminded me to fix breakfast for myself in the morning.

The first important decision I had to make was to find a job as quickly as I could since I was running out of money and I had to pay something for the lodging and food at my friends' home while I was staying there. I had already brought a street map of Los Angeles, so knowing the address of the printer's union offices I took my car downtown to speak to the union president, show him my union traveler's card and see if they could offer me a job in some printer that was looking for a pressman.

In those days Los Angeles was nothing like it is today. There were only two freeways. One was the freeway that I arrived on from San Bernardino, the San Bernardino Freeway, and the other freeway was called the Hollywood Freeway. Looking for the address was not easy in a strange city but I did finally find it in downtown LA on a side street in the heart of old town Los Angeles.

Taking the elevator to the upper floors I was not too impressed by the location or the building that the union operated and did their business. Entering the office, I spoke to the receptionist explaining that I had come from the New York local union and wanted to see the president or the secretary of the local union of Los Angeles. She told me to wait and then returned accompanied by a tall slight build of a man who introduced himself as Hunter McCall, secretary to the union. He invited me into his office and offered me a chair and asked me what he could do for me. I explained that I was a union member from New York Local 23 and a qualified lithographic pressman looking for a position in a printer's plant now that I had arrived in his city. I remembered how he looked at me after I had announced my intentions. He explained Los Angeles County was experiencing a severe recession at this time and printers were not hiring. I was just astonished by this statement because when I had left the east coast there was no sign of any slowdown in printing and generally around the country business was quite good. I politely pointed out to him that I had crossed the continent to come to live in Los Angeles and needed a job. His only response was to come here every day at 8:00 am and sit in the hiring hall downstairs and wait for a call from a printer that needed a pressman. He did however warn me that most of the calls that did come in here were for working only one day or a night shift and that it was called jobbing and that it would be unusual for someone to call and want a full-time pressman as that was usually reserved for their permanent members. I reminded him that I had a valid union traveler's card that allowed me to work through any local of our union. I remember he shrugged and said if there is no work, there is no work. He again recommended that I come in every morning to catch a spare job that might come in. He was very unfriendly. I thanked him and asked if there was a problem if I contacted some printers in the city and asked if they had a position open and he said that he had no problem with that. He also made a strange statement to me saying that printers in California do not like to hire printers from New York since they worked too hard while out here and we take it slow and easy so nobody wants to rock the boat.

After leaving his office I went down to the basement where the union hall was located. It was packed with many out of work printers waiting for a call to come in. I registered my union number and name with the union man whose job it was to put me on the list. The hall was noisy and thick with cigar and cigarette smoke, with men playing cards, reading books and checking out the horse racing page in the Los Angeles Times for horses running at the track for the day. I spent the whole day there and although a few jobs came in they were taken by first come first served on the list and I knew that I was probably at the bottom of the list. Soon it became obvious that my luck had run out this day so I went to the parking lot where I had left my car and figured out a way to get back to my friend's apartment for the evening.

I arrived back at my friend's house in time for dinner and told them of my union hall experience. Patrick confirmed to me that jobs were scarce in 1960 Los Angeles and there were really only two kinds of jobs, those who were connected to the aircraft industry and the other to the entertainment industry, such as in a movie studio as an extra. He also said that the work was such a problem that there were engineers that were working as professional dog walkers just to get by. This was not good so I decided that the following day I would go back to the union hall and spend the rest of the week there checking out how many jobs were coming in and that would give me some idea on what the situation is and would be for the future.

I decided that I would also spend some time canvasing some of the printers I could see and if I could be lucky and just pick up a job. I appreciated to have a place to stay for a while without having to go into some motel or even the YMCA like I did when I first arrived in America two years ago. During the next day I called on many printers but had no luck and came home to my friend's home.

After dinner that night some of Patrick's friends came over for a small party which was about twenty or so people. They brought plenty of Guinness beer. They introduced me and seemed to be a happy group but they were all Irish. Then they all started to get drunk and began to sing anti-British songs and talked about the IRA which it appears that they were part of the local group of the IRA. They were a real rowdy lot so I excused myself and went to bed in the side room but could not help what they were talking about as they passed the beer around. As the time went on, I could hear them talking about the troubles of Ireland. They were active members of the local IRA and were talking about buying weapons and sending them over to Dublin. I could barely believe my ears. I was living in a nest of Irish revolutionaries that were funding weapons to use in England and Northern Ireland and I had overheard them through the small doorway to the living room. One of them said who do you have visiting you? Bernie explained that I had just arrived from New York and was only here for a few days. I feigned that I was asleep as I heard one of the men slowly open my door to see if I had heard anything. The revolutionary music kept playing on the record player and I fell asleep.

The next morning, I awoke to somebody shaking my shoulder and as I opened my eyes it saw that it was Bernie. She was saying wake up, wake up you have to leave. I asked her what was going on and she said that this was a mistake to have you stay here and you have to leave today. You must be gone by the time we come home from work tonight. I asked her what was the problem and she said that I could not stay any longer. I asked her where was my friend Patrick, she responded that he had already left for work and agreed with this decision and you must leave as soon as possible. I had a memory of this happening once before in New York City. I barely had time to thank her for putting me up for a few days. As she turned to lock the front door she said again to be out of here with your luggage before I come home tonight. I asked her was it because I was English, but she just made a rude gesture and was gone.

I now had to find a place to live instead of going over to the union hall to look for a job. Instead, I first had to buy the Los Angeles Times newspaper and look in the classified section for some apartment to rent for the future time of my stay in Los Angeles. I have often wondered over the years why this ugly thing happened and also wondered if Patrick really knew about this incident and what she told him when he found that I had left their home. I tried to call them afterwards later that night but I got only a phone ringing nobody picked up the phone. I tried to call about a week later and the phone company said that the phone had been disconnected. My belief on this was that they were involved with some kind of illegal activity with the Irish IRA having a military meeting at their house that night. Then realizing I might have heard too much while their drunken friends were talking that evening, she decided that I might be in some sort of danger from their friends. They were afraid that they may have been planning to take some action against me. I have never found out what the problem was but thinking about it know I am glad I was out of that activist mix. I never heard from them again although I did mail them a letter hoping it would be forwarded to my friend Patrick but I had no return mail.

I drove downtown to the union hall and bought a paper on the way and scoured the classified advertisings for a room or small apartment that I could afford. I saw an advertisement and made a phone call for an appointment for the late afternoon. I found a one room with a bath and kitchen on Sunset Boulevard and Normandy Avenue that seemed to suite my financial budget. It was very close to the famous Sunset Strip made famous by the Hollywood movies. I checked out the location and the area seemed good and I moved in that night paying one month's rent in advance to the very nice lady who took my rent. She was middle aged and very attractive. Next thing I had to do was to buy food at the market to fill my empty refrigerator. The rent included cleaning and change of linens twice a week. Living in a small studio was the normal type accommodation for young men in those days.

Next day I was back to the union hall and found a job for two days temporary work and then worked fairly regularly once they began to know me. Finally the foreman of one company I had previously worked called me and asked if I wanted to work full time on the day shift. I was becoming more comfortable with my new city of Los Angeles. The weather appeared to be strange to me. It was December and with the sun out most of the time it gave a golden hue to the light, almost like a pastel painting the sunlight seemed mellow. To me it seemed very strange but I supposed people that were living there for many years it was just normal any time of the year.

During the time I was working at this plant I had the opportunity to look around the area. One of the places I wanted to visit was Grauman's Chinese Theater movie house on Sunset Boulevard. I saw a movie called North to Alaska which was really a great movie. The theater was really like nothing I have ever seen in a movie theater. It was so opulent and it even looked gross with all kinds of hanging lanterns and statues in the lobby, different colors and large dragons carved into the side of the lobby. Outside on the sidewalk was the walk of fame where famous movie stars imprinted their hands in concrete and scrawled their name on the wet concrete square. The seating in the theater was lush and comfortable and a perfect to see the movie. I remember Stewart Granger was the lead actor and the song North to Alaska sung by Johnny Horton made me feel like a true pioneer heading west and that maybe in the future I could go anywhere, even north to Alaska.

I also had the opportunity to drive down to the Santa Monica pier standing out into the Pacific Ocean with all of its carnival rides and carnival atmosphere. Sometimes I would make a trip out to Malibu Beach where many of the movie stars have the beach houses. There was also a time I would drive up into the Hollywood Hills where all the movie stars mansions were visible. Buying a map from a street vendor showed which house a movie star lived. Sometimes I would go up on Mulholland Drive in the hills where the giant letters HOLLYWOOD are poised on top of one of the hills. This was a favorite place where the kids would park on the overlook seeing the beautiful views of the Pacific Ocean and their romantic dreaming. I was told that the famous landmark of the sign of Hollywood was done in the 1930's by a real estate company trying to sell houses in the Los Angeles hills and that named a track of land called Hollywood and the name stuck. Most of the houses were built on the sides of high hills like a terrace leading down from one road to another below.

I was soon out of work again and wondering if I should stay in Los Angeles. There were limited printing companies in those days and my money was running out again so I decided to give it another week or so and then head for San Francisco. Los Angeles at that time was nothing like it is today. It was not a very large city except for the downtown area. The rest of the area was made up of hundreds of houses perched on the sides of the hills. The city was located in a basin like geography, which is why there was at that time so much smog since the smog could not get out of the basin. There was not much industry at that time such as heavy manufacturing as in cities on the east coast. There were two major industries, large aircraft building and what would today be called the aerospace businesses. There was the movie business with giants such as M.G.M., Paramount, Disney and others who in later years would be merged or would change their name. I would be driving on the freeway and suddenly there was Paramount Studios on the huge back lot where they would be making a movie.

I saw an advertisement in the help wanted section of the Los Angeles Times for a sales representative in a department store so being short of money I thought I would take a look and see what it was all about. The store was a department store called The Emporium. I met the sales manager who told me that they were looking for a floor salesman for the men's department. The job was selling men's clothes from suits to shirts and ties and that I would be on a shift basis. My pay was a small salary with a commission on what I sold. Since I had nothing else to do and I was running out of money I tried the job and was fairly good at it. It

351

lasted for a few months but slowly my income was getting low again. I thought that since I would be soon running out of money, I should make a move at the end of the month when my rent ran out.

I decided to leave Los Angeles and head north up to San Francisco about five hundred miles up the coast. I thought also that maybe if that did not work out, I could continue north to Seattle or Alaska. I was told by some of my friends that it would be much colder up in San Francisco than in LA and that I would notice the difference as soon as I got a hundred miles north of LA. In Los Angeles 70 degrees was normal in the winter time but up in the northern part of the state it would be much colder. I made up my mind to move up to San Francisco, closing down my small apartment and making plans to drive up the Pacific Coast Highway known as the El Camino Real, Highway Route 101 north to San Francisco.

Los Angeles was definitely not working out for me and following my instincts I left and started my drive of over five hundred miles north of LA to my new life in San Francisco. I was on the move again. It did not take long to drive up on the highway for my first stop. The scenery driving north was spectacular as the road paralleled the beautiful blue Pacific Ocean coastline. The high cliffs and the bays were so beautiful that it just made such an impression on me. The EL Camino Real (The Kings Highway) was such a beautiful drive along the coast, but halfway up the coast the highway the road turned inland towards Vandenberg Air Force Base, which is where they tested the rockets that eventually would go into space.

After losing the coast road I passed through the most fertile country I have ever seen where there was just about everything that grows was growing in the green fields of California. If the mid-west of America was the bread basket of America then California is the orchard and grocery, since there were so many fields of vegetables growing. When I see movies and read books about how the first settlers and pioneers crossing the high Sierra mountains that eventually comes down out of the cold snowy mountains into this fertile land of California, I could understand how joyful they were to see this fertile landscape.

I do point out that at that time Los Angeles was very small in population and had only two named freeways crossing the city with no interstates having been built yet. Years in the future when I returned back to LA many times while travelling on business, I could see how it was then compared to when I returned some years later. When I worked out of my office in LA in Cerritos just south of LA, I noticed how large and spread out the city was.

As I traveled north on the Pacific Coast Highway 101 there were very few cars along this route, but the beauty of the landscape and the inland areas were burnt into my memories. I stopped in a town called Capistrano where I found an inexpensive motel for the night. I decided to look around this mission town that the Spanish priests built all the way up this highway. The Spanish missions started in San Diego in the south to Los Angeles and then on to Capistrano and San Francisco. These missions or churches were built to create small settlements built by slave labor of the local Indians by the monks which in turn built to become a small city. All were named after various saints and they were surrounded by farms. It was very tiring since the road twisted and turned and that made the driver of the car keep his eyes on the road ahead. I remember so clearly that the scenery of the coast was just beautiful and blue Pacific Ocean was so deep blue in color.

I arrived in San Francisco by late afternoon and immediately I started looking for a room to rent. I didn't know anyone in San Francisco where I could borrow a couch or something for the night so I rented a room in the YMCA first and began to ask around where would be the best place to find a permanent room. I again bought a newspaper and turned to the classified section to look for a studio type apartment. I searched for a more permanent place the next day to rent and then find a job.

I found a room downtown in a different kind of building that I had not seen before. This city was very different from Los Angeles. The hills dominated the whole city as it moved up each side of these very steep hills. The city seemed to be built on the grid system and the transportation was mostly by trolley car or by cable car that rattled their way up and down the hills of this city. The architecture of SFO was certainly different from LA. The rented room was clean and furnished but not the kind of place that I would want to stay for too long. They were right, it was colder than Los Angeles and I had to wear my coat. The city was very different. There were so many hills. Looking across the bay I could see the Golden Gate Bridge and in the evening twilight I could make out the hills across the bay and the famous Bay Bridge. This was the bridge I would drive across the next morning to visit the union hall in Berkley and see if there were any jobs available.

The next day I found a place to have breakfast and got to talking to the cook who came out of the kitchen. He had somehow heard my accent probably by the waitress and he came out since he was also English and we talked for a while. He was constantly giving me advice from when you are parking on a hill don't forget to turn your wheels into the curb to prevent it rolling down the hill. He also told me that this area was not good to find a place to stay so he was kind enough to give me directions to a part of the city which had large houses on the street that rented out rooms. I thanked him and followed his directions and knocked on the door of this beautiful old-style house that had rooms to rent.

It was located on Sacramento Street half way up a steep hill. I remember that the house was opposite a small public park with a huge palm tree that was more like a bush. Remembering the advice to turn in my wheels into the curb when I parked my car, I climbed up some long steps and I rang the bell. A matronly woman opened the door and asked what I wanted. I told her that the cook at the restaurant had recommended her house for me to rent a room and were there any vacancies since I was looking for monthly lodging. She invited me inside and we went into a small office. She asked me who I was and what was I looking for in the way of accommodations. The house was most impressive and full of polished brass objects and shiny wooden floors and was quite old, probably built after the great earthquake of 1905. It was very Victorian in style with turrets on each corner of the roof. There was a winding staircase leading to the upstairs part of the house with a polished bannister and paintings on the walls going up the stairs. On the second floor she stopped and opened a door, waiting for me to pass her, and enter into the room. The room looked very nice with one large bed and lots of closet space and a small, clean bathroom. I asked her how much per month she would rent the room and she replied that she only rents to young gentlemen and there were rules. She said that the rent was $65.00 per month which included laundry service, clean linen twice a week and a month's rent in advance. I was responsible for the cleanliness of the room myself with the vacuum cleaner provided in the closet. There was a small gas stove that I was allowed to use to cook minor meals, but no parties or any loud singing or playing of instruments. Certainly, no activity allowed after midnight for sure. Visitors were allowed in the room up until 10:00 pm but no ladies were allowed up in the upper rooms. There was a sitting room downstairs where ladies could be entertained but they must not go upstairs into any of the rooms. She was quite definite on that. She would stay in her office to make sure that nobody sneaked through while she was not looking. I did take the room.

The next day I had to begin to look for work so I looked in the telephone book and found that the printing union office for the district of San Francisco was in Oakland. I managed to find my way in traffic to go over to Oakland by crossing the long Bay Bridge. I could not believe how long that bridge was but finally I did find the union offices and introduced myself to the one of the officers of the union. They were not giving me a welcome. He was very direct in saying that there were no jobs available in the area and if there was it would be difficult to place me since I was from a New York local union. After that interview I decided to take the day off and feel my way about town and then I would find a job somehow.

I went back to my rooms and spoke to the landlady who told me that there was, not too far away, a museum of old saloon pianos from all over the old west and was located on an embankment underneath the Golden Gate Bridge. That was a great afternoon looking at old pianos that must have come from some of the saloons of the old west days. My vivid imagination again got the better of me and as I looked at these old pianos, I could feel the spirit of the west. Maybe this very piano may have been in some saloon where a sheriff was trying to stop a gun fight in the saloon. Suddenly the bad guy pulled out a gun shooting the sheriff, then ran out the door and jumped onto his waiting horse heading for the Mexican border. I heard in later years that the museum caught fire and destroyed all of the pianos.

The next day I started looking for a printing job and to do that I had to canvass all of the printers that I had listed in my Printers Blue Book. It located all the printers in each locality in the area of San Francisco. For two weeks I tramped on foot, most of the time to where all the printers were grouped together asking for some kind of job in their pressroom. It seemed that there were no jobs available, especially to a person that rode around the city in a car with New York plates. In desperation at this time, I decided that if I couldn't find a job in printing, I would return to a retail men's clothing store for a job thinking that in between something might come up in printing while I was working in retail.

There was a large department store in the downtown area that appeared to be like the store I worked in Los Angeles and surely they would have a men's clothing department. I went into the main office for personnel. I found the hiring office and spoke to the store manager. After a few weeks I quit the job since I really was not cut out to be a clothing floor salesman. I had a great feeling that I was destined to be better and other jobs that could be available. I was out on the street again looking for work and running out of money since San Francisco was very expensive to live.

My car was not running too well and I could feel the engine was getting tired yet there was a lot that I wanted to see in this city. I crossed over the Golden Gate Bridge a number of times and went weekends to see the California countryside in Marin County. There was an area called the Presidio which had been an old Army base for many years which I found interesting.

I was just beginning to get used to the area and settling in when I received a letter from my mother in England. She said that she had changed her mind and she had decided that she and my brother Colin would like to move permanently with me and now wanted to live in America. My emotions were running hot and cold at this situation. Suddenly I had that feeling again of my family responsibility. I had asked them and wanted them to live in America and could not refuse her decision. At the same time, I wanted to stay in California, but I had very few contacts here like I had in New York. I decided to return to New York where it seemed to be the better place. I knew a lot of people in New York and could easily find a job for mum and Colin. The more I thought about it the more decisive I was. I was going back to New York.

In that moment I was very surprised at this turn of events so I first thing to do was to write back and tell her that I would be pleased that they would come over to America live the good life and that I would take over the arrangements for their permanent visas and other documents for their entry into the US as soon as they gave me a date when they were arriving.

My world was now becoming very complicated. Here I was in San Francisco not doing too well and it had taken me some years to make a lot of friends in the New York area and find jobs for myself. I had not found a job here in San Francisco and finding a job here at best looked bleak. I would have to find an apartment for us all with at least two bedrooms, but where? It would be better in New York since I had many friends there. I could probably get jobs for them fairly quickly and I had established myself there with lots of people I knew. While here in San Francisco I did not know too many people and I was sure it would be hard to find jobs for them.

We continued to send letters to each other and to make the plans for the journey for both of them but I was surprised. She said in her letter that she would dispose of the flat in Leyton and would plan to sell all of the furniture to one house broker when the time came to make the move. This was quite a shock to me since I was just settling into my new city. I really had no money saved up for this venture and I did not know too many people here in San Francisco for her and Colin to meet. Taking all things into consideration, I decided that staying in San Francisco was not a good idea and decided then and there I should return to New York, but how? I knew it was too dangerous to drive my old Chevy car again across America since I knew it would never make it across the deserts and mountains. I decided to sell my car and take the Greyhound bus back to New York well in time before they arrived. I would have loved to take the train, but that was too expensive.

I had to sell the car, I drove about the city stopping off at the used car lots but because I still had New York plates and a New York car registration card, all the dealers I contacted were not interested in buying my car. They complained that New York State had very easy registration system and application for car registration forms that were easy to pick up at the department of motor vehicles and the car could have been stolen. I did find one young guy on the used car lot who looked it over and said that he would give me $100.00 for it on a spot cash deal right there and then. Once again, my luck proved good since I did not have much money, in fact I really was practically broke. I still owed the landlady for the rest of the month before I could move my stuff out of the room.

I walked down to the Greyhound bus station in the city which was about a mile from my room and asked them the cost of a one-way fare to New York. The man in the ticket booth said that it would be $89.00 one way to New York and the bus left every day at 8:00 am. I told him that I had some baggage to put in the luggage carrier inside the under-side of the bus. He asked me what kind of luggage and told him my TV, record player, two suitcases and some other pieces of electronics. He told me then that the rules of the Greyhound Corporation West were that no electronic equipment could be carried by the Greyhound Bus. He whispered to me that I looked like a good kid so he told me to go pick up some large empty cardboard boxes at the TV store next door and put the electronics in the large board boxes, packing them with clothes and write on the boxes that they were old clothes.

I drove down to the car dealer and he paid me $100.00 for my car. I said good bye to my old Betsy which had carried me across country, but was now on her last days. Then I walked back to the TV appliance store for some good boxes that were had flattened down. I struggled back up the hill to my room on Sacramento Street. I told the landlady that I was vacating the flat in two days and paid her what I owed her in rent and then started to plan to leave San Francisco two days later.

That evening I began to pack my clothes in my suit cases and then to fill up the cartons with my electronic equipment lining the left over spaces in the boxes. I looked at my financial situation taking into con-sideration after paying my rent and paying for the bus fare of $89.00 I now had only $11.00 for food for the four days that it would take to cross America coast to coast in a Greyhound bus. The evening before I was to leave San Francisco I literally dragged my boxes down the hill to the bus station to be put into the luggage area ready to be loaded on the bus the following morning prior to departure. It took me all evening to clear out my room, pack my clothes and take them all down to the bus station. The following morning, I walked down Sacramento Street to the bus station, checked in with my paid ticket, found my seat which was on the upper observation deck on a scenicruiser section in the front of the bus and I carefully watched them load all my boxes. I had numbered them to ensure they all went together.

At 8:30 am the Greyhound scenic cruiser, half double decker bus pulled out of the bus station gate and lumbered towards the Bay Bridge crossing SFO Bay. The city of San Francisco was cloaked in fog and was chilly, but as we got half way across the bridge I looked back and saw the city skyline. The fog began to clear falling away from behind me as we crossed the bridge. It was as if it was saying, sorry Roy that it did not work out. I also said a silent goodbye to the city by the bay.

I think that if it was not for my mother and Colin coming to the United States I might have stayed in California and eventually got a job. But I also felt I had those responsibilities to my small family and I thought that it was all for the best that I was returning to New York and to other adventures. Here I was on my way back to New York City and all of my friends that I had left behind, but I somehow knew I would be back. All my worldly belongings were in the luggage compartment on this Greyhound bus and I was on my way back to the world that I had left behind. It seems to me that I was destined to always wander across the world. It would seem I would never be satisfied with what I had and needed to push on to the next greener pasture. It was part of my makeup and I always enjoyed moving to other parts of the country.

We slowly travelled across the Bay Bridge into the Oakland side and being in the front seat of the upstairs front window I could see all of the country passing by. Since there were no interstate highways in those days, we followed a small two lane highway that passed through some beautiful country where the fruit was growing and people were picking the fruit by hand. The first hurdle was to pass over the foothills of the Sierra Nevada Mountains then over the mountains ranges that surrounded the west coast. The sky was blue and clear and the sun was shining and I finally felt good that I was leaving the city by the bay with all of its challenges left behind.

It was going to be a fine trip back across country to the city that I had always wanted to be at, the city of New York. It seemed like it was calling me back again across three thousand miles of country, rich in history and to more adventures heading east. The road started to climb the foothills of the high mountains and began to grab the tires of the bus as it zig zagged up the mountainsides trying to reach the summit and pass through and over the top. Snow began to appear as we climbed up into the higher elevations of six-thousand-foot level and soon everything was covered in snow. At the peak there appeared a sign which said Donner Pass. I remembered then that this was where a terrible tragedy occurred in the mid 1800's. Suddenly my history kicked in when I saw that sign. The story of those pioneer settlers who crossed the country from St. Louis were west bound heading for the fertile valleys of California in 1800's. The secret in crossing the Sierra Nevada mountain range in those years was the exact timing of the year. To get through the pass safely before the heavy snow began to fill up the passes, the wagon train had to leave Ft. Smith by August of that year. For some reason the wagon master left much later in September, which caught them off guard and suddenly the wagon train was caught in an early snow blizzard crossing the Sierra Nevada valleys. The snow was so bad that they had to halt since the trail became impassable so they camped in a valley deep in snow. Soon they ran out of food and could not find any game to hunt. The wagon master decided that a small group of settlers with snow shoes could push their way through the mountains and find help for the wagon train left behind. History tells us that those left behind were dying of hunger and actually it was suggested that they became cannibals from those that had died from hunger and cold. The group that did leave did get across the mountains into the green valleys of California and managed to get help and with that help they returned to the camp, but very few settlers were left alive.

It was so very dangerous to cross the country one hundred and fifty years ago. Now here I was in a warm and comfortable bus passing the same area where this terrible event had taken place so many years before. I am sure there were many more disasters like the Donner party during that period of time in other places in America, but people were determined to reach their dream destination and I could surely understand that.

I soon began to feel a downward pull as we descended down from this mountain range that had taken the lives of so many pioneers of men, women and children that had pushed across so long ago. Suddenly the bus driver pulled into a bus station somewhere in the middle of nowhere and announced that it was a lunch stop at a small bus station. Keeping in mind I only had eleven dollars to spend on food for four days. I had a grilled cheese sandwich with fries for about 75 cents and a coke for 5 cents. Everything in those days was cheap compared to today's prices.

I do not recall the many small towns that we passed through as we traveled into the afternoon but the bus driver had said over the bus PA that the dinner stop would be in Salt Lake City and we would have an hour layover at the bus station. I did not get to see much of Salt Lake City since the day was winding down and it was getting dark. We pulled into the city when I saw flashing lights coming up behind the bus. It was a cop telling the driver of the bus to pull over to the side of the road. The cop came on board and asked the driver for his license. The bus driver had run a red light back down the road and he was giving the driver a ticket. I am not sure of the outcome of this incident, but we did finally pull away and soon we were in the bus station filled with other Greyhound busses with the destination lights all lit up as we pulled into a park slot for the bus to park. I got off the bus leaving my personal belongings on my seat so that nobody boarding the bus would take my seat and moved into the bus station. It was not a very clean place with lots of people all going somewhere on different busses. It really was a bus terminus for all destinations.

There were lots of military serviceman moving either to their homes on leave or returning back to their base. I remember it was a very busy place with bright lights, neon signs everywhere and everybody bustling around waiting for their particular bus and plenty of fast food. I found a small restaurant in the bus station and had a sandwich and French fries for dinner after using the bathroom since I do not recall there being a bathroom on the bus like today. I find that interesting since we were driving for about four hours at a time so we must have stopped for a few minutes as we drove along to use some facilities on the road but did not remember how often. I know that the bus driver had to keep a strict schedule and be on time at each of his stops. While in the bus station as the departure time approached the bus driver would walk around the bus station and call out that the New York bus is ready to leave in ten minutes.

We continued on through the night after leaving Salt Lake City. It was difficult to sleep the first night on the bus which is not unusual for me. I always seem to be constantly peering out the window as we went along the highway. They had changed drivers in Salt Lake City in the middle of the night. We were now heading into real open country and I could not see much of the land features off the road into the dark because the headlights of the bus were pointing forward, but suddenly the bus started to slow down and I saw a figure of a man waiting on the side of the dark road. As the bus stopped, in its headlights I could see a man carrying a saddle over his shoulder. It was a cowboy flagging down the bus. I realized that this was an official bus stop on this desolate road and the cowboy was going to board our bus at about three in the morning. When the bus had stopped the driver left the bus and lifted up the handle of the luggage compartment under the bus where all my worldly possession was located and the cowboy heaved his saddle into the compartment and boarded the bus. He climbed up the bus stairs to the upper deck where I was seated and he sat next to me.

Although it was about three in the morning, I was wide awake and was eager to talk to this man who came out of the night with only his saddle. My first thought was where is his horse? Did he shoot the horse somewhere in the desert I wondered? He was tall, very tall about six foot two plus and as he sat down in his seat his legs were bent towards his chin. Not much room for a tall cowboy with long legs. He looked at me looking at him and seeing I was awake he said howdy. I began to speak with him and his name was Shorty but no way did his name describe his build. I was awestruck about being able to speak again to a real working cowboy. He was dressed in a checkered shirt with a bandana around his neck, chino pants and beautiful boots etched leather. I very carefully looked at his waist and sure enough there was a gun belt with cartridges and sticking out of the holster was a gun. The laws of this state allowed passengers to carry guns anywhere any time.

Looking back over the years I just could not see in today's world a public bus stopping to pick up a passenger in the middle of the night in the middle of the desert. One lone man with a saddle over his shoulder and carrying a gun, unconcealed and gun belt allowed on a bus. I think the bus driver would have dialed 911 if it was on the East Coast and the police would have arrived very quickly. But no, this was in the days when all this was normal and people went around doing their own business any way that they wanted. It was as America was, not like it is now.

He was an easy guy to speak with and we had a long talk about what he did for a living. I recall him saying that he was heading for the rodeo in Casper, Wyoming and had been on another bus coming up from the south waiting to pick up our east bound bus that did not arrive until this time of the day. I asked him how long he had been waiting for our bus and he said about three hours but he was in a saloon most of that time while he was waiting. I did not see any kind of saloon in this wilderness but who am I to dispute his words. He must have had some of his pals with him in the saloon so it must have been a rowdy night in that saloon when these cowboys were in there. I said good luck to Shorty who was going to try his luck at the rodeo for the upcoming weekend. His face was the color of walnut being out in the sun all day. I could not determine his age with the sun wrinkling and hardening his features but I think he was about thirty years old which would have made him about seven years older than me. He said that his family owned a ranch some place in Wyoming and now he was an itinerant ranch hand doing odd jobs wherever his location was at the time. He had a horse that he had shipped to the rodeo location in Laramie, ready for him to arrive. By the next breakfast stop we were approaching Cheyanne, Wyoming where he got off of the bus. I said my goodbyes as we got off of the bus. I saw him go to the luggage compartment and pull out his saddle and threw it across his wide shoulders walking into the bus station. He was a fascinating man, a real composite of a western cowboy wandering around the west working the rodeo's trying to make some money while he was still young to do that kind of work.

The rest of the passengers went into the Wyoming bus station to get some breakfast. I had to be very careful about the cost of each meal since I had only eleven dollars for food at the beginning of the trip across country. At times I did without food, just lived through the day without lunch just having breakfast and dinner. Suddenly I heard the bus driver calling out for us to board and I found that most of the original bus passengers had reached their destinations or had to change their busses to end their journey somewhere else. There was a new bunch of people that had boarded our bus. They were mostly college kids all about my age and a young girl came and sat next to me. As we rode along on the bus some of the kids began playing guitars and singing songs. I began to get acquainted with this young lady that had sat next to me and she said that they were all from the University of Arizona in Phoenix. She was going home for the Christmas break and that she lived on a farm in Waterloo, Iowa. I do not recall her name but we talked all the way to Omaha, Nebraska where she was to get off to change busses to go north to Waterloo. By the time we got to Omaha we were the best of friends and she asked me if I would like to break my journey to New York and stay with her and her family on their farm for the Christmas holidays. I thought it was very kind of her to invite me, a stranger into her home. I would have liked very much to have taken her up on that invitation but I was very embarrassed that I was down to about five dollars and could not go to her home without any funds so I reluctantly said I could not break my journey as much as I would like to have done. She was such a nice young lady and I often wondered what would have happened if I had taken up on her offer. I may have inherited the farm and become a ranch hand with a large spread. Here I go again, my imagination was taking hold of me but here in America is where you can easily do that.

Very soon we were approaching Chicago. Here I had to change busses since the Greyhound bus company at that time had two divisions. One was the Western Division and the other was the Eastern Division and I had to change busses in Chicago to board an eastern division bus. We pulled into the Chicago bus terminal. I took my time to leave the bus, since the driver told us over the PA bus system that the New York bound bus was alongside of us and suggested we wait and watch to be sure that our luggage was transferred out of our bus and put onto the next bus alongside for its destination to New York. I waited for a while until no more luggage were being transferred then I looked and saw my luggage was still on the bus and had not been unloaded. I told the bus driver who picked up my luggage who was kind enough to personally transfer my entire checked luggage on to the bus that was going to New York. The bus could easily have left with my sole life possessions going to anyplace in America. When I was sure that my luggage was transferred on to the New York bound bus I boarded my new bus. The bus driver using his microphone was making sure his entire passenger's final destination was going to be New York City by way of other cities along the way. As soon as all was confirmed and everyone was aboard, we began to back out of the bus station and move out of the area. We were driving onto the main highway. I was on my way back to New York after travelling from coast to coast and back again this time by way of the northern route back to New York.

We drove out of the bus station, up the ramp on to the main highway which is named Lake Shore Drive not knowing that ten years into the future I would be returning to this very location as a printing press salesman attending the printing trade shows at McCormick Place exhibition hall. We passed by Wrigley Field where the Chicago Cubs play baseball, but I was not to know that at the time which building was for a baseball stadium. Passing by Migs Field which is a private airport running alongside of the lake, passing the Science and Industry Museum, we were soon out of the city heading to the state of Indiana. As we left the city of Chicago, we were soon on our way east through Gary, Indiana and passed the farms and fields of Indiana. I did notice at the time many industries with large smokestacks in the vicinity of the city of Gary, but that soon passed and we were in the state of Ohio making a stop in Cleveland discharging and picking up new passengers at the bus station café. After leaving Cleveland we were in the open farm country and before I knew it we were crossing the great Ohio River into the city of Pittsburgh in the western part of the state of Pennsylvania. By this time, it was time to stop for a dinner break so here I was eating another grilled cheese sandwich for dinner.

By now my money was really running out and I had to check out how many dollars, quarters and dimes that I had to carry me through to New York City which was a full day away. I was really getting very low in cash and hoped that I would have enough to last me to the end. We were now on the Pennsylvania Turnpike and only a few hours away from arriving in New York. I calculated that if I was careful, I would still have enough to get me there if I skipped lunch. Soon we were in Philadelphia not knowing that one day, some years ahead I would be living near this city.

As the day drew to an end, we were driving along the New Jersey Turnpike approaching New York City. I could see the skyscrapers in the distance of the skyline that seemed to be beckoning me back home after the thousands of miles I had travelled. Soon we were passing through the Lincoln Tunnel under the Hudson River and there was the end of the tunnel coming into sight. The next stop would be driving up the ramp towards the 40th Street Bus Terminal. I was back in New York with less than a dollar, just small change in my pocket, as we pulled into the gate assigned to my bus and finally stopped. I left the bus and ensured that I had found my all of luggage from the baggage compartment of the bus. I asked the bus driver where I could store my luggage since I had no money for a cab, so he suggested I put it in a secure caged area in Greyhound luggage claim. I moved the boxes over to the enclosed luggage area, received a ticket and sat down on a bench to decide what I was going to do.

1961, Back in NYC

I DECIDED TO call Mae Mollick, the landlady that rented me my room before I left to go to California. I checked my financial situation and found I had 75 cents left in my pocket. I decided to invest a dime of that for a local phone call to her to see if she had a room that I could rent. I phoned her and she was so surprised to hear from me she asked me how was I able to call her long distance from Los Angeles to New York. Laughing, I told her I was back in New York and needed her help, did she have a room that I could rent for the night? To my delight she said she had a room, in fact she said my old room was available, the same room that I had rented before I left on my great adventure. I explained my financial condition and she said no problem. I could pay her as soon as I got a job. It was incredible that everything was falling back into place.

I needed to free up one suitcase and remove it from the luggage cage and get on the subway to Mae's house in Queens. In those days a subway fare was only ten cents anywhere on the system so it did not cost me much to reach her house. Travel weary I arrived at her house and it was so good to see her. I told her some of my adventures across the country from coast to coast. She asked me if I was alright for cash. I said I was a little short because now I was down to 55 cents. She told me to wait and briefly left the room. When she came back, she had a five dollar bill in her hand and very kindly told me she knew what it is like to be cash short so take these five dollars and pay me back when you get a job. I was so surprised I wanted to hug her. Then she gave me a small pie out of the refrigerator and a bottle of coke and I was off to bed in my old room. Soon I was fast asleep and the end of my journey of over six thousand miles by car and bus had been completed and I was back in New York where it had all started. Tomorrow I would find a job and prepare for mum and Colin's arrival which would be only three months away in April. I had a lot to do in by then.

As soon as I could get myself ready, I was off to catch the bus from Main Street, Flushing to the subway terminal which would take me to downtown Manhattan and the printing union hiring hall where hopefully I could get a job as a printer again. Downstairs at the union offices was the hiring hall that was filled with other men that were also looking for work, either for the week or the day. The room was full of cigar and cigarette smoke. Men were playing cards and checkers; some were reading the newspapers. Every now and then the union hiring man called out in a loud voice that some company needed this and that pressman and the next one on the list would be given a ticket to show the foreman of the printing company that they were sent by the union for the job. Suddenly, to my surprise my name was called. When I went to the hiring desk the hiring agent said there was a phone call for me, I was to take the call upstairs. I was so surprised since I wondered who knew that I was back in town after over two years of absence. I picked up the phone that was offered to me and a voice that I was delighted to recognize, a familiar voice. It was Dave Jenkins my old foreman at Publishers' Printing in Long Island City. He said hey, my old friend what was I doing back in New York. He asked me to go outside to a public phone booth in a nearby candy store luncheonette and call him back on a public pay phone. He wanted to speak to me. I left the union hall and found a phone and called him. To my surprise he asked me if I would like to come back to work. I immediately told him yes, when can I start? He replied the next day would be good for him if I would like to start that soon.

America had come through for me again just as the union man had said to me years before that the Lady in the Bay would take care of me. I asked him could I be back on the day shift and he said yes. The next day I reported to his office and was back on the press in my old job on the day shift, which I wanted in the first place before I had left for California. To me it was amazing how things eventually turned out. Someone was watching out for me for sure. I could not believe my good luck. I was on a roll again. So here I was back in my favorite city in my same room, the same company to work for and life was beginning to look up for me at last. I had a lot of work to do to prepare for the family reunion during the month of April 1961 since that was the time that mum had decided on when she and Colin would be arriving in New York.

Dave Jenkins asked me if I was a bit short on cash and I replied that I was, so he put his hand in his pocket and gave me $50.00 dollars to get me through next payday and I could pay him back then. I reported for work at 8:00 am and what a reunion it was with all of the men. I was really welcomed back by the men. They slapped my back and shook hands and said the limey Roy was back and after a while it seemed like I had not left. Very little had changed. The same people doing the same job on the same presses except now I had my evenings to be able to find an apartment for mum and Colin before they landed in a few months. I had to find an apartment big enough for three people. Looking at the ads in the newspaper I found a single house that rented out the upper floors with one bathroom and two bedrooms at a reasonable price. It was close to the Belmont Park Racetrack which I could see from the upper floor windows and watch the horses race around the track.

I was back to where it all started but that was only the beginning, for now came the interesting part of my life. There in the future would be some wonderful opportunities for me that would only add to the story of myself, a young man in America from the East End of London, that changed my life. My American journey had only just begun and I would soon be proud to be called an American.

April 1961, A Second Beginning

I HAD RETURNED from my western travels knowing that I had to prepare the way for my mother and young brother Colin so I would be able to ease them into American society. I had to get a job for them lined up and also an apartment for us to live in. I had found an apartment large enough for the three of us in the borough of Queens which was a very nice.

The next thing I had to find was some second-hand furniture. One of the members in the British War Veterans club had a brother who was in the used furniture business. After meeting him one evening we travelled to his warehouse to look over some second-hand furniture that he had available. I picked out some living room furniture, a dining room set and two single beds for Colin and myself. I was concerned that I had to get some decent furniture before they arrived in a new country with better living conditions than what they left behind in England, plus I had only a certain amount of money to do this prior to their arrival. I visited some of the large department stores and found a good mattress that would fit the frame and box spring that I had already bought ready for mum. I decided on Gimbels department store and found the right mattress for her. I had bought all of the sheets and other necessary items to prepare for a home to be ready for when they arrived in three months on April 1961.

Now I had to work some double shifts to earn enough money to buy all of the kitchen items such as cutlery, tablecloths and other smaller items. I wanted everything to be complete before they arrived in three months' time. I arranged for delivery of all these items since I did not have a car yet. It was early January 1961 and I knew that even when working overtime in my job it would be difficult to save up enough money to pay for all of these items and set up a complete home so I decided to shut down my evening entertainment and not go out anywhere. I added up my possible expenditures and if I did not go out and spend money I would have just enough money to be able to keep three people in housing and food until everyone was employed. I knew it was going to be tight.

I went back to work on a day and a half night shift so I could get half a night extra shift overtime and then I got a job in a grocery store supermarket on odd hours as a checker on weekends bagging groceries. Sometimes I would not finish until 3:00 am in the morning when I would catch the subway train uptown to 42nd Street and change trains and then catch a bus in Flushing to the rooming house that I rented for myself. I finished up all of the official immigration documents for them and all the paper work I did when I first applied. I got them permanent residence visas and they already had passports. When all of the paperwork was ready and sent to her, she was ready to leave for America.

I did not have a car yet since I left my last car in San Francisco so the next item on the agenda was to find a good used car. One of the members of the British War Vets was an insurance agent and he found me an insurance company that would put me into the assigned risk pool and now I was ready to drive. I had to buy a used car so since I had a good relationship with the owner of Chesterfield used car dealer in Flushing, NY, I went back there. I found a nice used 1957 Mercury hard top and drove it off the lot and it felt good to have wheels again. Just as before, I paid cash for the car but had I had to finance the car insurance. It had many more gadgets on this car than I had in the 1952 Chevy that I left behind in San Francisco, so I was very pleased with my new set of wheels.

I was still going over each Saturday night to the British War Veterans Club and attending their weekend functions but that was just about all that I could afford. My mother was keeping in touch with me but she was not telling me what was going on in England and I could not understand why. In later years I did find out from my brother. Apparently, my mother had decided to sell the contents of the house to one person taking everything that was in the house. That included all my old toys, trains, lead soldiers which would be very valuable today. They also took the piano and all of the beautiful dishes and other china cups that we had in a glass cabinet in the formal front room of the house. I was in shock when all the items that she did ship over finally arrived from the ship prior to her arrival. Most of the items that came over on the boat must have been lashed to the outside deck of the ship, since most of the items were damaged by salt water and rusted by the sea.

When I took possession and the furniture was delivered to me at the apartment, I was very disappointed and tried to get an answer as to why the shipment was so damaged and how this had happened but the shipping agent had no response why. My mother did not ship a lot of the remaining items from England and she had not arranged for any special insurance with the shipping line and I suspect that they had left all of the furniture on the open deck and it was corroded by the salt spray and became rusted. There were some smaller items that we could save but most of it was also rusted. I went over to the freight line offices in Manhattan to complain about the condition of the goods delivered but I did not get much sympathy from the freight line without being insured. After sorting out the damaged items I went and replaced as much as I could and waited until they arrived.

The apartment in the house was very nice since it was the upstairs part of large two story house that was rebuilt into two apartments. The couple who owned the house lived downstairs were a quite elderly couple so there was plenty of space in the upstairs apartment for my mum, Colin and myself. It was a start and very nice for them to arrive in America and have a complete home when they arrived.

I still did not go out much on a Saturday night and was still working the double night shift for which I was paid time and half, so I was making quite a nice wage and put it mostly in the savings bank ready for the big day when they would arrive. They were flying to America this time to New York's Idlewild Airport serving the New York area. It was a slow airplane since it took over 24 hours to fly from London airport. It was scheduled to arrive at about 10:00 am so after making everything ready, I left the house to go to the airport to meet my family who would soon be residing in America. I remember it was a very nice day with plenty of sunshine for the month of April. I got into my car and went to meet my family at New York Idlewild Airport soon to be known as JFK New York International a few years later.

I did not know at that time but I discovered about forty years later from my brother that my mother had not discussed this major move with Colin or even asked if he would like to go to America. He told me that he had not been consulted about this move to leave England, leaving all his friends and family. I was quite upset when he told me this at the time since I thought I was doing the right thing for us all to have a better life in the best country in the world.

As I stood on the upper floors of the airport building, I saw the plane carrying mum and Colin landing on American soil. They had arrived and I was so pleased now that they were here and I would be able to offer them a better life than they had in England. I waited a while before they came through customs and immigration and there was my mother and my brother Colin together in a new world. My mother was fifty-one years old at that time and Colin was sixteen. It was April 21, 1961. After going through baggage claim we walked out to the parking lot and they were surprised to see my new long-bodied, wide Ford Mercury which was two tone, maroon and white.

In England all the cars were painted basically black and were quite small so, just like me when I first arrived in America three years before, they also were overwhelmed by the different colors of all the cars. We exited from the airport onto the main highway eastbound on Long Island's Southern State Parkway towards Belmont where their first home was waiting for them to move in. When we arrived at the new apartment, they were very happy about their new home but I am sure that it must have been very strange for them as it was for me. Also, they were very tired since they had been on that aircraft for over 24 hours from London making stops only to refuel. No jets had yet been available to cross the Atlantic Ocean during those early days of air travel because the days of trans-Atlantic tourism had not really arrived yet. They had arrived tired and hungry and also it was early morning about 10:00 am. So when we arrived at the apartment I cooked some food for them and made them a great breakfast of eggs and bacon, made tea for them and they both headed for some rest until they had recovered from their travels.

As soon as they were ready, I showed them the kitchen devices such as a dishwasher and how it worked, the gas stove and went through the house showing mum her room, which I had already prepared the bed and all of the dresser furniture ready for her to use. I had a television set installed in her room so that she could go to bed to watch TV. The furniture that she had shipped via sea was all put in order. I had cleaned off the rust on some of the items which I had put on the mantle so they then prepared to unpack their luggage and settled in. She was fascinated with the TV programs and so many channels to watch. After they had some afternoon tea, I took them for a drive around the neighborhood showing them the local supermarket which of course at that time did not yet exist in England and we bought some groceries that would be needed. I also had bought a larger TV screen in the living room for family viewing, putting my older smaller TV in mum's room. To get a good reception from the TV station in those days were the rabbit ears that had to be constantly re-adjusted and moved from side to side and up and down and of course all TV programs were in black and white.

We cooked the first dinner which my mother seemed to take to very quickly and now we had our first Yorkshire pudding in America together. I realized at the end of that day they were quickly settling into their new home and their new country. Colin and I shared a room with two single beds and as soon as dinner came and passed, we were each in our beds each sleeping off their tiredness and jet lag. Tomorrow would bring another day for them to explore America.

I had to go to back to work after the first week and I had to think of getting a job for Colin and my mother. Both were in the printing business but also Colin had a problem. Since he was only sixteen, which in England he had legally finished school, but here in America the kids had to stay at school until eighteen. Colin wanted to find a job like the one he left in England as a printing press operator.

To find out what we had to do I took him over to the local high school and spoke to the principle. I explained the situation asking if I could he get permission for Colin to go to work and not have to go back to school. The principle understood the problem and said that he felt that the schools in England at that time were much better than in the USA (how wrong he was) so he filed a petition to the school district to exempt Colin from returning to school so that he could find some work. In a few days a letter of confirmation arrived that he had finished his school curriculum and was finished with school.

The next thing was to find work for my mother since her experience was in printing also but in the book bindery part of the factory. She had a lifetime of experience in this kind of business so prior to their arrival in America I had contacted some friends of mine in New York who spoke to some other friends and I was advised that when she arrived she should contact the president of the bindery union in New York. After she was here for a few weeks and could move about more comfortably we took a subway ride into Manhattan and met with the bindery union local representative. They discussed what she could do and was told that they would find her a job as a bindery woman when she felt she was ready to go to work. They settled for a company in New York City and my friend in the union got her a start date within two weeks and she was back at work making friends almost as soon as she arrived. I found a print shop job shop in a nearby town which was perfect for Colin as a startup job, which he was able to fit in with the knowledge he had found in London so he was set up well.

I still attended the meetings at the British War Veterans of America so each Saturday evening Colin would stay at home and mum and I would go to the Saturday dance that they had. She immediately met new friends and seemed to fit in with the other English women of the club. Colin was a different situation because it was difficult for boys of his age to find friends for him. I managed to get him to join the Explorers organization, which was something like the Boy Scouts and he liked that very much and found some friends in that area. One of these boys at the Explorers became life-long friends with Colin and they still keep in touch and visit each other when possible.

After they had been here for a few weeks summer had arrived and we went on many picnics with the British War Vets. My mother liked the beach so we would go to Jones Beach which was only about half an hour away and she just lay in the sun which she just loved the suns heat. Colin also liked the beach since he would go body surfing. It seemed that after about three months things were just fitting together. Colin had a job doing what he wanted and mum and got a job in Manhattan at a large printing plant with a bindery. Although she had to take the subway to work on her own, she seemed to be happy with that and both of them were fitting in well. Both of them immediately loved the hot summer weather, since the weather in England was so cold and damp even in the summer season.

During this time, I was starting to going out on a Saturday night myself as I did before they arrived. I did not want to change my habits and mum was finding lady friends and Colin was finding friends of his own age, so I would still go out on a date or with some of the guys. I met a girl from Germany whose name was Perky and I never did find out what her last name was. She had come to America to go in the fall to the nursing college in Newport News located in Virginia at the Newport News Hospital. I brought her home to meet my mother and Colin during that summer so when September came for her to leave for college, we all drove her down to the Newport News Hospital and she checked into the nursing school. The nursing college had rules for visitors that were very strict for the students. They had a house mother who checked us out and made sure that we were the kind of people that would be good friends for a student nurse in her hospital. I was being checked out. I often wonder where she is now and even if she is even alive since she was the same age as me.

I decided I needed to take a vacation so first I would buy myself my first new car. I bought a light green Ford Falcon which was one of the first compact cars in America's small car options. It was small but not much shorter than the standard American car. It was supposed to get lower gas mileage, but I did not agree with that statement although gas was cheap at 29 cents per gallon.

Before I left for vacation, on Saturday night I decided that I would go back into Manhattan and visit Roseland, the giant dancehall with two bands on their rotating bandstand. While I was there looking for a partner to dance with, I met two girls that were together for the evening, one named Maryanne and the other Patty. I asked Patty if she would like to dance and she said no, but I replied are you sure. She hesitated then said yes and had a few dances and then had a drink at the bar and got acquainted. They both lived on Long Island so I asked if they wanted a ride back to Long Island when the dance was over. They both agreed so I drove them back to their homes. Patty and I went out on dates for a while and I explained that I was going on vacation and that I would call her when I got back.

The first Saturday morning of my two weeks vacation I found myself driving down the New Jersey Turnpike southbound heading to Miami. I was cruising along the highway listening to all those great songs of 1962 like Ahab the Arab and Alley-oop. I soon passed Washington, DC and drove into Virginia staying the first night at a motel on the Virginia and North Carolina state line. In the state of South Carolina, I saw my first palm tree and I knew that Miami Beach was only a day away. Then I crossed over into the State of Florida and now I saw lots of palm trees and the sparkling blue waters of the rivers and beaches of Florida. I felt like I was in paradise.

To reach Miami Beach I had to drive across the causeway from the city of Miami on into Miami Beach. One of my favorite TV shows at that time was Surfside 6 where they shot the outside scenes located on Collins Avenue and sure enough there was an address listed there but it really was only a private dock. I had made a reservation for two weeks at the Seville Hotel on the beach and checked into this huge luxury hotel, but after a few days I found that it was not the kind of hotel that had imagined it to be. I decided to check into another one of the hotels along the beach called the Fontainebleau which was much better with younger people as guests.

After enjoying a nice dinner, I went into one of the night clubs that offered dancing. While I was being seated at my table, I noticed a girl that was sitting alone. I got up from my table and introduced myself asking her to dance. As we danced, she told me that her name was Diane Ferrin and she was from the Chicago, Illinois area. She had already been there at the hotel for over a week and although she had arrived alone, she was now with two other couples and was waiting for them to enter the night club. Soon her friends arrived and they invited me to join their table. That was the first time I met Diane and I mention this only because she became a lifelong friend which lasted for over fifty years until she died. She had told me when we first met that she had had a big argument with her boyfriend Buddy, and that she had decided immediately to leave Chicago to get away for a while. She did go back to Chicago and eventually married her boyfriend Buddy. At times we would fly out to Chicago and spend a few days with them and we met at a rendezvous location at Niagara Falls for a long weekend. Her friends that were with us at the hotel were also a good group and we all had a great time during the week that I was there with them.

I was the only one with a car so we all piled into my car somehow and went on many trips in the Miami Beach area. One of the interesting places was visiting the Castaway Hotel at the northern end of Collins Avenue. This was a bar that had large windows behind the bar where you could see through a glass window below the surface of the pool watching the swimmers go by. I also remember taking the whole group into the Everglades swamp and looking for alligators. Everglades State Park was one of the highlights where airboats were available with a guide to show tourists the alligators and other wildlife. Airboats are flat bottom boats with a giant fan located at the stern which acted as a propeller and pushed the boat forward. The airboat having a flat keel enabled the boat to skim over the shallow swamps where the alligators and other wildlife could be seen. There were also very large birds of prey such as eagles, condors and kestrels in their nests, usually in the top of a very tall tree. The kestrels also lived at the top of telephone poles where the county had put up nesting platforms for them to keep their young in the nests.

The beaches along Collins Avenue were just perfect and everyone seemed to have a very good time, but soon it became time to get them over to leave for the airport. I drove each of them to the airport in my car in plenty of time to catch their flights back to a destination they called home somewhere across the country.

Driving back to New York took me three long days since in those days there were no interstate highways and the road I was travelling on broke into a four lane highway so it was an easy drive. I followed the old US Highway 301 heading north passing through Georgia, South Carolina, North Carolina, Virginia, Maryland into New Jersey on into New York and home to Long Island.

Arriving home, I was happy to find that my mother and Colin were doing just fine as if I had never left. It was now almost at the end of the summer of 1962. We still went down to the beach where the Atlantic was still fairly warm, but not like the warm Atlantic Ocean that was in Miami Beach. I went back to work the following Monday after a weekend to shake off the return travel time.

After returning, Patty and I were equally fond of spending an evening at a club called the Three Guitars, which was a Russian night club. They served a Russian dinner with black bread. The food was good and after being cleared away and sent back to the kitchen the after dinner show began. The show always had a Russian flavor and an artist dressed up as a Russian Cossack. He was dressed as a tribesman that threw large knives at his lady partner who stood against a board and he barely missed her outlined figure. Then a curtain would be pulled apart to show seven dancers dressed in Russian peasant costume playing the triangular instrument called a balalaika playing various peasant songs. As they were playing three others appeared also dressed with leather belts across their chests with ammunition inserted in each slot. Then their leather bandoliers sat-kicked their traditional music bending their knees out and back almost to the floor all at a high rate of speed to the sound of the balalaika music.

Living on Long Island we were only a short distance by subway to Manhattan and its entertainment venues. We could easily visit the theaters of Broadway and the many clubs that played Dixieland Jazz until the early morning hours. All of the good supper clubs were in Manhattan and for the charge of about ten dollars we would get dinner and a great show of very famous entertainers like Frank Sinatra, Dean Martin and Jerry Lewis. These night clubs had two dinner shows each night one at 8:00 pm and one at 10:00 pm. There was a dress code which meant that diners must wear formal attire. Ladies should wear an evening gown and men had to wear a suit and a shirt with a tie. At the door there was usually a doorman who directed you to the club door. If a guest walked in and did not wear a tie the doorman would provide a tie for you to wear while you were on the premises. We would then be shown into the dining area where we were seated by the maître d dressed in formal evening suit and he would give us a menu. The menu was quite complicated at times but the waiter would explain what was on it and asked if we required a drink first. There was usually a small band like a quintet playing in the background or a piano player singing quietly in the background.

There were other great clubs on Long Island which we went on a Saturday night. One was called the Oaks. This club was located further out on the Island and was a great club with a permanent band playing great music where we would dance until closing time which was about three in the morning. Patty and I would always go out on Friday and Saturday night to great places to drink and dance to the music and we would dance away the evening. I recall that this time of my life was very happy, in fact the best years.

Jones Beach on the Atlantic Ocean side of Long Island is a large beach with fine sand. During the early summer months, the water was a little cold, but as the summer days got longer the sun warmed up the ocean and by August and September the water was quite warm. I was still a member of the British War Veterans and they organized trips for the members and one night they arranged a trip to Jones beach at the Jones Beach Oceanside Theater, located off the beach in a great arena. This particular time the show that was playing was a musical called Song of Norway. The stage was surrounded with water. The Viking boats that were taking part in the show would sail around the arena with each boat fighting Vikings as well as singing.

1963, Lithographic Institute, Tennessee

I WAS STILL working at the same job but I could see that the printing industry was going through a new phase in its technology. I had worked in an old process known as letterpress with moveable type which had been a standard type for many years. I belonged to the local printing union of New York City and the union owned a lithographic school in Tennessee near the small town of Rogersville. It was named the Lithographic Institute and they were offering a six month printing course about a new print process called offset printing which promised to be the printing of the future. It was located in the foothills of the great Smokey Mountains of Tennessee.

This school was to enable printing firms that were presently using old letterpress printing machines to send one of their pressmen and take this special course since some firms were at that time changing over to offset (lithography) printing equipment. Many companies had sent their best pressmen to take this course. When they completed the course, they would train their pressman in the company's pressroom for this new printing system. In turn, the other personnel in their press room would be able to be trained in the principles of lithography or as it became known as offset. This new system would then be born into the industry and letterpress was basically outdated.

I knew that this new printing system would be the future of printing so I intended to somehow take this offered course. The trouble was that the company I worked for had to pay for the six month tuition. I tried to get my company to send me to the Lithographic Institute where they would pay for the tuition, but they would not agree to do that so here was another dead challenge for me to try and get through. I started to save my money again and I made enough money working days and half nights in the pressroom which earned me enough to pay for the tuition, lodging and board for six months. Although it was difficult to work ten hours per day it was good money at that time and I soon gathered enough to be able to send me to the six month offset printing course.

I wrote to the student director of the school to see if I could get on their schedule if I paid for the course. Finally, after some persuasion I was able to be offered six months of training as long as I paid for the course for the six months education plus living costs such as food and lodging. This did not include having an income while I was there, so here I was again saving up to get something that everybody else got for free. I got permission from my company that I could take a leave of absence for six months to learn this new process and they agreed to keep my job open until I came back six months later. It was an inexpensive benefit to them because I would return to work after I had completed the course and they would have an experienced pressman that knew the process and I could train others and it was also a great experience for me.

I decided to discuss this with my mum and Colin. My mother said that it would better my future if I took this opportunity and leave for six months of school education. I gave in again to my wandering foot and started to prepare for my journey south to the state of Tennessee. I had been sent some brochures of the course how the school was to teach me this new printing process. These brochures had outlined the costs which were high, but I had saved up enough to cover my tuition and living expenses so that I could secure my future. Here was another pending adventure by leaving New York to live temporally in Tennessee. It reminded me of the popular song and TV series called Davy Crockett. In the song about Davy Crockett he allegedly killed a bear when he was only three? Somewhat a stretch of the imagination, but it could have happened in eighteenth-century America.

On the first day of March 1963, I left New York to attend school in Tennessee and left Queens Village, NY, for a very long two-day drive to what was then a small town called Rogersville, Tennessee. At that time in the early sixties, it really was a small town. It almost could be described as a wild west town, but I could not even begin to think of the many adventures that I would have during these six months in a place they called Happy Valley.

Here I was saying goodbye again to my mother and Colin. It was difficult but they had been in America now for two years and they were both working at good jobs and seemed to know their way about so I felt comfortable about leaving them just for a short period of six months. It seems again that I had a wandering foot as others had before me to discover America! This would be the second time I started to load up my car with some of the necessary possessions in the trunk and on the back seat. After saying goodbye to my mother and Colin I started down the road to my new destiny, southbound towards the state of Tennessee heading this time southwest. I first had to drive towards New York west on the Long Island Expressway to cross over the newly built Verrazano Bridge that would take me across Staten Island. Soon I was on the New Jersey Turnpike heading south to join up with the Pennsylvania Turnpike going west to Harrisburg, PA. There I turned off onto a smaller road Route 15 South which would carry me most of the way through to my destination to Rogersville, Tennessee. In those days there still were not many interstate highways that had been built. After leaving Harrisburg, the state capital of Pennsylvania, I headed south on a two-lane federal highway Route 11-15 driving inland passing through Maryland, Virginia, then into Tennessee.

Three days later I arrived at my destination, the small town of Rogersville, Tennessee. At that time in the early sixties, it really was a small town. It could almost be described as looking like a wild-west town, but I could not even begin to think of the many adventures that I would have during these six months. It had one street named of course Main Street, but the sidewalks were raised off of the road on each side of the street like an old western town with a muddy main street through the town. It was so small that you could drive through it in a blink of an eye. After driving down Main Street to the end I had to find out where the location of the Lithographic Institute was and how to get there to check into the school. Most of the men in town were wearing overalls with shoulder straps and most of the ladies wore bonnets and old-fashioned clothes. I had definitely entered a different era like I had entered the Twilight Zone and had been pushed back in time about 100 years.

I asked around some of the stores the location of the Lithographic Institute and found that the there was a small dirt road that led in the direction of my destination. I was told it was located nearby and I drove slowly down this dirt road through a full fifteen miles of unpaved road full of muddy ruts to the entrance to the property of the Lithographic Institute. It was an interesting drive since I passed by many old houses with a front porch. Each house had people sitting on their front porches watching me. As I passed each house the family appeared at almost every house with members of the family sitting on the front porch watching the world go by usually each sitting on rocking chairs. Each of these homes had a small garden in the front with small green plants covered with white muslin cloth which I later found out the muslin was to protect the growing tobacco plants. In about half an hour I came to the entrance of the Lithographic Institute and I had to stop and see what my future home would look like for the next six months. It was surely a beautiful place looking down the valley. The property lay in a lovely long valley between two high ridges of mountains each about 2,000 plus feet high. They appeared to be the lower part of the Smokey Mountain range which I could see far off in the distance. True to the source of their name was a smoky blue haze hanging in between the folds of each mountain range and valley. I followed the road that twisted and turned for another three miles or so and there appeared a beautiful old plantation house with six tall plantation style pillars in the front of the house and was about three stories high. It was indeed a historic plantation house. There were two other buildings nearby and alongside of this was a small golf course.

I turned my car into the front drive of the main house and parked in the front parking lot then walked up to the front of the house opened the door. I could see it was like a hotel with a hotel lobby and front desk. There was no receptionist so I rang a small bell on the front desk and soon a man came to the counter and I introduced myself as a student, having a reservation and wanting to check into my room since school was starting the following day. He checked my reservation and found my assigned room. Confirming that I had previously paid for my room and meals and also for my tuition he showed me around the hotel. He explained to me that there was a restaurant in the hotel which served three meals a day giving specific times of breakfast, lunch and dinner all included in my plan.

That afternoon the rest of the incoming class that had driven from all over the country wandered in and registered. That evening we began to settle in since the following morning classes would start. I soon discovered that I had landed in a "dry" county. No one was allowed in Hawkins County to drink any kind of liquor or buy a beer or anything that was alcoholic. However, some of my new friends had come prepared and we had happy hour which lasted a while. By that late hour since everyone had been travelling all that day and some longer, we were ready for bed so we turned in, wondering what would tomorrow bring when we would begin school classes.

The following morning, which was a Monday, classes would begin at 9:00 am in one of those buildings that were part of the school. Also the next morning there would be an orientation period with the head instructor who would explain about the various classes. Then we would be organized into our special group for the rest of the time we would be at school. My room was very quaint but comfortable and at dinner I met many of the young printers that had come from all over America. We all belonged to the same union but different cities. There were local unions from across the country and we had about fifty printers that were there to learn this new type of process called offset printing.

The following day I went down to breakfast at 7:00 am since they wanted us ready to start at 9:00 am. The breakfast was very good, lots of food and anything you wanted, you just asked the waiter and he would get it. They served their famous southern biscuits which were baked on the premises and were large and fluffy. I recall that I had a wonderful omelet and home fries. Alongside of the omelet there was some white porridge that looked like mashed potato. I tasted it and nearly gagged since it tasted horrible. It was hominy grits that was unknown to me but it is a common dish very popular in the southern states. Other than that, the food was great and continued to be good until the end of the six month printing course. I never complained about the cuisine at the school.

We were now off to the first day of school to learn this new process of lithography. Entering this other brick building which I found out was the classroom area we went into the one room designated as orientation room where the instructor would give us all the information about the course and other local information that we needed to know such as a laundry located in town, one movie theater, a diner restaurant and other than that nothing much else.

The instructor seemed to be good and ready to start the course and the rest of the class members had arrived and soon enough the instructor had gone over the whole curriculum. He showed us all of the press equipment they had for us to work on and gave an overall talk on what the offset process was. At the end of the day, he told us that tomorrow we would start working on the presses with the individual instructors that would be assigned.

The weather at the school was quite nice even though it was in early March and since we were much further south than NY it was like early spring. I remembered that all of the springtime flowers and blossoms were already out and the weather was quite mild. The Great Smoky Mountains were always in the background looming in the far distance, mountains of ridges, green scenery of forests and small farms with the mountains as a background.

As we passed through the first week and the upcoming weekend everybody was asking the big question, where could we get a drink since we were in a bone-dry county and could not buy any beer or liquor. The only place we could get beer was at the American Legion Hall and of course we could not go in there since none of us had been in the American military. After a week or so we found that if we drove down to Knoxville, which was only sixty miles south on Route 11W Highway, we could buy cases of beer there and drive back to the school. The problem was the Hawkins County sheriff and his deputies would hide in the bushes on a Saturday night and set up a trap to catch the beer runners coming up from Knoxville with the beer. If these beer runners were caught the car would be impounded until the fine was paid. However, most of the time somehow the beer runners brought the cases of beer that somehow popped up at the school. We had great parties at the other end of the lake on the property.

One Saturday night we were partying alongside of the lake located on school property and looking across the lake coming towards us was a police car flashing its lights. The sheriff pulled up alongside of us and he wanted to know where we got the beer from. We said we did not know and that we had just found the case. He warned us that it was against the law to drink beer in Hawkins County and if he caught us again, we might end up in jail. We assured the sheriff that we would not do such a thing as break the law. He asked what brands of beer are yo' boy's drinking? We showed him a bottle and he grabbed it and drank the beer emptying the bottle in one swallow. I remember him saying that he was pleased that you boys were buying the best beer around since it was his brand of beer and he then drove off. We did see him regularly after that incident and sometimes he drove over in his police cruiser and sat around the bonfire grabbing another bottle. He was a great officer of the law and enjoyed his job very much.

We had all heard of white lightening which is illegal homemade liquor made in stills in the hills. Being somewhat interested we asked around where we could get ahold of some moonshine to try. We all thought that while we were in the south we might as well try it. I asked around where we could obtain this liquor and was told to go into the one diner in town and ask the waitress about getting some of this local homemade liquor. We did that and asked her if we could get some. She said that for five dollars paid in advance she could get some if we were to come back in one hour. They would leave it behind the toilet tank in the men's room. Taking a chance on losing our money we came back in one hour like she had said and went into the men's room and looked behind the toilet tank there would be a brown bag with a bottle. We did look and yes there it was. After taking a look at it we left the diner and went back to the lake. We had been told that if you were to buy white lighting liquor you must do a test first to see if it was good liquor or bad. We were advised that we should take a tablespoon and fill the spoon with the white lightening, then light it with a match and if the flame turned orange throw it away it was bad. However, if it burned into a fine blue flame then it was good to drink. We went back to our small camp by the lake and tried it. I can personally attest and say that I would never try it again since it was so strong it burned my throat. I nearly threw up it was so strong. Never to be tried again.

After the first week it became time to look for a laundry to do my wash so I asked around and someone told me that there was a coin operated laundry in town. It was a Saturday morning and just about everybody came into Rogersville on Saturday in their blue dungarees doing their shopping and meeting up with some old friends and family. It also seemed that a Saturday was a market day for Rogersville where everyone came into town not only to buy groceries, but to find their friends and sit around talking family business. I found the laundromat and figured out how to work the washing machines and put in my white underwear with the normal soap and bleach. When the cycle was finished, I began pulling out my wet clothes ready to put into the dryer. To my horror I saw that they had changed color to pink. I pulled them all out of the tub and there at the bottom of the drum was a stick of lipstick left behind by the previous user. It took a long time to get the pink out of my underwear with lots and lots of bleach.

The state of Tennessee is truly a beautiful state. It has plenty of rain and most of the foliage is green. It lies snuggled in the foothills of the Great Smoky Mountains which could be seen to the south. After about the second week I received some mail from my Long Island girlfriend Patty who sent me a letter giving me all the news back on Long Island.

While I was in the first few weeks of school there was some very exciting news over the local radio and TV. We were located about thirty miles from the state line of the state of Kentucky which was bordered on the north side of Hawkins County, Tennessee. The state of Kentucky just across the state line was a wet county, so liquor and beer were available to anyone who wanted to buy their favorite drink just across of the state line out of Tennessee into Kentucky. There was a high rated criminal trial being conducted in the State Capital in Knoxville, Tennessee whereby the chief constable of Hawkins County, Tennessee was continually being caught crossing over the state line from Kentucky on a Saturday night while he was going back into Tennessee. He got himself drunk each time and on each occasion the sheriff's deputies immediately would put him in jail for the night. It appeared that after many weeks this constable decided he had enough of being put in jail. One

Saturday night he changed his normal pattern after crossing the state line into Tennessee. He had gathered a group of his family down in a small dip or hollow in the mountains to wait in ambush with their guns, so he began to slow down ready to be stopped by the sheriff's deputies as usual. He led the deputies off the main road by making a sharp right turn down into the hollow where his family members were waiting in ambush with their shotguns fully loaded. The deputies followed the constable down into the hollow and there they were ambushed with shotguns. Three or four of the deputies were shot and killed, others wounded. The constable was now in court in Knoxville. The court case went on for quite a while, but by the time I had left to go back to home after the course was completed they still had not come to any conviction so I do not know how it all ended.

One Sunday afternoon a group of us decided to climb up the mountain ridge that surrounded us. After lunch we slowly walked up a winding road that took us through the lower part of the ridge where people still lived. It was tough going since the climbing was quite steep. Slowly as we climbed, we left the houses behind and were now in deep forest, climbing at a very steep angle. Every now and then we found a break in the deep forest and could see the valley far below where we could still see our plantation house. In about two hours we were approaching the summit but just before the top we noticed that there was a small well-trodden pathway leading off to the right. It seemed that the pathway had been used quite often so we decided to make a turn onto this pathway to find out where it would lead us. Everyone was very cautious since we knew that there were a lot of illegal liquor stills in the area and the owners could become very violent if we trespassed on their property. We walked slowly along the pathway and soon we came to a clearing in the woods. Holding our breath we waited to see what we could see from this small pathway. There in front of us was a small clearing in the woods with a small wooden hut with no windows. It felt creepy to me and I felt like eyes were watching us so I turned around slowly and told everyone to back off slowly and do not to run. We did that and had no difficulty in getting back on to the main track and then soon came back to the main path leading to the top of the mountain. We were all very sure that that hut was a bootleg still making lots of moonshine. I could feel that there were people inside the hut since we could see smoke coming out of the chimney.

We soon reached the summit of the mountain which was covered with large rocks and caves. The view was just fantastic looking across about 40 miles of rolling green mountains as far as the eye could see. Most of the scenery was of complete wilderness and it would not surprise me if it had never been explored. It showed a smoky blue haze across those 40 miles deep in the valleys which is why they call this part of the mountain range the Great Smokey Mountains. It looked like smoke from a fire but the smoke color was blue mist rising up from the valley in between each mountain range. These rolling mountains of Appalachia appeared to me like huge waves on an ocean moving towards me. The beauty of this part of eastern Tennessee was beyond comparison and seemed very American. I felt like I was an explorer in the 1800s following old Indian trails. The Appalachian Mountains runs as a ridge from Georgia as a long spine all the way up to the state of Maine, maybe 2,000 miles from south to north. Hikers use this trail as a rite of passage to hike this Appalachian Trail every year from top to bottom and bottom to top.

While we were at the summit of the three thousand foot plus mountain we started jumping across the rocks. As I jumped over these rocks, I heard below around my feet a rattle like a baby's rattle so looking down I could see below the rocks a coiled rattle snake ready to strike. I somehow twisted my body to land on another rock and avoided a nasty snake bite at the top of a mountain with help at least two hours away on foot. I considered myself very lucky to avoid the snake striking me which could have been fatal being that far from any kind of medical help. Being bitten by a rattler is not fatal if you are near a medical facility and can get some anti-venom into the foot quickly after being bitten. Since there was nothing to do now except admire the view that we had reached the summit it was time to go back down to the valley. It took half a day to climb up to the top of the mountain, but since it was now downhill it took less than hour to reach our plantation house in Happy Valley.

Upon returning from class I found that I had received a phone call from the principal of Rogersville High School. They had heard that an

English student was at the printing school and they had asked me if I had time to give a small lecture to the graduating high school kids all about what English schools were like and describe what my school curriculum was like. I was flattered and excited that they had asked me to do this for the kids so I immediately responded and said yes, I would love to do that, and just tell me the details when this event would take place. We settled on a date and time and it turned out to be a very interesting evening. I described how our school system worked and had told them what my school was like. I found the students were quite interested in how the British school system operated. I told them that tradition was very important to English education. They had a question time at the end and I was surprised how good the questions were. I answered all of their questions as best I could and I think they learned something. It reminded me of when an American came to our school when I was young.

While I was in the diner in town one evening, I got very friendly with one of the local waitresses who invited me to her house for dinner. She lived with her mother and father up in the hills. To get to her parents' home was an interesting drive since the roads twisted and turned and climbed up the hills in the dark. When I reached her home, I found it to be a small house with a front garden that was growing tobacco. When I reached her front door, her father came out to greet me and he was wearing his best ironed overalls and white shirt buttoned up to his neck. He wore a strange hat. Her mother looked like an old-fashioned granny with a bonnet and gingham blouse and long black skirt with button shoes. They really welcomed me and were very hospitable towards me. I am not sure what I ate for dinner but I did the best I could not to imagine what it was that I ate. I hope it was not roadkill!

On my way back down the mountain I had to drive off the road to reach another road. Crossing a dry field, I saw a car parked in the middle of the field. It was about midnight at the time when there was bright full moon shining like day. Sitting on top of a car roof clearly seen in the bright moonlight I could see a man carving on a wooden stick with his very long knife. I very carefully slowly drove passed by him and looked at him and he looked at me but we just passed by each other and although I was a little concerned, I slowly passed him by safely keeping an eye on what he was doing with his knife.

One of the students was from Chicago who drove a long sleek convertible car so we all went out for a drive with the top down. We were all piled into the car and we were driving across some wooded area that looked like a road, but wasn't, just a dusty track. We were driving along this dusty road when we came across a bunch of teenagers walking bare foot along the road. We stopped and started a conversation with them. They asked us where we all were from and our driver said that he was from Chicago. One of the kids walked around the back of the car and checked the car's license plate which was engraved as the state of Illinois and the kid returned to the front and said naw you ain't from Chicago, you are from Illinois. Everyone knows that Chicago is in the state of Illinois.

One of my favorite memories in Happy Valley was on a Saturday night we would build a campfire alongside of the lake and drink beer. One of the students had a guitar that he could play really well and we would all sing along around the camp fire old cowboy and country songs. Other times we would use the small lake boat and go boating and sometimes fishing. We were in a southern state where there are many strange creatures swimming in the lake that we did not have up north. Many times, we would see a water snake swimming with its head sticking out of the water. There were also cottonmouth snakes named because a small white cotton material was hanging out of its mouth and was very poisonous. Also, there were copperhead snakes swimming in the lake which are also very poisonous and if bitten there was not much time to get to a medical facility.

Just before the last weekend of our six months stay, we had a group that decided to rent a pontoon boat on one of the many man-made lakes in the area. During that time most of eastern Tennessee had very little electricity in the outlying areas. The Tennessee Valley Authority was damming up all the small rivers creating recreational lakes to make plenty of water not just for people to drink, but to drive the turbines to pump water into their homes which in turn would create electricity for the people up in the hills and around the countryside. Many people at that time would have only oil lamps in their homes for lighting. By damming the rivers, they created some very large lakes. We rented a pontoon boat with a small motor on the stern and went out on one of those lakes, brought plenty of food we had stashed away and motored the pontoon boat into the middle of the lake. Some of the guys were fishing and drinking. Others were just jumping off the boat into the cold water. The pontoon boat had a small engine to power the boat and so we chugged off. We had about fifteen guys on the boat which was marginal safety for the boat at best. We all had a great time that day. Many of them fell off the boat for over indulging in adult beverages.

Before I left Happy Valley, I made a point to stop and visit the town and look around an old overgrown cemetery that I had discovered earlier on. As I looked at the overgrown headstones, I saw a grave that caught my eye. It was almost lost in the overgrown weeds and bushes but I saw a familiar headstone with a historic name. The name at the top was not too clear but it said here lies the Crocket family. Underneath was an inscription that said that this was the family grave of the Crockets and read that the people in the grave were the parents of Davy Crocket and all had been massacred by Injuns, 1735. History records that Davy Crocket himself was killed with every other defendant of the Alamo by the Army of Mexican General Santa Anna at the battle of the Alamo, Texas in 1836 when Texas was still a territory with full statehood still pending. The Americans were under siege by the huge Army of Santa Anna at this old Spanish mission. Davy Crocket was killed at the Alamo with the other 135 defenders of American volunteers under siege by the Mexican Army of fifteen thousand Mexicans soldiers. The battle has been designated a massacre since the Mexicans blew on their trumpets The Royal which meant that general Santa Anna ordered to take no prisoners. Today native Texans hold this place as a shrine to the men who died. Just looking at this headstone I felt I was living in history. The state motto of Tennessee is called The Volunteer State. They were all volunteers at the Alamo. Most of the defenders of the Alamo were not all professional soldiers, but included a rag-tag group of mountain men and explorers who believed that Texas, not Mexico, belonged to the United States and they fought and died for that to become part of America. Later Sam Huston built an Army and repaid in kind the massacre at the Alamo and won the battle for the US and then it became part of Texas. A Texan created a saying that will always be heard to echo Remember the Alamo.

Very soon August 1st came along and it was end of the training period. The time came and we were ready to leave Happy Valley in Rogersville, Tennessee and return back to each of our home destinations. In my hand I had a diploma for finishing the course, which I could show any prospective employer.

During our last night at the plantation house we were hosted a farewell party by my trade union officers and we had a great time. Fortunately, even though Hawkins County was still a dry county they managed to smuggle in some bottles of moonshine and beer so that we all went to bed happy and ready to go home the next day. I do remember that when I started to leave for home I did not feel very well because of the moonshine from the night before. I never learn!

I left early the next morning to head back to New York which was about seven hundred miles away. Other students headed home for other cities such as Los Angeles and the mid-west and all were going back home in different directions. Each promised to each other that they would keep in touch with everyone, but really none ever did. I often wonder if any of these guys have survived during these past fifty years.

I had been in weekly contact with my mother and Colin during the past six months so I knew that all was well. The two full days drive back to Long Island, New York and home to mum and Colin was uneventful, taking the same return route back as I did when I first drove to Tennessee. When I arrived home on Long Island in Queens Village, I had a grand welcome and I felt glad to be home again. All was well with both Colin and mum. We now had an extra member of the family, a pure white cat that answered to the name of Fluffy. Now I had to start looking for some work and try out my new training skills of this new print process.

While I had been away at school Patty, my girlfriend and eventually my future wife, had been writing to me quite often. Her family had been very kind to me before I left and I did contact her as soon as I got back but I needed to find a job first. I wanted to have a job that allowed me to travel in sales and make a living as an offset press salesman. But first I had to get back over to the New York union hall once again to find a job which I knew would not be easy. The printing industry had changed but the opportunities were still there just as they were when I first arrived in America. I did have an edge over the others and that edge was that I understood all about this new process called offset printing and that was when I realized I could now do whatever I wanted to do. I could travel the US in printing machinery sales where I had an expense account and entertained customers and had the ability to travel the world.

Once again, I was looking in the help wanted advertisements in the New York newspapers. I found a printing company, a small printer called Drum Litho in downtown Manhattan that had offset presses like the kind that I had been trained on and I was asked to start my new job the following Monday. They showed me a printing press similar to one that I was taught on at school, but not quite the same. They asked me to set up the press and start up the printing job on the machine. I did well setting up the press, but a big mistake; I forgot to turn on the dryer sprayer that dried the ink on the sheets of paper almost immediately after it was printed. In just a few hours the pile of paper in sheets were wet but dried solid like a block of wood within the hour. Nobody could pry the sheets of paper apart and they were stuck hard as a solid brick. The stack of paper was so stuck together that one sheet of paper could not be pried for the other sheet. I lasted in that job for one half day and was fired before lunch. I had never been fired before in my whole life and it was not very pleasant.

I had some friends in the printing industry and I spent a lot of time contacting them to see if I could find a job. I found a company called De La Rue Banknote Company, which was a printer of stocks, shares and money. Best of all, my mother was working there and she knew the boss who did hire me. The location was not very far away from our home so I went for the interview and was hired on as an assistant on a lithographic printing press. Not the job I really wanted but it was a start. It was a clean, modern building and the foreman named George Beck took a liking to me and I began my new job the following day. Mum was working there in the bindery and we were back again as a printing family in America. Colin had settled in with the Explorers that were like the Sea Scouts so he easily made friends. He also had a good job in a printing company and did well there.

I was still a member of the British War Vets so I attended their weekly meetings and once a month attended one of their Saturday night dances at their headquarters so we were a happy united family again mum, Colin and I. I was pleased that my mum and Colin had settled in so well in America. Mum had changed so much from an English lady to becoming more like an American and it appeared that to me she was very happy in her new country. Summertime on Long Island is very pleasant. We usually all went to Jones Beach which was just half an hour drive away from home for the day. It was a beautiful beach and a hot summer sun, not like the chilly English beaches that was cold on an English summers' day. Colin liked to body-surf and mum just loved the hot sunny weather. The British War Vets had picnics that we attended at various places and the summer was turning into a very pleasant time of the year. The music on the radio was all rock and roll and everyone had their favorite artist and song and driving down the highway with the radio blasting it felt great. I was happy because all of my planning for my family to be happy in America was working out well and we looked forward to some good times in the future.

I was now going out with Patty quite often and we regularly went out to night clubs as soon as I finished work. I was working the evening shift until eleven pm so by the time I picked her up at her house we would be out late. On weekends we would go into Manhattan for dinner and show and night clubbing all over town. During the late summer of 1963 we talked of getting married and I spoke with Patty's mother and father and a date was set for the wedding for the next year on July 18, 1964. As the year progressed plans were being made for the wedding. It was decided that the reception would be held in Patty's family garden and would be a catered affair.

October turned into November and autumn was upon us. Many Americans felt a strong sense of pending problems. President Kennedy had won the presidential election in November 1960 by a very small margin of votes and he was gearing up for re-election in November 1964. Now there was also the beginning of a civil rights problem in the southern states with daily demonstrations and marches in major cities of America against all kinds of civil unrest. Even worse there was war on the horizon in a faraway country in Southeast Asia called Vietnam.

There were rumors about Americans who were already fighting there, but officially they were first called advisors. President Kennedy denied that we were going to war in Vietnam to fight the northern communists. There were marches and demonstrations in New York organized by people that were in favor of going to war and others doing the same thing who were against such action causing serious controversy. There was also a huge generation changeover from the older generation and the so-called baby boomers born after World War II. This later generation had very different political ideas and trouble was brewing. It all happened so quickly. Our country going from being so calm with American people united together to becoming unstable, arguing for and against these sudden civil problems. There was even worse to come that brought our country to a mental and physical standstill. During late November 1963, President Kennedy was assassinated in Dallas, Texas. This shook the very foundations of the Republic. Vice President Johnson was sworn in as our new President and flew back to an undisclosed location since we all did not know what really was happening.

1963-1964

DURING DECEMBER WE had an engagement party at Patty's home with all of the two families attending. With Patty's Uncle George around it was a lively party for sure. We did not go out to many places during this time. After Christmas we were saving up our money for the wedding. Some Saturday evenings we would visit Patty's family and play roulette on a homemade roulette board for the evening. It was only a nickel and dime game, but while the game was going on it turned their living room into a mini-Las Vegas.

Soon the date would be approaching and during the spring we had begun to look around for an apartment to move into prior to our wedding in July. We settled on an apartment that had just been built in the town in eastern Long Island called Port Jefferson. It was located about fifty miles from my home and we settled on the price terms. It was a one bedroom apartment and within a 45 minute drive from mum, Colin and Patty's family. We then went shopping for furniture. We were very fortunate since during the engagement party we had been given many gifts for the kitchen.

The ceremony was held at the Christ Lutheran Evangelical Church which was around the block from Patty's house. A band was hired to play at the reception after the church service. Patty's mother had a band that played regularly at her nightclub located in the next town and they were our band. The service was really nice and we all came back to the house for the reception. Patty's house had a large outside patio with a pool and a dance floor to dance to the band's music. Everything went well on the day of the wedding except for a few details. One big disappointment was the photographer that we had hired did not bring color film for the photos. All of the wedding photos were in black and white.

The time came to leave for the airport. We had arranged for a limo driver to drive us to JFK airport to catch our flight to Puerto Rico, then on to St. Thomas in the Virgin Islands. We waited and waited and no driver showed up so one of the guests volunteered to drive us to the airport. We managed to get on the plane and when we got to Puerto Rico, to our horror our bags went missing. They were left behind in NY. The bags did finally arrive and were delivered to our hotel.

The next morning, we boarded a small plane to fly to Charlotte Amalie, St. Thomas. When we arrived at our hotel it was located on a rocky stretch of beach on a bay and the room was full of bugs. Also across the bay was located a water distillery that took out all the salt in the sea changing it into drinking water. It made the sea very salty when the distillery returned the treated water into the sea and the bay.

St. Thomas in those days was undeveloped for tourists and there were very few built roads outside of town. I had to find another, better hotel immediately. To get around the island I hired a jeep with a canvas top. I left Patty at the hotel and drove a twisting road with a large drop-off cliff. As I drove up to the top of the mountain there was the Hilton Hotel and it also had a large pool. I managed to get a room and returned to check out of the buggy motel below and picked up Patty. We went to the Hilton Hotel on top of the mountain and after that event all went well and we had a good time on St. Thomas. The Hilton was an excellent hotel for the rest of the week. We did all the tourist stops, visited all of the beaches and various bays and events on the island. After a week's honeymoon we returned back to Long Island and moved into our new apartment in Port Jefferson. The apartment had just been built before we were married and we were very comfortable.

1965, I Started My New Sales Career

PATTY WAS NOW working at a hospital as a computer keypunch operator while I was still working for De La Rue Printing, but I was restless. I knew I could do something better. I needed to push ahead. One day I was in the pressroom when the ink salesman came in checking on our ink inventory. I went over to speak with him and asked how it was to be in sales. He said it was great because they pay your expenses and you get a company car and commission on the ink that you sell. A few days later the sales representative for small presses came into the plant. I also went over to him and asked him how it was working for the AB Dick Company who sold duplicating offset machines. He gave me the name of his boss and said give him a call. He might take me on since I know offset printing and the company was going to go into the offset business and nobody knew anything about it.

They needed a salesman to sell their machines that knew and understood the offset process. Once again luck was with me. I called the manager, Marvin Markowitz, who was a district manager in the New York office. They were located in mid-town Manhattan on 47th Street off of Madison Avenue. He set up an appointment and he interviewed me. I took the train into Manhattan where AB Dick had their corporate offices. The interview went well and he spent the morning explaining what they wanted in a new position that was to do with the new offset printing process. Their business was in office machines like copiers and mimeographs, but they did not understand offset presses. The corporate company in Chicago had decided to enter this new field since mimeo graphic machines were being replaced by small offset machines, so I was their man to help them enter this new field. By noon he had invited me to out to lunch. We had come to an understanding regarding salary and benefits.

I quit my printing press job the following day and started at the AB Dick Company selling small offset presses and supplies in Manhattan. My territory that I was assigned was the lower end of Manhattan. It was the beginning of my press equipment sales career, which helped me later to become the National Sales Manager for some very large corporations and to travel over half the world as a sales manager for manufacturing offset printing presses.

1965

IT WAS NOW mid-summer 1965 and Patty and I were considering a trip back to England. It was a good time to show Patty, my new wife, my relatives who lived in London and to show her what England was like. We planned to leave in the month of June when the weather was usually good at that time in the UK. We worked out the flight schedule which was a night flight and rented a room at a Holiday Inn at Swiss Cottage located north of London. Patty was able to take two weeks off from work and Roy worked it out with his manager.

That summer mum went on her first cruise to Bermuda on her own and she just loved going and meeting so many people on the ship. I took her down to the docks in Manhattan where the cruise ships would line up ready to leave for all of the tropical ports in the Caribbean Sea. First port of call was Bermuda and then on down the chain of islands into the Caribbean Sea. She had now become an American and also was pursuing the American dream.

All was well with the Phelps family who had arrived in America with high hopes for the future. We had jobs and we were all making money. We had good TV shows to see. The Phelps family was now together again and well on their way to become citizens of America, which was the direction that I had chosen to take those many years ago. Just as most Americans, we believed in America and would continue to support and enjoy this wonderful country. We never realized at the time there was something else just waiting for us just around the corner. The Vietnam War continued to grow and that seemed to be an endless war that would take more than 50,000 young American lives and tear this country apart from one generation to the next.

The Phelps family would be part of this terrible war since my young brother Colin would become involved. My brother Colin, being now eighteen years old, enlisted and served in the US Navy and was assigned as a Navy Corpsman. After completing his basic training in the Great Lakes Naval Training Center, he was assigned to the US Naval Air Station in Jacksonville, Florida. My mother and I were very relieved at his assignment believing that he would be either on a ship or on a shore base during this military conflict. After a few months of service in Jacksonville, Florida I received a phone call from my brother Colin. He was phoning from San Francisco with the news that he was assigned as a corpsman with the First Marine Division and was on his way to Vietnam. He had been assigned with the US Marines as a corpsman, the last place that we wanted him to be. A Navy Corpsman was like being a doctor in a platoon with the infantry in the field of battle. He was in one of the most dangerous positions since the enemy would try and kill the corpsman first. If the corpsman went down there was no other medic in the platoon to treat the wounded. He was in-country for the first six months assigned to an eight-man platoon and was sent out in helicopters each morning in the most active places. Colin finished his four year tour at the Chelsea Massachusetts Naval Air Center in 1972 unharmed except for a small leg wound which earned him a purple heart. While he was there, he met a Navy nurse and within a year he had married her and came to live near us on Long Island.

In 1971 I heard that Mrs. Heath had died at the age of 86 years. I was so sorry to hear that news since she was so much a part of my life as my surrogate mother for the most important years of a young boy's life. She had been so good to me during those bad war years. She gave me not only her love but a great education with her stories about history and what the world was all about. I feel I was very lucky to have had her as a surrogate mother during those very difficult years. Thank you, Auntie Ellie. She turned a young boy into a full grown man that learned to understand responsibility to his future family.

With her passing, the door closed on my early experiences as a young man yearning to go to America. I was now a citizen of America, married with a beautiful daughter who would be born in 1970. I was to become a traveling business man and make a life in America. The Echoes of My Footsteps continue.